How To Overcome
THE MOST
FRIGHTENING
ISSUES
You WILL Face
This Century

How To Overcome
THE MOST
FRIGHTENING
ISSUES
You WILL Face
This Century

Angie Peters, Shane Connor, Sue Bradley, Dr. Stanley Monteith, Debra Rae, Thomas and Nita Horn, Joseph R. Chambers D.D., D.S.L., Christian J. Pinto, Bill Salus, Dr. Michael Heiser, Dr. Gianni DeVincenti Hayes, J. Michael Bennett, Ph.D., Wilfred Hahn, Terry James, Thomas Glessner, Phillip Goodman, John P. McTernan, Patrick Heron, Carl and Althia Anderson

DEFENDER

A DIVISION OF ANOMALOS PUBLISHING HOUSE

CRANE

How To Overcome The Most Frightening Issues You Will Face
This Century

Defender
Crane, Missouri 65633
© 2009 by Thomas Horn
All rights reserved. Published 2009
Printed in the United States of America

10   3

ISBN 10: 0982323573 (paper)

ISBN 13: 9780982323571 (paper)

A CIP catalog record for this book is available from the Library of
Congress.

Cover illustration and design by Daniel Wright

Contents

chapter one

Bible Prophecy: Fulfillment, Not Fear

by *Angie Peters*

Horned beasts…Revelation…Old Testament books whose pages remain stuck together along the edges from nonuse…Israel…the number 666…Armageddon…the Rapture…the Antichrist…Tribulation.

These and other words and images, combined with my lack of knowledge about them, painted for me such an alarming and hazy portrait of biblical prophecy and end-time matters that my habit as a born-again Christian since age nine was to tune out any discussion about the subject.

"It's all Greek to me," I would dismissively say. "That's better left to scholars, preachers, and theologians." With all the sad and tragic events going on in the world, I didn't really want to dwell on the doom and gloom of the end times. Wasn't reading the headlines or watching the evening news frightening enough?

But one day several years ago, as a freelance writer and editor by profession, I landed right in the middle of a project editing, of all things, books about biblical prophecy for a man named Terry James, a Christian scholar and prolific writer whose eyesight happened to be quickly failing him because of degenerative retinal disease. Terry needed to recruit someone—as it turns out, me—to help him do things he was no longer visually able to do, such as help with research, transcribe dictated chapters, and edit manuscripts for the books he wrote and co-authored about eschatology, geopolitics, and other ominous-sounding topics.

As excited as I was about Terry's willingness to become not just my "boss," but my beloved friend and mentor, and as relieved as I was about the prospects of having a new project on my plate, I wasn't too crazy about the subject matter I would be dealing with. Why didn't he write books about spiritual growth? Bible study? Child-raising? Those were more my cup of tea. Actually, *anything* would be better than Bible prophecy, I figured. But, determined to succeed at the new job the Lord had handed me, I went to work to try to make sense of the foreboding subject as I went along. Surely *something* would be in there that I could understand—and maybe I would even find some tidbit of biblical truth in all those "dreary" topics, something that I could use to enhance my personal walk with God.

So I started combing the material I was working on for useful information. I picked Terry's brain, asking him to tell me in plain English what "all that apocalyptic jargon" meant. If he explained something to me and I still didn't get it, "explain that again," I would insist. I set out to find out what the new world order, humanism, the mark of the Beast, apostasy, and geopolitics had to do with me, a wife and mom whose worries centered far more on keeping peace between my kids at the dinner table than on the ongoing peace process in the Middle East.

What I learned from Terry, and from reading the material of other writers and scholars he was working with, surprised me: Prophecy isn't just about the end of the world system as we know it. It's much more personal than that. It has everything to do with me and my family—not just in that far distant, hard-to-imagine "last day," but *today*. Maybe that's why we're promised a specific blessing for reading the most end-times prophecy-saturated book in the Bible, the book of Revelation:

"Blessed is he that readeth, and they that hear the words of this prophecy" (Revelation 1:3).

Prophecy Hits Home

Unfortunately, many Christians neglect the study of prophecy for many of the same reasons that I did for so many years—fear, plus lack of understanding. But if we will learn even a little bit about the subject, then we will be blessed with the realization that every detail of our lives directly relates to God's prophetic Word.

For example, we'll know that evolution, the effort to explain the origin of life without God, is a part of the widespread and increasing deception described in 2 Timothy 3:13. We'll "get it" that e-mail, faxes, overnight mail, texting, and even Twitter are compelling us to "run to and fro" to manage both our business lives and our personal lives at a breakneck speed, like the prophet Daniel hinted at in chapter 12, verse 4, of the book that bears his name. We'll never fail to be sickened, but we might not be as surprised, when we read of parents murdering their own children because we'll recognize those activities as a symptom of the "unnatural affection" described in 2 Timothy 3:3.

We'll regard the Internet, one of the most staggering technological advances of our lifetime, as a "knowledge-increasing" tool (Daniel 12:4) that's uniting the world into a cozy "global village" in which the stage is being built for a world leader called Antichrist to one day play out his role as predicted in Revelation 13.

We'll see that the earthquakes, hurricanes, and other natural disasters shaking the foundations from under families like ours all across the world are some of the signals Christ himself said would be happening as our time on this planet marches on.

My growing understanding of biblical prophecy and the Revelation brought my blurry worldview into such clear focus that I soon wondered how I had missed seeing and making sense of all these signals before.

No More Fear

The best news of all wasn't simply that my understanding—my "head knowledge"—of these matters had increased. It was this: I learned that I no longer had any reason to be frightened about what I was seeing on news broadcasts, reading in headlines, and even experiencing myself.

Why not?

Because studying Bible prophecy nourished my trust in God and fortified my faith in His promises.

From the birth of Christ—foretold beginning in Genesis 3:15 and fulfilled in the Gospels—to the rebirth of Israel as a nation—foretold in Isaiah 66:7–9 and fulfilled May 14, 1948—countless prophecies have been fulfilled to date. How incredible, that words penned thousands of years ago outline with great and accurate detail events that have already happened and/or are beginning to happen right now! Seeing today's events unfold breathes life into the prophecies sketched out in the Bible. It builds my faith, pushes my focus forward, and draws my heart heavenward, giving me all the more reason to "smile at the future" as the remarkable woman of Proverbs 31 is said to have done.

So, when terrorists slammed their planes into the twin towers of the World Trade Center on September 11, 2001, sparking panic across our nation, fear might have been my first response, but it wasn't my lasting response. My study of Bible prophecy reminded me that God is always in control, that He always takes care of His children, and that He always keeps his promises. That's what enabled me to put one step in front of the other during those long days of watching the horrendous news unfold following that awful event.

And when headlines about global warming, mass murders, and natural disasters prompt "it's-the-end-of-the-world" speculation to echo across the playground, down the high school hallways, and across college campuses, alarming my three kids—a grade schooler, a high school senior, and a college sophomore—I can calm their fears, too. "Hey," I can remind them, "God's Word promises us that we will be taken out of this world to be with Him before things get too bad. We can believe it, because we know He keeps His promises!"

Bright Hope during Dark Days

It's been more than fifteen years since I tackled my first Bible prophecy book project with Terry James. Back then, belief among Bible prophecy scholars was that surely we were living in the last days. The headlines, geopolitical events, societal changes, and other signals strongly indicated that the earth age really might be wrapping up. But today, the message that we're surely living in the last days rings even more loudly and clearly.

Certainly the "frightening issues" that we faced in the mid-nineties have become even more "frightening" today. The topics featured in this book attest to that: The prospects of nuclear Armageddon, pandemics, World War III, food and fuel shortages, financial collapse, persecution of Christians, and other dreadful possibilities are more real than ever before. What makes them even more real is the fact that many of us have already experienced some of them firsthand. If the days leading up to the Tribulation are predicted to get continually worse and worse, my goodness, just how much *worse* can things possibly get?

The gifted and dedicated Bible prophecy scholars, speakers, researchers, and writers I've been honored to work with in this collaboration agree—and are single-mindedly trying to get the word out to everyone they possibly can—that the signs are certainly clear and our days are in fact numbered. They've made it their mission to prepare readers like me and others for what's likely to come by sharing their specialized knowledge and equipping us with practical strategies for overcoming the obstacles we'll undoubtedly face in the coming days. Forewarned is forearmed, as the adage goes, and this group of writers is doing a great job of both forewarning *and* forearming us.

But they don't stop there. Each author makes it evident that he or she is not about to discuss the "bad news" without bringing in the

Good News of the hope we have in Christ. Christ, after all, is love itself...and you know what the Bible says about love: "There is no fear in love, but perfect love casteth out fear" (1 John 4:18).

Taking Courage

I know I'm still a long way from grasping some of the more difficult issues in biblical prophecy. And reading some of the contributions to this book reminds me that I still have many, many things to learn about how life might possibly be in the days to come. But I have at least made some sense out of a lot of the words and phrases related to the subject that used to intimidate me. I'm no longer reluctant to open my Bible to the book of Revelation, or to think about the sequence of events that will lead up to the last days of the world as I know it.

So, if the purpose of this brief chapter I'm writing is to share with you "how to overcome the most frightening issues you will face this century," as our book title promises, here's my advice: Remember that "fear" is never God's choice for His followers. Courage is His preference for us, and it's ours for the taking. He has given us that courage wrapped up in a package the apostle Paul described as a spirit "of power, and of love, and of a sound mind" (2 Timothy 1:7).

- With *power*, the power of the Holy Spirit, we are equipped to understand spiritual matters we couldn't otherwise hope to grasp and to accomplish things that we couldn't otherwise begin to accomplish.
- With *love*, we can continue to forge meaningful relationships, encouraging fellow believers, pointing the lost toward Christ, and serving one another as He urges us to do.
- And with *sound minds*, we can take God's prophetic teachings to heart: "A wise man will hear, and will increase learning; and a man of understanding shall attain unto wise counsels" (Proverbs 1:5).

When we accept these gifts from God, we will find that we have no reason to fear sudden disaster (Proverbs 3:25) or the days to come— whatever "frightening issues" they may hold.

—

Angie Peters, a professional writer, editor, and speaker, is the author of several books and Bible studies, including her newest releases, The Life of David *and* The Life of Solomon *("Smart Guide to the Bible" series, Thomas Nelson). Visit her website at www.justwords.me or contact her at angiedpeters@att.net.*

Nuclear Armageddon

by Shane Connor

Some people might be tempted to skip or skim over the topic of nuclear Armageddon because they assume the event will be overwhelming or not survivable. Unfortunately for their families, however, those who pass up reading this chapter will miss out on essential, life-saving "good news."

What possible "good news" could there ever be about nuclear destruction coming to America, whether via dirty bombs, terrorist nukes, or intercontinental ballistics missiles (ICBMs) from afar?

In a word, those events are all survivable for the vast majority of American families—that is, for families who know what to do beforehand and who make even modest preparations.

Tragically, though, most Americans today don't give much credence to—much less seek out—such vital, life-saving instruction because they have been misled by our culture's pervasive myths that say nuclear destruction isn't survivable. In fact, most people think that if nukes go off, then everybody will die—or will wish they had. That's why we hear such absurd comments as: "If it happens, I hope I'm at ground zero and go quickly."

This defeatist attitude was born as the disarmament movement ridiculed any alternatives to its agenda. The sound civil defense strategies of the sixties have been derided as largely ineffective, or at worst as a cruel joke. With the supposed end of the Cold War in the eighties, most Americans neither saw a need to prepare for nuclear destruction nor believed preparing would do any good. Today, with growing prospects of nuclear terrorism, we see emerging among the public either paralyzing fear or irrational denial. People no longer can envision effective preparations for surviving a nuclear attack. In fact, the biggest surprise for most Americans, if nukes really are unleashed, will be that they are still here!

Most people will survive the initial blasts because they won't be anywhere close to ground zero—which, of course, is the target of a missile or bomb—and that is very good news. Unfortunately, though, few people will be prepared to survive the subsequent radioactive fallout, which eventually will kill many more than the blast itself. However, there is still more good news: Well over 90 percent of the potential casualties from the fallout can be avoided if the public is trained through an aggressive national civil defense educational program. Simple measures taken by a trained public immediately after a nuclear blast can prevent agonizing injury and death from radiation.

"The National Planning Scenario No. 1," an originally confidential internal study conducted by the Department of Homeland Security in 2004, cited the above survival odds when it examined the effects of a terrorist nuke going off in Washington, D.C. The study revealed that a ten kiloton nuke (about two-thirds the size of the Hiroshima bomb in 1945), detonated at ground level, would cause about 15,000 immediate deaths and another 15,000 casualties from the initial blast, thermal flash, and radiation release. As horrific as that sounds, the surprising revelation here is that more than 99 percent of the residents in the D.C. area will have just witnessed and survived their first nuclear explosion.

Clearly, the good news is that most people will survive the initial blast. However, the study also determined that another 250,000 people could receive lethal doses of radiation from the fallout drifting downwind toward them after the blast. These much larger casualty numbers are avoidable—and that's more good news, but only for those who are prepared by a civil defense program teaching them what they should do before that ill wind arrives.

Another study released by the Rand Corporation in 2006 looked at a terrorist ten-kiloton nuke arriving in a cargo container and being exploded in the Port of Long Beach, California. The study estimated that more than 150,000 people would be at risk downwind from fallout—again, that number is much higher than the number of casualties from the initial blast itself. Other, more recent, studies continue to show the same much higher population percentages at risk downwind from fallout and away from the ground zero blast.

Today, without any meaningful civil defense program, millions of American families continue to be at risk and could perish needlessly because they lack essential knowledge that used to be taught at the grade school level. The public urgently needs to receive instruction again on civil defense basics, which include:

- "Duck and cover"—This tactic prevents people from running to the nearest window to see what the big flash was just in time to be shredded by the glass imploding inward from the shock wave.
- Safe evacuation—Evacuating in a course that's perpendicular to the downwind drift of the fallout is the best way to avoid fallout contamination and injury.
- Sheltering in place—People must learn how to effectively shelter in place for a brief time if they can't evacuate. The radioactive fallout loses 90 percent of its lethal intensity in the first seven hours and 99 percent of it in two days. The majority of those who would need to shelter from the fallout would only need to hunker down for two or three days, not for weeks on end. An effective improvised family fallout shelter can be assembled at home both cheaply and quickly with proper instruction. (More on that a bit later in the chapter.)

Unfortunately, our government today is doing little to promote nuclear preparedness and civil defense instruction among the general public. Regrettably, most of our officials, like the public, are still captive to the same illusions that training and preparation are ineffective against a nuclear threat.

Secretary of Homeland Security Michael Chertoff demonstrated this attitude in 2005, when he responded to the following question in *USA Today*:

"Q: In the last four years, the most horrific scenario—a nuclear attack—may be the least discussed. If there were to be a nuclear attack tomorrow by terrorists on an American city, how would it be handled?

"A: In the area of a nuclear bomb, it's prevention, prevention, prevention. If a nuclear bomb goes off, you are not going to be able to protect against it. There's no city strong enough infrastructure-wise to withstand such a hit. No matter how you approach it, there'd be a huge loss of life."

Mr. Chertoff apparently failed to grasp that most of that "huge loss of life" can be prevented if the survivors of the blast and those downwind of the fallout know what to do beforehand. He only acknowledged that the infrastructure will be severely compromised and that responders won't be responding. Training the public before a nuclear event occurs is clearly the only hope for those in the fallout path. Of course, the government should try to prevent nuclear attack, but Mr. Chertoff might have better responded to the above question with the answer, "preparation, preparation, preparation," for when efforts at prevention fail.

The federal government must launch a national mass media, business-supported, school-based effort superseding our most ambitious public awareness campaigns to date, such as those addressing prevention of AIDS, drug abuse, drunk driving, and smoking as well as those advocating the use of seat belts and smoke detectors. The effort should percolate down to every level of society. Let's be clear: We are talking about the potential to save many more lives than all those other noble efforts combined!

Instead, Homeland Security continues to focus on two missions:

1. Interdiction—catching nuclear materials and terrorists before an event; and
2. Continuity of Government—ensuring government operations will continue when the first mission fails.

A third mission, the most important one, has been largely ignored:

3. Continuity of the Public—providing proven mass media civil defense training of the public that would make the survival difference for the vast majority of Americans affected by a nuclear event.

This deadly oversight won't be corrected until the crippling myth of nuclear un-survivability is banished by the good news that a trained and prepared public can, and ultimately must, save themselves.

We hope and pray each major political party will try to outdo the other in proposing aggressive national civil defense educational programs. We are not asking for billions of dollars for public fallout shelters for everyone (like the shelters that already await many of our top government officials). We are just asking for a comprehensive mass media, business, and school-based re-release of the proven practical strategies of civil defense education—similar to what already has been embraced in nations such as China, Russia, Switzerland, Israel, and even Singapore.

In the meantime, though, don't wait around for the government to instruct and prepare your family and others in your community. Start learning—today—how to establish your own family nuclear survival preparations. Begin by reading the following emergency guide, which is for families preparing for imminent terrorist or strategic nuclear attacks that are expected to cause severe destruction, widespread radioactive fallout downwind, and extensive disruptions of services.

What to Do if a Nuclear Disaster is Imminent

A Dirty Bomb Attack

(The vastly more devastating nuclear weapon blasts with fallout are discussed in the next section.) The United States Nuclear Regulatory Commission defines a dirty bomb as "one type of a 'radiological dispersal device' (RDD) that combines a conventional explosive such as dynamite with radioactive material."

In the event of a dirty bomb attack, expect localized and downwind contamination from the explosion and dispersed radioactive materials. If you are close enough to see or hear any local bomb blast, assume it includes radiological or chemical agents and move away from the blast area as quickly as possible. If the wind is blowing toward you from the direction of the blast, travel in a direction that is crosswise or perpendicular to the wind as you move away from the blast area. If possible, cover your face with a dust mask or cloth to avoid inhaling potentially radioactive dust.

When you reach a safe location, remove your outer clothing outside and shower as soon as possible. Refer to local news sources for additional instructions about sheltering or evacuation. The government is better prepared to direct and assist the public in a dirty bomb incident than it is to direct and assist the public during an actual nuclear weapon attack.

A Nuclear Weapon Attack

In a national crisis of imminent nuclear weapon attack, read all the way through this guide first, then take effective protective action with confidence—quickly!

1. Make a Decision: Stay or Go?

First, you must decide whether you need to prepare where you are or try to evacuate. The nature of the threat, your prior preparations, and your confidence in your sources of information should direct your decision. (If you already know you will be preparing to stay at your own home or in the immediate local area, see No. 2.)

If you are considering evacuation, your decision requires a very high level of confidence that it is worth the risk. You do not want to get stuck between your current location and your desired destination because you will probably find it difficult to return. If you fail to reach your destination, you might be exposed without shelter in a dangerous situation with little effective law enforcement, perhaps among panicked hordes of refugees. Whatever supplies you have then might be limited to what you can carry on foot.

Evacuation might be a viable option for a limited time if:

You are in a large city or near a military target.

You have relatives or friends in the country whom you know are awaiting you.

The roads between you and those family or friends are clear.

You have the means and fuel.

Do not attempt evacuation if all of the above are not clearly known, or if the situation is deteriorating too quickly to assure the complete trip. If evacuation truly is a viable option, do not wait—go now! Do so with as many supplies (listed in No. 6) as possible. It's better to arrive two days too early than to leave two hours too late and get snagged midway, potentially exposing your family to a worse fate than if you had stayed where you were. Because of the very real danger of being caught in a stalled evacuation stampede, almost all families are better off making the best of it wherever they currently are when events are moving too quickly.

2. Delegate and Prioritize

Your first priorities to assure your family's survival are food/supplies, water, and shelter. Because time is of the essence, delegate specific tasks to adult family members so they can be working on these priorities at the same time. While some family members are acquiring food and supplies, others can be constructing the shelter and collecting and arranging for water storage.

3. Gather Food and Supplies

Because food and supplies might quickly become unavailable, immediately assign someone to go to the stores with the list provided in No. 6. Stop to withdraw cash from the bank or automated teller machine first, but try to use credit cards at the stores, if at all possible, to preserve your cash.

4. Collect and Store Water

With one or more adults now heading to the stores for supplies, those remaining should begin collecting and storing water immediately. A lack of clean water will debilitate your family much more quickly and more severely than will a lack of food. Without water to drink, to use for continued cleanliness in food preparation, and to use for sanitary purposes in personal hygiene, debilitating sickness could rampage through your household, where you have little hope of receiving prompt medical attention. That is an avoidable disaster only if you have stored enough clean water.

So, fill every possible container with water right now. It will be very hard to have stored too much water. When the electricity/pumps stop working, or when the water pressure drops because everybody in your community is collecting water at the same time, what you have collected is all the water you might be able to get for a very long time. Empty soft drink bottles (one to three liters) are ideal for water storage; also fill up bathtubs and washing machine. (Remember, you also have water in your hot water tank.) If you have any plastic swimming pools or water beds, fill them up, too. (Water from a water bed should be used only for bathing or cleaning, not for drinking, because it might contain traces of algaecide and/or fungicides.) It's important to fill up anything that will hold water—and do it right now.

Two of the items on your shopping list (see No. 6) are new garbage cans and liner bags, which you'll also use for storing water. If you can't buy new garbage cans, scrub any you already have with bleach, then put in a new liner bag and fill with water. You can even store water in liner bags inserted into sturdy boxes or dresser drawers.

When you fill garbage cans with water, give some thought to where you will do that because they won't easily be moved once full, and many of them together could be too heavy for some upper floor locations. Ideally, water storage cans need to be very near where your shelter will be constructed; in fact, they can actually add to the structure's shielding properties, as you'll see below.

Don't forget: You cannot collect and store too much water! Do not hesitate; fill up every possible container right now.

5. Construct a Shelter

The principles of radiation protection are simple, with many options and resources families can use to prepare or improvise very effective in-home fallout shelters. But before we look at how to protect yourself against radiation, it's important to understand the source of the danger and how it occurs. Radioactive fallout is the particulate matter (dust) produced by a nuclear explosion and carried high into the air by the mushroom cloud. It drifts on the wind, and most of it settles to earth downwind of the explosion. The heaviest, most dangerous, and most noticeable fallout first "falls out" close to ground zero, possibly arriving minutes after an explosion. The smaller, lighter dust-like particles typically arrive hours later because they drift much farther downwind, even up to hundreds of miles. Whether easily visible or not, fallout accumulates and blows around everywhere, just like dust does on the ground and roofs. Wind and rain can also concentrate the fallout into localized hot spots of much more intense radiation, with no visible indication of its presence.

This radioactive fallout is dangerous because it emits penetrating radiation energy (similar to x-rays). This radiation (not the fallout dust) can go through walls, roofs, and windows. Even if you manage to keep from inhaling or ingesting the dust, keep it off your skin, hair, and clothes. Even if none gets inside your house, the radiation penetrating your home from the fallout outside is still extremely dangerous, and can injure or kill you.

Radioactive fallout from a nuclear explosion, though very dangerous initially, loses its intensity quickly because it gives off so much energy. For example, fallout emitting gamma ray radiation at a rate of 500 R/hr (fatal with one hour of exposure) shortly after an explosion weakens to only one-tenth as strong seven hours later. Two days later, it's only one-one hundredth as strong, or as deadly, as it is initially.

That is all really very good news, because it means that our families can easily survive it if we get them into a proper shelter to wait in safety as the fallout becomes less dangerous with every passing hour.

The goals of your family fallout shelter are:

Location: Maximize the distance between you and your family and the fallout outside on the ground and roof.

Protective shielding: Place sufficient mass, the heavier the better, between your family and the fallout to absorb the deadly radiation.

Livability: Make living in the shelter tolerable while the radiation subsides.

To shield your family from radiation, simply put mass—anything weighty—between them and the radiation source. Like police body armor stopping bullets, the mass stops (absorbs) the radiation. The thicker and denser (heavier) the mass, the more radiation it stops. Thus, it is more effective with every inch you add.

The Location of Your Shelter

Although you can build a fallout shelter anywhere, your best options are inside or near your home. Some other existing structures might provide significant shielding or partial shielding; you can enhance those for adequate protection. If you don't have a basement, you can use the techniques shown below in any above-ground structure, but you'll need to use more mass to achieve the same level of shielding. Also consider using other solid structures nearby—especially those with below-ground spaces, such as commercial buildings, schools, churches, parking garages, large and long culverts, and tunnels. Using some of these structures might require permissions and/or the acquisition of additional materials to minimize any fallout drifting or blowing into them if they have openings. Buildings with a half-dozen or more floors that did not sustain blast damage often provide good radiation protection in the center of the middle floors. This is because of both the distance and the shielding the multiple floors provide from the fallout on the ground and roof.

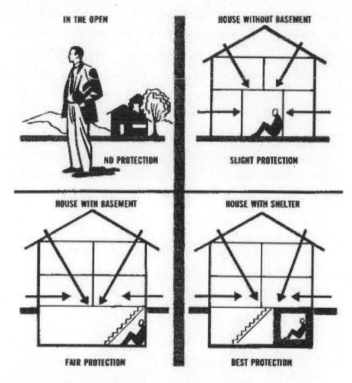

The bottom line: Choose a structure nearby with both the greatest mass and distance between the outside, where the fallout would settle, and the shelter occupants inside.

If you (or a nearby friend or relative) have a basement, your best option is probably to fortify and use it (unless you have ready access to a better structure nearby). For an expedient last-minute basement shelter, push a heavy table (one that you can get under) into the corner that has the highest level of soil on the outside. The ground level outside ideally needs to be higher than the top of the table shelter inside. If no heavy table is available, create one by taking internal doors off their hinges and mounting them across supports.

Protective Shielding: Placing Mass between Your Family and the Radiation

Now it's time to accomplish your second goal: placing sufficient mass between your family and the fallout to absorb the deadly radiation. To do this, pile any available materials on and around the table; you can use books, wood, cordwood, bricks, sandbags, sacks of cement or feed, heavy appliances, full file cabinets, full water containers, food stocks, and boxes and pillowcases full of anything heavy, like dirt. This pile of material will help absorb and stop radiation from penetrating, so the thicker the layer of materials, the better. (By the way, lead is nothing special for stopping radiation, it's the same as anything else pound for pound; it just takes fewer inches compared to less weighty materials.) Be sure to reinforce your table and supports so you do not overload it and cause it to collapse.

SHIELDING REDUCES RADIATION		
Material	Thickness (in inches) needed to reduce the radiation to 10% of initial intensity	Thickness (in inches) needed to stop 99% of the radiation
Steel	3.3	5
Concrete	11	16 solid brick or hollow concrete blocks filled with mortar or sand
Earth	16	24 (packed) 36 (loose)
Water	24	36
Wood	38	56

You might not have enough steel, but any materials you use have mass and can enhance your shielding; it just takes more thickness of lighter wood, for example, than heavier earth, to absorb and stop the same amount of radiation.

Also, adding mass to the floor above your chosen basement corner and outside against the walls opposite your shelter can dramatically increase your shielding protection. Every inch of thickness adds up to more effective life-saving radiation shielding.

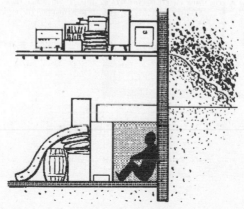

Livability: Making Living in Your Shelter Tolerable

Finally, you'll want to turn your attention to the practical aspects of spending time in the shelter. For example, you'll need to be able to get into and out of it, so create a small crawl-through entrance to the space underneath the table. Near that entrance, place more mass that you can easily pull in after you to seal the opening.

You'll also need to ensure adequate ventilation. Leave at least two four- to six-inch square air spaces in the protective layer of material—one high at one end and one low at the other end. Create more air spaces if you're crowded and/or in a hot climate. Use a small piece of cardboard to fan fresh air in if the naturally rising warmer air convection current needs assistance in moving the air along. This incoming air won't need to be filtered if the basement has been reasonably sealed up; however, any windows or other openings in the basement will require solid mass coverage to assure glass does not break, and to provide additional shielding protection for the basement. (More details on that in No. 7.)

Of course, with more time, materials, and carpentry or masonry skills, you could even construct a more professional fallout shelter.

Pre-built wood components
stored
in the basement
may be
assembled
and filled
with bricks
or concrete blocks
for emergency protection.

HOME FALLOUT SHELTER
lean-to shelter-
basement location

FEDERAL EMERGENCY
MANAGEMENT AGENCY

What Results Can You Expect?

As cramped as that crawlspace fallout shelter might seem, the vital shielding provided by simply moving some mass into place can mean the difference between exposure to a lethal dose of radiation and the survival of your family.

An effective fallout shelter constructed in a basement can reduce your radiation exposure by one hundred to two hundred times or more. Thus, if the initial radiation intensity outside were 500 R/hr (fatal in one hour), the basement shelter occupants might only experience 2–5 R/hr or even less, which is survivable, especially with the radiation intensity decreasing by the hour.

The majority of people requiring any sheltering at all will be many miles downwind, and they will not need to stay sheltered for weeks on end. In fact, most people will only need to shelter full-time for a few days before they can start coming out briefly to attend to quick essential chores. Later, they can begin spending even more time out of the shelter daily, only returning to sleep. As miserable as it might seem now, you and your family can easily endure that, especially compared to the alternative.

6. Basic Supply List for Family Member(s) Tasked with Store Run

If stores are still stocked and it's safe to go, try to buy as many of the following items as possible immediately. No quantities are listed for food items because family sizes vary and because, as the emergency and panic widens, many items will quickly become sold out or quantities will be restricted. At a minimum, try to gather enough provisions for two weeks; at best, aim for collecting enough to last two months or longer.

It's important to remember that if and when we are attacked, it will be a very long time before anything about our communities returns to normal again. Hurricane victims can attest to the prolonged misery and disruptions from even a localized disaster (and that's with the rest of the country being able to help out). Nobody can imagine how bad the suffering and disorder will be, or how long they will continue, once nuclear weapons have gone off—especially if they do so in multiple locations.

The first few items on the list below are primarily for use during the time spent in the shelter. They are mostly ready-to-eat items that require no cooking or preparation, just a can opener at most. (Note: The iodine solution is included here because of its importance for its thyroid-blocking topical use detailed below, but it's never to be ingested or swallowed.) The foods listed below the first grouping are additional staples for use during the extended recovery period. After that is a list of general non-food supplies, tools, and equipment.

The important thing to remember is: Acquire it all now—act quickly! It's much better to risk being a little early rather than a few hours too late when securing your family's essential food and supplies.

For Use in the Shelter
- Bread and cooler of sandwich meats
- Canned goods (pasta, soups, chili, vegetables, fruit, tuna, meats, beans, peanut butter, etc.)
- Drink mix flavorings (Since you won't have cold drinks and will have only water, kids will appreciate these.)
- Fruit (bananas, apples, oranges, grapes, etc.)
- Iodine solution such as Betadine, 16 ounces (Note: Not to be ingested or swallowed!)
- Ready-to-eat foods (toaster pastries, raisins, cheese, granola/energy/protein bars, puddings, etc.)
- Vitamins (multi-vitamins, vitamin C, etc.)

For Use during the Extended Recovery Period
Note: Purchase the largest boxes, bags, or jars of the following supplies you can find, and purchase enough to last your family a minimum of two weeks but preferably two months.
- Additional large stock of canned and ready-to-eat food
- Baking powder
- Baking soda
- Beans

- Bottled water (especially if home supplies are not secured yet)
- Cooking oil (2 gallons or more)
- Dried milk (can be used inside shelter, too)
- Flour
- Honey
- Macaroni and other pasta
- Pancake and biscuit mix
- Potatoes
- Quick oats and other grains and cereals
- Rice
- Spice assortment
- Sugar
- Syrup

Non-Food Items
- Ammunition (if you have weapons)
- Baby wipes (for personal hygiene)
- Batteries (at least three sets for each battery-operated device)
- Bleach (5.25 percent, without fragrance or soap additives)
- Bucket (5-gallon) and corresponding liner bags (for use as toilet)
- Camping supplies such as a cook stove, fuel, water filters, and portable toilet
- Diapers
- Duct tape
- Feminine hygiene products
- Fire extinguishers
- First aid kits
- Flashlights (ideally LED)
- Garbage cans and liner bags (for water storage and waste storage)

- Kitchen matches and disposable lighters
- Manual can opener (2)
- Medications: Over-the-counter medications and first-aid supplies (aspirin/acetaminophen/ibuprofen, stomach relief medications, alcohol, hydrogen peroxide) as well as prescription drugs (as recently filled as possible, and with as much extra as possible)
- N95 dust filter mask respirators (These are inexpensive; buy a large supply.)
- Paper or plastic plates/bowls/cups/utensils
- Plastic hooded rain ponchos (These are also inexpensive; purchase plenty for everyone.)
- Plastic sheeting
- Radio (portable, and preferably more than one)
- Staple guns and staples
- Toilet paper
- Toilet seat (or use one from your house) if no portable toilet is available

7. Essential Details

If you've secured your supplies, stored water, and built your family fallout shelter, congratulations! You have improved the odds of your family's survival by a hundred times or more. Now, you need to expand your knowledge and fine-tune the tactics that will make the most of your family survival strategy. Following is a round-up of information for quick reference.

What to Expect from the Government

Government information and guidance are vital resources as you respond to a nuclear crisis, but for many reasons that information might be late, incomplete, misleading, or simply incorrect. While evacuation might be prudent for individuals who act quickly in response to a threat, governments will be slow to call for mass evacuations because of their potential to create panic and gridlock. As the recent government calls for people to gather duct tape and plastic sheeting caused stores to run out of those items, ignited public anxiety, and touched off derision by the press, the government will be greatly reluctant to issue similar alarms again. If you want to assure successful evacuation or shelter, with adequate food and supplies for your family, you must act before the panic and without first waiting for government instructions that might never come or that might not come as urgently as warranted. You alone are ultimately responsible for your family survival.

Ensuring Air Quality

Filtering the air coming into your basement inner shelter from the basement itself won't be required. Air does not become radioactive, and if your basement is reasonably snug, there won't be any wind blowing through it to carry the radioactive fallout dust inside. Simply sealing any basement windows and other openings will prevent significant fallout accumulation within. To improve the radiation shielding inside the basement and to protect the windows from being broken and letting fallout blow in later, cover them with wood. Then, if possible, also cover them with sandbags, solid masonry blocks, or earth on the outside and/or inside. If the basement air becomes oppressively stale, you can re-open a door into the upper floors of the still-closed house. It's also important to know that a common furnace air filter is effective in filtering radioactive fallout; therefore, you can later cover an outside air opening (such as a window) with one of those to safely improve air circulation.

Contamination of Food and Clothing

Any food or water stored in sealed containers will be safe to use after brushing or rinsing off any fallout dust that has accumulated on the surface of the container. As long as the dust does not get inside the container, whatever radiation penetrated the container from the outside will not harm the contents.

If you suspect that your clothes have fallout dust on them, remove your outer clothing before you go inside—and leave the contaminated clothing outside. An inexpensive plastic hooded rain poncho that can be easily rinsed off or left outside is a worthwhile investment. Also, keep a supply of water and baby shampoo near the entrance so late-arriving family members can wash and thoroughly rinse any exposed skin and hair before entering the house. (Baby shampoo is easier on the eyes for both children and adults, especially if limited rinse water is available.) Exposure to fallout radiation does not make one radioactive, but you need to ensure that you don't bring any of the fallout dust inside. (The indication of radiation sickness, which is not contagious, is typically temporary nausea. When it's a mild case, you can expect a full recovery.)

Protecting Outdoor Items

Before fallout arrives, cover with plastic tarp any outdoor items or vegetable gardens to make it easier to rinse off the fallout dust once it's safe to come out and do so.

Radios

If you haven't had enough time to acquire radiological instruments such as Geiger counters (which measure intensity of ionizing radiation) and dosimeters (which measure dose absorption of radiation), you'll need to be certain that portable radios function properly from inside your shelter, and that you have plenty of fresh batteries in stock. Without radiological instruments, listening for official guidance about the radiation threat levels in your area will be the only way you can learn when it will be safe to venture out. It might also be the only way you'll know when you need to take your initial maximum protective action. When not in use, radios should not be attached to any outside antenna, nor should their own antenna be extended. Further, wrap the radios in any non-conducting insulation, like layers of paper, cloth, or bubble wrap plastic, then store them in a metal container or wrap them in aluminum foil to minimize the potential of electromagnetic pulses ruining the electronics.

Having back-up radios is very prudent. Keep one additional radio tuned to a station in the closest likely target city. If that station suddenly goes off the air, you will know an attack might have occurred.

What Happens First

If you are close to a target, your first indication of a nuclear detonation may be its characteristic bright flash. The first effects you might have to deal with before radioactive fallout arrives, depending on your proximity, are blast and thermal energy. Promptly employing the "duck and cover" strategy will protect you from flying debris injuries and minimize thermal burns. Those very close to the blast will experience brief tornado strength winds, and should quickly dive behind any solid object or into any available depression or culvert. Even if you're out in the open, lying flat on the ground can reduce your chance of being hit by shrapnel or becoming airborne shrapnel by eight times. A very large, 500-kiloton blast two and a half miles away will arrive about eight seconds after the detonation flash with a very strong, three-second wind blast. That delay is much greater farther away, and it provides plenty of time to "duck and cover" if you're trained and alert. Once you do that, stay down for up to two minutes. Most people won't be near a ground zero, and will—like the vast majority of people—only need to deal with the fallout later.

Waiting for the Fallout

When fallout is anticipated but hasn't yet arrived, anyone who isn't already sheltered should begin wearing an N95 dust protector filter mask and a plastic hooded rain poncho (both of those items are available at most hardware or home supply stores). Everyone should also begin taking potassium iodide (KI) or potassium iodate (KIO3) tablets for thyroid protection against cancer-causing radioactive iodine, which is a major product of nuclear weapons explosions.

The farther you are downwind, as all the two hundred or so radioactive isotopes released become ever more dissipated over distance, radioactive iodine becomes the greater relative threat because it re-concentrates itself in the tiny thyroid gland where other isotopes disperse more evenly in one's body with comparatively less harmful effects. If no KI or KIO3 tablets are available, you can apply an iodine solution such as tincture of iodine or Betadine topically (on the skin) for a similar protective effect. (Warning: Iodine solutions are never to be ingested or swallowed.)

Recommended Use of Iodine

Apply the following amounts of a 2 percent tincture of iodine by painting the solution on the abdomen or forearm each day, for a maximum of ten days, ideally beginning at least two hours before initial exposure.

Adults 19 and older	8 ml*
Children 3 to 18 years (and under 150 pounds)	4 ml
Children under 3 and older than 4 weeks	2 ml
Newborns up to 4 weeks old	1 ml

*If you don't have a medicine dropper graduated in milliliters, it will help you to know that one measuring teaspoon is about 5 ml. Also, if your iodine is stronger than 2 percent, reduce the dosage accordingly.

Absorption through the skin is not as reliable a dosing method as using the tablets, but research shows that it is still very effective for most people. Do not use if allergic to iodine. If at all possible, ask your doctor now if there is any reason anyone in your household should not use KI tablets, KIO3 tablets, or iodine solution on their skin in a future nuclear emergency, just to be sure.

Sealing the House

When you know that the time to take protective action is approaching, turn off all the utilities coming into the house and make sure windows, doors, vents, and any other openings are sealed up and locked down. Also, place near your shelter additional tools, crow bars, and car jacks for use later to dig out, if required. Keep fire extinguishers handy. And have on hand a collection of building supplies, tools, plastic sheeting, and staple guns for covering any holes caused by damage. Your basement should already be well sealed against fallout, but you will need to use duct tape to seal around the last door you use to enter the shelter, especially if it's a door that leads directly outside.

Food

Don't risk fire, burns, and asphyxiation by trying to cook anything in the cramped shelter space. Stock your shelter with a can opener, canned goods, and other non-perishable foods that are ready to eat. Leave additional food and water right outside the entrance so you can pull those in quickly as needed when it's safe to do so.

Light

A couple of small LED flashlights or LED headlamps will help stretch the life of the batteries in your flashlights. Avoid using candles if at all possible.

Sleeping

Pack in a small, thin mattress, sleeping bags, cushions, blankets, and pillows.

Passing the Time

Bring in some books for yourself and books, puzzles, and games for the children.

Restroom

To create a makeshift restroom, if you don't have a portable toilet, improvise a toilet by mounting a seat (purchased or borrowed from one of your house bathrooms) on a five-gallon bucket lined with garbage bag liners of the appropriate size. Position it near the wall with the outgoing upper air vent, and hang a sheet or blanket around the facility to provide privacy. Stock the "restroom" with toilet paper and pre-moistened cloths.

For disposal, keep a full-size, bag-lined garbage can with a tight-fitting lid very close to the shelter entrance for depositing used (tightly sealed) liners when it is safe to do so quickly.

Pets

What to do about your pets? That is a tough call. Letting dogs or cats run free is not a humane option because of the possibility that they will have to endure a miserable death from radiation exposure outside and/or because they will put others at risk, especially if they become diseased or join one of the inevitable packs of other abandoned pets. Caring for them within the shelter, then, is ideal—if it's truly realistic and doesn't drain your limited resources. Putting pets down might eventually become a painful but necessary reality if the disruption of services and food supplies is long-term and you haven't secured sufficient food for them.

Water

Boiling or bleach water treatments will be used for cleaning your stored water later for drinking. (This is for killing bacteria, not for radiation contamination, which is never a concern for any stored and covered water containers or even sealed food.) Tap water recently put into clean containers before the crisis won't likely need to be purified before using. To purify questionable water, bring it to a rolling boil and keep it boiling for at least ten minutes. If you don't have the fuel to boil the water, kill the bacteria by mixing in ten drops of good quality household bleach (at least 5.25 percent pure, such as Clorox) per gallon. Then let the water sit for at least a half-hour. But be sure the bleach you use has no additives such as soap or fragrance. You can get rid of the flat taste the water takes on after boiling or some of the chlorine taste caused by the bleach by pouring the water from one container to another several times.

Additional Information

There's much more that you can learn to help you better understand what you are up against and what you can do to help your family survive a disaster such as this. The basic strategy for securing the safety of your family during a nuclear emergency is simple: Maximize your distance from the fallout radiation source, minimize your time exposed to fallout radiation, and utilize the most effective available shielding for your designated shelter space. When time allows, and if the Internet is still up and running before the nuclear event, you or someone in your family should do further research and acquire more detailed information.

The information in the following section explains the different kinds of radiation and their health effects. (See www.radshelters4u.com.)

The Difference between Alpha, Beta and Gamma Radiation

Everything in nature would prefer to be in a relaxed or stable state. Unstable atoms undergo nuclear processes that cause them to become more stable. One such process involves emitting excess energy from the nucleus. This process is called radioactivity or radioactive decay. The terms "radiation" and "radioactivity" are often confused. The proper relationship between the terms is that "radioactive atoms emit radiation."

There are three main types of nuclear radiation emitted from radioactive atoms and included in all fallout:

1. Alpha: These are actual particles that are electrically charged and are commonly referred to as alpha particles. Alpha particles are the least penetrating of the three primary forms of radiation, since they cannot travel more than 4–7 inches in air, and a single sheet of paper or the outermost layer of dead skin that covers the body will stop them. However, if alpha particle-emitting radioactive material is inhaled or ingested, the alpha particles can be a very damaging source of radiation with their short range being concentrated internally in a very localized area.

2. Beta: These are also actual particles that are electrically charged and are commonly referred to as beta particles.

Beta particles travel faster and penetrate deeper than alpha particles. They can travel from a few millimeters to about ten yards in open air, depending on the particular isotope. They can also penetrate several millimeters through tissue. Beta particle radiation is generally a slight external exposure hazard, although prolonged exposure to large amounts can cause skin burns, and it is also a major hazard when interacting with the lens of the eye. However, like alpha particles, the greatest threat occurs when beta particle-emitting radioactive material is inhaled or ingested, because it can also cause grave internal damage.

3. Gamma: Gamma rays are similar to x-rays; they are a form of electromagnetic radiation. Gamma rays are the most hazardous type of external radiation, because they can travel up to a mile in open air and penetrate all types of materials. Since gamma rays penetrate more deeply through the body than alpha or beta particles, all tissues and organs can be damaged by sources from outside of the body. Only sufficiently dense shielding and/or distance from gamma ray-emitting radioactive material can provide protection.

The bottom line: All three of the primary types of radiation can be a hazard if emitted from radioactive fallout that has been inhaled or ingested. Protected food and water, and even a simple inexpensive dust protector face mask, can go a long way toward blocking this route of entry. However, for the penetrating gamma rays, it is essential to be able to identify the best protected shielding and distance options available.

Measuring Radiation

Since nuclear radiation affects people, we must be able to measure its presence. We also need to relate the amount of radiation received by the body to its physiological effects. Two terms used to relate the amount of radiation received by the body are *exposure* and *dose*.

When you are *exposed* to radiation, your body absorbs a *dose* of radiation.

As in most measurement quantities, certain units are used to properly express the measurement. For radiation measurements they are:

Roentgen: The roentgen measures the energy produced by gamma radiation in a cubic centimeter of air. It is usually abbreviated with the capital letter "R." A milliroentgen, or "mR," is equal to one one-thousandth of a roentgen. An exposure of 50 roentgens would be written "50 R."

Rad (Radiation Absorbed Dose): Rad recognizes that different materials that receive the same exposure may not absorb the same amount of energy. A rad measures the amount of radiation energy transferred to some mass of material, typically humans. One roentgen of gamma radiation exposure results in about one rad of absorbed dose.

Rem (Roentgen Equivalent Man): Rem is a unit that relates the dose of any radiation to the biological effect of that dose. To relate the absorbed dose of specific types of radiation to their biological effect, a "quality factor" must be multiplied by the dose in rad, which then shows the dose in rems. For gamma rays and beta particles, 1 rad of exposure results in 1 rem of dose.

Other measurement terms: Standard International (SI) units that may be used in place of the rem and the rad are the sievert (Sv) and the gray (Gy).

These units are related as follows:

1Sv = 100 rem

1Gy = 100 rad

Two other terms that refer to the rate of radioactive decay of a radioactive material are curie (Ci) and becquerel (Bq).

Fortunately, cutting through the above confusion, for purposes of practical radiation protection in humans, most experts (including those at the FEMA Emergency Management Institute) agree that roentgen, rad and rem can all be considered equivalent for radiation emergencies. The exposure rates and doses you'll usually see will be expressed simply in terms of roentgen (R) or milliroentgen (mR). Remember, too, that a milliroentgen, or "mR," is equal to one one-thousandth of a roentgen "R."

When Radiation Exposure Becomes Dangerous

Several government publications outline the levels of radiation and their effects on a person's health. Here's a look at the expected health effects for an adult assuming the cumulative total radiation dose (all received within a week's time). Note that for children, the effects can be expected at half these dose levels.

TOTAL DOSE	ONSET & DURATION OF INITIAL SYMPTOMS & DISPOSITION
30 to 70 R	**From 6-12 hours:** Zero to slight incidence of transient headache and nausea; vomiting in up to 5% of personnel in upper part of dose range. Mild lymphocyte depression within 24 hours. Full recovery expected. (Fetus damage possible from 50R and above.)
70 to 150 R	**From 2-20 hours:** Transient, mild nausea and vomiting in 5-30% of personnel. Potential for delayed traumatic and surgical wound healing, minimal clinical effect. Moderate drop in lymphocyte, platelet, and granulocyte counts. Increased susceptibility to opportunistic pathogens. Full recovery expected.
150 to 300 R	**From 2 hours to three days:** Transient to moderate nausea and vomiting in 20-70%; mild to moderate fatigability and weakness in 25-60% of personnel. At 3 to 5 weeks: Medical care required for 10-50%. At high end of range, death may occur to maximum 10%. Anticipated medical problems include infection, bleeding, and fever. Wounding or burns will geometrically increase morbidity and mortality.
300 to 530 R	**From 2 hours to three days:** Transient to moderate nausea and vomiting in 50-90%; mild to moderate fatigability in 50-90%. At 2 to 5 weeks: Medical care required for 10-80%. At low end of range, less than 10% deaths; at high end, death may occur for more than 50%. Anticipated medical problems include frequent diarrheal stools, anorexia, increased fluid loss, ulceration. Increased infection susceptibility during immunocompromised time-frame. Moderate to severe loss of lymphocytes. Hair loss after 14 days.
530 to 830 R	**From 2 hours to two days:** Moderate to severe nausea and vomiting in 80-100%; **From 2 hours to six weeks:** Moderate to severe fatigability and weakness in 90-100%. At 10 days to 5 weeks: Medical care required for 50-100%. At low end of range, death may occur for more than 50% at six weeks. At high end, death may occur for 99% of personnel. Anticipated medical problems include developing pathogenic and opportunistic infections, bleeding, fever, loss of appetite, GI ulcerations, bloody diarrhea, severe fluid and electrolyte shifts, capillary leak, hypotension. Combined with any significant physical trauma, survival rates will approach zero.
830 R Plus	**From 30 minutes to 2 days:** Severe nausea, vomiting, fatigability, weakness, dizziness, and disorientation; moderate to severe fluid imbalance and headache. Bone marrow total depletion within days. CNS symptoms are predominant at higher radiation levels. Few, if any, survivors even with aggressive and immediate medical attention.

The response to radiation varies widely, and the longer the time frame over which a specific dose is accumulated, the better your body can respond to and recover from the radiation damage. In other words, a normally fatal (to 50 percent of a group exposed to it) cumulative dose of 530 R, if received all within a week, would create few noticeable ill health effects at all if it was received but spread out over a year's time at the rate of about 10 R per week.

Think of the difference in acquiring a suntan gradually over a year at a rate of about a half-hour per day compared to packing that year's worth of sun exposure (182 hours) into one non-stop week, night and day. The health effect difference is obviously very dramatic when the body is overwhelmed and does not have time to keep up with repairs.

Radiation Exposure Time Chart

ACUTE EFFECTS	ACCUMULATED EXPOSURE (R) IN ANY:		
	1 WEEK	1 MONTH	4 MONTHS
Medical Care Not Needed	150	200	300
Some Need Medical Care; Few If Any Deaths	250	350	500
Most Need Medical Care 50%+ Deaths	450	600	*

* Little or no practical consideration
SOURCE: National Council on Radiation Protection and Measurements

Remember, promptly removing yourself from the radiation source would have you no longer absorbing and adding to that cumulative dose. And, that can make all the difference between absorbing a dangerous radiation dose or getting only a tiny fraction you might not even be able to later notice.

The Bottom Line

The above guide was written assuming it would not be read by the majority of its intended audience until a nuclear crisis is already fully upon us—when time and resources will be extremely limited. If you are fortunate enough to have read this well before a nuclear threat occurs or appears imminent, there's a great deal more you can learn and should do beyond the scope of this guide.

Surviving the initial threats of a nuclear event and radioactive fallout is relatively easy with the proper knowledge and even modest preparations, as detailed above. The ongoing bigger challenge will be the one brought on by extensive and long-lasting disruption of services after you survive the nuclear event and emerge safely once the fallout radiation threat has diminished. You may go many months with little or no new food supplies arriving, disruption of water, sewer, gas, electric, and telephone services, little or no gasoline, and severely limited medical services, banking services, law enforcement activity, and fire protection.

With more time to research, make plans, and order supplies, families are well served to acquire more in-depth training, reference books, long-term food and water supplies, fuel, medical equipment, personal security, communication equipment, radiation monitoring instruments, and tools. Many informative web sites and suppliers make available all of the above, including ready-to-eat meals, dehydrated and freeze-dried foods, as well as buckets of beans, rice, and grains. They also offer solar cookers, water purifiers, water barrels, compost toilets, comprehensive medical kits and manuals, shortwave and local two-way radios, alternative energy systems, long-term packaged seeds, gardening tools, and canning equipment.

Starting Small

If all of this preparation seems daunting, here's one strategy to making it a little less overwhelming: Think in twos. First, acquire all the supplies your family would need to survive for two weeks if totally cut off from stores, utility services and municipal services. It might help to consider all you would need during an extended camping trip in any season. Then, once you've accomplished that, expand your preparations to meet the goal of surviving at home for two months with no utilities or services.

After that, continue adding provisions for even more months, with the eventual goal of gathering enough supplies so that your family can survive under these distressed conditions for as much as a year. A year might seem terribly long, but you'll no doubt discover that in any disruptive event, numerous friends, neighbors, and relatives will be in need—and you will want to help them if you can. Of course, ideally, they should also be preparing their own families for survival during a nuclear disaster, so sharing this information with them might help get them started. Also, for your own family's security, you will want to try to surround yourself with like-minded people who are also doing the right things to prepare so they will become helpful allies instead of draining your limited resources. (They could possibly even become a threat if severely unprepared and difficult circumstances were to drag on and became ever more desperate.)

It Won't Go to Waste!

If you're trying to convince yourself or a spouse to make the investment in supplies, keep in mind this fact: Many of the supplies save money because buying in bulk is less expensive than buying smaller quantities. Further, if nothing bad ever happens, you can eventually eat or use most of the supplies. They will also be useful in many disasters besides nuclear events. For example:

Job loss—Having two to four months of food at home would certainly relieve much of the stress of losing your job and being without an income while looking for another.

Pandemic—We could someday see a pandemic unleashed that would require families to self-quarantine themselves at home for many weeks to avoid catching the disease. Having these supplies and having made these preparations would make that difficult time go much more smoothly.

Natural disaster, economic dislocation, civil disruption—You could ride out any number, or cascading combination, of these events in much better shape if you are sufficiently prepared.

Being prepared and stocking up makes sense on numerous levels, especially during this age when costs for essentials such as food, fuel, and ammunition will surely continue to increase.

How People Act in Times of Trouble

When tough times come, you'll likely discover that people today, overall, are not as resilient as they were in times past. For many of us, our grandparents' generation included a higher percentage of self-reliant, rural folks who "made do" on less, and who grew and raised their own food and livestock. Today, more people are far removed from the land and the routine of being responsible for supplying their own food; many even have a government-dependent entitlement mentality. The morality that both sustained and restrained previous generations during tough times is not as widely evident in this present population. As a result, more people will more quickly succumb to rationalizing theft, robbery, looting, and rioting when they fear hunger and deprivation. Crime is already a problem today—even with nobody being hungry, and even with law enforcement in place. Crime, then, could explode when hunger and disruptions escalate and law enforcement deteriorates concurrently. It is therefore prudent for anyone making serious preparations to also include plans for maintaining their own security if law enforcement is either unavailable or cannot keep pace with the demands of a greatly increasing crime wave. If you do not own or use guns, I would strongly urge you to reevaluate your personal security. If you find it lacking, acquire some guns and ammunition immediately, and get some safety and practical tactical training in their use. Ask a clerk at your gun store to point you to local resources for that kind of training.

For those who already have weapons, be sure they are effective models and calibers for self-defense, and that you have stocked plenty of ammunition and high-capacity magazines if needed. Weapons and ammo will quickly disappear—or it will become prohibitively expensive or restricted once the essential need is more widely recognized.

Financial Concerns

Once you are well on your way to acquiring your family's preparation tools, equipment, and supplies, consider gathering extra items to help others and to use as future barter goods. You might be able to trade extra garden seeds, batteries, antibiotics, water filters, and ammo for other needed products or services. Some people are even converting a small percentage of their traditional paper investments into some gold and/or silver coins for trading purposes, as well as for prudent wealth diversification. Having wealth in forms other than solely paper dollars, plastic credit cards, or a 401(k) account might make the critical difference in one day being able to get your gravely ill child to the front of a mile-long line to see the only overworked doctor or dentist in town. It'll sure beat waving around a copy of your last monthly investment or banking statement then.

A Final Word

To better avoid unhealthy and overwhelming angst trying to prepare for all future dislocations and disruptions, keep in mind, too, that each step is like acquiring medical insurance. We all hope and pray we won't need that insurance, but if we ever do, our families won't find us lacking in stepping up to our fundamental responsibility of providing for their safety and welfare.

Once you've started making these preparations, strive to stay balanced. Thank God that you have begun, and begin to relax within your new alert status. You'll now be able to more fully enjoy life with your family confidently knowing you're better able to handle just about any event that might occur in this quickly changing world.

Shane Connor is the CEO of www.ki4u.com and www.nukalert.com, consultants and developers of civil defense solutions to government, military, private organizations and individual families.

Pandemics and Emerging Diseases

by Sue Bradley

In 1818, Mary Shelley first described her expedition into "murky sub-terranean passages" within the trapezoid cavern of Cumaean Sibyl near Naples, Italy. It was here in the cave so frequently described in Virgil's first century *Eclogues* and *Æneid* that Shelley asserts she discovered the ancient apocalyptic writings of the Roman prophetess Cumaean Sybil recorded on oak leaves. Translating and editing the *Sibylline Prophecies*, Mary Shelley published *The Last Man* in 1826.

Described as "a memory at the end of history," *The Last Man* begins, "let me fancy myself as I was in 2094," and continues to describe an horrific plague that destroys mankind as a species. *The Last Man* would become the first modern account of an apocalyptic pandemic, and, disturbingly, would be written as a nihilist narrative in a post-human era.[1]

Contagion, the transmission of disease, has always been a unique entity, surpassing all potential cataclysms with its singular characteristic of being entirely sovereign and non-discriminatory. Borderless, apolitical, and smugly defiant, disease has spread, multiplied, and mutated—and has historically shown deference to no one.

A Pox on Both Your Houses
Ring Around the Rosy: Ashes, Ashes

Though mortality estimates of pandemics throughout history are often unreliable (if not entirely unknown), their impact has often been measured only by these statistics, with less examination of concurrent societal disruption. With the exception of medical and scientific study, epidemics were understood mostly within their literary and classical context. Children's songs, nursery rhymes, and colloquialisms would hint of their impact, but nothing in recent memory would demand the serious attention of many in western society. The sustained scourge of AIDS is familiar in concept, but easily dismissed unless there is direct involvement. Ebola, cholera, plague, Marburg, SARS, and anthrax are serious sounding, but largely irrelevant to the generations raised in a society of "eradication," vaccines, and fix-'em-fast antibiotics.

There has been growing concern among experts of the fast-rising density of human populations and the immediate need to strategize to avoid high death tolls in inevitable natural disasters. Similarly, public health experts warn that vigilance and speed in tracking and responding to disease outbreaks is vital to limit the chances of a pandemic.

Every age in history has had its plagues, wars, and disasters. What *is* different about our world today is the enormous potential of a catastrophic pandemic situation. A public health emergency at this level would be far more catastrophic than any other type of naturally occurring, accidental, or other instigated event the world has ever experienced.

Who's WHO?
The Names behind the Letters

In early September 2000, 152 heads of state, the largest assembly of world leaders in history, gathered at the United Nations headquarters in New York City for The Millennium Summit, with the purpose of adopting The UN Millennium Declaration, which commits the nations to a "new global partnership to reduce extreme poverty and setting out a series of time-bound targets, with a deadline of 2015."[2]

These "target" purposes are outlined in eight specific objectives and are defined as "The Millennium Development Goals (MDGs)," and were adopted by all 189 member states of the United Nations General Council and have been proclaimed as "a defining moment for global cooperation in the 21st century."[3] These eight objectives are:

Goal 1: Eradicate extreme hunger and poverty

Goal 2: Achieve universal primary education

Goal 3: Promote gender equality and empower women

Goal 4: Reduce child mortality

Goal 5: Improve maternal health

Goal 6: Combat HIV/AIDS, malaria, and other diseases

Goal 7: Ensure environmental sustainability

Goal 8: Develop a global partnership for development

It is under "The Millennium Declaration Goal No. 6 (MDG 6)" that the united global effort to combat disease would commit financial, academic, field, and trial resources and through which all ensuing programs and commitments would be ultimately patrolled and controlled.[4]

September 25, 2008, at the historic midpoint of the MDGs program, leaders from around the world once again convened to reaffirm their governments' commitment to reach the articulated goals. This convention would be given the designation of "UN High-level Event."

"I am grateful for all the energy invested in this High-level Event by developed and developing countries, civil society, faith groups, foundations and the private sector.... My great hope for today was that all development partners would join forces to accelerate MDG progress. We have succeeded. We did this together. And now, we must forge ahead. We must make it happen."

UN Secretary-General Ban Ki-moon
September 25, 2008[5]

During the years that the nations of the world pursued collaborative energies to effectively meet "Millennium Declaration Goal No. 6,"
through health and social programs for developing and substandard
nations, Hollywood had begun a program of inoculating the more
comfortably preoccupied masses with remarkably prescient bio-threat
scenarios such as *I Am Legend, Outbreak, The Stand,* and *V for Vendetta.*
And it was during these years that very real and prolific research programs began to notice that life forms confined to the microscopic realm
were changing—rapidly, sometimes predictably, often unpredictably,
and in some instances, chillingly purposefully.

It has been only within the past five years that serious attention
and discussion of infectious threats have taken place at a popular level,
and these have been limited, for the most part, to ingestible mad cow/
Creutzfeldt-Jakob disease and avian influenza strains. These too, however, are fast succumbing to the social fatigue of media hype. No one
can identify a specific pandemic agent with absolute certainty, but it
might be possible to determine the most likely.

Under the Internet umbrella is a massive collection of data, documentation, and detail—and perhaps a deterministic hint. The propor-
tional ratio of available literature and guidelines for influenza is, by
comparison to other potential pandemic threats, in such stark contrast
that one could entertain the suspicion that influenza pandemic is actually an orchestrated effort.

> "Some will say this discussion of the Avian Flu is an overreac-
> tion. Some may say, 'Did we cry wolf?' The reality is that if
> the H5N1 virus does not trigger pandemic flu, there will be
> another virus that will."
> Secretary Mike Levitt
> Department of Health and Human Services
> November 2, 2005[6]

Newly developed and otherwise newly emerging strains are designated "novel": their patterns are not yet determined. The World

Health Organization's guidelines for humanitarian agencies explains that, "When a major change in surface proteins occurs spontaneously, a new subtype can emerge that has not previously circulated in humans, and to which no one will have full immunity. If this new virus also has the capacity to spread efficiently and in a sustained manner from person to person, an influenza pandemic can occur."[7]

But while pandemics are broad in effect, the toxicity of the operative pathogen needs to be carefully balanced. A pandemic virus emerges via two principal mechanisms: reassortant and adaptive mutation.

The World Health Organization describes past pandemics as the "epidemiological equivalent of a flash flood," often beginning abruptly, without warning, and sweeping "through populations with ferocious velocity,"[8] leaving considerable damage in their wake. WHO also notes a predictable feature of pandemics: the tendency to recur in waves, often with a stronger, more virulent mutation of the affecting agent: "Subsequent waves often began simultaneously in several different parts of the world, intensifying the abrupt disruption at the global level."[9]

The United States Department of Homeland Security projects the potential effect of pandemic influenza on the United States population: "The clinical disease attack rate will be 30 percent in the overall population during the pandemic. Illness rates will be highest among school-aged children (about 40 percent) and decline with age. Among working adults, an average of 20 percent will become ill during a community outbreak."[10]

The eventuality of a global pandemic of unprecedented scope has been the singular priority within the international response community for years. There has never been a discussion of "if" there will be another global pandemic; there have only been the best estimates of "when," and within the space of weeks a pandemic could affect multiple communities, nations, and regions simultaneously. Likewise, there are coincident factors that would depend upon the status of regional (or available) infrastructure, and all include variables at different, and often unstable, levels.

These "Critical Infrastructure and Key Resources" (CI/KR) are the focus of the U.S. Department of Homeland Security's *Pandemic Influenza* guide. The eighty-four page document introduces the crucial nature of infrastructure integrity in section 1.3:

The "Situation"

The mounting risk of a worldwide influenza pandemic poses numerous potentially devastating consequences for critical infrastructure in the United States. A pandemic will likely reduce dramatically the number of available workers in all sectors, and significantly disrupt the movement of people and goods, which will threaten essential services and operations within and across our nation's CI/KR sectors.

Industries in every sector of the critical infrastructure will experience pandemic impacts. Given today's highly mobile population, disease outbreaks may occur simultaneously throughout the country, making the reallocation of human and material resources more difficult than in other disaster or emergency situations.[11]

As thorough preparedness at every level is imperative, it is prudent to examine the manner of response contingent upon sociobiological realities, specifically, a pandemic "situation" as it would be managed with:

Comparatively intact critical infrastructure/key resources
(CIKR)
Substantial impairment of critical infrastructure/key resources
(CI/KR)

Exotic Threats

In 2008, WHO published the *Operational Procedures for Event Management* for international public health security, drafted within the context of communicable diseases, but adoptable for all hazards—chemical, biological, radio-nuclear, etc.[12] Having established guidelines for risks or events which are or have the potential to be of international concern, WHO's *International Health Regulations* (2005) identifies and mandates protocol when public health security across international borders is threatened.[13]

The parameters themselves can vary widely within WHO's 193 member nations. International collective oversight permits the management and distribution of resources to appropriately designated vectors from the most technologically superior western standard to the less developed and often balkanized nations.

If specific threats are identified as "extreme and rare," the director-general of WHO may declare events to be "Public Health Emergencies of International Concern" (PHEIC) with provision to assess, coordinate, and manage the identified emergency. It is through WHO's *International Health Regulations*, IHR, that rules are established that member states *must* follow in the identification and management of disease outbreaks.[14]

Dr. Margaret Chan, Director-General of WHO, said in a news release, "Given today's universal vulnerability to these threats, better security calls for global solidarity…International public health security is both a collective aspiration and a mutual responsibility. The new watchwords are diplomacy, cooperation, transparency and preparedness."[15]

As if in precise commemoration of the 91st anniversary of the H1N1, Spanish flu pandemic that began on March 11, 1918, the spring months of March and April 2009 brought a "quadruple reassortant" novel virus of two genes of European and Asian swine, one of avian origin and one human element, triggering alarm within the scientific community who recognize the anomalous construction of the agent.[16]

In accordance with the prescribed initiatives for pandemic guidelines, the World Health Organization's operational procedures were immediately launched. While the elevated status Public Health Emergencies of International Concern (PHEIC) is by internal documentation an "extraordinary event," Director-General Margaret Chan took little time before pronouncing a pandemic emergency in late April. Shortly thereafter, WHO elevated the threat phase from 4 to 5: one phase below full pandemic status.[17]

While the strategic benefits of cooperative oversight and management are enormous, the language, range, and levels of control contained within the official documents are boldly unambiguous and broadly comprehensive. There are specific and repeated references to "legal" compliance.

Participating as necessary in the event management process to advise on the **legal adherence** to the IHR (2005).

International Health Regulations (2005) [IHR (2005)] **—International legal instrument that is binding on 194 countries, including all the Member States of WHO.** Their aim is to help the international community prevent and respond to acute public health risks that have the potential to cross borders and threaten people worldwide.[18] (emphasis added)

In the United States, a federal or local public declaration of a health emergency is essentially considered to be a suspension of long-held constitutional rights. The suspension of personal sovereignty, even on a temporary basis, is difficult under the best of circumstances. Many who carefully scrutinize temporary or drill/preparation scenarios have genuine and defensible concerns.

The use of private property, the rationing of health care services and supplies, the threat or the actual implementation of isolation and quarantine procedures, and the possibility of enforced curfew or a martial law situation raise reasonable and presumably expected apprehension. As of this writing, there is the appearance of limited pandemic control, but there is also a sustained public recognition of the potential for abuse of authority, even due to poor communication, during these periods.

Comparatively Intact Critical
Infrastructure/Key Resources (CI/KR)

First world status implies access to reasonably intact and operative modern medical standards, and while pandemic crises are not trivial, they are not likely to be catastrophic. Though it is far too early to accurately assess the April 2009 outbreak of H1N1, it would appear that this is a very limited example.

Living conditions in many regions of central Mexico have historically been crowded with limited access to medical facilities as well as somewhat sub-standard baseline nutritional and overall health. The same biological agent responsible for increased morbidity and mortality in Mexico had significantly lesser effect on comparable hosts in the United States and Western Europe.

Such findings have been historically demonstrated by contrasting cultures, geography and demographics. Risk areas are assessed, disease progression surmised, and trends projected through regional and global monitoring. Statistical models are then developed and event management directed and coordinated.

Substantial Impairment of Critical
Infrastructure/Key Resources (CI/KR)

Vulnerability Assessment: CI/KR

Using present-day North American and Western European models as context in a pre-event assessment of CI/KR, consideration must be given to the likelihood of limitations to regional and international traffic and commerce as a *causative*: a result of the event itself. The reason(s) for impairment, whether single or multiple, would not necessarily be immediately evident. This model would also carry no expectation of near-term abatement or available response or support infrastructure.

Although the endless roster of variables within a catastrophic scenario would be far too lengthy to enumerate, all additional consequences would amplify already severely limited resources. Additionally, it would be expected that within even the most sophisticated cultural situations, there would be limited experience in the management of contaminated environments.

Dark Agendas: Biowarfare's "Invisible" Army

The unpleasant reality of biological warfare begins in its ancient past and ends in a time yet forward. Ancient lore speaks of Apollo as a god who could bring ill health and deadly plague as well as the one possessing the ability to cure. Legends describe Apollo shooting plague-infected arrows into the Greek encampment during the Trojan War. From poisoning enemy wells, hurling corpses over city walls, or giving smallpox-ridden blankets to American Indians, it is difficult to grasp the concept of being assaulted by a living, albeit microscopic, enemy.

But the plagues of history past bear little resemblance to their emergent constructs. As science continued its quest for unlocking DNA, a parallel priority—with a far more sinister agenda—was already growing, and on the loose. Designed for maximum casualties and high emotional impact, this nano-army can be crafted for ethnic-specific targeting.

> "Genetic engineering for biological agents? There'd be no protection. These are weapons of the future and the future is coming closer."
> William Cohen
> U.S. Secretary of Defense
> 1998[19]

If history could teach mankind anything, it would be that we've not yet chosen to understand it. Despite warnings and flags, these unseen warriors are eager to meet their new hosts and are prepared to launch a new campaign, promising to reveal themselves in all of their horror in an unprecedented spectacular finale.

In Plague Wars: The Terrifying Reality of Biological Warfare, authors Tom Mangold and Jeff Goldberg assert:

Biological weapons are both more immoral and more lethal than their pestilential cohorts in the nuclear and chemical armoury, for infecting the enemy aggressor can infect his own side; the pathogens blur the lines between peace and war as they silently spread through the ranks of families and non-combatants... [20]

...To contemplate their use is to wink at evil, for pestilence and poison are afflictions as much as weapons. [21]

National security and intelligence must function in a complex and increasingly unsteady international environment. The element of strategic surprise can be a formidable weapon or a powerful adversary.

Authors M. Wheelis, L. Rozsa, and M. Dando analyze the often contradictory historical developments of three central issues of biological weapon research since World War II in *Deadly Cultures, Biological Weapons since 1945*:

Why have states continued or begun programs for acquiring biological weapons? Why have states terminated biological weapons programs? How have states demonstrated that they have truly terminated their biological weapons programs?

Despite the shifting view of the nature of the BW [biological weapon] threat, it has been evident for over sixty years that biological agents can be used to cause mass casualties and large-scale economic damage...

...Contemporary concerns relate largely to the threat of BW acquisition and use by rogue states or by terrorists. However, the BW threat has much deeper roots, and it has changed markedly...

...During most of the Cold war period, major global powers invested substantial resources to develop a strategic BW capability aimed at the military forces, civilian populations, or agricultural resources of their adversaries. Indeed, early in this period BW were considered to rival nuclear weapons in strategic importance.[22]

In a little over a hundred years we have moved from a situation of almost total ignorance to a significant understanding of pathogens and the diseases they, and the toxins they produce, cause in humans, animals and plants. Our already considerable capabilities to use this knowledge for good or, regrettably, for ill are being profoundly enhanced by the ongoing genomics revolution in the life sciences. There must indeed be a risk that in the coming century such knowledge may be used for hostile purposes and in warfare.[23]

With the comparatively recent explosion within microbiological field study, and specifically DNA, it is becoming increasingly popular to advance biologic "novelties." Glow-in-the-dark pups, fish, and plants vie for media attention and capital while less glamorous but decidedly more dramatic are the bio products that find their places in dark circles but seek a more pernicious and indelible glow.

Exotic Threats
Some More Exotic than Others

Plum Island

Located off the northeast coast of Long Island, New York, beyond Montauk, the Plum Island Animal Disease Center (PIADC) is a Level 3 Biosafety Agriculture facility. Transferred in 2002 from the U.S. Department of Agriculture to the U.S. Department of Homeland Security, Plum Island is a federal facility for the research and investigation of foreign and domestic animal pathogens. Plum Island's offshore status allows the study of forbidden mainland organisms, but has recently been the subject of serious East Coast tsunami-related vulnerabilities and concerns.

Plum Island's mission of diagnosis, research, and education permits the housing of freezers that contain samples of polio and other microbial diseases that can be transferred from animals to humans that have, in the past, been compromised by weather-related issues. Plum Island's directives are managed under Homeland Security Presidential Directive, HSPD-9.[24]

NEST
Nuclear Energy Support Team,
U.S. Department of Energy
(Formerly the Nuclear Energy Search Team, NEST)
Operating under the U.S. Department of Energy's Nuclear Safety Administration, the Nuclear Emergency Support Team, NEST, is one of seven emergency response branches of the NNSA. Information from the *Bulletin of Atomic Scientists* indicates that NEST has the ability to deploy up to six hundred people in the event of a nuclear incident alongside the Federal Bureau of Investigation's Domestic Emergency Support Team or the State Department's Foreign Emergency Support Team.[25]

In February 2004, *Popular Mechanics* magazine featured a cover story, "When UFOs Arrive." Within the seemingly whimsical text, article writer Jim Wilson hinted:

...State Of Emergency:
If ET turns up at NASA's doorstep bearing that invitation, it is in for a surprise. Instead of getting a handshake from the head of NASA, it will be handcuffed by an FBI agent dressed in a Biosafety Level 4 suit. Instead of sleeping in the Lincoln Bedroom at the White House, **the alien will be whisked away to the Department of Agriculture's Animal Disease Center on Plum Island,** off the coast of New York's Long Island. Here it will be poked and probed by doctors from the National Institutes of Health. A Department of Energy (DOE) Nuclear Emergency Search Team (NEST) will tow away its spacecraft.

Unfriendly as this welcome may seem, it is the chain of events that most likely will follow the visitor's arrival. Unique as the appearance of an alien-piloted spacecraft may be, **the event incorporates elements of three situations familiar to federal emergency response workers: a plane crash, the release of radioactive material, and the capture of an animal suspected of harboring a contagious disease. Responsibilities in these situations are spelled out in Presidential Executive Orders...**[26] (emphasis added)

High-Energy Physics
Biological Warfare Implications

Traditionally unpopular within the western scientific community, the study of high energy, torsion physics is rapidly gaining interest and acceptance. The reunification of Germany in 1988–1989 greatly facilitated the exchange of support documentation from formerly Eastern bloc nations for experimentation.

One of the most astounding, albeit highly controversial, areas of scientific development is the consideration and implementation of scalar interferometry and its effects on matter and time itself.

In *Aids, Biological Warfare*, Ret. Lt. Col. Tom Bearden describes and documents the results of repeated independent studies of Dr. Vlail Kaznacheyev, director of the Institute for Clinical and Experimental Medicine in Novosibirsk, Siberia:

The Soviets reported detecting near-ultraviolet photons—bioluminescence—as carriers of the death/disease pattern. However, scientists at the University of Marburg in West Germany also duplicated the effect in the infrared. This shows that bioluminescent photons in the near UV and in the IR can definitely carry "disease and death" information between cells. Further, integrating a continuing input of such photons coherently integrates the disease or death pattern from the virtual state into the observable state.[27]

Note also that portions of the infrared spectrum are a subharmonic of the near ultraviolet. **Harmonics are well-known in nonlinear oscillator theory, and biological systems are filled with nonlinear oscillators.** It may be that harmonics and subharmonics are directly involved in the death pattern...[28]

...[in] other words, one can create the healing pattern—the antidote, if you will, for any biological warfare agent. Cancer, leukemia, AIDS, viral diseases, bacterial diseases, whatever. One can create the antidote within minutes after the first symptoms of the disease or death pattern appear.[29]

One can then simply add the negating (healing) signal to power line signals, television and radio signals, special transmitters, etc.—and immediately start to "administer the antidote" to the irradiated population one wishes to protect. **Now one can see why the Soviets are so ready to expose the entire world to something like AIDS. It doesn't represent a real problem to them, the instant they decide to negate it...**[30]

...There are other even more diabolical possibilities, but these should be quite sufficient to illustrate the point.[31]

...Pandora's box has already been spilled, and the end of humanity is ticking away like a time-bomb. It's already nearly midnight, and the watchman hasn't even sounded the alarm yet...[32] (emphasis added)

In the DVD presentation, *Tom Talks Tesla*, Lt. Col. Bearden describes the profound significance of scalar implications:

Looking at it along the lines of scalar interferometry, and dealing with something [that] can [have] some rather astounding weapons effects, we can see...

...Now, what does that **imply**?...

...Those radiators [scalar] could conceivably create within a mass population, the instantaneous spread of mass diseases of all kinds.

They would be anomalous, you could be dying, for example, of bubonic plague and you wouldn't have the organism.... But if that part is true, it represents a biological weapon of incredible implications for population warfare.

I hope to God I'm wrong...but I don't think I am[33] (emphasis added).

Summary

It would be unrealistic for any country with a centralized infrastructure and bureaucracy to consider that it could prepare and implement a detailed and comprehensive pandemic plan in weeks or even months. We have recently seen and experienced an extremely limited local, regional, national and global response to a potential pandemic situation.

Specific pandemic identification, protection, and response strategies are continually evaluated and reconsidered, but all will have varied implications and efficacy within and across multiple sectors. A multisectoral approach means the involvement of many levels of government and people with various specialties including policy development, legislative review and drafting, animal health, public health, patient care, laboratory diagnosis, laboratory test development, communication expertise, and disaster management.

All are health strategies necessary to limit social interactions and disease spread, reducing illness and death, and mitigating, as much as possible, the direct economic impacts. All also have potentially significant side effects and social outcomes which, coupled with the health impact assumptions, substantially compound the direct effects on personal, private, corporate, military, and government operation.

Conclusion

As of this writing, the current World Health Organization's alert phase continues to be at phase 5 with officially reported cases of influenza A (H1N1) at 984.

The official WHO *Guidelines for Humanitarian Agencies* are presumably currently in effect although there is no urgent, unusual, active, or ongoing communication. There persists, however, a perceptible uneasiness, perhaps a consequence of performing extensive background documentation and research.

But...

Perhaps this April 2009 H1N1 "Situation" is following far too closely the prescribed regimens for the described scenarios within the ridiculously copious official directives.

Perhaps this April 2009 H1N1 "Situation" is mirroring the unusual spring timing of the first H1N1 pandemic ninety-one years ago.

Perhaps this April 2009 H1N1 "Situation" is following the "wave" pattern as the first H1N1 pandemic did, recurring with a strong, "unusually virulent" mutation the following August.

Perhaps this April 2009 H1N1 "Situation" is following the second "wave" pattern as WHO Director-General Margaret Chan has warned—and may strike "with a vengeance" in August or September. (V for Vendetta)?

Or just perhaps it is the WHO guidelines of April 2006 that end with instruction point number 6.6.6: "Management of dead bodies," or the reminders that the Black Plague began 666 years ago in 1343. Or might it be, as author Sharon Gilbert suggests by noting the pale horse of pestilence and death, "It's a convergence of three sixes, in a crazy sort of way: WHO Protocol Phase 6, The Millennium Goal 6, and Revelation 6."[34]

As a culture engorged with death, taking morbid pleasure in temporary vicarious misery, do we in some way *prescribe* our misery? Consider the cover description of Stephen King's *The Stand*, self-described as "the greatest horror *novel* ever written:"

It is an apocalyptic vision of the world, when a deadly virus runs amok around the globe. But that lethal virus is almost benign compared to the satanic force gathering minions from those still alive to destroy humanity and create a world populated by evil.[35]

Another post-human sequence that gathers its "minions" from an insurgent and ravaged humanity before complete usurpation: Pan*demonium*.

While Mary Shelley's *The Last Man* has been popularly recognized as a first-generation science (fiction) *novel*, it is worth remembering Shelley's *insistence* that this work is a *translation* of the nine ancient *Sibylline* Books as recorded by the priestess Cumaean Sibyl while presiding over the Apollonian oracle.

The ancient Roman descriptions of an *apocalyptic pandemic plague of unprecedented magnitude in the twenty-first century* are difficult to ignore as the penetrating proclamation of April 30, 2009, by WHO Director-General Margaret Chan that "all humanity is under threat," chillingly punctuates the Sibyl's macabre echo.[36]

—

Sue Bradley is an international geopolitical writer and researcher. Her articles have appeared in The International Jerusalem Post, The Electronic Telegraph, Jane's Intelligence Group, *and* Raiders New Update *in addition to several private intelligence newsletters. She has prepared and provided information for various U.S. and international governmental agencies for support documentation and background.*

Totalitarianism and World War III

by Dr. Stanley Monteith

"Some of the biggest men in the United States, in the field of commerce and manufacture, are afraid of somebody, are afraid of something. They know that there is a power somewhere so organized, so subtle, so watchful, so interlocked, so complete, so pervasive, that they had better not speak above their breath when they speak in condemnation of it."—President Woodrow Wilson, *The New Freedom*, 1918[37]

"An understanding of the forces that shaped the events of past centuries is predicated not on facts to be learned, but rather on secrets to be discovered."—Author unknown

"The idea gleaming and dancing before one's eyes like a will-of-the wisp at last frames itself into a plan. Why should we not form a secret society with but one object, the furtherance of the British Empire, and the bringing of the whole uncivilised world under British rule, for the recovery of the United States, for the making the Anglo-Saxon race but one Empire."— Cecil Rhodes: Confession of Faith, 1877 (punctuation added)[38]

"The Trilateral Commission is international.... It is intended to be the vehicle for multi-national consolidation of the commercial and banking interests by seizing control of the political government of the United States."—Senator Barry Goldwater, *With No Apologies*, 1979[39]

We live in a wonderful country, but it is changing. Have you ever wondered why the United States is changing? Is someone, or some group, responsible for the growing federal effort to monitor and control the American people? Should we be concerned that:

- Social Security numbers are used to identify and track American citizens.
- The Defense Department's Defense Advanced Research Projects Agency (DARPA), the Federal Bureau of Investigation (FBI), and the National Security Agency (NSA) maintain dossiers on American citizens.
- Companies maintain an electronic record of every item purchased with credit cards and grocery cards.
- Telephone companies maintain permanent records of every fax, cell, and telephone call made.
- The NSA monitors every fax, e-mail, and telephone call through Project Echelon.
- When you use a cell phone, government agencies can determine your location and monitor your conversation.
- Some cell phones contain a remote-activated switch that lets government agencies monitor conversations when the cell phone is turned off.
- Google keeps a record of every Internet site you visit.
- Many new automobiles are equipped with a GPS device that tracks your location and where you have been.
- Some cars have electronic devices that facilitate their use of toll roads and toll bridges.
- Video cameras are being installed in banks, stores, schools, offices, hallways, government buildings, and parking lots;

at intersections; and along highways to monitor American citizens.

- U.S. military satellites monitor activity in the United States.
- Government bureaucrats want Americans to carry an identification card.
- New U.S. passports contain a Radio Frequency Identification (RFID) chip.
- Every farm animal must have an RFID chip or other type of identification.
- Most cats and dogs have been chipped.
- International and domestic shipments are tracked via RFID.
- Government bureaucrats want to "chip" every U.S. citizen.
- Recent privacy legislation permits government surveillance of medical records.
- Congress appropriated $82 million to refurbish the World War II Japanese concentration camps.
- Congress appropriated $385 million to build concentration camps in the United States.
- Recent legislation permits the president to mobilize the National Guard, and use the units to control American citizens.
- The Posse Comitatus Act prevents the use of army units against American citizens, but President George W. Bush said he didn't have to obey that law.[40]

Why are these things happening? Does someone, or some group, want to establish a dictatorship in the United States? Could the U.S. government become a totalitarian regime?

The 1966 *Encyclopedia Americana* describes totalitarianism as: "a highly centralized form of government, controlled by a despot or clique, which admits of no political opposition and seeks to regulate all aspects of the citizen's life."

White's Political Dictionary defines a totalitarian government as one that "interferes with, affects, and regulates every aspect of the life of the individual. ... A reaction against parliamentarianism...in favour of a 'totalitarian' or unitary state, whether Fascist or Communist. Fascist Italy, Nazi Germany, and Communist Russia are typical totalitarian regimes."[41]

Why is America changing? Why is every level of government restricting our freedom? What does the future hold?

Ninety-five years ago, my grandfather told my father there was a secret cabal that controlled our nation. Was there a secret cabal at that time? Does it exist today?

Ninety years ago, President Woodrow Wilson recognized the danger and wrote:

Since I entered politics, I have chiefly had men's views confided to me privately. Some of the biggest men in the United States, in the field of commerce and manufacture, are afraid of somebody, are afraid of something. They know that there is a power somewhere so organized, so subtle, so watchful, so interlocked, so complete, so pervasive, that they had better not speak above their breath when they speak in condemnation of it.

They know that America is not a place of which it can be said, as it used to be, that a man may choose his own calling and pursue it just as far as his abilities enable him to pursue it; because to-day, if he enters certain fields, there are organizations which will use means against him that will prevent his building up a business which they do not want to have built up; organizations that will see to it that the ground is cut from under him and the markets shut against him.

American industry is not free, as once it was free; American enterprise is not free; the man with only a little capital is finding it harder to get into the field, more and more impossible to compete with the big fellow. Why? Because the laws of this country do not prevent the strong from crushing the weak. That is the reason, and because the strong have crushed the weak the strong dominate the industry and the economic life of this country.[42]

What were "some of the biggest men in the United States" afraid of? What did they fear? On pages 184 and 185 of his book, *The New Freedom*, President Wilson discussed the powerful men who controlled the American economy at that time. Although he didn't mention their names, they were: J.P. Morgan, John D. Rockefeller, the Whitneys, the Mellons, and the Rothschild agents—Jacob Schiff, Paul Warburg, and the Lehman brothers.[43] These people eventually died, but most of the financial institutions they created exist today and direct the economic destiny of our nation. The influence of the Whitney family and the Mellon family eventually diminished and their banks merged with other banks, but J.P. Morgan Chase, Morgan Stanley, and Citigroup are largely controlled by the Rockefeller dynasty, and the Rothschild dynasty controls several major banks in the United States today.[44]

President Wilson wrote:

However it has come about, it is more important still that the control of credit also has become dangerously centralized. It is the mere truth to say that the financial resources of the country are not at the command of those who do not submit to the direction and domination of small groups of capitalists who wish to keep the economic development of the country under their own eye and guidance. The great monopoly in this country is the monopoly of big credits. So long as that exists, our old variety and freedom and individual energy of development are out of the question. A great industrial nation is controlled by its system of credit. Our system of credit is privately concentrated. The growth of the nation, therefore, and all our activities are in the hands of a few men who, even if their action be honest and intended for the public interest, are necessarily concentrated upon the great undertakings in which their own money is involved and who necessarily...chill and check and destroy genuine economic freedom.

This money trust, or, as it should be more properly called, the credit trust...is no myth; it is no imaginary thing. It is not an ordinary trust like another. It doesn't do business every day. It does business only when there is occasion to do business...I have seen men who...were put "out of business by Wall Street," because Wall Street found them inconvenient and didn't want their competition.[45]

In the years that followed, J.P. Morgan, the Rockefeller family, and the Rothschilds precipitated a series of senseless wars. They incited World War I because they wanted to create a world government (the League of Nations). Why did the United States enter the Great War? J.P. Morgan and his associates purchased the editorial policy of twenty-five major U.S. newspapers and launched a coordinated propaganda campaign to convince the American people the U.S. had a moral obligation to enter the conflict. Congressman Oscar Callaway's February 8, 1917, *Congressional Record* article described what happened. He wrote:

In March 1915, the J.P. Morgan interests...got together twelve men high up in the newspaper world and employed them to select the most influential newspapers in the United States and sufficient number of them to control generally the policy of the daily press of the United States.

These twelve men worked the problem out by selecting 179 newspapers, and then began, by an elimination process, to retain only those necessary for the purpose of controlling the general policy of the daily press throughout the country. They found it was only necessary to purchase the control of twenty-five of the greatest papers. The twenty-five papers were agreed upon; emissaries were sent to purchase the policy...of these papers; an agreement was reached; the policy of the papers was bought, to be paid for by the month; an editor was furnished for each paper to properly supervise and edit information regarding the questions of preparedness, militarism, financial policies, and other things of national and international nature considered vital to the interests of the purchasers.[46]

During World War I and every subsequent U.S. war, the banking dynasties financed both sides of the conflict and prolonged the engagements until both sides were exhausted, disheartened, and bankrupt. Most of the historians who have studied the Great War believe the banking dynasties prolonged the conflict because they wanted to make money, but I believe the financiers prolonged it because they wanted to increase the number of casualties and develop support for world government.[47]

What was the true reason for World War II? The banking dynasties and the corporations they controlled financed Adolf Hitler and built the armaments that were used by the Allied forces and the Nazis during the terrible conflict. Why? Because the banking dynasties wanted to create the United Nations and a world government. Can that be verified? Certainly. I suggest you read *Wall Street and the Rise of Hitler* by Antony Sutton; *Who Financed Hitler?* by James Poole; and *Trading with the Enemy* by Charles Hingham.

In addition, when I researched Col. Edward Mandell House's papers at Yale University in 1980, I discovered a letter that Ambassador William Dodd, the U.S. ambassador to Germany, wrote to Col. House on October 29, 1936. Ambassador Dodd was concerned because U.S. corporations were arming the Nazis. He wrote:

It seems to me that a very large part of the wealth of every country is now devoted to rearmament—the completest armament that Europe has ever known. This would remind you sadly of what you saw here in June 1914…

I might say to you that in spite of all the debts and all the huge losses since the great war, more than a hundred of our great corporations have subsidiaries here, and are of course involved in a great deal of the acute business which goes on. At the same time no corporation can take profits out of the country...., This entanglement of great business relations all over the world would seem to me to argue strongly for peace. Yet a great many of these corporations are supplying the means for rearmament, actually supplying arms. It's strange to me that they are willing to risk the property of their stockholders in such a way. But you know how unwise bankers were between 1923 and 1928; also how much they lost for their depositors. Is it not possible some way to avoid a repetition of such tremendous losses.[48]

General Motors, General Electric, Standard Oil, ITT, IBM, Ford, Dow Chemical, and dozens of other U.S. corporations built the German weapons that killed millions of English, French, Russian, and American servicemen during World War II, but the information has been kept from the American people.[49]

The banking dynasties and their corporate allies involved the U.S. in a series of no-win wars that were fought under the auspices of the United Nations—i.e., Korea, Vietnam, Gulf War I, and Gulf War II. Why? Because they wanted to destroy the moral fabric of our nation, accumulate wealth, and promote support for a world government.[50]

The financial dynasties used the military and economic power of the United States to install authoritarian leaders in foreign nations—i.e., Lenin and Stalin in Russia; Adolf Hitler in Germany; Benito Mussolini in Italy, Chairman Mao in China, Fidel Castro in Cuba, the Mullahs in Iran, and Robert Mugabe in Rhodesia (Zimbabwe). Why? Because the financial dynasties needed a foreign enemy to justify increasing the power of the U.S. government and expanding domestic surveillance.[51]

The effort to establish a totalitarian world government has existed since Nimrod tried to unite the nations five thousand years ago. There have been numerous attempts since that time, but they invariably failed because most people don't want to be ruled by other nations. The Egyptians, the Babylonians, the Persians, Alexander the Great, and Rome tried to conquer the world, but they all failed, and the western segment of the Roman Empire collapsed in 476 A.D. Three hundred and fifty years later, Charlemagne established the Holy Roman Empire, and that government ruled Europe until 1806, when Napoleon Bonaparte defeated the Austrian army. During the years that followed, Napoleon conquered most of Europe—and he might have conquered the world if his attack on Russia had succeeded in 1812. Two years later, in 1814, Napoleon was forced into exile, but he returned the following year and fought his final battle two miles south of a Belgian village called Waterloo.

Have you ever wondered how Napoleon Bonaparte was able to win dozens of battles? Was he a military genius? Was he lucky? Thousands of books have been written about Napoleon's life, but only a few of them mention the fact that he obtained a copy of *The Book of Fate* when he was in Egypt, and accessed the esoteric knowledge that guided the remainder of his military career. Why is that important? Because "an understanding of the forces that shaped the events of past centuries is predicated not on facts to be learned, but rather on secrets to be discovered."

Was the esoteric knowledge Napoleon learned in *The Book of Fate* the source of his military success? If you research that subject on the Internet, you will discover several sites support that thesis, and other sites that discuss the fact that many military leaders and philosophers have been involved in astrology and/or the occult—i.e., Pythagoras, Socrates, Plato, Aristotle, Alexander (the Great), Hitler, Cecil Rhodes, Winston Churchill, Theodore Roosevelt, Franklin Roosevelt, Harry Truman, Richard Nixon, Ronald Reagan, Nancy Reagan, Hillary Clinton, J.P. Morgan, Andrew Carnegie, Henry Ford, the Rothschilds, and members of the Rockefeller family. If you would like to verify that information, search the Internet for the person's name and the word "occult." I also suggest:

www.paranormality.com/napoleon_fate_book.shtml
http://en.wikipedia.org/wiki/Hitler_and-the_Occult

The Eye of the Phoenix, DVD, Adullam Films
The Secret Mysteries of America's Beginnings, DVD,
    Adullam Films
The Dark Worship, Toyne Newton
Brotherhood of Darkness, Stanley Monteith
The Secret Destiny of America, Manly P. Hall
The Life of Alexander, Plutarch[52]

If my premise is correct, why did the occult force that guided Napoleon abandon him at Waterloo? I believe the men who controlled the British government at that time were also involved in the occult, and they utilized the amazing power of "fractional reserve banking" to purchase the weapons and mercenaries that defeated Napoleon Bonaparte.

Can I verify that premise? No, but I can verify the fact that leading members of the British aristocracy have been members of "The Order of the Garter," an occult organization,[53] and they have used the hidden power of "fractional reserve banking" to finance their effort to unite the world—from 1694, when William Paterson established the Bank of England,[54] until 1918, when the Round Table (a front group for Cecil Rhodes' secret society) ceded control of its program to an American group led by J.P. Morgan, who was deeply involved in astrology and the occult.[55] Three years later, in 1921, J.P. Morgan and his followers founded the Council on Foreign Relations, which is an integral part of the "invisible government" that rules the United States today.[56] What is the group's objective? To establish a world government, a world financial system, and a world religion.

To verify that statement, I suggest you read:

Tragedy and Hope: A History of the World in Our Time, Carroll
    Quigley
The Anglo-American Establishment, Carroll Quigley
None Dare Call it Conspiracy, Gary Allen
The Naked Capitalist, Cleon Skousen

Brotherhood of Darkness, Stanley Monteith

All of the books discuss Cecil Rhodes' secret society, but my book, *Brotherhood of Darkness*, discusses the spiritual force that is directing the current effort to unite the world.[57]

Who was Professor Carroll Quigley, and why is his information important? Quigley researched Cecil Rhodes' secret society and the banking dynasties that control the world. He wrote:

The commanders in chief of the world system of banking control was Montagu Norman, Governor of the Bank of England. ... In government, the power of the Bank of England was a considerable restriction on political action as early as 1819, an effort to break this power by a modification of the bank's charter in 1844 failed. In 1852, Gladstone, then chancellor of the Exchequer, and later prime minister, declared, "The hinge of the whole situation was this: the government itself was not to be a substantive power in matters of Finance, but was to leave the Money Power supreme and unquestioned."

This power of the Bank of England and of its governor was admitted by most qualified observers. In January 1924, Reginald McKenna, who had been chancellor of the Exchequer in 1915–1916, as chairman of the board of the Midland Bank told its stockholders: "I am afraid the ordinary citizen will not like to be told that the banks can, and do, create money. ... And they who control the credit of the nation direct the policy of Governments and hold in the hollow of their hands the destiny of the people."[58]

Note Reginald McKenna's statement that "banks can, and do, create money. ... And they who control the credit of the nation direct the policy of Governments and hold in the hollow of their hands the destiny of the people."

Is that true? Does the U.S. Congress control the Federal Reserve

System (the U.S. Central Bank), or does the U.S. Central Bank (the Fed) control our nation? Tragically, the latter is the case, but most people don't understand what has happened. Why is that important? Because the banking dynasties that control the Fed are working with the central banks of other nations to establish a feudal (totalitarian) system that will rule the world.

Professor Quigley wrote:

> The powers of financial capitalism had another far-reaching aim, nothing less than to create a world system of financial control in private hands able to dominate the political system of each country and the economy of the world as a whole. This system was to be controlled in a feudalist fashion by the central banks of the world acting in concert, by secret agreements arrived at in frequent private meetings and conferences. The apex of the system was to be the Bank for International Settlements in Basle, Switzerland, a private bank owned and controlled by the world's central banks which were themselves private corporations. Each central bank...sought to dominate its government by its ability to control Treasury loans, to manipulate foreign exchanges, to influence the level of economic activity in the country, and to influence cooperative politicians by subsequent economic rewards in the business world.[59]

What is their goal? They want to establish a feudal (totalitarian) government that will rule the world. What is the origin of that concept? When I examined Professor Quigley's research papers at Georgetown University in 1980, I discovered a copy of Cecil Rhodes' "Confession of Faith" (1877), which states: "The idea gleaming and dancing before ones eyes like a will-o-the-wisp at last frames itself into a plan. Why should we not form a secret society with but one object the furtherance of the British Empire, for the bringing of the whole uncivilized world under British rule for the recovery of the United States for the making the Anglo-Saxon race but one Empire."[60]

The Council on Foreign Relations in the United States and the Royal Institute for International Affairs in Great Britain were the major front organizations for Cecil Rhodes' secret society until David Rockefeller created the Trilateral Commission (TC) in 1973. Senator Barry Goldwater tried to warn the American people about the danger of the organization in 1979 when he wrote:

> The Trilateral Commission is international.... It is intended to be the vehicle for multinational consolidation of the commercial and banking interests by seizing control of the political government [of] the United States.... In my view, the Trilateral Commission represents a skillful, coordinated effort to seize control and consolidate the four centers of power—political, monetary, intellectual, and ecclesiastical. The Commission emphasizes the necessity of eliminating artificial barriers to world commerce— tariffs, export duties, quotas.... What it proposes to substitute is an international economy managed and controlled by international monetary groups through the mechanism of international conglomerate manufacturing and business enterprise.... Freedom—spiritual, political, economic—is denied any importance in the Trilateral construction of the next century.... What the Trilaterals truly intend is the creation of a worldwide economic power superior to the political governments of the nation-states involved. They believe the abundant materialism they propose to create will overwhelm existing differences. As managers and creators of the system they will rule the future.[61]

Does the Trilateral Commission control "the political government of the United States" today? There are only eighty-seven members of the North American Group of the Trilateral Commission, yet since 1976:

> Three of the last four chairmen of the Federal Reserve System (Arthur Burns, Paul Volker, and Alan Greenspan) have been TC members.

Six of the eight presidents of the World Bank have been TC members.

Eight of the ten U.S. trade representatives have been TC members.

Seven of the twelve secretaries of state have been TC members.

Nine of the twelve secretaries of defense have been TC members.

Every president and/or vice president of the U.S. has been a member prior to the Obama administration.[62]

At present, eleven TC members hold key positions in the Obama administration. The current secretary of state's husband, Bill Clinton, was a member.[63]

If that is true, why hasn't someone told the American people? It is very difficult to disseminate information in the United States through regular channels because members of the TC, the CFR, and the Bilderbergers control most of the major media outlets. TC members currently control:

David G. Bradley, chairman, Atlantic Media Company

Lee Cullum, TV commentator

Donald E. Graham, chairman of the board of the *Washington Post* and *Newsweek* magazine

Karen Elliott House, former senior vice president, Dow Jones (publisher of *The Wall Street Journal*)

Richard Plepler, co-president, HBO

Charles Rose, editor, Charlie Rose Special Edition, PBS

Fareed Zakaria, editor, *Newsweek International* magazine

Mortimer B. Zuckerman, editor-in-chief, *U.S. News & World Report*[64, 65]

Do they control the major banks and financial institutions? Certainly. Here are some of the corporations currently controlled by members of the Trilateral Commission:

Alan R. Batkin, vice chairman, Eton Park Capital
Management
Sylvia Mathews Burwell, president, Global Development
Programs, Bill and Melinda Gates Foundation
E. Gerald Corrigan, managing director, Goldman, Sachs &
Co.
Jamie Dimon, chairman and chief executive officer, J.P.
Morgan Chase & Co.
Roger W. Ferguson, Jr., board of governors, U.S. Federal
Reserve System
Stanley Fischer, governor, Bank of Israel; former president,
Citigroup International; vice chairman, Citigroup;
former first deputy managing director, International
Monetary Fund
Michael B.G. Froman, director, head of Infrastructure and
Sustainable Development, Citi Alternative Investments,
Citigroup, Inc.
Timothy F. Geithner, former president, Federal Reserve Bank
of New York; current secretary of the Treasury
Charles R. Kaye, co-president, Warburg Pincus, LLC
Michael Klein, chairman and co-chief executive officer,
Citi Markets & Banking; vice chairman, Citibank
International
John A. MacNaughton, chairman, Business Development
Bank of Canada (Canadian citizen)
Sir Deryck C. Maughan, managing director and chairman,
KKR Asia; former vice chairman, Citigroup
Robert S. McNamara, former president, World Bank
Arthur F. Ryan, chairman and chief executive officer,
Prudential Financial, Inc.
Paul A. Volker, former chairman, board of governors, U.S.
Federal Reserve System; current economic advisor to
President Obama.[66][67]

Members of the Trilateral Commission and their ancillary organizations created the housing crisis that is destroying the financial structure of our nation and other nations throughout the world. How did they do it? The three previous Fed chairmen were TC members; they flooded the world with fiat money, expanded the world economy, and laid the foundation for the economic collapse that is destroying the world today. Ben Bernanke, the current Fed chairman, doesn't belong to the TC, but he attended the secret Bilderberger meeting held in Virginia in June 2008, and met the men who control the TC—i.e., David Rockefeller and Henry Kissinger. What they discussed is "secret," but we can determine what lies ahead by reading Henry Kissinger's January 12, 2009, *International Herald Tribune* article, "The Chance for a New World Order." Kissinger wrote, "As the new U.S. administration prepares to take office amid grave financial and international crises, it may seem counterintuitive to argue that the very unsettled nature of the international system generates a unique opportunity for creative diplomacy.... The nadir of the existing international financial system coincides with simultaneous political crises around the globe. Never have so many transformations occurred at the same time in so many different parts of the world.... The alternative to a new international order is chaos."[68]

Why do the men who control the banking dynasties, the Trilateral Commission, and their ancillary organizations want to establish a world government? I believe they are energized by the same dark spiritual force that energized Nimrod, the Greek philosophers, and the leaders who have tried to unite the world down through the ages. Will they succeed this time? I believe the men who rule our nation are going to plunge the United States into a nuclear war...World War III. Why would rational men do that? For the same reason their predecessors fomented World War I, World War II, the Korean War, the Vietnam War, Gulf War I, and Gulf War II. I believe they want to use the coming devastation to unite the world. A detailed explanation of that concept is beyond the scope of this article, but if you would like to know how Pakistan acquired the technology and material that was used to build their nuclear weapons, I suggest you read my January 2008 Radio Liberty letter titled "State Secrets" at www.radioliberty.com. The article describes Sibel Edmonds' effort to tell the American people about the U.S. program that transferred nuclear technology to the Moslem world.

Why is the U.S. economy collapsing? Why are we facing the threat of a nuclear war? I believe there has been a spiritual battle between good and evil—between God and Satan—since the beginning of time, and I believe the final battle is being waged today. What can you do? You can tell your friends and relatives about the events ahead, and pray that a spiritual revival will sweep across America and restore the religious foundation of our nation.

What does the future hold? Only God knows the answer to that question. We are called to do our best, and to trust in Him for provision, protection, and salvation.

—

Dr. Stanley Monteith, a retired orthopedic surgeon, has traveled throughout the world interviewing prominent leaders in an effort to understand the "hidden force" that directs the course of international and domestic events. He describes his shocking findings in his book, Brotherhood of Darkness, *and currently does five hours of talk radio every day on programs heard worldwide.*

Globalism: Utopian Dream or Luciferic Nightmare?

by Debra Rae

Globalism: An "Interlocked, Complete, Pervasive Power" Not to be Questioned

In the field of medicine, an ultrasound diagnostic image exhibits shadowy, computer-generated movements of a developing fetus. Globalists likewise monitor *in utero* movement—but on the grander screen of geopolitics. Their one-world love child is spawned by what many call the "shadow government." According to Nelson Rockefeller in *The Future of Federalism*, this new order of one-world government is "struggling to be born."[69]

A foretaste of full-term globalism, the opening ceremony of the 2008 Olympics showcased selected features of "one world" at its best. At the Bird's Nest in Beijing, the planet's best athletes bedazzled an ecstatic audience of ninety-one thousand onlookers, not to mention some four billion at-home viewers.

Sober reverence and a-biblical religious metaphors attending

Olympic events echo ancient times when even the sweat of competitors was decreed sacred. This declaration alone warrants close scrutiny by Christians, many of whom are surprised to learn that the torch lighting and bearing were instituted by Nazi propagandists in the Berlin Olympics (1936).[70]

Though Hitler's hope was to prove Aryan superiority, none dare challenge the custom. To speak against Pierre de Coubertin's Olympian dream for global solidarity, peace, and friendship is ridiculed as ignorant and intolerant.[71]

This we've heard before. Prior to passage of the *Federal Reserve Act* in 1913, the means by which globalists seized control of American finances, President Woodrow Wilson described the burgeoning, one-world phenomenon as "power so organized, so subtle, so watchful, so interlocked, so complete, so pervasive" that no one dares to speak out against it.[72]

Globalism: Who Will Be Prime Minister of the Planet?

As capsulated in the 1994 *UN Report on Human Development,* the one-world premise is simple enough: Given that mankind's problems no longer can be solved by national governments, world government is deemed necessary.[73]

In 1928, former Fabian Socialist H.G. Wells published *The Open Conspiracy: Blue Prints for a World Revolution.* In Wells' view, before the shadowy new order's character is "plainly displayed," existing governments first must be "weakened, effaced, incorporated, and superseded."[74]

Democratic Socialists of America insists that "now is the time to press for the subordination of national sovereignty."[75] Yet eliminating an effective global system of checks and balances based on nation-states begs the question, "If not sovereign nations, then who's to be in charge?"

Consider this: Wells further distinguished "plain display" of the face of globalism as "a world religion."[76] You read it right—"a world religion." That said, could God himself emerge as the globalists' candidate of choice as Prime Minister of the planet?

Not a chance. Signatories of the third *Humanist Manifesto* (2003) included twenty-one Nobel laureates who joined predecessors in supplanting traditional religion with decidedly incompatible albeit grandiose ideals of Darwinism,[77] ethical naturalism,[78] and empiricism[79]—in a word, secularism.

The same three manifestos (1933, 1973, 2003) that expressly deplore division of humankind on nationalistic grounds likewise demean religion as sentimental, wishful thinking and, therefore, devoid of power. No deity will save us; we must save ourselves.[80]

Plainly, a theocracy is not what globalists have in mind.[81] Therefore, our question remains: If not nation-states, if not God, then who's to be in charge of a border-free new world order?

Follow the Clues

The Bible provides needed clues to this pressing question. About six hundred years before Christ, Daniel's apocalyptic visions accurately prophesied and characterized major world governments to follow the Babylonian Empire—specifically, Medo-Persia, Greece, Rome, and Rome revived.[82]

Once revived, a new Rome will resemble the ancient counterpart with respect to its universal belief system, global impact, and destined collapse. Although Charlemagne, Mussolini, and Hitler tried to resuscitate ancient Rome, none could accomplish what the Antichrist alone can at his given hour.[83]

Scripturally, the joint work of Antichrist and his false prophet is called "the mystery of iniquity."[84] Furthermore, the work of Satan through the Antichrist is clearly rooted in the prophecies of Daniel. Indeed, Daniel's account of the "little horn"[85] references this last-day visionary and mother of all dictators who, while at the helm of end-time world government, will *oppose* Christ, all the while pretending to *be* Christ ("the anointed one").[86]

In prophetic imagery, this conquering counterfeit of Christ, a powerful "free-world, supra-national, political being,"[87] sits on the white horse of a godless, one-world system. With a deceptively silent weapon of war in hand (a bow) Antichrist demonstrates shrewdness; that the bow lacks arrows signifies his empty promise of peace.[88] In this picture, Antichrist imitates the infinitely greater white horseman called "Faithful and True." However, instead of delivering peace, plenty, and abundant life as offered by Christ, Antichrist releases the red horse of warfare, the black horse of famine, and the pale horse of death.[89]

Globalism: One Size Fits All

"Shadow government" is an oft-used euphemism for the developing one-world system also known as global restructuring (*perestroika*), the global village, the new paradigm, sustainable society and, yes, even "glo-bologna" (compliments of Clare Boothe Luce).

It's not just the new world order anymore. Any one (or combination) of the following characterize globalism's many facets: global transformation, world religion of Open/Aquarian Conspiracy,[90] vision for world peace, enlightened eco-socialism, economic integration, multinational institution building, collaborative partnerships, global democracy, interdependence, collective security, federalized world government, transnational federal government, and more.

In testifying before the Senate Foreign Relations Committee (1950), international financier James P. Warburg insisted we shall have a world government—either by consent or conquest.[91] To this end, globalism extends a hook to everyone—you name it: the bleeding-heart liberal, the pacifist, the activist, the idealist, the spiritually enlightened, the atheist, the underdog, and the uninformed.

It's as if globalism were a chameleon whose unique body language enables it to change color when attracting potential mates. This metaphor suggests that globalists quickly and opportunistically adjust their values so as to win others to a one-world point of view.

Case in point: In a speech delivered at the Institute for the Study of

International Affairs at Copenhagen, historian Arnold Toynbee documented high-level "discreet workings" to wrest sovereignty out of the clutches of local nation-states, all the while denying with one's lips what is being done with one's hands.[92]

To carry the global agenda, minus sovereignty of nation-states to its zenith, international treaties, conventions, and environmental regulations are detailed in *Our Global Neighborhood*, written by the United Nation's Commission on Global Governance.[93]

Correspondingly, in 1992 the United States ratified a UN *International Covenant on Civil and Religious Rights*. In reality, the covenant is yet another con intended to swap U.S. sovereignty for international courts, taxes, and military.

Globalism: Warranted by an International Disaster Key

Mikhail Gorbachev was awarded the Nobel Peace Prize in 1990 but in 1991 was criticized globally for his harsh repression of nationalist demonstrations in the Baltic States. Having served as president of the Soviet Union and Communist Party leader, Gorbachev hardly qualifies as the planet's hero that he's become.

Gorbachev and his foundation actively work on behalf of the New Paradigm at a former U.S. military base. The Presidio in San Francisco serves as a sort of White House on the West coast. In 1995, for instance, the foundation hosted the State of the World Forum attended by world leaders Mikhail Gorbachev, Maurice Strong, Margaret Thatcher, and George Bush, among others.

Proclaiming the *cosmos* (universe) as his god, Gorbachev handpicked deep ecology as the handy "international disaster key" required for establishing global governance driven by civil society, or non-governmental organizations (NGOs). To this end, Gorbachev calls for integrated global policies that smack of Native American earth servitude.[94]

Gorbachev further insists that necessary environmental regulations be imposed worldwide. His is a type of planetary commandment rooted in the 1992 Rio Earth Summit. Called the *Earth Charter*, this key document is one of three designed to solidify political, economic, social, and religious changes deemed essential in a new world order. The other two are the *UN Charter* and the *International Declaration of Human Rights.*[95]

Globalism's Central Organizing Principle: Sustainable Development

While propelling the misleading ideal of "global democracy," today's borderless, one-world state operates under the United Nations' guiding principle of sustainable development. While the term "sustainable development," or "smart growth," has a noble ring, its agenda is by no means faith-, family-, or America- friendly.

In 1948, a preliminary draft of a *World Constitution* includes the right of a Federal Republic of the World to seize and use property in sustainable society.[96] Keep in mind that Point One of the *Communist Manifesto* likewise calls for outright abolition of private property; and sustainable development is described, not in any of our nation's founding documents, but rather in the 1997 *USSR Constitution* (Chapter #2; Article 18).

In his letter to President George Bush dated December 25, 2000, Mikhail Gorbachev insisted that America's extraordinary privilege is not tenable over the long run. To the contrary, the one-world vision demands "equitable distribution" of the world's finite resources. This Robin Hood approach to wealth distribution is classic Marxism.[97]

Indeed, the Marxist-Leninist maxim of earning one's keep on planet earth is at the heart of sustainability.[98] To merit this coveted status, enlightened communities must limit growth, eliminate suburbs, establish ethnic/economic equality, and curtail consumption patterns consistent with America's middle class.

The socialist principle of government-managed development, sustainable development calls for revamping the very infrastructure of our nation away from private ownership and control of property to nothing short of a national zoning system through which producers are expected to provide for non-producers.[99] Good global citizens are herded out of the suburbs into urban clusters more easily controlled and regulated by UN-empowered special interest groups.

Land-Grab Bully on the Global Block

Worldwide, hundreds of scenic and cultural treasures are UN regulated. Disturbingly, the United Nations has designated as Heritage Sites dozens of monuments across our nation. In fact, through the *World Heritage Convention*, the lion's share of our national preserves, parks, and monuments (e.g., the Statue of Liberty and Independence Hall) already fall under protection of the United Nations Educational, Scientific, and Cultural Organization (UNESCO).[100]

Furthermore, the federal government owns some 40 percent of the entire land mass of our nation; and states own a big hunk as well. When it comes to land use under UN control, there is no clear distinction between federal and privately owned land.

Purposing to "wild" fully half of U.S. land, the United Nations' *Wildlands Project* describes biosphere core- and buffer- zones (with corridors) as places where, in the words of University of Florida Professor Reed F. Noss, "collectivist needs of non-human species must take precedence over the needs and desires of humans."[101]

Contained in Agenda 21, the *Desertification Treaty* claims jurisdiction over some 70 percent of the earth's land. Although no enforcement mechanism is in place, the UN works to prevent land use that lends to desertification—e.g., converting forests to pasture, or pasture to row crops, or crop lands to subdivisions. A convention adopted in Paris (1994), the *Desertification Treaty* is integral to the global agenda.[102]

The same holds true for the earth-centric Gaia hypothesis. In Greek mythology, Gaia is goddess of the earth, now perceived as an interconnected, living ecosystem whose delicate nature demands protection of world government. In 1982, British atmospheric chemist James Lovelock expounded the basis for sustainability. Lovelock's Gaia hypothesis warned that, unless humans halt their technical assault on the planet,

Mother Earth cannot heal herself and, for that reason, faces certain destruction.

To the contrary, anthropocentricity celebrates humans as the very crown of God's creation—not a blight on it. Yet a new breed of eco-theologians insists that human activities like eating meat or previously frozen fast foods, consuming fossil fuels, and using air conditioning and appliances are, well, simply unsustainable.[103]

Maurice Strong's 1,100-page *Global Biodiversity Assessment* (GBA) implements policy of a treaty signed at the 1992 Rio Earth Summit. Put out by Cambridge University, the GBA suggests a cure for "human-pox": Simply cut the world's population by approximately 80 percent and then establish a feudal lifestyle short on amenities, tall on earth servitude *à la* Gorbachev.[104]

Moreover, Canadian billionaire and 1992 Rio Earth Summit secretary-general Strong contends that global ecosystems will be preserved only when affluent nations significantly lower their standards of living.[105] Never mind that the Genesis account sanctions basic human need-meeting as fully compatible with biblically mandated earth stewardship.[106]

Stewardship or Earth Servitude?

Compulsory green living is not found anywhere in the Bible; furthermore, theologian Wayne Grudem rightly questions the likelihood that God would design a world in such a way that, over time, mundane human activities (such as breathing, cooking, traveling, and keeping warm) would somehow devastate His handiwork. Yet in an apparent effort to counter the culture of abundance with "a rite of atonement for the sin of excess," increasingly more evangelicals devote themselves to saving the planet. [107]

By a letter dated March 1, 2007, Dr. James Dobson joined an impressive array of pro-family Christian leaders requesting that the National Association of Evangelicals refrain from endorsing controversial and divisive environmental causes, such as human-induced global warming.[108] Now, *planet preservation* trumps the traditional call to *earth conservation*.[109]

Deep Ecology—In Pursuit of Planetics

Contrary to politically correct dogma, the science assigning human blame for catastrophic warming of the planet is by no means settled. The truth remains that, when it comes to environmental health, science trumps passion and politics. Nevertheless, self-proclaimed eco-experts continue to elude hard-hitting challenges to their theory, as posed by colleagues of equally impressive credentials. Some follow:

If we are in global warming crisis, how is it that 24/7 data-collecting satellites and weather balloons demonstrate imperceptible temperature rises?

If CO_2 threatens to endanger world food output, how is it that an increase in CO_2 yields more (not less) bio-mass production?

If global warming can be blamed on carbon emissions due to human activities, how come distinguished scientists believe that CO_2 generally lags behind temperature changes by some eight hundred years?

How exactly are humans to blame for global warming evident on Mars and other planets, and why was the fifteenth century every bit as warm as the twentieth when only the latter experienced an industrial revolution blamed for it?

Since the McIntyre and McKitrick Report discredited the "hockey stick curve" due to a computer glitch, why continue to use it as proof, and why was the *BH98 Report* (or "hockey stick curve") never audited?

In 1941 a plane crashed in Greenland. From the date of the crash to 1992, ice accumulated up to 268 feet atop a well preserved plane. Why so much ice if land mass sloughs due to global warming have dangerously escalated throughout the decades?

Finally, why do studies challenging, say, ocean-flow data (its role crucial in global warming) appear on the tenth page of city newspapers when earlier studies (apparently not settled science, as the public is lead to believe) merit front-page status?[110]

Through the *UN Climate Change Treaty* and its subsequent *Kyoto Protocol*, globalists favor foreign interests by forcing regulatory control and limitations on U.S. economic growth. When not ratified by the U.S. Senate, international treaties employ back-door means, as executive orders, to implement key components of the global eco-agenda.[111]

Population Control

Surprising to some, the Total Fertility Rate (TFR) is declining worldwide. In developed countries, the rate is below zero growth.[112] President Allan Carlson of the Howard Center for Family, Religion, and Society in Rockford, Illinois fingers depopulation (not overpopulation) as the dominant twenty-first century issue. Nevertheless, sustainable development calls for population control of Malthusian magnitude.[113] It's no wonder that death by suicide, physician assistance, abortion, and euthanasia enjoy high-profile, big-money, organizational clout.[114]

The United Nations' Year of the Family is a campaign to redefine the nuclear traditional family in support of cohabitation, single-parent households, and same-gender partnerships.[115] Intolerance for homosexual unions is decreed a global threat because non-proliferating alternative lifestyles, as theirs, bear the sustainability seal of approval. The same applies to legalized, nonproductive, and allegedly safe, voluntary prostitution, likewise advanced by an international bill of rights for women called the UN *Convention on the Elimination of All Forms of Discrimination against Women.*[116]

In 1932 American Birth Control League founder Margaret Sanger published a *Plan for Peace* in which she called for coercive sterilization. Incredibly, Sanger demanded mandatory segregation and rehabilitative camps for "dysgenic stocks"—i.e., Blacks, Hispanics, American Indians, and Catholics. I kid you not!

And, yes, this is the same Margaret Sanger who founded Planned Parenthood, best known for globally promoting and performing "fully-accessible-to-all" abortions.[117] Today, the U.S. government gives tens of millions of our tax dollars to Planned Parenthood and similar organizations; furthermore, industrialized nations provide some $1.5 billion annually for UN population control.

Natural Selection

English biologist Charles Darwin validated the supposed humaneness of nature, which destroys the weak to give place to the strong. In search of a superior species better suited for higher levels of existence on our ever-evolving planet, humanist bio-ethicists condemn some lives as not worth the living. Examples include useless eaters (the newborn called non-person neonates); the comatose, disabled, or terminally ill; those severely depressed or mentally impaired; the elderly; and eventually (I'm guessing) independent thinkers.[118]

To the globalist, no one can or should live the anthropocentric fable found within a presumed-to-be-archaic, sanctity-of-human life ethic. While animals are "not ours to eat, wear, experiment with or use for entertainment," nonproductive human life is justifiably expendable and subject to medical experimentation for the greater, global good. Baby pesticides and neo-mort harvesting naturally follow the Kevorkian practice of physician-assisted suicide.[119]

Globalism: Strategic Demise of America

Today's culture of death extends beyond individuals to entire nation-states. Former governor of Colorado Dick Lamm fleshed out what he recognized as a genius strategy for destroying our country. To spark tension and turmoil, one first must turn America into a bi- or multilingual and bicultural country. Next, to level the playing field, one must invent multiculturalism and, in the end, celebrate diversity over unity.

No more the "melting pot," America instead must establish her metaphoric identity with the "salad bowl." In so doing, each societal component maintains its own language and culture, dual citizenship, and thus divided loyalties. Any effective down-with-America strategist worth his or her weight in gold knows to under-educate America's fastest growing demographic group.

By recruiting big foundations and businesses to invest generously in the grievance industry, strategists milk the cult of victimology so that even undocumented workers feel entitled to jobs along with all the rights and privileges of American citizens.[120]

Attorney Phyllis Schlafly of Eagle Forum suggests that amnesty for tens of millions dwarfs when compared to temporary guest workers for whom American citizens are expected to pay staggering entitlements as Medicaid, Social Security (with credit for Federal Insurance Contributions Act [FICA] taxes paid under false numbers), Supplemental Security Income, Earned Income Tax Credit, the Women, Infants, and Children (WIC) program, food stamps, public and subsidized housing, Temporary Assistance to Needy Families (TANF), and federally funded legal representation.[121]

Add to these the exorbitant costs of public schooling (lunches included), and some surmise that under the titanic weight of diversity, multilingualism, and entitlement even for lawbreakers, America's already begun her downward descent. Once the rate of immigration exceeds that of assimilation, chaos is unavoidable.

Globalism: Political Correctness, Its Philosophical Base

In an ironic twist, postmodern liberals believe that standardized tests are racist, but racial quotas and set asides, reverse discrimination, and cultural entitlement are not. Though laden with laughable absurdities and inconsistencies, political correctness (PC) is serious business. It forms the philosophical base for globalism, and many -isms huddle under its umbrella. United causes include civil/gender/sexual orientation rights, and radical environmentalism.

The one-world agenda surpasses all other considerations. Politically correct thought police brand counter arguments as mere anecdotal evidence, and simple word choices—e.g., illegal aliens instead of "undocumented workers"—are tagged racist. Though the law distinguishes a domestic partnership from lawful marriage between one man and one woman, any free-thinking individual who does so is labeled "homophobic," intolerant, and oppressive.

In spheres of education and employment, the government-endorsed policy of positive discrimination favors minority ethnic groups and women; but nepotism is no small matter. By expediting government control over hiring, firing, and other business practices, conceptual political correctness actually hinders assimilation and hope for economic improvement.

Already, the workforce development program of Goals 2000 is considering a national job registry whose computer database contains Myers-Briggs-type indicators of the job candidate's political and even religious leanings. Loopholes allow governmental intrusion into beliefs and values of students and their parents—this, through subtle psychological evaluation. Resulting high-efficiency databases merely masquerade as accountability when, in fact, they smack of excessive governmental control.[122]

Costly Consensus

Over the last three decades, bilingual education, expanded welfare, the hyphenated identity, and radical historical revisionism have served well the global cause, but not without consequence. Sadly, affirmative action has been twisted into a legalized quota system that hurts everyone, most particularly qualified minorities.

No matter, to bring about desired group thinking under peer pressure, Hegelian dialectic or conflict resolution, otherwise known as the Delphi Technique, is the globalist's attitudinal and behavior modification tactic of choice. In the dialectic process, ends always justify means; through it, bureaucrats, politicians, and educrats handily discredit notions of fixed rights or wrongs in exchange for a new earth global civic ethic as endorsed by Professor Carroll Quigley of Georgetown University.

In *Tragedy and Hope* (1966), Quigley wrote about an international network of handpicked, likeminded Ivy Leaguers. Having declared war on the world's alleged disease of nationalist individualism, this elitist shadow government virtually controls America and rightfully so in Quigley's view.[123]

The stealth, though costly consensus process primes world citizens for transformation to a new, politically-correct, and collectivist paradigm that insiders embrace, Quigley affirms, and Gorbachev portrays as "one human family and one Earth community with common destiny."[124]

Globalism: Bound to Christianity-Free Religiosity

Held together by the Council on Foreign Relations, America's pre-eminent non-governmental foreign affairs organization, Eastern liberal establishment insiders superintend the burgeoning one-world system. Council of Foreign Relations spin-offs wield three arms of interrelated power: *economic* (Bilderberg Group),[125] *spiritual* (Club of Rome),[126] and *political* (Trilateral Commission).[127] The Bible accurately predicts a central, end-time authority to control its citizens' power to buy and sell. Even a portion of the church (Laodicea) will be increased with goods of the global economy and will consider itself to be rich and in need of nothing, but erroneously so.[128]

Once plainly displayed, H.G. Wells' open conspiracy will manifest as a world religion that serves higher consciousness, as promulgated by theosophists who fancy themselves part of the god-force and identify the voice of god within as "your voice and mine."[129] Promising an emerging new age in concert with the new world order, theosophy plaits religious, philosophic, and scientific thought into the tangled braid of new age mysticism.[130]

In Latin religion means "to bind"—that is, to a belief or philosophy that might or might not involve worship of a god or gods. Powerful incentives of guilt and/or fear beckon the gullible to one-world dogma, as expounded in globalism's bible, the *United Nations Charter*.[131] Forget the Ten Commandments. The UNESCO *Declaration of Tolerance* (1995) essentially elevates rejection of moral absolutism to the status of legal requirement in one-world politics.[132]

Ordo Ab Chao

In the mid-1940s, Fred Emery explained that, when confronted with various crises, folks go into psychological retreat. In the face of looming chaos, these readily forfeit personal power ·in hopes of reestablishing desired order. Fantasy and addiction that trail cognitive dissociation serve only to strengthen the grip of control.

A Latin motto *ordo ab chao* means "order out of chaos." It works like this: First, one identifies—or, if necessary, creates—a problem. The so-called Law of Five advanced by late Grand Patriot of the Jacobin Society Adam Weishaupt gives rise to threatened chaos and, then, discord, confusion, and micromanagement—all followed by an aftermath of frustration and/or alienation.[133]

With this in mind, opportunistic control mongers lick their chops at the prospect of any old crisis—be it real (moral decay), imagined (vast, right-wing conspiracy), or manipulated (man-made environmental catastrophe). A wearied public becomes well conditioned to being warned, shamed, rebuked, and mocked under pretext of becoming informed (actually, manipulated) by "those in the know." That being the case, folks more readily identify with Liesel von Trapp of *Sound of Music* fame.

Admittedly young and inexperienced, this sweet sixteen-year-old was in need of someone older and wiser telling her what to do. Boyfriend Rolfe (then seventeen going on eighteen) waited in the wings, ever-eager to take care of her. Unfortunately, this nature-takes-its-course liaison served only to bring down Liesl's once-privileged world by means of the 1938 Anschluss of Austria when Nazi Germany took control.[134]

Globalism: A-traditionalism toward World Peace

In clearing the way for global governance, proponents undermine all that is traditional. For example, alternative lifestyles lauded for their inherent sustainability supplant traditional families. Bible truth gives way to universalism, and the *U.S. Constitution* takes on the attribute of a "living" document subject to the whims of politicians.[135] Once "up for grabs," this supreme law of our federal government yields to international law in the form of UN conventions and treaties to which American citizens are bound.[136]

Endorsing world dominion of ruling elitists, South African Cecil John Rhodes established the secret Society of the Elect (1891) to found "so great a power as to hereafter render wars impossible."[137] Recall that in the wake of Vietnam, John Lennon only imagined "nothing to kill or die for"; and in similarly troubled times, talk-show hostess Oprah Winfrey bolsters peace as prompted by "a civil rights movement for the soul."[138]

Purportedly spirit-channeled in 1965 through Oprah's longtime friend Marianne Williamson, the alleged new revelation from Jesus embedded in *The Course on Miracles* presumes to guide humanity through such a time as this.[139] Given that sin, evil, and the devil are thought to be illusory, there remains nothing to kill or die for in Ekhart Tolle's *New Earth*.[140]

Benjamin Franklin once mused, "There never was a good war or a bad peace," but I disagree. Christians are called to "fight the good fight of faith."[141] Authentic peace is possible only as it flows from its source, the Prince of Peace himself; otherwise, it's a hollow counterfeit.

Globalism: Evangelized by the Mainstream Media

Politician-industrialist Cecil Rhodes once reasoned that, "The press owns the minds of the people." He was not alone in that belief. Journalist, playwright, and essayist Arthur S. Miller pinpointed "a pervasive system of thought control" in the United States—this, by employment of the mass media coupled with the system of public education. Both, he added, tell people what to think about.[142]

In an op-ed piece about the role of the Council on Foreign Relations media members, *Washington Post* ombudsman Richard Harwood once characterized their membership as "an acknowledgement of ascension into the American ruling class." These are not restricted to mere analysis and interpretation; they "help make" foreign policy.[143]

Left or Right?

In December of 2004 the Associated Press News Service referenced PBS journalist Bill Moyer for his indictment of "an ideological press that's interested in the election of Republicans." Though likeable and highly regarded, Moyer overlooks that reporters, writers, and others in the media vote overwhelmingly for liberal Democrats; and a substantial majority is pro-choice, pro-gun control, pro-separation of church and state, pro-feminism, pro-affirmative action, and supportive of gay rights—all left-centric and globalism friendly.[144] Even Peter Jennings acknowledges that for many years the media has been more of a liberal persuasion.[145]

Hard or Soft News?

On a recent segment of "Bill Moyer's Journal," Moyer admitted to ending each day with Comedy Central's "The Daily Show." Whereas comedian-host Jon Stewart boasts of "faking the news," Moyer credits him for delivering real news with extraordinary impact. Increasingly, young people look to Stewart for hard news; older fans lap up Stewart's infectious satire. Admittedly, he's tickled my funny bone more than once.

"The Colbert Report" is a spin-off and counterpart of "The Daily Show." Both critique and satirize personality-driven politics. The fictional Stephen Colbert is portrayed as a fact-averse, self-aggrandizing anchorman. In my view, many segments of "The Colbert Report" are downright hilarious; still, Colbert's character is a hyper-patriotic, theologically bereft, right-wing egomaniac feigning to hate liberals.

In reality Colbert is a registered Democrat. Problem is "The Report" is all too often embraced as non-satirical journalism. Even the reputable dictionary publisher Merriam-Webster named as its 2006 "Word of the Year," a term Colbert coined ("truthiness").[146]

Media Nannies

Neither Ann Coulter nor Michael Moore ranks high on the "nicey-nice" scale. But it's the former who took a pie in the face—literally! Moreover, media elitists criticized over forty citations within Coulter's book, *Slander*. The upshot of Coulter's treachery, they reasoned, is that casual readers are certain to be misled by her scathing accusation of liberal bias and unfair representation of conservatism in the mainstream media.

Presuming the American public to be inept at analysis, media nannies work hard to protect dim-wits from the likes of Coulter. At the same time, true-to-form liberal bastions as *The New York Times* and the *Washington Post* praise Michael Moore for his sharp "populist instincts" and "admirable forbearance."[147]

Key Omissions by Design

In 1990 when the World Federalist Association faulted the American press for being slow at grasping most global developments, the WFA failed to reveal that, more likely than not, key omissions were by design.[148]

Just ask David Rockefeller. At a Bilderberg Society meeting in Baden, Germany, he thanked attendees from the *Washington Post*, the *New York Times, Time Magazine,* and other distinguished publications. For nearly forty years, he gushed, these friends of global governance had "respected their promises of discretion." Now that the world was adequately primed to welcome a new world order and the cat was out of the bag, globalists were free to go public. This, too, was by design.[149]

Globalism: Evangelized in State Schools

In 1983 the Education Department issued a broadly circulated report, *A Nation at Risk*. "If an unfriendly foreign power had attempted to impose upon Americans the mediocre educational performance that exists today," it cautioned, "we might well have viewed it as an act of war." And so we should. This stunning declaration fittingly shook the education establishment to its core.[150]

Conveniently, the traditional family took the fall when, according to columnist John Steinbacher, Dr. Chester Pierce of Harvard University allegedly suggested that every child in America entering school at the age of five is "mentally ill." Educators must make these "sick" children well by creating and nurturing "the international child of the future." Over time, social engineering to reverse pesky behavior patterns picked up at home, in churches, and in synagogues was coupled with systematic legal drugging of millions of youngsters.[151]

Therapeutic Restructuring

Today, millions of school-aged children are chemically restrained with psychotropic drugs for Attention Deficit Disorder (ADD), Attention Deficit Hyperactivity Disorder (ADHD), or Oppositional Defiance Disorder (ODD) in children five years of age and younger.

Systematic drugging is turning millions of school-aged children into patients. Consequently, Title I programs fund a flood of psychiatrists, psychologists, social workers, and the like to address any languishing self-esteem arguably resulting from colossal failure of the state school system. By the mid-1990s, child psychologists, psychiatrists, counselors, and special educators in and around U.S. public schools nearly outnumbered teachers, themselves touted as change agents.

The fitting question arises, "Have too many children been labeled and subsequently medicated?" A December 1999 report by the surgeon general revealed that a purported 20 percent of American children suffer from "psychiatric disorders."

In a lengthy, well-researched paper, Dr. Fred A. Baughman, Jr., suggests that few if any questions can be addressed properly without an honest answer to this: "Is ADHD a disease with a confirmatory physical (including chemical) abnormality, or isn't it?"

The good doctor agrees with his colleagues that some three decades of research have offered no definitive answer for warranting the medication of one in five American youngsters.[152]

By ensuring subdued compliance, widespread drugging does, however, serve the unfolding global agenda.

Curriculum Restructuring

The late U.S. Senator Sam Hayakawa lamented that the functional task in today's education is no longer to acquire knowledge and skills. Rather, it is therapy. Forget that little Johnny can't read. Schools harp on self-esteem, ethnic pride, alternative lifestyles, global citizenship, safe sex, diversity, drugs, mandated volunteerism, and death/dying—all globalism-friendly themes.[153]

With Big Brother wrestling the family reins from parental grasp, Mom and Dad eventually forfeit power to exercise their God-given authority. If ratified, the UN *Convention on the Rights of the Child* (1989) could prosecute parents who deny their own children access to violent movies, music, videos, or computer games.[154]

That the focus has shifted dramatically from home to state schools and from academics to emotional health begs the question, "How is this working?" Apparently not well. Whistle blower Charlotte Thomson Iserbyt uncovered the mother lode, armed herself with it, and then fled the U.S. Department of Education for which she had served as senior official.[155]

Grooming Human Resources for Cosmic Citizenship

In December 1980, the UN General Assembly formulated *The United Nations Global Education Project* as a model for global education and course for teacher training and curriculum development of all nations. The project is based on mystic Dr. Robert Müller's UNESCO prize-winning, holistic *World Core Curriculum*.[156]

Theosophist Dr. Shirley McCune offers her own prescription for "sick" children—that being a "quantum leap" to higher, group (or collaborative) consciousness. In a speech she gave at the 1989 Kansas Governor's Conference on Education, Dr. McCune claimed that "we no longer see the teaching of facts and information as the primary outcome of education." Instead, she added, we look to a "total transformation of our society."[157]

In *Creating the Future*, edited by Dee Dickinson, Dr. McCune proposes the direction of desired change toward universal societal transformation—namely, "moving out of the business of schooling and into the business of human resource development."[158]

Apparently McCune embraces the cradle-to-grave vision for lifelong learning as conceived by Marc Tucker and former First Lady Hillary Clinton. Increasingly, world citizens are viewed as mere human resources to be groomed and fitted in the global economy as workers, not thinkers; followers, not leaders; group members, not individuals.

"The Possibilities Mind"

Longtime colleagues and friends Drs. Shirley McCune, Andrew Griffin, and Robert Carkhuff share interest in the disturbingly esoteric study of the paranormal and human potential. See for yourself in *The Light Shall Set You Free*[159] and *The Possibilities Mind*[160] by Drs. McCune and Carkhuff, respectively.

In pursuit of transpersonal psychology, Dr. Carkhuff applies his own make-believe formula (Energy=PE^213) to measure human energy toward self-actualization, clarified by McCune as looking to "the Light within" in our collective journey. Cosmic mindfulness is entered into through altered states of consciousness. The way to that "Light," McCune claims, is to increase one's "vibration frequency."

Sounds to me like a spiritual experience. True, Dr. McCune has the constitutional right to believe as she does; however, the path to power, in her view, "requires a whole new curriculum and set of guidelines." Don't think for a moment that this federal liaison refrains from exposing children to her arcane theological grid.[161]

Be sure the utopian brave new world of infinite possibilities, purportedly achieved by Carkhuff's *Links Project,* costs taxpayers millions of dollars in federal grants, yet he identifies "the possibilities mind" as god—yes, *god*—who allegedly co-processes with us to illuminate mysteries.[162]

If this isn't weird enough, "the possibilities mind" discards what is dubbed dysfunctional, traditional math for constructivist learning. Forget numerals. Students are required not to solve a problem with its correct answer, but rather to use their team voices to think about mathematics and how it makes them feel. Carkhuff advances a similarly troublesome new science of possibilities.[163]

Globalism: Revolution-Ready Products of the System

For progressive liberals to unhinge the establishment in the name of egalitarianism, student-led reform is called to bat. Founded by Adam Fletcher in April 2000, the left-wing Free Child Project promotes radical democracy toward achieving a fair, sustainable, and peaceful world. A youth-driven training ground, the project serves as think tank and advocacy group, especially for minority races, gays, women, and animals.

Marxism assumes center stage in directing the global social revolution against national sovereignty, traditionalism, and capitalism. By accessing the Internet and liberal media, young activists pit themselves against youth-fearing grown-ups (otherwise known as "ephebiphobic" adult authorities). Incited youth bemoan the digital divide, oppose captive breeding, denounce medical testing, and champion "my-body—my-choice."[164]

Hard-core direct action propelled by a spirit of resistance frequently involves civil disobedience, boycotts, and occupation. Says the late Redwood Forest tree-sitting anarchist, the late Anita Roddick, this is "the rent we pay to live on the planet."[165]

Globalism: Laissez-faire Left Behind

In the wake of the autumn 2008 U.S. banking crisis, France's president and Germany's finance minister (Nicolas Sarkozy and Peer Steinbrueck, respectively) agreed that the Anglo-Saxon capitalist system had run its course. To end the folly of that post-war, U.S.-dominated, but finished system, new global banking rules are indicated.[166]

Enter the World Trade Organization. A product of the *General Agreement on Trade and Tariffs (GATT)*, the WTO is all about central control of world markets.[167] By locking nations into regulations that exceed authority of their own constitutions, it is perhaps the closest thing we have to world government on this planet.[168]

Similarly, German-born U.S. diplomat Henry Kissinger described the *North American Free Trade Agreement* (1989) as a "first step toward a new world order."[169] Achieved by fast-track legislation, the North American Union (its backdrop, NAFTA) will be a super-state roughly patterned after the European Union.[170]

Some years back, presidential candidate Ross Perot warned about "the giant sucking sound going south."[171] His apprehension was not new. George Washington, Thomas Jefferson, Henry Clay, and Abraham Lincoln likewise opposed the global theory of free trade that siphons off America's wealth.

On the other hand, Karl Marx favored free trade to break up old nationalities and, thus, hasten the social revolution. More recently, in 1977 Chinese Foreign Minister Huang Hua revealed that his country would use it in the U.S. to foment revolution and to build socialism.

Today's European community and NAFTA appear to be regional economic groups forming basis for this up-and-coming world socialist scheme.[172]

Officially under the Department of Commerce, the *Security and Prosperity Partnership* was created at a summit in Waco, Texas (March 2005) and thereafter affirmed in Cancun (March 2006). A planned ten-lane international corridor will be the first leg of what has been dubbed the NAFTA Superhighway. With no congressional oversight and no signed agreements, our nation's merged future with Canada and Mexico allows freer flow of people, goods, and capital under joint military command with a tri-national data base. By 2010, biometric identifiers will facilitate even freer passage throughout our region.[173]

Globalism: Twenty-First Century Prototype, European Union

With dawn of a new millennium has come a formidable superpower threatening to end American geopolitical supremacy. Accordingly, attempts were made in Prague (March 2004) to further enlarge the pan-European vision by creating under a single banner a true continental political unification. Complete with Euro- culture and currency, this New Europe is destined to morph into a United States of the World.

Rhodes Scholar Strobe Talbott (Council on Foreign Relations member) believes "a politically united Europe will advance our common goal to terminate nationhood as we know it and replace it with a single authority."[174] International power-elitists as Talbott purpose first to regionalize Europe, then the world, in the forcible race to global governance.

Adopted by twenty-five countries at the second session of the World Constituent Assembly, the 1977 *Constitution for the Federation of Earth* proposes an administrative structure of twenty world electoral and administrative regions with ten mega-regions. Already the Club of Rome has divided the world into ten political-economic regions referred to as "kingdoms."[175]

Founded in 1968, the Club of Rome is responsible for today's United Europe. Its 1972 report, the *Limits of Growth*, served as blueprint for this gutsy new political, economic, and military union. A prelude to full-blown globalism, the EU has emerged first in position and in preeminence.[176] The European Monetary Union with common currency for participating member-states represents about one-fifth of the world's economic output and trade, and the *Lisbon Strategy* (2000) is poised to render it the most competitive and dynamic knowledge-based economy in the world.

In February 2004 Witton Park Meetings in England looked to expanding the European security force and its relationship to the U.S., UN, and NATO.[177] The world's largest two-way trade and investment relationship amply motivates and propels the burgeoning U.S./EU partnership.

Egalitarianism may sound good for its supposed advocacy of political, economic, and legal equality for all when, in fact, it is no more than a specious buzzword for supplanting America's hegemony. The eventual goal of the global brain trust is to incite planetary class conflict, resulting in transformation to democratic transnationalism, which weds free-market capitalism with communism. This being the case, the divinely inspired and unique political perspective of what Trinity Law Professor James Hirsen identifies as "the grand experiment we call America" is imperiled.[178]

Globalism: Global Law

Our founding fathers clearly understood the critical nature of establishing law and order. They saw to it that the very essence of the Ten Commandments coupled with New Testament amplification would serve as overarching worldview for our legal system.[179]

By way of contrast, laws of the universe (i.e., cosmology) regulate conduct in the emerging new earth. Given a skewed world view favoring cosmic humanism, lawful authority resides entirely within the individual, for every person is god, and god is every person.[180]

Even more, the universe itself is god. Because planet earth allegedly was meant to be a place of worship, it stands to reason that a simple rule of reference for planetary management is to fashion earth into some sort of utopian paradise. Green strategies for doing so include shopping locally, recycling waste as a resource, consuming materials sparingly, and gathering and using energy efficiently—all rational choices for good earth stewardship.

But, wait! In today's global economy, many requirements favor green products over conventional ones for use in construction; but if truth be told, green labels more reflect a company's environmental campaigns and political activities than any realistic ecological impact.[181]

A new, up-and-coming eco-science credited to Janine Benyus takes inspiration from nature's models and elevates nature as supreme ecological standard and mentor. Nature itself dictates how humans must live out inherent connections in life. This is known as the Law of Biomimicry.[182]

To enable light, love, and power to restore the illuminist's plan on earth, God-given law must bite the dust. In its place, soft law addresses ecologist Garrett Hardin's overshadowing argument that "freedom in a commons brings ruin to us all."[183]

To avoid this inevitable fate, citizens of the world are held accountable for achieving rapid transition to community sustainability. Unfortunately, the same demands totalitarian control—this being the only way to enforce laws needed to prevent humans from messing up biodiversity.

At the global level, soft law represents unenforceable agreements between nations. By appearing to represent global consensus, these have a way of evolving slowly into enforceable international law in the form of agreements, conventions, declarations, executive orders, pacts, summits, and treaties. UN resolutions represent a kind of international common law to which national courts have already begun to refer.

Historically, U.S. power was vested in government solely through a legal conveyance from the people—i.e., the *Constitution*. Of late, progressively more international agreements are being used to control even domestic matters. Already, state law has been invalidated by using words of United Nations' international treaties. This judicially renders the *UN Charter* the supreme law of our land.

Disturbingly, old international treaties can be resurrected years and even decades after taking what attorney Phyllis Schlafly calls a knock-out punch. One such example is the old UN *Convention on the Law of the Sea.* LOST created the International Seabed Authority (ISA) which exercises total jurisdiction over all the oceans and everything in them—fully seven-tenths of the world's entire surface.

Were the U.S. to ratify LOST her vote in the ISA would equal that of Cuba's. Furthermore, the treaty empowers the restriction-free ISA to levy international taxes under the guise of assessments, contributions, fees, payments, or permits; to impose production quotas; and to restrict intelligence-gathering missions by U.S. submarines. As is the case with most soft law, LOST is more about international control than it is about stewardship.[184]

Globalism: Soldiers in Spiritual Warfare

Good news! Article 19 of the *Universal Declaration of Human Rights* upholds the right to freedom of thought, conscience, and religion; but (now the *bad* news) Article 29 limits these rights to the purposes and principles of the United Nations.[185]

Furthermore, the *International Covenant on Civil and Political Rights* (April 1992) sets open-ended limits on religious freedom and peaceful assembly.[186] As a result, Christians and Jews gradually forfeit the same liberty afforded politically correct earth pagans who worship Gaia; Muslims who worship the Moon God, Allah; and neo-pantheists who worship "the god within."

Be that as it may, some are surprised to learn that God himself favors one-world government. The book of Revelation describes a season of one thousand years during which time deception is quelled, wars cease, the animal kingdom is subdued, and believers rule and reign with Christ. Worldwide knowledge of the glory of God likewise distinguishes Christ's millennial, one-world reign.[187]

Not so with the *Novus Ordo Seclorum* ("New Secular World Order of the Ages"). Globalism is a godless counterfeit of God's intended plan. Deceived backers from among "peoples, multitudes, nations and tongues" are destined to share "one mind" with respect to globalism's empty promises. Anticipating a mass planetary shift to enlightenment, duped global citizens will put their trust in lying wonders. In the end, sudden destruction, not peace, will be their unanticipated recompense.[188]

So What to Do?

To be separate and "touch not the unclean thing" presupposes identification with God's truth as opposed to any counterfeit of it.[189] In order to discern accurately between truth and a credible counterfeit, one first must know the real thing inside-out, top-to-bottom. This is accomplished through lifelong, Spirit-directed study of God's Word line upon line, precept upon precept.[190] Knowing the Bible and yielding to the Holy Spirit alert believers to distracting winds of doctrine and deceit by the sleight of men.[191]

In all matters, one's first and primary allegiance is to the Lord, but American people of faith also have a duty to engage the representative form of government with which God has blessed our nation. To whom much is given, much is required.[192] Though each must pick his battles wisely and determine his own appropriate level of involvement, all believers can and must nurture love for what God loves, hate for what God hates.[193]

Today's essential warfare is decidedly spiritual, as are the most powerful weapons in combat.[194] All are not qualified to grasp and grapple with globalism's multifaceted agenda, but Christians everywhere can and must release faith, fight the good fight, and pray fervently.[195] In so doing, believers ask largely in the name of Jesus, always in accordance with God's expressed will.[196]

Our hope as Christians is not in a political party, a candidate of preference, partisan activism, or emergency preparedness.[197] It is in

Jesus Christ and none other.[198] While maintaining unruffled trust in the creator and sustainer of life, Christians are called to apply God-given common sense to faith-propelled, proactive preparedness.

That none can turn the tide of globalism is not to say that political activism is useless. Mandated civic responsibilities include obedience and godly action.[199] Believers are compelled by creed and action to uphold liberty, defend the traditional marriage-based family, support the sanctity of human life, preserve parental rights, promote community standards of decency, protect children, and champion wise checks and balances (e.g., sovereignty of nation-states).[200]

Spiritually, Christians must seek God's will and remain in it as best they can. Morally, they must set and keep godly standards. Politically, they can vote and, as God leads, assume leadership positions on key battlefronts for which they are equipped and called to enter. Mentally, they must work at being fully informed and engaged, but never lose sight of Jesus.[201]

These choices are before Christians: scoff at the threat of globalism, join the movement, beat it down, or use it for good and thereby restrain its full expression.

Scoff at It

Many scoff at the sky-is-falling rhetoric of globalism naysayers. In similar times, a committed preacher of righteousness named Noah warned corrupt contemporaries of an impending flood so that they might repent. Sadly, scoffers refused to listen and, as a result, were excluded from safety on the ark. Correspondingly, contemporary Christians mustn't scoff at what God fingers as very real contemporary threats.[202]

Join It

True, Christians anticipate a golden era of unprecedented opportunity, peace, and worldwide collaboration when Christ rules and reigns in the Millennium. To the undiscerning, the right use of energy among intuitive friends united by earth stewardship, sustainability, collectivism, and illumination sounds like the real deal; but it isn't. The Bible warns even Christians that, if not wary, they too are subject to strong delusion.[203]

Globalism's promises of unlimited well-being, transcendence to one's higher self, and universal brotherhood are compellingly seductive; however, in the end, a one-world religious system as enforced by the false prophet obliges all to worship Antichrist or face certain death for noncompliance. From biblical perspective, to join this order guarantees spiritual death.[204]

Beat It

Some might not like to hear this, but attempting to beat down the system is as useless as pounding mole hills with a baseball bat. As I understand biblical eschatology, one-world government is a given. Rome will revive; and world financiers, acting as kings without kingdoms, will rule with Antichrist for a predetermined and bounded time span.[205]

It is by God's permission that Satan empowers malevolent men and seducers to advance their errant agendas;[206] nonetheless, in God's time, and with the brightness of Christ's coming, the enemy's schemes will be revealed and utterly paralyzed.[207] Even as dark clouds gather and loom overhead, Christians are all the more empowered to overcome evil and to fulfill their destinies simply by retaining spiritual purity.

Christians' Two-Fold Charge:
Use It for Good and Restrain It

While living in this world, Christian believers are not party to it.[208] In his first letter to the church at Corinth, Paul allowed using the whole world order (*cosmos*) for godly purposes as long as they not overly use it, or rely on it wholly.[209] With eternal citizenship elsewhere, believers are as pilgrims; they remain riveted to their Lord more so than to a world system destined in time to pass away.[210]

Perhaps unexpectedly, twenty-first century global trends have much to offer Christian kingdom-builders. For example, open borders promise ease of entry for Bibles and ministers of the gospel. Technological genius and limitless information invite broad access to biblical knowledge on big or small screens, in radio, and by means of the Internet. The universally spoken English language facilitates networking while abundant resources/cashless transactions support/assist global ministries of transformative spiritual impact.[211]

What some would use for wrongdoing, Christians can and must use for good. God's call to resist and restrain the "mystery of iniquity" falls to the universal body of Christ whose charge is to restrain iniquitous use of the system. This is not accomplished by American Christians acting alone, by any specific political administration, or under orders of some standing army security counsel.[212]

For such a time as this, some among us are raised to leadership and action, as was Queen Esther, who risked her own life to champion her people before King Ahasuerus. Though not all lead in the church, in business, or in politics, all Christians defend righteous judgments in the civic arena.[213]

Conclusion

It is not appropriate for Christians to herald planetary doom, thereby attracting and drawing together the fearful. Nor should they yawn in the face of impending calamity by escaping into a comfortable world of complacency, fantasy, or addiction. Instead, Christians must be wise as serpents, gentle as doves.[214] To win over doubters requires wisdom, not stealth; prevailing prayer, not brute force.[215]

Perhaps more now than ever before, it's time to shake sleep, study to show ourselves approved, maintain spiritual sobriety, and exercise vigilance.[216] Being well-read and up-to-date on vital issues is a great start; but more exactly, believers must heed biblical mandate by praying diligently, exercising faith, and practicing charity.

Even if one were to achieve all of the above and willingly face martyrdom, it's never enough if God's love evades the equation.[217] Just imagine the magnetic draw of a surrendered life led in Christ-blessed abundance, one that is tempered by balance and lived victoriously and joyfully to the glory of God and in service to others.

This, my friend, is the restraining power of the church: experiencing the Christ life, humbly but powerfully; circumspectly but with a single eye for the Savior; no longer I, but Christ.[218]

The Bible assures us that we can do all things through Christ who strengthens us.[219] By divine enablement, *yes, we can.* By God's grace, *yes, we will.*

—

Debra Rae holds undergraduate degrees in education and theology, and graduate degrees in special education and Christian ministries. She has traveled Asia, Africa, North and South America, Europe, and Australia. Co-host of WOMANTalk Radio, she is a regular contributor to online news magazines. Debra is the author of ABCs of Globalism *and* ABCs of Cultural-Isms.

Nanotech, Biotech, Genetic Mutation, and Transhumanism

by Thomas and Nita Horn

Not long ago, a writer for *Wired Magazine* named Elizabeth Svoboda contacted me to let me know she was writing an article about "research advances using transgenic animals to produce pharmaceutical compounds." She had come across an editorial by me raising caution about this kind of experimentation, and wondered if I might be willing to provide points for her article, elaborating areas where I saw producing transgenic animals as potentially harmful. She stated that most of the scientists she planned to quote were "pretty gung-ho about the practice," and thought it would be important to provide some balance. I thanked her for the invitation, and sent a short summary of some, though not all, of the areas where concerns about this science could be raised.

When the article was finally published by the magazine, I was surprised that none of my notes had made it into the story. I contacted Elizabeth and asked why, and she replied, "Unfortunately, my editors cut your quotes during the editing process, which were originally included in my article, 'Pharm Animals Crank Out Drugs.'" She apologized and said she hoped the experience had not soured me on dealing with *Wired Magazine*.

"It doesn't sour me," I assured her. "I just think the reporting by most agencies is lopsided and missing the opportunity to thoroughly engage such an important issue."

The article was mostly positive on transgenic research and concluded with a scientist by the name of Marie Cecile Van de Lavoir saying that potential human health benefits from transgenic research "justify tinkering" with nature's plan. "If a transgenic animal produces a great cancer therapy," she said, "I won't hear anyone saying, 'You shouldn't do that.'"

Van de Lavoir's comments were undoubtedly in response to some of my observations before they were cut, because in offering caution I had specifically used the phrase "tinkering with nature's plan." Van de Lavoir's short-sighted approach, like that of many bioethicists engaged in the current debate, is as scary as the science, in my opinion. I wanted to contact her to suggest that she watch the film *I Am Legend*, which opens appropriately enough with a scientist announcing the cure to cancer using a genetically engineered virus that blends animal and human genetics. If you've seen the film, you know the "cure" results in a human form of rabies that wipes out most life on earth, a real possibility given the scenario.

While I believe some positive things will come from biotechnology, nanotechnology, synthetic biology, and related fields, below is the short list—by no means a complete list—of areas where I suggested to *Wired Magazine* that caution could be raised about transgenic and related science, and that need to be addressed for any balanced treatment of the field:

NUMBER ONE: What will be the long-term impact on the environment and health-related issues? As we have seen with genetically modified (GM) crops, unpredictable things can occur when living organisms are modified in unnatural ways. Transgenics is one of the fields in biotechnology where the DNA of one species is blended with the DNA of a different species, thus crossing the species barrier—something that neither creation nor evolution allowed for. In the past, I have cited laboratory results reported by Dr. Arpad Pustai and repeatedly verified by Irina Ermakova that showed GM food had surprisingly ill effects on the health of test rats, including organ deterioration, shortened life span, and cancer development. The independent experiments led to the biotech industry suppressing the findings and an eight-year court battle with biotech corporations, which did not want the results made public. Recently the suppressed report was in the news again as Greenpeace activists published evidence from the Russian trials verifying the ramifications of the negative health issues related to transgenic foods. Additional research on the significant health dangers represented by GM foods is available in the book section of www.SurvivorMall.com.

NUMBER TWO: Transgenic research that includes inserting animal DNA into humans and human DNA into animals at the embryonic level could escape its control environment, thereby passing the altered DNA into nature. Once this happens, it would be impossible to put the genie back in the bottle, and could lead to hybrid viruses, prion contamination, or new diseases that we can neither foresee nor prepare for.

NUMBER THREE: Animal rights activists have raised questions in this area that have to do with the ethics of altering animals in ways that could be demeaning to them. For instance, creating zombie-like creatures that grow in feeder labs and gaze off into space from birth until death; militarized animals that behave in unnatural, unpredictable ways; humanized animals that become "self-aware," or animals that produce human sperm and eggs, which then are used in in vitro fertilization to produce a human child. Who would the parents be? A pair of mice?

NUMBER FOUR: Questions are evolving now over "patenting" of transgenic seeds, animals, plants, and synthetic life forms by large corporations, which threatens to impact the economy of rural workers and farmers.

NUMBER FIVE: Biotech "patenting" of human genes. Consider Michael Crichton's piece for the *New York Times* last year, "Gene patents aren't benign and never will be," in which he claimed that people could die in the future because they might not be able to afford medical treatment as a result of medicines owned by patent holders of specific genes related to those persons. Some of these gene modifications and patents are growing out of transgenic research.

NUMBER SIX: Redefining basic human rights. Some advocates of transhumanism actually want transgenic chimps and great apes uplifted genetically so that they will have basic human cognitive ability as a way of proving that certain cognition and not "humanness" should be the key to constitutional protections and privileges. Such changes to intrinsic sanctity of human life could pave the way for harvesting organs from people like Terry Schiavo, due to a loss of cognitive ability. Adopting "personhood" theory based on specific cognitive abilities would be to deny what some bioethicists champion as "human exceptionalism," the idea that human beings carry special moral status in nature and special rights, such as the right to life, plus unique responsibilities, such as stewardship of the environment. Some, but not all, believers in human exceptionalism base this concept on a biblical worldview: Genesis 1:26 states, "And God said, Let us make man in our image, after our likeness: and let them have dominion over the fish of the sea, and over the fowl of the air, and over the cattle, and over all the earth, and over every creeping thing that creepeth upon the earth." Others who do not necessarily have a biblical worldview are nonetheless concerned about the unnatural alteration of living organisms and the unknown repercussions.

NUMBER SEVEN: Transhumanist views of biotechnology including transgenics are opening the door for a new eugenics and social Darwinism, which we already see developing in "Right to Die" laws and related issues. The whole idea of transhumanism is to use the fields of biotechnology, nanotechnology, robotics, mind-interfacing, and related sciences to create a superior man. The result could lead to classifications of persons—the enhanced and the not enhanced—ultimately giving rise to a new eugenics.

Besides the short list above that I provided to *Wired Magazine*, more immediately there are key reasons to be cautious about biotechnology, synthetic biology, genetic engineering, transgenic animals and plants, and associated fields of new technology. Part of the reason for this is that, frankly, it represents an area where neither science nor nature can account for unintended consequences. In recombinant DNA technology, for instance, a "transgenic" organism is created when the genetic structure of one species is altered by the transfer of a gene or genes from another. Given that molecular biologists classify the functions of genes within native species but are unsure in many cases how a gene's coding might react from one species to another, not only could the genetic structure of a modified animal and its offspring be changed in physical appearance as a result of transgenics, but its evolutionary development, sensory modalities, disease propensity, personality, behavior traits, and more could be changed as well.

Many readers will be astonished to learn that in spite of these unknowns, widespread transgenic tinkering is already taking place in most parts of the world, including the United States, Britain, and Australia, where animal eggs are being used to create hybrid human embryos from which stem cell lines can be produced for medical research. On March 9, 2009, President Barack Obama signed an executive order providing federal funding to expand this type of embryonic research in the United States. Not counting synthetic biology, where entirely new forms of life are being brewed, there is no limit to the number of human-animal concoctions currently under development in laboratories around the world. A team at Newcastle and Durham universities in the United Kingdom recently announced plans to create "hybrid rabbit and human embryos, as well as other 'chimera' embryos mixing human and cow genes." The same researchers more alarmingly have already managed to reanimate tissue "from dead human cells in another breakthrough which was heralded as a way of overcoming ethical dilemmas over using living embryos for medical research."[220] In the United States, similar studies led Irv Weissman, director of Stanford University's Institute of Cancer/Stem Cell Biology and Medicine in California, to create mice with partly human brains, causing some ethicists to raise the issue of "humanized animals" in the future that could become "self aware" as a result of genetic modification. Even former President of the United States George W. Bush, in his January 31, 2006, "State of the Union Address," called for legislation to "prohibit...creating human-animal hybrids, and buying, selling, or patenting human embryos." His words fell on deaf ears, and now "the chimera, or combination of species, is a subject of serious discussion in certain scientific circles," writes senior counsel for the Alliance Defense Fund, Joseph Infranco. "We are well beyond the science fiction of H.G. Wells' tormented hybrids in *The Island of Doctor Moreau*; we are in a time where scientists are seriously contemplating the creation of human-animal hybrids."[221]

Not everybody shares Infranco's concerns. A radical, international, intellectual, and quickly growing cultural movement known as "transhumanism" supports the use of new sciences including genetic modification to enhance human mental and physical abilities and aptitudes so that "human beings will eventually be transformed into beings with such greatly expanded abilities as to merit the label 'posthuman.'"[222]

I have personally debated leading transhumanist Dr. James Hughes on his weekly syndicated talk show, "Changesurfer Radio." Hughes is executive director of the Institute for Ethics and Emerging Technologies and teaches at Trinity College in Hartford, Connecticut. He is also the author of *Citizen Cyborg: Why Democratic Societies Must Respond to the Redesigned Human of the Future*, a sort of bible for transhumanist values. Dr. Hughes joins a growing body of academicians, bioethicists, and sociologists who support "large-scale genetic and neurological engineering of ourselves...[a] new chapter in evolution [as] the result of accelerating developments in the fields of genomics, stem-cell research, genetic enhancement, germ-line engineering, neuro-pharmacology, artificial intelligence, robotics, pattern recognition technologies, and nanotechnology...at the intersection of science and religion [which has begun to question] what it means to be human...."[223] While the transformation of man to posthuman is in its fledgling state, complete integration of the technological singularity necessary to replace existing Homo sapiens as the dominant life form on earth is approaching at exponential speed. *National Geographic Magazine* speculated in 2007 that within ten years, the first transhumans would walk the earth, and legendary writer Vernor Verge recently stated that we are entering a period in history when questions like "what is the meaning of life?" will be nothing more than an engineering question. "Within thirty years, we will have the technological means to create superhuman intelligence," he told *H+ Magazine*. "Shortly thereafter, the human era will be ended."[224]

In preparation of the posthuman revolution, Case Law School in Cleveland was awarded a $773,000 grant in April 2006 from the National Institutes of Health to begin developing guidelines "for the use of human subjects in...the next frontier in medical technology–genetic enhancement." Maxwell Mehlman, Arthur E. Petersilge Professor of Law, director of the Law-Medicine Center at the Case Western Reserve University School of Law, and professor of bioethics in the Case School of Medicine led the team of law professors, physicians, and bioethicists over the two-year project "to develop standards for tests on human subjects in research that involves the use of genetic technologies to enhance 'normal' individuals."[225] Following this study, Mehlman began in 2009 offering university lectures such as "Directed Evolution: Public Policy and Human Enhancement" as well as "Transhumanism and the Future of Democracy" addressing the need for society to comprehend how emerging fields of science will, in approaching years, alter what it means to be human, and what this means to democracy, individual rights, free will, eugenics, and equality. Other law schools, including Stanford and Oxford, have hosted similar "Human Enhancement and Technology" conferences where transhumanists, futurists, bioethicists, and legal scholars have been busying themselves with the ethical, legal, and inevitable ramifications of posthumanity.

As the director of the Future of Humanity Institute and a professor of philosophy at Oxford University, Nick Bostrom (nickbostrom. com) is another leading advocate of transhumanism who envisions re-manufacturing humans with animals, plants, and other synthetic life forms through the use of modern sciences. When describing the benefits of man-with-beast combinations in his online thesis *Transhumanist Values*, Bostrom cites how animals have "sonar, magnetic orientation, or sensors for electricity and vibration" among other extra-human abilities. He goes on to include how the range of sensory modalities for transhumans would not be limited to those among animals, and that there is "no fundamental block to adding, say, a capacity to see infrared radiation or to perceive radio signals and perhaps to add some kind of telepathic sense by augmenting our brains."[226]

Bostrom is correct in that the animal kingdom has levels of perception beyond human. Some animals can "sense" earthquakes and "smell" tumors. Others, like dogs, can hear sounds as high as 40,000 Hz, and dolphins can hear even higher. It is also known that at least some animals see wavelengths beyond normal human capacity. Incidentally, what Bostrom may also understand and anticipate is that, according to the biblical story of Balaam's donkey, certain animals also see into the "spirit world." At Arizona State University where the Templeton Foundation is currently funding a series of lectures titled *Facing the Challenges of Transhumanism: Religion, Science, Technology,*[227] transhumanism is specifically viewed as possibly affecting *supernatural* transformation, not just physical. Called "the next epoch in human evolution," some of the lecturers at ASU believe radical alteration of Homo sapiens could open a door to unseen intelligence. Consequently,

ASU launched another study in 2009 to explore communication with "entities." Called the SOPHIA project (after the Greek goddess), the express purpose of this study is to verify communication "with Deceased People, Spirit Guides, Angels, Other-Worldly Entities / Extraterrestrials, and / or a Universal Intelligence / God."[228]

Imagine what this could mean if government laboratories with unlimited budgets working beyond congressional review were to decode the gene functions that lead animals to have preternatural capabilities of sense, smell, and sight, and then blended them with Homo sapiens. Among other things, the ultimate psychotronic weapon could be created for use against entire populations—genetically engineered "nephilim agents" that appear to be human but who hypothetically see and even interact with invisible forces.

While the former chairman of the President's Council on Bioethics, Leon Kass, does not elaborate on the same type issues, he provided a status report on how real and how frightening the dangers of such biotechnology could imminently be in the hands of transhumanists. In the introduction to his book *Life, Liberty and the Defense of Dignity: The Challenges of Bioethics,* Kass warned:

> Human nature itself lies on the operating table, ready for alteration, for eugenic and psychic "enhancement," for wholesale redesign. In leading laboratories, academic and industrial, new creators are confidently amassing their powers and quietly honing their skills, while on the street their evangelists are zealously prophesying a posthuman future. For anyone who cares about preserving our humanity, the time has come for paying attention.[229]

The warning by Kass of the potential hazards of emerging technologies coupled with transhumanist aspirations is not an overreaction. One law school in the UK where CSI students are taught crime scene investigation is already discussing the need to add classes in the future devoted to analyzing crime scenes committed by posthumans. The requirement for such specially trained law enforcement personnel will arise due to part-human part-animal beings possessing behavior patterns not consistent with present-day profiling or forensics understanding. Add to this other unknowns such as "memory transference" (an entirely new field of study showing that complex behavior patterns and even memories can be transferred from donors of large human organs to their recipients), and the potential for tomorrow's human-animal chimera issues multiply. How would the memories, behavior patterns, or instincts of, let's say, a wolf, affect the mind of a human? That such unprecedented questions will have to be dealt with sooner than later has already been illustrated in animal-to-animal experiments, including those conducted by Evan Balaban at McGill University in Montreal, where sections of brain from embryonic quails were transplanted into the brains of chickens, and the resultant chickens exhibited head bobs and vocal trills unique to quail.[230] The implication from this field of study alone suggest transhumans will likely bear unintended behavior and appetite disorders that could literally produce lycanthropes (werewolves) and other nightmarish nephilim traits.

As troubling as those thoughts are, even this contemplation could be just the tip of the iceberg. One-on-one interpersonal malevolence by human-animals might quickly be overshadowed by global acts of swarm violence. The possibility of groups of "transhuman terrorists" in the conceivable future is real enough that a House Foreign Affairs (HFA) committee chaired by California Democrat Brad Sherman, best known for his expertise on the spread of nuclear weapons and terrorism, is among a number of government panels and think-tanks currently studying the implications of genetic modification and human-transforming technologies related to future terrorism. *Congressional Quarterly* columnist Mark Stencel listened to the recent HFA committee hearings and wrote in his March 15, 2009, article, "Futurist: Genes Without Borders," that the conference "sounded more like a Hollywood pitch for a sci-fi thriller than a sober discussion of scientific reality...with talk of biotech's potential for creating supersoldiers, superintelligence and superanimals [that could become] agents of unprecedented lethal force."[231] George Annas, Lori Andrews, and Rosario Isasi were even more apocalyptic in their *American Journal of Law and Medicine* article, "Protecting the Endangered Human: Toward an International Treaty Prohibiting Cloning and Inheritable Alterations," when they wrote:

> The new species, or "posthuman," will likely view the old "normal" humans as inferior, even savages, and fit for slavery or slaughter. The normals, on the other hand, may see the post-humans as a threat and if they can, may engage in a preemptive strike by killing the posthumans before they themselves are killed or enslaved by them. It is ultimately this predictable potential for genocide that makes species-altering experiments potential weapons of mass destruction, and makes the unaccountable genetic engineer a potential bioterrorist.[232]

Not to be outpaced in this regard by rogue fringe scientists or even bio-terrorists, Defense Advanced Research Project Agency (DARPA) and other agencies of the U.S. military have taken inspiration from the likes of Tolkein's *Lord of the Rings*, and in scenes reminiscent of Saruman the wizard creating monstrous Uruk-Hai to wage unending, merciless war, billions of American tax dollars have flowed into the Pentagon's Frankensteinian dream of "super-soldiers" and "Extended Performance War Fighter" programs. Not only does the EPWFP envision "injecting young men and women with hormonal, neurological and genetic concoctions, implanting microchips and electrodes in their bodies to control their internal organs and brain functions; and plying them with drugs that deaden some of their normal human tendencies: the need for sleep, the fear of death, [and] the reluctance to kill their fellow human beings," but as Chris Floyd in an article for *CounterPunch* a while back continued, "some of the research now underway involves actually altering the genetic code of soldiers, modifying bits of DNA to fashion a new type of human specimen, one that functions like a machine, killing tirelessly for days and nights on end…mutations [that] will 'revolutionize the contemporary order of battle' and guarantee 'operational dominance across the whole range of potential U.S. military employments.'"[233]

For these reasons and more, careful consideration should be given to the control environments where fields of study are being made. That has not always been the case, and given what we are seeing in open studies today involving genetically modified plants, animals, and even humans at the embryonic level, the public and the environment we depend on are the guinea pigs for the time being.

So what can you do about it?

Plenty.

First, you can pray. We believe that prayer changes things and is integral to our personal lifestyle and worldview.

Second, do not underestimate yourself. If you are unfamiliar with such terms as "biotechnology," "nanotechnology," "genetic modification," and so on, do not discount your ability to clearly understand the basics of these issues in order to speak up on the subject where ethical or other areas concern you. In the age of the Internet, Google, Wikipedia, and other information-highway resources, it will not take you very long to gather a basic understanding of terms like "biotechnology" or "transhumanism."

Third, get engaged in the public forum. No matter how young or old you are, your opinion matters, and you have access to groups of people through social networking, blogs, websites, school, college, church, or even the bingo hall!

Fourth, contact your representatives in government. A single call or letter to your congressman is considered by most legislators to reflect the opinion of many thousands of other persons. Remember, the only thing necessary for evil to prevail is for good people to do nothing. To find the United States governors, senators, and representatives for your area, visit http://directory.usayfoundation.org/.

Fifth, participate in the political process. You can talk to local educators, call the local talk radio show, attend campaign rallies, and, when appropriate, town hall meetings. Form a citizen's group of four or five people, educate them on the issue, and meet privately with your representatives and senators if your state is considering laws that would allow genetic experiments on embryos, or perhaps where a corporation is looking to move into your state to conduct experiments with genetically modified crops or animals. Many congressmen report that small citizen groups like this are the most effective way to get legislation on your side.

Please note that this chapter is a brief adaptation from the new book, *Apollyon Rising 2012: The Lost Symbol Found and the Final Mystery of the Great Seal Revealed* by Thomas Horn, and as such, is an introductory primer to what we consider singularly the most overlooked issue of our day. To find out more about biotechnology, genetic modification, synthetic biology, and related issues, visit the book section at www. SurvivorMall.com, where you will find *Apollyon Rising 2012* and several other titles on this topic.

—

Thomas and Nita Horn are best-selling authors, founders of the top-ranked internet news service RaidersNewsNetwork.com, and CEOs of Survivor Mall (SurvivorMall.com), one of the foremost discount suppliers of survival gear and supplies, long-term storage foods, wholesale books, media, and thousands of other relevant items.

Occultianity, Dominionism, Institution Collapse

by Joseph R. Chambers D.D., D.S.L.

The Bible states clearly, "If the foundations be destroyed, what can the righteous do?" (Psalm 11:3). It is impossible to build a spiritual house unless the foundation is pure and biblical. When a religious event is based on a foundation totally apart from the solid truth of Scripture, then that event cannot be accepted as New Testament or biblical. The fruit that issues from an unbiblical religious experience or event may appear real, but will prove to be rotten fruit.

We often hear modern preachers say "the test is in the fruit," and that is true if the test is a biblical test, not just a religious one. Thousands of people become religious by joining the Mormons or the Jehovah's Witnesses. Often, they quit grievous lifestyles to follow one of these cults, but they are still lost without Jesus Christ and His finished work. Millions of individuals are attending apparitions of Mary and claiming great conversions and miracles, but Mary has no power to redeem one's soul.

The modern occultic or false anointing revival is producing identical fruit to a Marian apparition or a cultic guru. Lives brought under the influence and conversions of any unbiblical phenomena are actually in greater danger than honest sinners who know they are lost and are in need of Jesus Christ.

I want to show you the foundation stones of the modern New Wave revival. It is spreading throughout the major Pentecostal denominations and the Baptist, Methodist, Episcopal, etc., and independent churches. If these foundation stones are not biblical, they are really nothing but shifting sand bars, and will leave ruins in their wake. Many lives will be destroyed, many will be deceived, and many will eventually reject biblical Christianity totally, believing that all of us are similar to this false noise and manifestations.

This New Wave revival in a broad sense is based upon or embraces at least eight concepts or ideas. There is a lot of variation from minister to minister and ministry to ministry. The best title for this occultic revival is "Latter Rain Theology," or "Manifest Sons of God." It is occultic, and is teaching a form of postmillennialism called Dominion Theology. Look carefully at the following eight concepts.

Concept One

This theological idea teaches that an unusual and clearly false paranormal revival will occur at the end of the church age, which is above, greater, and more complete than any revival of the Second Testament church. There is certainly truth to this because the "latter rain" promised in Joel and James is yet to occur, but it will be a pure and sovereign work of the Holy Spirit, and not anything similar to the present New Wave confusion.

Bob Jones, a Vineyard minister and one of the original Kansas City Prophets, stated:

> They will move into things of the supernatural that no one has ever moved in before. Every miracle, sign and wonder that has ever been in the Bible—they'll move in it consistently. They'll move in the power that Christ did. Every sign and wonder

that's ever been will be many times in the last days. They themselves will be that generation that raised up to put death itself underneath their feet and to glorify Christ in every way…and the Church that is raising up in the government will be the head and the covering for them. So that that glorious church might be revealed in the last days because the Lord Jesus is worthy to be lifted up by a church that has reached the full maturity of the god-man![234]

Dr. Jack Deere, a former teacher at Dallas Theological Seminary who has converted to New Wave, stated the following:

Heretofore in history we have only had one Moses on the scene. Only one Elijah. Only one Elisha at a time. Now, among the Apostles, we only have one Paul, then John, and Peter, a few of those that are really outstanding.

Heretofore we have only had one or two mighty servants of God on the face of the earth at a time. It is not true any longer. When this army comes, he says, it is large and it is mighty. It is so mighty that there has never been anything like it before. Not even Moses. Not even David. Not even Paul. What's going to happen now will transcend what Paul did. What David did, what Moses did, even though Moses parted the Red Sea. Something greater is coming in this army. And there won't be just one Moses. They'll be a numerous company. *See, Revelation hints at this when it talks about the 144,000 that follow the Lamb wherever He goes* [emphasis added]. And no one can harm that 144,000. See, that's a multiple of twelve. What's twelve? Twelve is the number of the apostles. Twelve is apostolic government. And when you take an important number in the Bible and multiply it that means you intensify it. So 12,000 times 12,000 equal 144,000. That is the ultimate in apostolic government. Revelation talks about that. Well, here Joel is talking about it now in different words. A powerful and mighty army with many Pauls, and many Moses, many Davids.[235]

It does not take great discernment to see the arrogant attitude of these modern heretics. According to recent statistics that I have heard, upwards of 50 million people worldwide have bought into this religious doctrine.

Concept Two

This concept teaches that there must be a restoration of all prophetic and apostolic offices to accompany this end-time revival.

Mike Bickle with the Kansas City Prophets and Vineyard Church stated the following:

> There's Apostles, there's Imminent Apostles and there's MOST IMMINENT APOSTLES.... There's various levels of Apostles and the Lord was showing that...out of this movement there would be thirty-five apostles...that will be of the highest level of apostolic ministry...the whole government of this movement in its highest level in all places it goes...the government rests on Apostles and Prophets.... Though I believe there will be hundreds of apostles in this movement and every movement will have its apostles and prophets, I believe God, He's merging Apostles in a number of movements now and He's going to add prophets to the prophets that are already there and He's going to bring us to higher statures.[236]

Rick Joyner, in great reputation among the New Wave churches, stated, "The dismantling of organizations and disbanding of some works will be a positive and exhilarating experience for the Lord's faithful servants...a great company of prophets, teachers, pastors and apostles will be raised up with the spirit of Phineas."[237]

A book written by Richard Kelly Hoskin entitled *Vigilantes of*

Christendom describes these warriors. He says of them, "As the Kamikaze is to the Japanese, As the Shiite is to Islam, As the Zionist is to the Jew, So the Phineas priest is to Christendom."[238]

It is easy to see that this occultic move will serve the Antichrist after the Rapture. It will be part and lot of the "Mystery Babylon" religion of Revelation 17. The promise of great position and authority over multitudes of people gives strong impetus to this movement. Daniel described their method in his prophecy, "And such as do wickedly against the covenant shall he corrupt by flatteries" (Daniel 11:32a).

Concept Three

New Wave adherents believe that Joel's army, as described by the prophet Joel (Joel 2) and John the Revelator (Revelation 9), will be a Christian army taking dominion for Jesus Christ on the earth.

Paul Cain was in the Latter Rain movement in the 1940s and 1950s, but was rejected for this strange message. Presently, he is a big name in New Wave circles. (Recently, he was found to be a homosexual and an alcoholic.) Here are his words regarding the New Wave movement and what he says is going to occur:

Joel's Army will be in training there (Kansas City) and other places until it graduates into the stadium where Shriners are going to be raised from the dead and everything else. Praise the Lord, that's really getting wild, but a right understanding of the plan of God for this generation bring this tremendous conclusion, God's offering to the believer of this generation what I thought He was offering it to the believers of that generation (40s & 50s) when I preached this, but they didn't want it, but you want it? You got it! God's offering to you, this present generation, a greater privilege than was ever offered to any generation at any time from Adam clear down through the millennium. Such a declaration, I think, would be absolutely stupid and out of place if it wasn't for the fact that I have found proof that nobody else has been looking for it. Seemingly, thirty-five years ago they weren't.

I'm not making fun of that, but I want you to know people who really feel the Holy Ghost conviction, really feel the power of God and you see a dead Mason rise up more than 33 1/3 degree, let me tell you that's going to do something. And when you see CBS, NBC, ABC news anchormen come one and they say, "Hello there, ladies and gentlemen, we have no news to report. All of the stadiums and all of the ballparks are filled with hundreds of thousands of people. They have hearses lined up, ambulances lined up, they have hundreds of stretcher cases and all that and there are men standing there in the pulpit, there are women standing there that haven't had a change of raiment in three days. They haven't had a drink of water. They haven't had any food and they're preaching under the mighty power." Why, did you see that last night on ABC? Did you see that fixed pose? They stood there for twenty-four hours in a fixed pose worshipping and praising God and hundred of thousands came by and fell on their face and nobody pushed them and nobody shoved them. They fell under the power of God—and everybody everywhere is crying, "Oh, this is God and Jesus is Lord." It seems like the whole world is turning to God.[239]

Here are the words of another proponent, Bill Britton, who is well respected in this company. He stated, "Beloved, it is people in human, flesh bodies who shall conquer this world and defeat Satan...Jesus defeated Satan and overcame him for us and put all of hell's forces to an open shame. And He did this in a flesh body. Since He is the Head of the Body, it is now in order for the Body to follow in the pattern, which He has set for us. This Body of Christ, the Overcomer, shall come forth in mighty power to manifest the fullness of Christ in the earth. They are known as the Manifested Sons of God, and this place they occupy is the High Calling of God in Christ Jesus."[240]

A magazine entitled *New Beginnings* gives a clear picture of the end of such biblical tampering. Paul Mueller writes, "Following His baptism by John, the heavens were opened to Yahshua ["Jesus" in Hebrew], and He saw the Spirit of Yahweh descending upon Him. The Father's voice then proclaimed, 'This is my beloved Son, in whom I am well pleased.' As Yahshua was baptized and acknowledged as the Father's Son, so shall we be also. A new baptism awaits all the sons of Yahweh in this hour. It will be the baptism of the fullness of the seven Spirits of Yahweh unto our transformation, thereby identifying and acknowledging us as mature and perfected sons of Yahweh."[241]

Francis Frangipane, another voice in the New Wave theology, says the same thing in his book, *The Three Battlegrounds:* "The Lord is raising up His Army…There are a growing number of churches around the world who are being gathered together by the Lord for war."[242] These men are teaching that Jesus became the incarnate Son when the Spirit descended upon Him. They then continue to show that in the same way we will become incarnate or "manifest sons of God." This is the root of this doctrine and what is now called New Wave theology. We are then to take over the world for Jesus. He describes the city church idea being promoted by these deceivers: "The devil knows that when we become one with Christ and, through Him, one with each other, it is only a matter of time before this Jesus-built church will destroy the empire of hell!"[243]

This is a powerful idea that appeals to the haughty flesh of unsanctified people. To believe we are going to be a Christian army with power to take control of the earth and establish the kingdom actually dates back to the Jewish expectancy in Christ's day. They were looking for an earthly kingdom for which to fight, instead of a gospel message for which to die.

Concept Four

Many within this movement believe that the church has the right of dominion over all institutions and powers of government, commerce, education, and judiciary.

Gary North, one of the leaders preparing for this world takeover, said, "We are now witnessing the beginning of a true paradigm shift... the Christian community in the United States has at last begun to adopt the intellectual foundation of a new world view, and this is always the first step in the replacement of a dying civilization which is based on a dying world view...the rotten wood is ready for burning, and a new civilization is being prepared to replace it."[244]

Rick Joyner expresses his concept of the New World Order that he believes the church is going to establish:

We are all members of one another and we must start acting like the church—as a body. I believe the same thing could be said today that was said before the Revolutionary War—because I tell you, we've come to a time of a *spiritual revolution*. What Benjamin Franklin said, "We've gotta join or die," is becoming increasingly applicable to the Church. Those that refuse to tear down the wall—if the leaders refuse to tear down the walls, I tell you the people are going to do it. They are going to come down. And just as those of the former ORDER—who did not recognize that a NEW ORDER had come, they got swept away with the changes when they came. If we do not recognize the times in which we live—if we do not recognize the NEW ORDER has come upon the Church—that there is a NEW ORDER TODAY. There is a Revolution taking place in the church today. I tell you, if we do not recognize that, if we do not become a part of that, we are going to be swept away by these changes when they come because they are coming—they are irresistible. The Kingdom of God is coming and I'll tell you, there is nothing that we can do to stand against it....

I remember some of the most penetrating scenes that I saw in the news last year were the communist leaders who just weeks before were some of the powerful men in this world, were on their knees begging the people to listen to them and the people were saying, "Away with you, we will not listen to you because you were part of the OLD ORDER, we will never listen to you again." A NEW ORDER has come. I tell you, you are going to see the *same thing* taking place in the church. If you wait until it becomes *politically expedient* to jump on the bandwagon, I tell you, it will be too late. Today is our day of visitation. Now is the time to stand up for that which is coming. There are changes. The Lord is going to bring down every wall that separates His people.[245]

Concept Five

Many in this movement believe the rapture doctrine in its pretribulation form was nothing but escapism theology. Some believe He will come only after they take dominion over the earth. Others believe that the full manifestation of the sons of God on earth is actually the biblical Rapture.

Rick Joyner was quick to announce the death of a rapture doctrine. He stated, "The doctrine of the rapture was a great and effective ruse of the enemy to implant in the church a retreat mentality, but it will not succeed. Already this yoke has been cast off by the majority in the advancing church, and it will soon be cast off by all."[246]

Francis Frangipane appears to teach that the Rapture is the final perfection of the "manifest sons of God":

Most of true Christianity shares a doctrine commonly called the "rapture" of the church (1 Thessalonians 4:16). And while study and debate surround the timing of this event, Scripture assures us it will occur before Jesus Himself returns. However, before the rapture occurs, there will be a time of unusual grace in which the living church of Jesus Christ, like a bride, makes "herself ready." In this unparalleled season of preparation, those who are alive in Christ shall realize a level of holiness and blamelessness of the quality in which Jesus Himself walked.

The result of this new level of holiness will be a new level of unity.

During the rapture our bodies will be changed. But our *character*, that is, the essence of who we have become, will remain intact. There will be no regrets or wondering how "those from that church" made it, for the living bride will be a church built together in love, meeting in separate buildings but serving the single Lord.

It is highly significant that the Scriptural term for the rapture is called "the gathering together." What ultimately will be consummated in our gathering together *physically* to the Lord will be precipitated by a *spiritual* gathering together of His body on earth. Concerning the "end of the age," Jesus taught that the "good fish" shall be "gathered...into containers."

The pastors of the last Christian Church will be undershepherds to the Lord Jesus; they will be anointed to gather together His remnant and under that anointing shall be "fruitful and multiply."

Indeed, right now, in the context of humbling ourselves and submitting our hearts to His will, we are participating in being "gathered together" [Mr. Frangipane's new rapture]. And that process will progressively increase until the barriers between brethren are melted by the overcoming nature of Christ's love. Before Jesus returns, we will truly be "one flock with one Shepherd." We will be a holy and blameless sheepfold, meeting in different buildings, but baptized into one body. [247]

Restorationist Rick Godwin expresses his view of the Latter Rain results, while also speaking clearly against the pretribulation rapture. "The Lord is going to have a 'Glorious Church' before He returns... The Glorious Church is to be a mighty army of over-comers through whom God reveals and demonstrates Himself to man...We are to be an army on the offensive, taking the fight to the enemy, instead of sitting around waiting for the Rapture. We are not instructed to 'Hold the Fort'—we are to TAKE THE LAND!...Over infatuation with the Rapture produces a stagnant and sterile people. The OVERCOMER doesn't care WHEN Jesus comes—He is simply 'occupying until He comes.' "[248]

Concept Six

Another aberrant teaching of New Wave thought is the idea of the "Manifest Sons of God." I heard Kenneth Hagin, who is now deceased, tell a large church filled with his ministers and followers that this "New Wave" will perfect them until their body works perfectly.[249]

Francis Frangipane teaches this idea in a very prolific manner. He stated:

> In another sense, Mary, the mother of Jesus, also was "a body [God] had prepared" (Heb 10:5). When Christ first entered our world as a child, it was Mary whom God chose to give Christ birth. Mary's life symbolized the qualities the church must possess to walk in the fullness of Christ.... Like Mary, our humble state as the Lord's bond slaves is but a preparation for the coming forth of Christ in our lives.... Indeed, our purity, our spiritual virginity as the body of Christ, is nothing less than God Himself preparing us, as He did Mary, to "give birth" to the ministry of His Son. Even now, in the spiritual womb of the virgin church, the holy purpose of Christ is growing, awaiting maturity; ready to be born in power in the timing of God!
>
> Through intense prayer and the agonizing of the Holy Spirit, in groanings too deep for words, she embraces her appointed destiny—until the very voice of Christ Himself is heard again through her prayers: "Lo, I have come to do Thy will, O God!" Birthed in His Spirit and in His power, fused together through love and suffering, this holy people becomes, as it were, a "body [God] hast prepared."
>
> Even now, hell trembles and the heavens watch in awe. For I say to you, once again the "virgin is with child."

Before Jesus Himself returns, the last virgin child shall become pregnant with the promise of God. Out of her travail the body of Christ shall come forth, raised to the full stature of its Head, the Lord Jesus.... Yet in the midst of darkness, the visible, powerful glory of the Lord Jesus shall rise upon the virgin church.... Radiant shall they appear, for their hearts shall possess the beautiful Star of the Morning. In holy array, from the womb of the dawn, their light shall exult like the dew! (Quotes from New American Standard Bible)[250]

It is amazing to learn that this is not a new idea at all, but it comes right out of New Age doctrines. M. Scott Peck, a noted New Ager, has said almost identical words: "I think what is meant by the Second Coming is not the bodily return of that one solitary man, but the coming of the mystical body of His True Church; the coming of the spirit of Christ to everyone, sweeping through the world. Father, make us like Mary... to give birth to Your Son; to give Him to everyone. This is the time of the Second Coming. Whether we like it or not. There's no alternative except self-annihilation...it is the time of the Second Coming...The time when we must choose is upon us. Father, make us like Mary."[251]

How do we describe such fantasy? Not one Scripture supports such New Age deception. This is in perfect harmony with the similar doctrine that we are little gods instead of fallen humans. It fits the next concept perfectly. In his book *The God Chasers*, Tommy Tenney states that the Bible is where God was in the past, but revelation is where God is in the present.[252]

Concept Seven

One of the greatest sources of false teaching within the Latter Rain movement is its acceptance of new revelations on equal par with Holy Scripture. The entire landscape of the movement's theology is filled with strange interpretations of Scripture dreams and visions and ideas that are totally foreign to the Bible.

Here is a quote out of Rick Joyner's book, *There Were Two Trees in the Garden:*

"Here is wisdom. Let him who has understanding calculate the number of the beast, for the number is that of a man; and his number is six hundred and sixty-six" (Revelation 13:18). The number 666 is not taken arbitrarily. Because man was created on the sixth day, the number six is often used symbolically in the Scriptures as the number of man. This number is further identification of the spirit of the beast, which is the spirit of fallen man. In verse 11, we see that this beast "comes up out of the earth." This beast is the result of the seed of Cain having been a "tiller of the ground" or earthly-minded. The beast is the embodiment of religion that originates in the mind of man. It comes up out of the earth in contrast to Christ who comes down out of heaven.[253]

The Toronto Airport Church website announced the following vision and prophecy, which was assigned to John Arnott and Tony Black. Here are the exact words:

At a conference in Birmingham attended by people from the UK, Ireland, USA and Brazil, and during a time of prayer for the healing of the nations, I was blessed with this vision: I saw a very large sword which was laid upon the top of an altar. It had gleaming handles of solid gold, and was beautifully crafted. My first impression was—wonderful; we are being given a new sword of authority! But the Lord told me this was not so. This was THE SWORD OF THE LORD. I asked our Father what was the significance, and then I was shown many small swords being tossed into an open furnace, melted down to make this one new larger sword. I believe He said this to me:

"I am bringing My Church to a place at the end of her own understanding and devices, so that they have begun turning to one another, seeking strength through unity. Those who are relying upon the old ways must now learn that the old swords are useless for the battles which are ahead. Behold! I am doing a new thing. If my people will forget their former ways, and allow my Spirit to melt them as one, then will I command such a blessing as has not been seen before...And this I will do: I will take up My Sword, and will ride upon My White Horse. But now you must wait, pray and prepare. The day is soon coming when you will hear my trumpet sound as I ride throughout the earth, causing great consternation amongst the Nations. After this, you will follow, armed in the knowledge of mercy, not sacrifice, and with a new Sword. Thus, when you give your battle cry of 'FREEDOM'...they shall be free indeed. For none shall be able to stand against the authority of my Word."[254]

Another prophecy was assigned to Marc Dupont. Here are excerpts:

"But now I am doing a new thing. I am pouring out a new vine. This is a deeply intoxicating wine. The bouquet releases a fragrance that immediately beautifies any church it is released in. I am again, intoxicating My disciples with a great revelation of My heart. Those that have refused this wine, are like their wine skins growing still and set in their ways. They too, are My children but not all of My children run to me. When Adam and Eve ate of knowledge they became cursed with learning their own ways devoid of intimacy with Me. Many today, although I love them dearly are set on their own ways of doing My things, and are operating out of their head knowledge of what I can do and how I can do it. I say to you just as My ways are above your ways and My thoughts are beyond your thoughts so is the outpouring of My Spirit going to be in these coming days. None of the group of My 120 disciples in the upper room could have imagined that in one day, I would add thousands to join them in worshipping Me, right in the center of Jerusalem I tell you that those that drink of this new wine are truly going to have the boldness of the Lion of the Tribe of Judah. You have heard the Lion Roar. Now you are going to see the Lion go after the prey that He has been roaring at…I say to you the veil is being torn. Up until this time you have only seen a little. You have seen what is coming with a mist. But now I am tearing the veil, I will, just as I said I would, speak to you of the things yet to come by My Spirit. I will heal your blindness. I will cover your nakedness…Again, I say the veil is being torn."[255]

Concept Eight

The latest and most deceptive of the Latter Rain teachings are confused doctrines concerning Jesus Christ and His death.

Look at Benny Hinn's teachings concerning Jesus and the nature of Satan:

Ladies and gentlemen, the serpent is a symbol of Satan. Jesus Christ knew the only way He would stop Satan is by becoming one in nature with him. "What did you say? What blasphemy is this?" No, you hear this! He did not take my sin, He became my sin. Sin is the nature of hell. Sin is what made Satan. You remember, he wasn't Satan till sin was found in him. Lucifer was perfect till Ezekiel says, sin was found in thee. It was sin that made Satan. Jesus said, "I'll be sin. I'll go to the lowest place. I'll go to the origin of it. I won't just take part of it. I'll be the totality of it." When Jesus became sin, sir, he took it from A-Z and said no more. Think about this. He became flesh that flesh might become like Him. He became death so dying man can live. He became sin so sinners can be righteous in Him. He became one with the nature of Satan so all those who had the nature of Satan can partake of the nature of God.[256]

Now, let's look at Kenneth Hagin's teaching on this same subject: "He [Jesus] tasted spiritual death for every man. And His spirit and inner man went to hell in my place. Can't you see that? PHYSICAL DEATH WOULDN'T REMOVE YOUR SINS. He's tasted death for every man. He's talking about tasting spiritual death." [257]

Look at the same idea from Kenneth Copeland:

The Spirit of God spoke to me and He said, "Son, realize this." Now, follow me in this. Don't let your tradition trip you up. He said, "Think this way. A twice-born man whipped Satan in his own domain," and I threw my Bible and I said, "What?!" He said, "A born again defeated Satan. The first born of many brethren defeated him." He said, "You are the very image and the very copy of that one." I said, "Goodness, gracious sakes alive!" And it just began; I began to see what had gone on in there. And I said, "Well, now, you don't mean, you couldn't dare mean that I could have done the same thing." He said, "Oh, yeah, if you've known and had the knowledge of the Word of God that He did, you could have done the same thing, 'cause you are a reborn man, too."[258]

Conclusion

There is no possibility of a true revival issuing from a theological landscape so different from historic biblical truth. Some thread of truth is seen in a few places, but even then the final teaching confounds the whole idea. Our compassionate Father has given revival to His faithful children in every generation. The offices of prophetic and apostolic ministry have not ceased since Acts 2. These offices were not occupied by attention seekers, but by quiet, godly men who were usually unsung by their generations. A few names on that incredible list are A.W. Tozer, G.H. Lang, Joseph Seiss, and Charles Finney.

This generation needs men and women who will surrender their own wills, be totally submerged in the grace of God and biblical righteousness, and be filled with a fresh anointing of the Holy Ghost. I believe such a class of godly individuals is being prepared, and will carry on His great Kingdom work as time may allow. While we prepare to be used, we must be ready to be raptured.

Doctrines that are contrary to Holy Scripture must be taught carefully and progressively if a movement such as the New Wave is going to succeed. One way to teach contrary doctrines is to fill the music with both the spirit and emotion of those doctrines. New Wave music is having a powerful effect in exactly that fashion.

This entire false movement of occultic "Christianity" is going to collapse. Each so-named prophet who appears on the scene takes false doctrines to a lower level. It's all a part of the same nature as the signs produced by the magicians in Egypt as they devoted themselves to resisting Moses and the pure words of God. It is encouraging to watch and hear the preposterous things coming from the foolishness of these apostates because such blasphemy demands the intervention of our Sovereign God. The Heavenly Father always reveals himself and confounds the ways of the wicked. A sovereign move of God's grace is on the horizon. The foolishness of men will be confounded and the Heavenly Father will have the last word.

This entire New Wave of occultianity and dominionism is a form of replacement theology. The book of Revelation has promised the true church that we will be His bride, and that this false religious movement will bow at our feet: "Behold, I will make them of the synagogue of Satan, which say they are Jews, and are not, but do lie; behold, I will make them to come and worship before thy feet, and to know that I have loved thee" (Revelation 3:9).

Almost all religious error in Christianity will fail in two main truths. First, there will be a departure from the infallible Word that will be connected to distaste for the honest believers who adhere strictly to Scripture. Second, there will be a rejection of Israel's prophetic future and an intense distaste for Jewish people. This plainly establishes that heretical doctrines are indeed doctrines of devils.

We find perfect safety in the Word of God. No truth or eternal hope exists without the Holy Scripture. This false system will collapse; in fact, I believe it is teetering on the edge of collapse as I write. Truth will prevail!

—

Dr. Joseph Chambers, director of Paw Creek Ministries, pastors a church in Charlotte, North Carolina, and operates "Open Bible Dialogue," a two-hour weekly radio program. Dr. Chambers speaks and writes about a wide range of topics, but he specializes in exposing false teachings in the body of Christ. Visit his website at: http://www.pawcreek.org.

The Church and Secret Societies

---

by Christian J. Pinto

The Patriotic Faith

Perhaps more dangerous than yoga, psychology, or any of the New Age doctrines that have crept into modern churches is the ongoing love affair some believers have with *patriotic Christianity*. Many Christian leaders who can easily spot the lies of the New Age movement abandon all discernment when it comes to the history of America and the idea that this country was founded as a Christian nation. Yes, they are well able to recognize the *kundalini* serpent crawling up the spine of believers at the gym, but can't seem to figure out that the Washington monument is a pagan phallic symbol that glorifies a demonic entity. They are unable to discern that certain Freemasons writing "Glory to God" on it does not make it a Christian icon.

Christians who live in America understand that we are soldiers of Christ who are strangers and pilgrims upon the earth, and who happen to be stationed in a place called America. *American Christians,* on the other hand, believe that the United States represents the kingdom of God on earth, and their purpose is to promote American values and the revolutionary principles of democracy rather than the message of life eternal. They politely refrain from being too forward about such sensitive issues as heaven and hell; but boldly speak about freedom of speech and the right to bear arms. "I don't want to intrude my beliefs on yours," they say, "unless it comes to my Constitutional rights!" If their zeal for the Lord Jesus were equal to their love for America, we can only wonder what great things might be done for the sake of the truth.

As believers living in America, we must ask: Is the core message of Americanism, even at its best, really that of the Bible?

Church and State

Those who study these elite societies at any length quickly realize that their religious views cannot be separated from their political machinations. Their insistence on a separation of church and state does not mean they want to separate religion from government. It means they want to separate the *church* (i.e., Christianity) from the state. This is why they demand that all Christian icons (such as the cross and the Ten Commandments) be removed from government buildings, seals, etc. Yet the pagan icons such as the Statue of Liberty, the Eye of Horus, and the Washington Monument, along with countless other celebrations of the occult religions, are never threatened. Yes, the Ten Commandments must be taken away from the front of the courthouse, but the statue of the blindfolded Themis, the Greek goddess of justice, can remain unfettered. The message is clear: *The devils can stay, but God must go.*

The Founding Fathers of America

Many Christians are repeatedly told by their pastors, teachers, and church leaders that America was founded as a Christian nation. This assertion would not be so bad if it were confined to the arrival of the Puritans at Plymouth and the early development of the new world. If that were the case, it would be an accurate statement, in this writer's opinion.

The problem arises when one marks the foundation of our country at the American Revolution and the establishment of the United States. It is at this point where all Bible-believing Christians should be very wary, since the working of occult societies during this era was at an unprecedented height. Some historians even argue that you simply cannot understand the history of the world for the past few hundred years if you do not take these societies into account. Their members have been the planners, leaders, and engineers of a global agenda, one that they do not readily share with the rest of the world. More importantly, they often use "religion" as an instrument to manipulate the masses, their belief being that the end justifies the means.

For Christians, our concern should be not for their *conspiracy* to take over the world, which is simply the fulfillment of God's prophecies and proof that His Word is true. Rather, our concern must be their corruption of the faith of Christ from within our ranks.

The Bible vs. Secular Terminology

It is often given out that certain founders were "deists," "theists," or some other such thing. Unfortunately, such secular terminology is very misleading and does not represent a biblical world view. Jesus said: "He that rejecteth me, and receiveth not my words, hath one that judgeth him: the word that I have spoken, the same shall judge him in the last day" (John 12:48). According to Scripture, it is in no way wrong to examine the faith of those who claim to be Christians. We are not expected to politely accept their confession, especially if we are given cause to doubt it: "Beloved, believe not every spirit, but test the spirits whether they are of God; because many false prophets are gone out into the world" (1 John 4:1).

In the pages ahead, we will examine some of the beliefs of the key founding fathers, whose own words prove that these men were *not* Christians and had no intention of founding a Christian country. As you read the words of these men, consider the following passage: "Who is a liar but he that denieth that Jesus is the Christ? He is antichrist, that denieth the Father and the Son" (1 John 2:22).

Thomas Paine

While often overlooked or marginalized by modern historians, the American Revolution, in many ways, began with Thomas Paine. The Marquis de Lafayette said, "A free America without her Thomas Paine is unthinkable."[259] Paine wrote the famous pamphlet, *Common Sense,* which is called "the most influential tract of the American Revolution"[260] by not a few historians, who also maintain that it influenced Jefferson's writing of the Declaration of Independence. Paine also published *The Crisis* pamphlet series, some of which were read aloud by George Washington to his troops during the revolution. John Adams is known for saying, "Without the pen of Paine, the sword of Washington would have been wielded in vain." These words (sometimes attributed to Joel Barlow) are engraved on the very tombstone of the revolutionary author, whose words are said to have "stirred the American colonies to independence." Another quote appears on his tombstone, saying: "History is to ascribe the American Revolution to Thomas Paine." With these things in mind, consider that Paine said about the Bible: "...when I see throughout the greater part of this book scarcely anything but a history of the grossest vices and a collection of the most paltry and contemptible tales, I cannot dishonor my Creator by calling it by his name."[261]

Deist or Antichrist?

While some will tell us that Paine was a *deist* and critic of Christianity, the reality is that he was an *antichrist* by biblical definition. Paine did not merely disagree with Christianity, but specifically made it his business to denounce it. He wrote: "I do not believe in the creed professed by the Jewish church, by the Roman church, by the Greek church, by the Turkish church, by the Protestant church, nor by any church that I know of. My own mind is my own church."[262]

Reason, the God of the Revolution

Paine, a mere man, worshiped the thoughts of his own mind. This is idolatry of the highest order. His most nefarious work was *The Age of Reason*, wherein he glorifies his own ability to *think* above the revealed words of God. The concept of "reason" is not merely to think soberly or to *be reasonable*, as we are taught in Scripture; it is specifically the rejection of things divinely inspired by God in favor of the natural reasoning powers inherent in men. Yet the Scripture makes it clear that the wisdom of God is not as the wisdom of man: "…we speak, not in the words which man's wisdom teacheth, but which the Holy Ghost teacheth; comparing spiritual things with spiritual. But the natural man receiveth not the things of the Spirit of God: for they are foolishness unto him…" (1 Corinthians 2:13–14).

The above Scripture perfectly describes the condition of Paine, Jefferson, and those who embraced the ideas of *reason*, pitting their own minds against what they called the *superstition* of believing the miraculous things of God. By this, they were usually referring to the virgin birth, the resurrection of Christ, inspired revelation, etc. This argument was also supported by John Adams, who wrote: "When philosophic reason is clear and certain by intuition or necessary induction, no subsequent revelation supported by prophecies or miracles can supersede it."[263]

If you read more of the writings of Adams, Paine, and Jefferson in particular, you will learn that what they are collectively saying is: "If something in the Bible does not make sense to our natural understanding, we must reject it."

To say that reason was worshiped by the revolutionaries is no exaggeration. Men like Paine, Jefferson, and Benjamin Franklin spent years interacting with the revolutionary Masons in France, who even set up a goddess they called "Reason" in the midst of the French Revolution. This was done specifically to denounce Christianity, which the French attempted to destroy completely from their midst. What French occultists tried to do literally overnight, the American Civil Liberties Union (ACLU) and other leftist groups in America have been working to accomplish over a number of decades.

There can be no question that Paine (along with others like Thomas Jefferson) was in lock step with the intellectual Masons of France. Here are two more quotes from the leading author of the American revolt:

"What is it the Bible teaches us?—rapine, cruelty, and murder. What is it the Testament teaches us?—to believe that the Almighty committed debauchery with a woman engaged to be married, and the belief of this debauchery is called faith."[264]

"It is the fable of Jesus Christ, as told in the New Testament, and the wild and visionary doctrine raised thereon, against which I contend. The story, taking it as it is told, is blasphemously obscene."[265]

The evil fruit of men like Thomas Paine, and as you will see, Jefferson, Franklin, and Adams, continues to fuel the fires of atheism to this day.

The Culture War

The current cultural conflict in America is not between conservatives and liberals; it is a contest between Christianity and the occult—a battle that can be traced to the very beginning of our country, and one that reached a peak during the revolutionary era. A leading historian, Dr. James H. Billington, said, "The revolutionary faith was shaped not so much by the critical rationalism of the French Enlightenment (as is generally believed) as by the occultism and proto-romanticism of Germany."[266]

The above reference to Germany has to do with Bavaria, in particular, and the influence of the Bavarian Illuminati founded by Adam

Weishaupt. Billington goes on to say, "If Freemasonry provided a general milieu and symbolic vocabulary for revolutionary organization, it was Illuminism that provided its basic structural model. The organizational plan...was simply lifted from the Bavarian Order of Illuminists."[267]

Paine and the Illuminati

Not only was Thomas Paine *not* a Christian, but he was an especially immoral man for his day. According to Billington, "Thomas Paine... lived in a *ménage a trois* with [Nicholas] Bonneville and his wife from 1797 to 1802."[268] A *ménage a trois* is when a married couple and a third party live together and have sexual relations. It is also worth noting that Paine's associate in this adulterous affair, Nicholas Bonneville, was directly involved with the Bavarian Illuminati. We read that "Nicholas Bonneville was...the decisive channel of Illuminist influence. He was converted to Illuminist ideas during the first of two visits to Paris (in June 1787) by Weishaupt's leading associate...Christian Bode."[269]

Adam Weishaupt's indirect association with Paine seems to have come years after the American Revolution, yet they may have been associated earlier. Nevertheless, Paine's writings were entirely in keeping with Weishaupt's own antichrist philosophies and those of the French Revolution.

Paine and Freemasonry

Like many other founders, Paine's involvement in Freemasonry is debated. He wrote a history on the *Origins of Freemasonry* as if he knew about it personally. Paine was specifically brought to America by Free-mason Benjamin Franklin. It was Franklin who (with the support of Freemason George Washington) made Paine's "great swelling words" an acceptable sensation in the American colonies. He published *Common Sense* after having been in America for less than a year. It is almost as if his entrance into the country and subsequent popularization were planned with a specific intent.

We read that: "Paine's writing skills and friendship with Franklin and Washington enabled him to stay at the forefront of the political action and he was made secretary to Congress' Committee for Foreign Affairs from 1777–79. After Paine left this position, he continued to be active in foreign affairs, and letters from Paine to Washington reveal a personal friendship at this time, Washington arranging a hefty salary for Paine."[270] When Paine left America, he joined up with the revolutionaries in France and "with the help of friends like Freemason, the Marquis de Lafayette, he entered the political arena, assisting in forging the new French Constitution."[271]

While in France, Paine lived for a time with Freemason (and later, U.S. President) James Monroe; while his close friend Nicholas Bonneville was also a Freemason. "A number of (Masonic) lodges in the USA were also named after Paine, and when he died many lodges throughout America honoured him."[272]

The Death of Paine

Even in his parting words to the world, Paine was defiant with his dying breath. An account is recorded of an old Christian woman visiting him before he died. We read the following from *The Life of Thomas Paine*, as recorded by Moncure D. Conway:

While Paine was one day taking his usual after-dinner nap, an old woman called, and, asking for Mr. Paine, said she had something of great importance to communicate to him. She was shown into his bed-chamber; and Paine, raising himself on his elbow, and turning towards the woman, said: "What do you want with me?" "I came," said she, "from God, to tell you, that if you don't repent, and believe in Christ, you'll be dammed." "Poh, poh, it's not true," said Paine; "you are not sent with such an impertinent message. Send her away. Pshaw! God would not send such a foolish ugly old woman as you.

Turn this messenger out. Get away; be off: shut the door."
And so the old woman packed herself off.[273]

Other accounts reveal that Paine was repeatedly warned. Christians of every denomination came to his home over and over and literally told him that "whosoever does not believe in Jesus Christ shall be damned."[274] Paine rejected every warning. In his last will and testament, he listed what he thought were his great contributions to the world, in which we find the following: "I, Thomas Paine, of the State of New York, author of the work entitled *Common Sense*...which awaked America to a Declaration of Independence...author also of a work lately published, entitled, *Examination of the Passages in the New Testament, Quoted from the Old, and called Prophecies concerning Jesus Christ, and showing there are no Prophecies of any such Person.*[275] Apparently, Paine wanted to be sure he got in the full denial of Christ in the title of his "lately published" work right before he died. Ask yourself: Was this the man *God* sent to help start the *Christian Revolution?* If the pen of Paine was the spirit behind the war of independence, what spirit was it? "And every spirit that confesseth not that Jesus Christ is come in the flesh is not of God: and this is that spirit of antichrist, whereof ye have heard that it should come; and even now already is it in the world" (1 John 4:3).

"Religion" Defined

It seems now appropriate to speak about the idea of "religion" or "the Christian religion," or even "the religion of Jesus Christ" as spoken of by certain founders. Such quotes are often given as proof that this founder or that one was a Christian. But the idea of being a *Christian* to this era often had more to do with *moral conduct* than faith in Christ. According to Scripture, rejecting the *doctrine* of Christ is to be without God: "Whosoever transgresseth, and abideth not in the doctrine of Christ, hath not God" (2 John 9).

Next, consider this nineteenth-century view of religion. In spite of all that he clearly denied concerning the gospel, here is what the editor of his published writings tells us about Thomas Paine: "His attack on Christianity was indeed directed at the gross corruptions of it...Few or none of his sneers affect the religion of the New Testament."[276] Notice that "the religion of the New Testament" had nothing to do with believing that Jesus Christ is the Son of God. In other words, the *Christian religion* they often refer to is not Christianity at all!

Thomas Jefferson

If there were ever a man utterly ruined and spoiled by vain philosophy, it was surely Thomas Jefferson. Along with Thomas Paine, he was America's greatest deceiver and antichrist—*if you judge him according to the Scriptures*. Jefferson, perhaps more than any other, typifies the last days "scoffers, walking after their own lusts" warned about in the Bible (2 Peter 3:3). Jefferson said this about the book of Revelation in a letter to General Alexander Smyth on January 17, 1825: "It is between fifty and sixty years since I read it and I then considered it as merely the ravings of a maniac, no more worthy nor capable of explanation than the incoherences of our own nightly dreams."[277]

Through the rest of his letter, Jefferson makes it clear to the general that he had not repented of his formerly held view. Some have tried to whitewash Jefferson because he thought Jesus was a fine teacher of morality; here is what he said: "The greatest of all the Reformers of the depraved religion of his own country, was Jesus of Nazareth. Abstracting what is really his from the rubbish in which it is buried, easily distinguished by its luster from the dross of his biographers, and as separable from that as the diamond from the dung hill."[278]

The above passage describes the approach Jefferson took in writing his so-called *Jefferson Bible* (properly titled *The Life & Morals of Jesus of Nazareth*). What he claimed he was attempting to do (and wrote about extensively) was to separate the "true" sayings of Jesus from the things he believed had been added to the gospel accounts. But he did not really believe in the authority of the Bible, Old Testament or New. In a letter to John Adams, he wrote: "...where get we the ten commandments? The book indeed gives them to us verbatim, but where did it get them? For itself tells us they were written by the finger of God on tables of stone, which were destroyed by Moses.... But the whole history of these books is so defective and doubtful, that it seems vain to attempt minute inquiry into it; and such tricks have been played with their text, and with the texts of other books relating to them, that we have a right from that cause to entertain much doubt what parts of them are genuine" (Jefferson, letter to John Adams, January 24, 1814).[279]

As seen earlier, Jefferson's view of the New Testament was no better. In the same letter to John Adams, he wrote: "In the New Testament there is internal evidence that parts of it have proceeded from an extraordinary man; and that other parts are of the fabric of very inferior minds. It is as easy to separate those parts, as to pick out diamonds from dunghills."

When one reads *The Jefferson Bible*, it becomes clear what Jefferson was referring to when he mentioned "dunghills." He specifically removed the virgin birth, the miracles of Christ, the Lord's resurrection and His ascension into heaven. Needless to say, the entire book of Revelation was omitted. These were among the things Jefferson believed came from "inferior minds." Concerning the Lord Jesus, Jefferson wrote: "Among the sayings and discourses imputed to Him by His biographers, I find many passages of fine imagination, correct morality, and of the most lovely benevolence; and others, again, of so much ignorance, so much absurdity, so much untruth, charlatanism and imposture...I separate, therefore, the gold from the dross...and leave the latter to the stupidity of some, and roguery of others of His disciples. Of this band of dupes and impostors, Paul was the...first corruptor of the doctrines of Jesus" (Jefferson, letter to W. Short, April 13, 1820).[280]

The Word of God is True

Far from being discouraged by the words of men like Jefferson, true believers should count it the fulfillment of all that the Scriptures warned us of.

The contempt that Jefferson had toward the gospel of Christ is explained by the apostle Paul: "For the preaching of the cross is to them that perish foolishness; but unto us which are saved it is the power of God. For it is written, I will destroy the wisdom of the wise, and will bring to nothing the understanding of the prudent" (1 Corinthians 1:18–19).

For Thomas Jefferson, the entire Christian belief was nothing more than "foolishness," and he said so in the most contemptuous ways possible. As Christian patriots charge forward to defend Jeffersonian democracy, and the wisdom of the other Christ-rejecting founders, they should consider the ultimate end of that wisdom. How will it fare in the consuming fires of the Most High God?

Benjamin Franklin

"Original sin was as ridiculous as imputed righteousness."— Benjamin Franklin

One of the most influential founding fathers, and the only one to have signed all of the original founding documents (the Declaration of Independence, the Treaty of Paris, and the U.S. Constitution) was Benjamin Franklin. Franklin was responsible for three important phases of America's development: 1) Unifying the colonists in their rebellion against England; 2) Philosophy concerning the rights of mankind; 3) Facilitating the American Revolution by publishing the writings of Thomas Paine. To Sir Walter Isaacson, Benjamin Franklin was "the most accomplished American of his age and the most influential in inventing the type of society America would become."[281]

Franklin and the Hellfire Club

Ben Franklin was, without question, deeply involved in Freemasonry and in other secret societies. Franklin belonged to secret groups in the three countries involved in the War of Independence: America, France, and England. He was master of the Masonic Lodge of Philadelphia, while over in France he was master of the Nine Sisters Lodge, from which sprang the French Revolution. In England, he joined a rakish political group founded by Sir Francis Dashwood (member of Parliament, advisor to King George III) called the Monks of Medmenham Abbey, otherwise known as the Hellfire Club. This eighteenth-century group is described as "... an exclusive, English club that met sporadically during the mid eighteenth-century. Its purpose, at best, was to mock traditional religion and conduct orgies. At worst, it involved the indulgence of satanic rites and sacrifices. The club to which Franklin belonged was established by Francis Dashwood, a member of Parliament and friend of Franklin. The club, which consisted of 'The Superior Order,' of twelve members, allegedly took part in basic forms of satanic worship. In addition to taking part in the occult, orgies and parties with prostitutes were also said to be the norm."[282]

Dead Bodies in London

On February 11, 1998, the *Sunday Times* reported that ten bodies were dug up from beneath Benjamin Franklin's home at 36 Craven Street in London. The bodies were of four adults and six children. They were discovered during a costly renovation of Franklin's former home. *The Times* reported that, "Initial estimates are that the bones are about 200 years old and were buried at the time Franklin was living in the house, which was his home from 1757 to 1762 and from 1764 to 1775. Most of the bones show signs of having been dissected, sawn or cut. One skull has been drilled with several holes."[283]

The article goes on to suggest that the bodies may have been the result of the experiments of Dr. William Hewson, who worked alongside the founders of British surgery and who was a friend of Benjamin Franklin. Hewson apparently ran his medical school from Franklin's home from 1772 to 1774. The suggestion put forth is that the bodies were probably "anatomical specimens that Dr. Hewson disposed of," but investigators admitted they were still "uncertain." For the record, the Benjamin Franklin House currently presents the bones as "the remains of William Hewson's anatomy school" and even has them on display for the public.

The original *Times* article reported that the bones were "deeply buried, probably to hide them because grave robbing was illegal." They said, "There could be more buried, and there probably are." But the story doesn't end there.

Science and Satan: Together Again?

Later reports from the Benjamin Franklin House reveal that not only were human remains found, but *animal* remains were found as well. This is where things get very interesting. From the published photographs, some of the bones appear to be blackened or charred, as if by fire. (See a photo of the bones on the Benjamin Franklin House website at benjaminfranklinhouse.org and look under "The William Hewson & Craven Street Bones Exhibition.") Needless to say, a number of researchers are doubtful about the "medical" explanation and have suggested that Franklin's involvement with the Hellfire Club might be the real answer. It is well documented that Satanists perform ritual killings of both humans and animals alike. Could Franklin and his Hellfire friends have been working with Hewson to provide the doctor with fresh bodies?

The uncomfortable questions are these: If the humans were medical cadavers, why were they disposed of like so much trash beneath the house? Why not give them some kind of proper burial? If grave robbers could sneak into a graveyard to steal a body, they could also sneak in to put one back. Furthermore, why were the human remains mingled with those of animals? It is worth noting that Dr. Hewson developed an infection from working on one of his cadavers, and he died from it.

Franklin and the Gospel

But what was Franklin's view of Christianity and of the Lord Jesus Christ? He answered that question directly shortly before he died. He wrote the following to Ezra Stiles, who was then president of Yale University. Stiles had inquired about Franklin's views on religion and of the Lord Jesus Christ: "As to Jesus of Nazareth, my Opinion of whom you particularly desire, I think the System of Morals and his Religion, as he left them to us, the best the world ever saw or is likely to see; but I apprehend it has received various corrupt changes, and I have, with most of the present Dissenters in England, some Doubts as to his divinity..."[284]

From the first part of his response, Franklin's views about Jesus seem very similar to those of Paine and Jefferson, making reference to "corrupt changes" in the gospel record. Like many others, he compliments the "morality" of Christ while rejecting His authority. This was typical of the founding fathers. But this is also what Paul warned the church of when he wrote of "perilous times to come" in the last days, when men will have a "form of godliness" but are "denying the power thereof" (2 Timothy 3:5). The power of godliness comes from faith in Christ himself. Without Him, the *form of godliness* men create through morality is a deception. This is why Paul tells believers, "from such turn away." In the rest of his reply, Ben Franklin goes on about the divinity of Jesus Christ, saying: "...it is a question I do not dogmatize upon, having never studied it, and I think it needless to busy myself with it now, when I expect soon an Opportunity of knowing the Truth with less Trouble..."[285]

Franklin's final words were looking forward to his own death, which would occur about a month later in April 1790. It is unfortunate that while at death's door he felt it "needless" to seek out the truth of Christ. The Bible says that without faith "it is *impossible* to please God" (Hebrews 11:6, emphasis added) and that faith "*is the evidence of things not seen*" (Hebrews 11:1, emphasis added). As John the Baptist testified,

"He that believeth on the Son hath everlasting life: and he that believeth not the Son shall not see life: but the wrath of God abideth on him" (John 3:36).

John Adams

"The divinity of Jesus is made a convenient cover for absurdity." —John Adams

John Adams was America's third president and a close friend of Thomas Jefferson. Adams, Jefferson, and Franklin worked together on the first committee to design the Great Seal for the United States. While it does not appear that Adams was a member of any secret group, he was a Unitarian and shared views of Christianity not unlike those of Paine, Jefferson, and Franklin. Adams wrote: "I almost shudder at the thought of alluding to the most fatal example of the abuses of grief which the history of mankind has preserved—the Cross. Consider what calamities that engine of grief has produced!" [286]

Treaty of Tripoli

It was during the presidency of John Adams that the much debated Treaty of Tripoli was signed in an attempt to "make peace" with Muslims. The treaty bears perhaps the most damning statement against the idea of the United States as a *Christian* nation. Article 11 begins with these words: "As the government of the United States of America is not in any sense founded on the Christian Religion; as it has in itself no character of enmity against the laws, religion, or tranquility of Mussulmen (Muslims)." [287] Despite the efforts of some Christian leaders to spin-doctor this document, the statement speaks for itself. If you read the whole treaty, it becomes clear that the statement serves absolutely no purpose whatsoever other than to appease the Islamic hatred for Christianity. Furthermore, this was approved by the entire U.S. Senate and then signed by President

Adams. Where was the outcry from the *Christian* senators? Perhaps the answer comes from nineteenth-century preacher, the Reverend Dr. Wilson, who investigated the faith of the founding fathers and concluded: *"Those who have been called to administer the government have not been men making any public profession of Christianity."* [288]

Imagine your church saying that it was "not in any sense founded on the Christian religion," or a member of your congregation telling his neighbor that his own personal faith was "not in any sense founded on the Christian religion." If such words are unfit for Christians and their churches, how are they acceptable in a Christian government? There is simply no context that justifies the statement—other than it being a deliberate denial of Christianity.

A Bold Assertion

At the risk of being anathematized by patriotic Christian zealots, I will make the following assertion: If you study the founders carefully, and put aside the word games concerning them, it becomes clear that the establishment of certain rights, such as free speech and freedom of religion, were to give scoffers the right to denounce Christianity and the Bible as they pleased, to call it "rubbish" if they liked, without suffering any consequence. They wanted these freedoms for themselves so they could freely express their contempt for the Christian faith and encourage others to do the same.

George Washington

Undoubtedly, the most famous man to have survived the American Revolution is the veritable "father of our country," George Washington—but was he a Christian? Many die-hard Christian patriots have insisted that he was, but history reveals that questions about his faith did not begin in the modern era. Even during his lifetime, many sought out a clear answer as to what George Washington believed about God and the Lord Jesus Christ specifically. While Washington was less vocal about his thoughts on religion than men like Paine and Jefferson, it is clear that he held similar views.

Several interesting character traits of this man were well known in his lifetime. First, he refused to take communion. On Sundays when communion was served, Washington would get up and leave the church. This information is well documented, and testified to by many sources. People repeatedly inquired about it, and some were very disturbed by the fact that such a great American refused to partake in the Lord's Supper.

It is only fair to say that others, including the wife of Alexander Hamilton, testified that on certain occasions, George Washington *did* partake of communion in the church. Nevertheless, that it was a point of contention for him is without question. The reason has never been fully answered.

Testimony of the Clergy Who Knew Washington

Bishop James White is known as the father of the Protestant Episcopal Church in America. It is also reported that: "During a large portion of the period covering nearly a quarter of a century, Washington, with his wife, attended the churches in which Bishop White officiated."[289] After more than twenty years of being a pastor to George Washington himself, the Reverend White was only able to give a vague testimony of Washington's faith. For obvious reasons, many people sought this man hoping he could give a clear declaration of Washington's Christian belief. His reply on one occasion was, "I do not believe that any degree of recollection will bring to my mind any fact which would prove General Washington to have been a believer in the Christian revelation further than as may be hoped from his constant attendance upon Christian worship, in connection with the general reserve of his character."[290]

In other words, beyond his generally moral character and the fact that he went to church regularly, there is no other proof that he was a believer.

The assistant to Rev. White was Rev. James Abercrombie, who also ministered to Washington for years. Years later, when questioned by Dr. Bird Wilson, it is clear that Rev. Abercrombie arrived at the following conclusion: "Long after Washington's death, in reply to Dr. Wilson, who had interrogated him as to his illustrious auditor's religious views, Dr. Abercrombie's brief but emphatic answer was: 'Sir, Washington was a Deist.'"[291]

In Philadelphia, certain Christian clergymen had even tried to obtain a confession of faith, or a clear denial, from Washington during his farewell address as president. Thomas Jefferson commented on this in his journal, saying:

> Feb. 1. Dr. Rush tells me that he had it from Asa Green that when the clergy addressed General Washington on his departure from the Government, it was observed in their consultation that he had never on any occasion said a word to the public which showed a belief in the Christian religion and they thought they should so pen their address as to force him at length to declare publicly whether he was a Christian or not. They did so. However, he observed, the old fox was too cunning for them. He answered every article in their address particularly except that, which he passed over without notice.... I know that Gouverneur Morris, who pretended to be in his secrets and believed himself to be so, has often told me that General Washington believed no more in the system (Christianity) than he did.[292]

The "Asa Green" mentioned by Jefferson was Dr. Ashbel Green, who was chaplain to the Congress during Washington's presidency. Dr. Green "dined with the President on special invitation nearly every week."[293] One of his relatives, A.B. Bradford (who was later appointed a consul to China by President Lincoln), gave the following testimony about the event Jefferson had described. Bradford related that what follows was "frequently" told to him by Dr. Green: "He explained more at length the plan laid by the clergy of Philadelphia at the close of Washington's administration as President to get his views of religion for the sake of the good influence they supposed they would have in counteracting the Infidelity of Paine and the rest of the Revolutionary patriots, military and civil. But I well remember the smile on his face and the twinkle of his black eye when he said: 'The old fox was too cunning for Us.'"[294]

Notice the reference to "us" as Dr. Green counted himself among the Christian clergymen who were trying to obtain a *clear* confession from President Washington. The quote continues, as Bradford says of Dr. Green: "He affirmed, in concluding his narrative, that from his long and intimate acquaintance with Washington he knew it to be the case that while he respectfully conformed to the religious customs of society by generally going to church on Sundays, he had no belief at all in the divine origin of the Bible, or the Jewish-Christian religion."[295]

Sacred Fire?

In recent years, an attempt was made by authors Jerry A. Lillback and Jerry Newcombe in their book, *George Washington's Sacred Fire,* to prove that Washington was a Christian. They penned a thousand pages of seemingly endless speculation and suggestive possibilities, but the only confession they could produce was a single quote from Washington on "the Religion of Jesus Christ." Moreover, the authors of *Sacred Fire* destroy their entire hypothesis by revealing the following ecumenical quote from Washington to his fellow Freemason, the Marquis de Lafayette: "Being no bigot myself to any mode of worship, I am disposed to indulge the professors of Christianity in the church, that road to Heaven, which to them shall seem the most direct, plainest, easiest, and least liable to exception."[296]

Notice how he refers to Christianity as "that road to Heaven" as if it were one of many. Washington's words are entirely Masonic, and the quote appears as if he is letting his hair down to a fellow Mason. Furthermore, the quote clearly shows that Washington viewed himself as an *outsider* to biblical Christianity, and suggests that he merely "indulges" the Christians by going to church, etc.

All who knew him would agree that in terms of moral conduct and his code of honor, the world viewed him (and he probably saw himself) as *a man of Christian character.* This did not, however, require that he believe that Jesus is the Christ, the Son of God, or that He died for our sins, and that by faith in Him alone, do we have eternal life.

Freemasonry and the Founders

In his book, *The Question of Freemasonry and the Founding Fathers*, author David Barton takes up the argument about whether or not the United States was founded by Masons. Despite the overwhelming evidence against him, he diminishes the role of Masonry, saying: "it is historically and irrefutably demonstrable that Freemasonry was *not* a significant influence in the formation of the United States."[297]

Nevertheless, in January of 2007, the first session of the 110th Congress (when Nancy Pelosi became speaker of the house) passed House Resolution 33, which recognized "the thousands of Freemasons in every State in the Nation..." The resolution goes on to say specifically, "Whereas the Founding Fathers of this great Nation and signers of the Constitution, *most of whom were Freemasons*, provided a well-rounded basis for developing themselves and others into valuable citizens of the United States" (H. RES. 33, as submitted by Congressman and 33rd degree Mason Paul Gillmor, emphasis added).

Christian Masonry?

Furthermore, Barton makes the assertion that Freemasonry was a "Christian" organization during the time of the founding fathers, but was then later corrupted by men like Albert Mackey and Albert Pike. As we show in the documentary, "Secret Mysteries of America's Beginnings,"[298] American Masonry can be traced to England during the time of Sir Francis Bacon (1561–1626), who is considered the first grand master of modern masonry. Even at this time, the inner doctrine of embracing all the world religions alongside Christianity existed; but they did not publish such things in formal declarations, for fear of persecution. The outer and inner doctrine of secret societies is something overlooked by many researchers who attempt to marginalize the influence of Freemasonry. These same men would also know little of Rosicrucianism, which was the forerunner of Masonry.

Satanic Roots of Masonry

Sir Francis Bacon's close associate during this time was Dr. John Dee, the court astrologer for Queen Elizabeth I. It is well known that Dee was a sorcerer who summoned demonic spirits to obtain secret knowledge; a practice used by Rosicrucians (of whom Dee was the chief in England) for centuries. The root word for "demon" means "a knowing one."[299] The Rosicrucians desired to know secrets of science (i.e., *knowledge*) and consulted demons to get information. Bacon also made contact with demonic spirits, including the goddess Pallas Athena, whom he claimed was his muse or inspiration. In time, Dee handed off the leadership of the Rosicrucian Society to Bacon, who would enfold the secrets of Rosicrucianism into the system of Freemasonry.

It is little wonder that Sir Francis Bacon would become the father of the modern scientific method and that men like Benjamin Franklin and Thomas Jefferson would follow his example in their scientific endeavors. Franklin and Jefferson are both claimed by modern Rosicrucians as being of their order.

Like the Gnostics, the Rosicrucians craved knowledge; and it was this desire that lead them to worship Lucifer. The secret orders regard Lucifer as the "angel of light" who, in the form of a serpent, bid mankind to partake of the tree of knowledge of good and evil so that their eyes would be open and they could become as gods. This is—and always has been—the inner doctrine of Rosicrucianism, Freemasonry, and all the secret orders. In the nineteenth century, when Masons like Pike and Mackey (along with leading occultists such as Eliphas Levi and Madame

H.P. Blavatsky) described this doctrine in their writings, they were only admitting in print what had been secretly known for centuries. The difference was that with the revolutionary movements, *freedom of religion* allowed them to publish such things without fear of persecution.

Secrets in Stone

Centuries before all this, in 1492, Rosslyn Chapel was built by Scottish Freemasons. To this day, the chapel is considered a puzzle because it is filled with carvings and icons of Christian and pagan religions. Why? The reason is because Freemasons have always had the inner doctrine of amalgamating religious beliefs. Much of this can be traced back to the Knights Templar, who are said to have fled to Scotland when they were persecuted in Europe (circa 1307). In fact, the red cross of the Templars is said to be a point of origin for the rose cross of Rosicrucianism. Furthermore, in the wake the Scottish Jacobite rebellions of the early 1700s, many Scottish Masons and Rosicrucians fled to America, bringing their occult doctrines with them. One of their power centers was the Fredericksburg Lodge No. 4, whose members included George Washington, James Monroe, and eight of the Revolutionary War generals.

The practice of carving their doctrines in stone continued in the new world with the building of Washington D.C. This is why one will find in our nations' capital countless images of gods and goddesses, along with zodiacs, the Washington Monument obelisk, reflecting pools, and a whole cacophony of pagan imagery. There are no monuments to Jesus Christ, the apostles, or anything having to do with the Christian faith.

The Reason for Masonic Deception

Manly P. Hall has been called "Masonry's Greatest Philosopher" in America's leading Masonic publication.[300] In his book, *The Secret Destiny of America,* Hall says that, in the past, secret orders intentionally made a pretense of Christian faith in order to avoid persecution. He writes: "The rise of the Christian Church broke up the intellectual pattern of the classical pagan world. By persecution…it drove the secret societies into greater secrecy; the pagan intellectuals then reclothed their original ideas in a garment of Christian phraseology, but bestowed the keys of the symbolism only upon those duly initiated and bound to secrecy by their vows."[301]

The "initiated" who were "bound to secrecy" is an obvious reference to those in secret societies. Hall argued that these groups have been operating in America for centuries, and that they were the authors of the American Revolution. Before dismissing his assertion as a *conspiracy theory*, ask yourself a question: Did *Christians* erect a bunch of pagan monuments to various gods in Washington D.C., and while doing it, just happen to omit Jesus Christ? Or was it done by men who outwardly *pretended* to be Christians, but who inwardly had a hidden agenda, just as their "greatest philosopher" tells us?

Classicism: The Veil of Lucifer

In his book on the founders and Masonry, David Barton defends the use of pagan symbolism with the following argument: "Americans in recent generations have not been trained in classical literature—a training that was routine in the Founding Era. Therefore, present-day Americans are not inclined to consider structures from the ancient empires (such as the pyramids), or to be familiar with their heroes (such as Cato, Cicero, and Aeneus), or even with their writers (such as Homer, Virgil, Herodotus, and especially Plutarch…)."[302]

If you take the time to look up the works of Homer, Virgil, and others, you will find that these ancient writer/philosophers were writing about the gods and goddesses of the ancient world. All of these gods are called "devils" in the Bible (1 Corinthians 10:20). The same deception is used to describe the Statue of Liberty where reference is made to "Liberty's classical origins." The placard on Liberty Island then goes on to say that the statue was based on the Roman goddess, Libertas. Were the statue judged from a biblical viewpoint, it would tell of "Liberty's *demonic* origins." The clever use of the word "classic" is simply more evidence of satanic duplicity. David Barton's incredible delusion seems to be that if Satan and his demons are put in a book marked "classical literature," then they are somehow sanitized and no longer offensive to God. But in the Bible, God says, "Thus shall ye say unto them, The gods that have not made the heavens and the earth, even they shall perish from the earth, and from under these heavens" (Jeremiah 10:11).

Why would any Bible-believing Christian want to build statues and monuments to exalt spiritual powers that God has condemned to destruction? Clearly, the modern references to "classical literature" by which demons become acceptable learning tools, are a clever veil of deception. This danger was defined two centuries earlier by the sixteenth-century scholar Erasmus concerning "classical" studies, who said, "...that under the cloak of reviving ancient literature paganism tries to rear its head, as there are those among Christians who acknowledge Christ only in name but inwardly breathe heathenism" (Erasmus, as cited by David W. Cloud, in *What About Erasmus?*).[303]

G.A.O.T.U. and George Washington

To enable their members to embrace any god they wish, Masonry developed vague terminology when referring to deity. Their favorite title is "Great Architect of the Universe." David Barton, in his attempts to call early Masonry a "Christian" organization, suggests that this idea developed *after* the founding era. He creates this argument in an attempt to justify the involvement of men like George Washington and others in early American Masonry.

In his book, Barton rightly states that in Christianity, "Only one God is worshipped—and that God is *not* the universalist deistic god that Masonry denotes as the 'Great Architect of the Universe' (G.A.O.T.U.)" (Barton, p. 20, emphasis in original). While saying this, he fails to tell his readers that George Washington (whom he insists was a Christian) referred to this same Masonic god when writing to the Grand Lodge of Free and Accepted Masons for the Commonwealth of Massachusetts on January 1793, when he wrote: "I sincerely pray, that the Great

Architect of the Universe may bless you here, and receive you hereafter into his immortal temple. George Washington."[304]

Notice that the idea of G.A.O.T.U. was not *invented* by Albert Pike or others who came later. It was well known among early American Masons. Could such a quote be the reason George Washington, in his thousands of pages of written correspondence, never made a clear confession of Jesus Christ? Or that the only quote anyone can find from him makes mention of "the Religion of Jesus Christ," but not of faith in the Son of God, according to the Scriptures? Could this be why Washington's own pastor called him a *deist*?

Pythagorean Masonry

While some patriot Christians will scoff at the idea that the Illuminati could have had anything to do with the design of Washington D.C., they are simply unfamiliar with Illuminati symbolism. The Illuminists (an inner circle of Freemasons) were high-minded intellectuals who exalted the teachings of the Greek and Roman philosophers of the ancient world (i.e., the so-called "classical" authors that Barton defends). Pythagorean philosophy was chiefly embraced by the revolutionaries of the founding era. The Pythagorean theorem is based on the right triangle of Pythagoras, and (according to Masonic author, David Ovason) is the reason Federal Triangle in Washington D.C. was designed as it is.

Dr. James H. Billington, in his book, *Fire in the Minds of Men,* writes about the revolutionary faith that was inspired by the Bavarian Illuminati. Bear in mind that Billington is not a "conspiracy writer," but the Thirteenth Librarian of Congress and a friend of the Bush family. He is as official a historian as you can find. President George W. Bush quoted his book in his 2005 inaugural address after he was elected for his second term. In his exhaustive work, Dr. Billington has a whole section titled *The Pythagorean Passion,* in which he says, "…a vast array of labels and images was taken from classical antiquity to legitimize the new revolutionary faith."[305]

Notice his reference to "classical" antiquity (i.e., pagan symbolism). He goes on to say that "Pythagoras, the semi-legendary Greek philosopher, provided a model for the intellectual-turned-revolutionary. He became a kind of patron saint for romantic revolutionaries..." (Ibid, p. 100). Adam Weishaupt, the founder of the Bavarian Illuminati, even named his "final blueprint for politicized Illuminism...*Pythagoras*" (Ibid, p. 100). Billington says that the "revolutionaries...repeatedly attached importance to the central prime numbers of Pythagorean mysticism: one, three, seven, and above all five." The number five is significant because there are five points to a pentagram. Pythagoras called the pentagram the *pentalpha*, which is why there are so many Pentalpha Lodges in modern Freemasonry. This may also be why there is a pentagram in the street layout of Washington D.C., as we detail in our documentary, *Riddles in Stone.*[306]

The Washington D.C. Pentagram

All serious researchers contend that the controversy over the pentagram is not about whether or not it is truly there. Arial photos clearly reveal it. Even the Masons, who deny that they are responsible for it, acknowledge its presence, but argue that Rhode Island Avenue does not extend all the way to complete the figure. As such, the debate is twofold: 1) Was the pentagram intentional, or simply the coincidence of geometric lines? 2) Why is the pentagram incomplete? The answer to the second part seems to reveal the first. As we explain in our film *Riddles in Stone,* the unfinished pentagram is a well known symbol in Freemasonry. As Manly P. Hall records in his writings, "The pentagram is used extensively in black magic, but when so used its form always differs in one of three ways: The star may be broken at one point by not permitting the converging lines to touch...When used in black magic, the pentagram is called the 'sign of the cloven hoof' or the 'footprint of the devil.'"[307]

Of course, Hall was writing in the twentieth century, but was this symbolism known by Masons during the founding era? The answer is yes. One of the most famous Master Masons of all time was Johann

Wolfgang von Goethe, who made use of such a pentagram in the play *Faust*, in which the character of Faust summons Mephistophiles (the Devil) to make a pact with him. As the Devil tries to leave, he is hindered. As a result, he and Faust have the following exchange:

MEPHISTOPHILES
Let me go up! I cannot go away; a little
hindrance bids me stay. The Witch's foot
upon your sill I see.

FAUST
The pentagram? That's in your way?
You son of Hell, explain to me,
If that stays you, how came you in today?
And how was such a spirit so betrayed?

MEPHISTOPHILES
Observe it closely! It is not well made;
One angle, on the outer side of it,
Is just a little open, as you see.[308]

The "open" or "broken" pentagram was used by Faust to summon the Devil in a black magic ceremony. The famous author of the play, Goethe, was not only a Mason, but also a well known member of the Bavarian Illuminati. To this day, Freemasons proudly acknowledge that his writings are filled with Masonic symbolism, while books have been written about his Illuminist involvement.

Goethe published his first edition of *Faust* in 1790 (called *Faust: ein Fragment*), and it was in the next two years that Pierre L'Enfant (with the possible help of Thomas Jefferson) came up with the street design for Washington D.C. (1791–1792). It is therefore provable that members of these secret orders were familiar with the idea of an unfinished pentagram *before* the street layout was complete. Admittedly, this does not of itself prove that the pentagram was intentional. Yet it is interesting that Goethe's play and the D.C. design were done during the same period. Because of the close interaction between the Freemasonry of America and that of Europe, it is entirely possible (and likely) that L'Enfant and Jefferson were familiar with the symbol and placed it intentionally.

Were They Masons?

Both Pierre L'Enfant and Thomas Jefferson are thought to have been Masons. The reason for doubting it is because modern American Masonry cannot find the initiation records of these two men. Some believe they were initiated in France and their records destroyed through the chaos of the French Revolution. Before believing those who deny their membership, bear in mind that Jefferson is listed among the Masonic presidents in the Harry S. Truman Presidential Library. Furthermore, the well known European publication *Freemasonry Today* maintains unequivocally that Pierre L'Enfant was a Mason: "Washington DC can fairly be described as the world's foremost 'Masonic City.' Its centre was laid out according to a plan drawn up by the French Freemason Pierre L'Enfant."[309]

Many other Masonic writers similarly state that Jefferson and L'Enfant were Masons, while some Masonic apologists debate the issue. When critics like David Barton or the History Channel *insist* that these men and others of the founding era were not Masons—and then blame the "conspiracy theorists" for passing on misinformation—they are either ignorant or deliberately withholding information.

America: The New Atlantis

In our documentary series, *Secret Mysteries of America's Beginnings*, we show how Freemasonry and Rosicrucianism existed in England during the Elizabethan era, and were directly involved in the colonization scheme. Yes, there were most certainly Christians who came to this country through the Puritan/Pilgrim movement, but they were not alone. With them came the secret societies that saw America as "the New Atlantis" envisioned by Sir Francis Bacon. There is even a 1910 Newfoundland six-cent stamp (with three sixes on it, no less) with the image of Bacon that reads: "Lord Bacon, the Guiding Spirit in Colonization Scheme."

Clearly, there were those who understood that the development of the new world was inspired by Bacon and his occult philosophies. It was Bacon who said, "Knowledge is power," and the pursuit of knowledge through scientific discovery has guided the success of America. If one reads *The New Atlantis*, where Bacon describes a society with tall buildings, flying machines, weapons of mass destruction, health spas, the magnification of sound, and experiments with poisons on animals for the purpose of curing human beings, it becomes readily discernable that our country has followed his blueprint from the start.

Rosicrucianism: Mask of the Ancient Mysteries

Once you understand that Rosicrucianism (the inner doctrine of Masonry) is the mingling of Christianity with paganism, many of the founding fathers make more sense. A Rosicrucian can readily quote the Bible, make references to "Christ," "Jesus," "the Savior," and so forth; but he will also exalt the teachings of Plato and the philosophers of old, and look upon the gods of the ancient world as examples of virtue and justice. Consider this passage from Bacon's *New Atlantis*, where a band of "Christian" sailors come upon an unknown island: "…the man who I before described stood up, and with a loud voice in Spanish, asked, 'Are ye Christians?' We answered, 'We were;'…at which answer the said person lifted up his right hand towards heaven, and drew it softly to his mouth, which is the gesture they use when they thank God, and then said: 'If ye will swear, all of you, by the merits of the Savior that ye are no pirates…you may have license to come on land.'"[310]

Below is a series of passages from the *New Atlantis* to show how the use of Christian sounding dialogue flows from Bacon's pen:

"He gave us our oath; 'By the name of Jesus and his merits;' and after told us that the next day…we should be sent…"[311]

"…let us look upon God, and every man reform his own ways. Besides we are come here amongst a Christian people, full of piety and humanity…"[312]

"Therefore for God's love…let us so behave ourselves as we may be at peace with God, and may find grace in the eyes of this people."[313]

At one point in the story, the sailors make an inquiry as to how "Christianity" came to the mysterious island they have stumbled upon. We read, " 'But above all,' we said, '…we…hoped assuredly that we should meet one day in the kingdom of heaven, for that we were both parts Christians, we desired to know, in respect that land was so remote…from the land where our Savior walked on earth, who was the apostle of that nation, and how it was converted to the faith?' "[314]

The answer Bacon provides to the above question is that the apostle Bartholomew sent forth an ark in the water with a copy of the Bible and the following letter: "I Bartholomew, a servant of the Highest, and Apostle of Jesus Christ, was warned by an angel that appeared to me in a vision of glory, that I should commit this ark to the floods of the sea. Therefore do I testify and declare unto that people where God shall ordain this ark to land, that in the same day is come unto them salvation and peace and good-will, from the Father, and from the Lord Jesus."[315]

Did you notice all the rich, majestic words that have every impression of godly Christian faith in them? Notice that mentioning "the Lord Jesus" and "salvation" is not a problem for Bacon in this Rosicrucian fable? How can he do it? It is because all of these things have another meaning to the Rosicrucian adept. This is what Manly Hall was referring to when he said the "pagan intellectuals reclothed their original ideas in a garment of Christian phraseology."[316]

If one reads the whole story, he will begin to notice that the flowery words of Bacon are not unlike the words of some revolutionary founding fathers.

Bacon's *New Atlantis* has also been called *The Land of the Rosicrucians,* (see *A New Light on Bacon's New Atlantis* by Mather Walker) and that is exactly what America has become, thanks to the secret societies. The rise of paganism in our country is no accident; it was planned from the beginning. The patriotic religion that demands "religious tolerance" and ends up teaching "many paths to heaven" is the ultimate doctrine these groups have always believed, and hoped to normalize in America.

What Saith the Scripture?

Even if Christians are ignorant of the history that has intentionally been withheld from them, they ought to know the teaching of Scripture. The patriot Christian seems spiritually blind to the fact that rebellion against authority is not a *Christian* virtue. It is, however, a very Masonic virtue to fight against those who will not submit to the occult philosophies of their secret order.

No, the followers of Christ did not dress up like wild Indians and besiege a ship in Boston harbor because they refused to pay a tax on tea. Imagine such a thing happening today! When the Minutemen went down to the Mexican border with cell phones, President Bush called them "vigilantes." Can you imagine what would have happened if they had hijacked a ship somewhere and thrown all the produce in the water? Would anyone, including men like David Barton, have said they were following in the "godly Christian" footsteps of the founding fathers? No! They would've said, "Those guys are nuts! What a terrible witness," and so on.

Revolution in Ancient Israel?

If there ever were a people who had the right to rebel against unjust authority, it would have been the Jewish people dwelling in the land of

Israel two thousand years ago under Roman occupation. They could have opened the Scriptures and said, "This is the land given to us by God! These pagans have no right to be here!" And indeed, the zealots of that time most surely took that view and fought against Rome. Why, then, did their Messiah *not* support their cause?

In fact, Jesus taught, "But I say unto you that ye resist not evil, but whosoever shall smite thee on thy right cheek, turn to him the other also.... And whosoever shall compel thee to go a mile, go with him two" (Matthew 5:39, 41).

As many teachers have noted, these instructions are in direct reference to the unjust treatment of Rome against the Jewish people. The second admonition had to do with a law that allowed Roman soldiers to force Jews to carry their backpacks up to one mile.

Notice that the Lord did not answer these issues with a diatribe on "human rights violations," but gave instruction to do the exact opposite of what our flesh is inclined to do. In other words, resist our rebellious and vengeful nature and yield ourselves to the character of Christ. Just after this, Jesus said, "Ye have heard that it hath been said, Thou shalt love thy neighbor, and hate thine enemy; But I say unto you, Love your enemies, bless them that curse you, do good to them that hate you, and pray for them who despitefully use you, and persecute you, that you may be the sons of your Father who is in heaven..." (Matthew 5:43–44).

Did the revolutionary founders obey the Lord in these things? Ask yourself: Why is it that while they had certain declarations about God, and sometimes even about Jesus; they almost never quoted from the teachings of the Lord himself? In all of David Barton's founding father quotes, there are no quotes from Jesus himself; there's only a rare mention of His name. Did the founders avoid His words because they knew in their hearts that their actions were contrary to His commands?

The Scripture warns us that "they are the enemies of the cross of Christ: whose end is destruction, whose god is their belly, and whose glory is in their shame, who mind earthly things" (Philippians 3:18–19). Though some of the founders said things like, "No king but King

Jesus," and made mention of "the Christian religion," of what value are such declarations apart from obedience to Christ? Jesus himself said, "And why call ye me, Lord, Lord, and do not the things I say?" (Luke 6:46). And elsewhere, He said, "Not every one that saith unto me, Lord, Lord, shall enter into the kingdom of heaven; but he that doeth the will of my Father which is in heaven" (Matthew 7:21). Is it a coincidence that the same founding fathers who did not obey Christ also did not believe He was the Son of God?

Conclusion

As the New World Order looms ever nearer, and many who can see the signs are wondering what to do, it is time to arm ourselves with the true Word of God. We should be as the sons of Issachar, "which were men that had understanding of the times, to know what Israel ought to do" (1 Chronicles 12:32). And if we die for something, brethren, let it not be for the vain wisdom of man, but for the gospel of our Lord Jesus Christ.

—

Christian J. Pinto is the founder of Adullam Films, a Christian ministry dedicated to promoting the gospel of Jesus Christ through film and video production. His documentary series, Secret Mysteries of America's Beginnings, *on secret societies in America, has won top awards at film festivals, and has received several Telly Awards. For more information, visit adullamfilms.org.*

chapter nine

The Final Century—
Christian Survival versus
Pagan Revival

---

by Bill Salus

"Behold, I stand at the door,
and knock: if any man hear my voice,
and open the door, I will come in to him,
and will sup with him, and he with me."

REVELATION 3:20

This chapter opens with the well-known quote from Christ to the "lukewarm" Christian church of Laodicea.[317] Christ warns of a time whereby the professing church will position Him outside its door as an ordinary stranger rather than its extraordinary Savior. This precarious end-times placement outside church confines causes Christ to long from His exterior location for either a soothing "cold" drink, be it a hot day, and/or a "hot" meal, should a cold night be in store—both equally satisfying. Conversely, He receives a lukewarm reception, which neither quenches His thirst nor satiates His appetite. As this final twenty-first century commences, do we see Christianity simmering down to this undesired temperature? Will a "lukewarm" Christian condition push Christ outside its door, making room for a pagan spiritual revival?

Three themes are developed in this opening paragraph that will characterize the content of this chapter. First is the possibility that this is likely the final century on this present earth's timeline. Second is the genuine concern that Christianity is faltering toward apostasy in these last days. Last is the likelihood that a "lukewarm" Christian religion invites the revival of paganism, also commonly referred to these days as "neo-paganism." Loosely defined, paganism is the practice of false polytheistic and/or pantheistic religious practices by humanity's heathen populations, and neo-paganism is the contemporary practice of paganism, such as Wicca.

Part 1
The Final Century

The Bible, in addition to several other religious books, identifies an expiration date on this present earth's timeline. Like the Bible, these other books tend to profess that divine judgment is forthcoming and that a new era filled with a brighter future will ensue in the aftermath. Could this be the final century? Are all the prophetic signs falling into place encouraging end-time, apocalyptic thinking?

Judaism, Christianity, and Islam, listed in the order of their religious origin, advocate that world judgment is coming on the nearby horizon and that this reckoning will commence and conclude at the end of time. These three predominant world religions believe in the monotheistic worship of a God, which separates them from Hinduism, Buddhism, and other alternative New Age religions that generally encourage the worship of self as a god among other gods.

Christian eschatologists like me are becoming increasingly convinced that humanity has been thrust beyond the point of no return into the last days. The prophetic signs reinforcing our views are abundantly clear. Scholars today are hard pressed to locate even a single prophecy—out of the myriad of Bible prophecies remaining to be fulfilled—that couldn't occur in the very near future. A few examples are listed below.

A climactic, concluding Arab-Israeli war. Psalm 83 foretells of an Arab confederacy comprised of Palestinians, Syrians, Saudis, Egyptians, Lebanese, Jordanians, and likely their terrorist bedfellows, the Hezbollah, Hamas, Al-Qaeda, and more. In my book, *Isralestine: The Ancient Blueprints of the Future Middle East,*[318] I write extensively about this prophecy and its nearby fulfillment. This prophecy could easily be fulfilled in the next one to two decades.

An invasion of Israel. Ezekiel 38 and 39 tell of the last days Russian-Iranian-led nuclear equipped consortium of nine populations that comes to invade the Jewish State of Israel. Today, Russia and Iran have become the best of national friends. Russia has helped Iran develop nuclear technologies and Iran has expressed a desire to "wipe Israel off the map"![319] This prophecy will likely occur in the aftermath of the Psalm 83 event, according to my assessments, and it could also easily occur in the early decades of this twenty-first century.

The mark of the Beast. Revelation 13 issues the infamous "666" prophecy, often referred to as the "mark of the Beast" (Antichrist). This prophecy declares that no one will be able to buy or sell unless he or she receives a mark upon the right hand or forehead. Many eschatologists believe that the apostle John, approximately two thousand years ago, attempted to describe a type of advanced computer technology that exists today. This prophecy, which seems to predict humanity's ability to conduct cashless commerce, was impossible at the time it was written, but is a definite possibility today. A one-world order coupled with a one-world banking system could evolve out of the current world economic crisis and such a system could effortlessly segue into the fulfillment of this prophecy.

Two witnesses. Revelation 11 informs us that a day will come when two evangelical witnesses will be killed by the Antichrist in Jerusalem for their Christian testimony. We are told that they will lie dead in the streets on full visual display for a period of three-and-a-half days. The prophecy declares that the entire world will see their dead bodies lay wasted in the street. In the nineteenth century, atheists would argue that this prophecy could never happen and that, therefore, the

Bible must be errant. However, in this century—with satellite television technologies—the whole world will be able to witness this prophetic spectacle. To international astonishment, these two witnesses will rise from the dead and ascend into heaven outside the range of television viewing.

These prophetic examples are just a few among a litany of others that suggest biblically that these are the last days, and that this is likely the final century. Extra-biblical sources suggest similar apocalyptic scenarios are about to occur, such as the growing number of those who believe the end of the world will occur in the year 2012 with the conclusion of the Mayan calendar. Additionally, many Muslims, like Iran's President Mahmoud Ahmadinejad, are predicting the nearby coming of the Mahdi, the Islamic Messiah who is foretold to arrive at the end of time.

Furthermore, as the world entered its first threshold decade of this century, it was greeted by turbulent events sequenced in fairly rapid succession, evidencing the disturbing possibility that this is the concluding century. Listed below are a few examples:

1. The Al-Qaeda terrorist attacks of September 11, 2001, that toppled the twin towers of the World Trade Center in New York City.
2. The Asian tsunami of December 26, 2004, which was generated by a magnitude 9.1 earthquake in the Indian Ocean killing an estimated 225,000 people in eleven countries. This was the deadliest natural disaster in recorded history.
3. Hurricane Katrina in August 2005, which ranks as the costliest hurricane in American history.
4. The financial crisis that began in 2007 that caused the collapse of numerous major banking and financial institutions worldwide.

Stockpile upon the list above the American invasion of Afghanistan in October 2001; Operation Iraqi Freedom, which commenced in

March of 2003; the sub-prime lending crisis of 2005; the thirty-four-day conflict in July 2006 between Israel and the Hezbollah; the Russian invasion of Georgia in August 2008; the twenty-two-day "Operation Cast Lead" campaign of the Israeli Defense Forces into Gaza in December 2008; and the burgeoning worldwide UFO phenomena, and we have further cause to consider this century being the time of the end.

Interestingly, Jesus Christ predicted approximately two thousand years ago in Matthew 24:7–8 that world wars would come and be followed by cataclysmic events like regional wars, pandemic pestilences, earthquakes, and famines in various places. He called it a time of travail, and likened it to a woman having birth pangs. His birthing illustration envisions catastrophic events occurring with greater frequency and intensity as the end of time nears, similar to the way a woman's contractions increase as her child begins departure from the womb.

Eschatologists tend to agree that "nation" already rose "against nation" in World Wars 1 and 2, fulfilling the first part of this prophecy. It is also commonly understood that "kingdom" coming "against kingdom" refers to regionalized conflicts[320] and those also have been and are still occurring in the aftermath of the world wars. Lastly, significant earthquakes spontaneously shaking assorted world locations have become an increasingly regular phenomenon. Jesus implies that these events would characterize creation in convulsion as it nears the time of the end.

Part 2
Christian Survival

If this is the final century, then what role will Christianity play within it? Will it survive and thrive in these final few decades, serving as a vibrant venue by which humanity can come to Christ, or is it destined for a less fertile future? According to prophecy, there appears to be both a yes and no answer. Yes, it survives and thrives through a sincere, Bible-believing base that will be "hot" on fire for the Lord. Purportedly, this Christian contingency continues to preach the Good News fervently from Jerusalem unto the uttermost parts of the world! However, against the backdrop of this evangelistic component emerges an increasingly lackadaisical, "luke-warm" element that spirals deeply downward into apostasy.[321]

These two groups seem to coexist up until the point of the Rapture, after which only the latter group remains. For the purposes of this chapter, these two groups will be called Philadelphia and Laodicea in association with two of the seven churches described in the book of Revelation. Philadelphia, which means "brotherly love," represents—again, for the purposes of this chapter—true, born-again Christian believers who overcome the last-days tendency toward lukewarm-ness that will characterize the Laodicean faction of the Christian church.

For readers not familiar with the powerful Rapture event, it is described in the passages that follow, which tell of a time when Jesus Christ returns in a nanosecond to *retrieve* His true, born-again believers miraculously in the air, and to *receive* them into the heavenly abode:

Behold, I show you a mystery: We shall not all sleep, but we shall all be changed, In a moment, in the twinkling of an eye, at the last trump; for the trumpet shall sound, and the dead shall be raised incorruptible, and we shall be changed. For this corruptible must put on incorruption, and this mortal must put on immortality. So, when this corruptible shall have put on incorruption, and this mortal shall have put on immortality, then shall be brought to pass the saying that is written, Death is swallowed up in victory. (1 Corinthians 15:51–54)

For this we say unto you by the word of the Lord, that we who are alive and remain unto the coming of the Lord shall not precede them who are asleep. For the Lord himself shall descend from heaven with a shout, with the voice of the archangel, and with the trump of God; and the dead in Christ shall rise first; Then we who are alive and remain shall be caught up together with them in the clouds, to meet the Lord in the air; and so shall we ever be with the Lord. Wherefore, comfort one another with these words. (1 Thessalonians 4:15–18)

There are conflicting opinions as to the timing of this event. Some suggest this event is imminent, which means it will occur at any moment and likely before the Tribulation period; others teach that it will occur either at the end or mid-point of the Tribulation period.[322]

Regardless of the reader's perspective, the event will likely occur in this final century, and in the aftermath the "lukewarm" Laodicean apostates will likely be those left behind. Furthermore, the occurrence of this event should severely impact the way the world thinks and operates in the minimal time remaining in this final century.

One of the several ways scholars confidently predict the condition of the Christian church in its final stage of development is through the prophetic interpretation of the seven letters to the seven churches in Revelation 2 and 3. Many eschatologists teach that these letters were partially intended to chronologically order the seven stages of church development throughout its earthly existence.[323] In essence, these letters include an intrinsic prophetic value intended to offer more than just contemporary instruction to the specific seven churches existing at the time of issuance. Fortunately, today's experts have the opportune advantage of looking back upon church history, which enables them to accurately make this association.

Below is an outline of the chronological development of the Christian church in accordance with the blueprints of the seven letters in Revelation.[324] This outline reveals that we are living in the final days of church development, the "days of Laodicea."

Ephesus (Revelation 2:1–7) (AD 30–100)

The first stage of Christianity was primarily an apostolic period. Christians operated in compliance with Matthew 28:18–20. It was a time of reconciliation whereby the disciples successfully preached the Good News gospel of Jesus Christ outwardly from Jerusalem into the surrounding Gentile populations of the world. This was Christianity in its infancy, and as a religion, it was rapidly spreading throughout the broader Middle East region and into the greater Roman Empire.

Smyrna (Revelation 2:8–11) (AD 100–313)

This segment of church history was characterized by a period of persecution. Rome was conducting wide-scale Christian executions in an attempt to prevent the growth and spread of the religion. Martyrdom was the unfortunate predicament forced upon the church by the Roman Empire during the Smyrna era. However, to Rome's chagrin, the persecutions actually bolstered the growth of Christianity. Christians dying for their faith caught the attention of multitudes that in turn fixated their focus upon Christ as their Savior.

Pergamos (Revelation 2:12–17) (AD 313–600)

The period of Pergamos, meaning "mixed marriage" in Greek, is associated with the paganization of the church. As the Roman Empire began its decline, it embraced Christianity as its state religion. This served two primary purposes. First, it began to fill deepening political rifts developing in the deteriorating Roman government; and secondly, it facilitated the survival of faltering pagan religious practices by cleverly integrating and incubating them into Christianity. Also, the martyrdom period of Smyrna that experienced Christianity flourishing became problematic for Rome. Each martyr's death brought new and renewed strength among fellow Christians. Thus Rome adopted the attitude, "If you can't beat them [kill all the Christians], join them." Throughout time, this Roman attitude eventually led many Christians to reciprocate and romanticize Romanism, and to believe that "when in Rome, do as the Romans do."[325]

During the Pergamos period, Christianity essentially was asked to compromise itself—and in so doing, create an end to the persecutions occurring during the Smyrna stage. By marrying up with Roman paganism, Christianity was insured its survival. Shortly thereafter, ancient Roman religious practices began to permeate and adulterate the church. Christian traditions such as Christmas trees and Yule logs can likely be traced to this Pergamos period of church history.

Thyatira (Revelation 2:18–29) (AD 600-Tribulation)

This church is commonly thought to represent the Roman Catholic Church, which evolved out of the Pergamos period. Thyatira tends to be a works-based rather than a faith-based church. In so doing, it emphasizes the religious rather than relational importance between God and humanity. Revelation 2:22 declares that an apostate element within Thyatira will exist in the end times and be cast into the "sickbed" of the Great Tribulation period.

Sardis (Revelation 3:1–6) (AD 1517-Tribulation)

This period is best described as the Protestant Reformation; however, it lacked true transformation. Salvation through faith rather than works was reintroduced within Christianity; however, the Reformation continued to be more about religion than about a personal relationship with God.

Philadelphia (Revelation 3:7–13) (AD 1648-Rapture)

Powerful, worldwide missionary movements beginning in the mid 1600s characterize the period of Philadelphia. In accordance with Matthew 28:18–20, this church answered the call to the "Ministry of Reconciliation." The Philadelphian period concludes with the Rapture. (More will be said about this church later in this chapter.)

Laodicea (Revelation 3:14–22)
(AD 1900-Tribulation)

This church began in the twentieth century and will continue on into the seven-year Tribulation period. This last-days church is guilty of preaching a social rather than a scriptural gospel. (More on this church later in this chapter.)

Many eschatologists believe that the world hourglass has made its final turn, and that the church alas has entered into the "days of Laodicea." However, they also believe that up until the Rapture, the Philadelphian component still will preside in the Christian equation.

As such, it is important to interpret through the prophetic lens the key passages contained in the pertinent sixth and seventh letters to the seven churches that validate this scholarly viewpoint.

Philadelphia–The Sixth Letter

And to the angel of the church in Philadelphia write: These things saith he that is holy, he that is true, he that hath the key of David, he that openeth, and no man shutteth; and shutteth, and no man openeth. I know thy works; behold, I have set before thee an open door, and no man can shut it; for thou hast a little strength, and hast kept my word, and hast not denied my name. Behold, I will make them of the synagogue of Satan, who say they are Jews, and are not, but do lie; behold, I will make them to come and worship before thy feet, and to know that I have loved thee. Because thou hast kept the word of my patience, I also will keep thee from the hour of temptation, which shall come upon all the world, to try them that dwell upon the earth. Behold, I come quickly; hold that fast which thou hast, that no man take thy crown. Him that overcometh will I make a pillar in the temple of my God, and he shall go no more out; and I will write upon him the name of my God, and the name of the city of my God, the new Jerusalem, which cometh down out of heaven from my God; and I will write upon him my new name. He that hath an ear, let him hear what the Spirit saith unto the churches. (Revelation 3:7–13)

Definite contrasts are observable between the sixth and seventh letters. This letter to the church of Philadelphia evidences that it is a beloved contingent within Christianity that has an open missionary door to the international community. Furthermore, it is a believing population that will escape "the hour of temptation which shall come upon all the world." It is commonly taught that this "hour of temptation" refers to the final, seven-year Tribulation period that concludes this present earth's timeline. Thus, this group will be removed sometime prior to the Tribulation period. Its departure will likely be the result of the Rapture event previously referenced.

As listed prior in the chronological outline of church history, this group still effectively espouses the gospel today throughout the nations of the world. Whereas the church of Philadelphia is loved and will escape the hour of trial, the church of Laodicea does not seem to share the similar blessings or the same fate. The seventh church letter below to Laodicea reveals a church component in need of repentance that disconnects from Christ, causing him to vomit it out of His mouth.

Laodicea—The Seventh Letter

And unto the angel of the church of the Laodiceans write; These things saith the Amen, the faithful and true witness, the beginning of the creation of God; I know thy works, that thou art neither cold nor hot: I would thou wert cold or hot. So then because *thou art lukewarm, and neither cold nor hot, I will spue thee out of my mouth.* Because thou sayest, I am rich, and increased with goods, and have need of nothing; and knowest not that thou art *wretched, and miserable, and poor, and blind, and naked*: I counsel thee to *buy of me gold tried in the fire,* that thou mayest be rich; and white raiment, that thou mayest be clothed, and *that* the shame of thy nakedness do not appear; and anoint thine eyes with eyesalve, that thou mayest see. *As many as I love, I rebuke and chasten*: be zealous therefore, and repent. Behold, *I stand at the door, and knock*: if any man hear my voice, and open the door, I will come in to him, and will sup with him, and he with me. To him that overcometh will I grant to sit with me in my throne, even as I also overcame, and am set down with my Father in his throne. He that hath an ear, let him hear what the Spirit saith unto the churches. (Revelation 3:14–22, emphasis added)

As we can decipher from these telling passages, this last-days church component is deceived into thinking it is something that it is not. Laodicea believes that it is a prosperous church having need of nothing; conversely, Christ considers it "*wretched, miserable, poor, blind, and naked.*" Furthermore, Christ encourages this church to abandon its prevailing problematic practices and purchase gold from Him that is refined through the fire. By the reference to gold refined through fire, Christ says that Laodicea is an impure and undisciplined church in severe need of repentance—a point further emphasized in the statement "*As many as I love, I rebuke and chasten.* Be zealous therefore, and repent."

This last-days group appears to dethrone Christ as Savior, minimize the value of the inerrant word of God, and enthrone itself instead. This makes the resurrected Jesus Christ ill, provoking Him to step outside of its confines in order to "spue" or "vomit" this element of the church out of His mouth, after which He makes His way back to knock upon its door for one last salvation altar call to humanity. Christ located outside of the church is a severe positional change, as noted in Revelation 1:12–20, which describes the Savior as clearly located in the midst of the Christian church at its point of inception.

This illness illustration infers that, unlike the church of Philadelphia, the preponderance of the church of Laodicea will not escape the Tribulation period. Thus, this represents a relatively large contingent within end-times Christianity that is not truly born again, which according to John 3:3–7 is a prerequisite condition of true belief and eternal salvation. This last-days church seemingly reshapes traditional Christendom into some new form of Christi-vanity that dethrones Christ, annuls the word of God, and essentially eradicates the Christian requirement of being born again. In so doing, it subjects itself to the daily dangerous ebbs and flows of emotional spiritualism.

By way of sound reminder, the prescription for eternal salvation is contained in the following passages and elsewhere in the Bible:

But what saith it? *The word is nigh thee, even in thy mouth, and in thy heart*: that is, the word of faith, which we preach; That if thou shalt confess with thy mouth the Lord Jesus, and shalt believe in thine heart that God hath raised him from the dead, thou shalt be saved. For with the heart man believeth unto righteousness; and with the mouth confession is made unto salvation. For the scripture saith, *Whosoever believeth on him shall not be ashamed.*

For there is no difference between the Jew and the Greek: for the same Lord over all is rich unto all that call upon him. For *whosoever shall call upon the name of the Lord shall be saved.* (Romans 10:8–13, emphasis added)

Homosexual bishops, lesbian Methodist ministers, name-it-and-claim-it prosperity teaching pastors, and mega "emergent church" congregations further evidence that we have entered into the final period of Laodicea. Many of today's prominent preachers refuse to deliver sermons purposed to take sinners to the foot of the cross where Jesus died for their sins. Furthermore, God's greatest twentieth-century miracle, the reinstatement of the Jewish State of Israel, hardly gets an honorable mention from church pulpits any more.

In these turbulent, terror-filled times, the world ponders legitimate evangelical and eschatological questions about the significance of the sacrificial death and subsequent resurrection of Christ and the biblical relevance of modern-day Israel. Unfortunately, the Laodicean church component provides warm and fuzzy, feel-good-about-yourself teachings that fail to adequately address either of these sincere secular concerns. Instead, the Laodicean component favors a social gospel and agenda in an attempt to win humanity over. This is becoming epidemic and reveals that Christianity today often feels the need to take pew-filling matters into its own carnal hands rather than modeling the Acts 2:46–47 church-building format.

Christianity is rapidly succumbing to the belief that it best grows through self-subscribed means whereby carnal methods of sustaining its congregational health and wealth are acceptable. It has indoctrinated the view that its survival is proportionate to its ability to successfully serve humanity's emotional rather than scriptural needs. This turnabout of church thinking segues well into Part 3 of this chapter, which is paganism, Christianity's recently revived competitor.

Part 3
Pagan Revival

Now the serpent was more subtil than any beast of the field which the LORD God had made. And he said unto the woman, Yea, hath God said, Ye shall not eat of every tree of the garden? And the woman said unto the serpent, We may eat of the fruit of the trees of the garden: But of the fruit of the tree which is in the midst of the garden, God hath said, Ye shall not eat of it, neither shall ye touch it, lest ye die. And *the serpent said* unto the woman, *Ye shall not surely die:* For God doth know that in the day ye eat thereof, then *your eyes shall be opened,* and *ye shall be as gods,* knowing good and evil. (Genesis 3:1–5, emphasis added)

When we discuss paganism, a safe starting location is in the Garden of Eden about six thousand years ago. In the above Genesis 3 account, we find that Satan encourages humanity to achieve its own godhead condition. He tells Eve that she can be like God. Furthermore, he accuses God of being a liar: God had told Eve that should she be disobedient, she would die, but Satan declared she "surely" would not "die." This episode lays the foundational groundwork for recognizing a fundamental difference between the monotheistic worship of God the claimant creator of the universe and the polytheistic worship of self as a god among a host of other gods.

Ultimately, God was right and Adam and Eve both died, and so has all of humanity since (barring the biblical exceptions of Enoch and Elijah, who were translated [raptured] from earth into heaven without experiencing death). Therefore, Satan turns out to be the liar, which Christ poignantly clarifies in John 8:42–44.

In keeping with his lying persona, Satan had to continue along the same deceitful path and create concepts like karma, reincarnation, and Christ consciousness in order to cover up his original lie in the Garden of Eden. Certainly humans die, but cleverly this most cunning serpent Satan had a logical explanation for the death phenomena. Eastern religions like Hinduism echo another ancient spiritual lie: that people reincarnate into another body, rather than their body ceasing to exist upon dying.

The cover-up lie probably sounded something like this: *"You will not surely die, you shall reincarnate and come back again in another life."* The truth according to Hebrews 9:27 is that man is appointed to die only once, not multiple times, as the theory of reincarnation espouses. Furthermore, the Hebrews passage declares that upon death, man subsequently experiences judgment. To counteract this truth, the devil injected the "karmic clause" into his reincarnation fantasy.

As the web of lies became more deceptively complex, one lie building upon another, the ensuing cover-up likely went something like this: *"You will not surely die and subsequently face God in final judgment; you will temporarily cross over and be evaluated by your good or bad previous life's deeds, at which point you will return to live and do better the next time."* This is how karmic law correlates with reincarnation according to Hinduism and several other offshoot New Age religions.

The goal of these polytheistic pagan religions like Buddhism, Hinduism, or their New Age counterparts is obtaining a utopian state of consciousness through a multitude of good works compiled through a series of reincarnated lives. Buddhism's nirvana, Hinduism's bliss, or the New Ager's Christ consciousness is the end game of these spiritual sojourners. The prevalent teaching inherent in these assorted religions is the age-old garden lie that *"you will be like God."*

According to most of these religions, Jesus Christ obtained this utopian state of consciousness, and therefore so can you. This theology that nirvana, bliss, or Christ consciousness, which has become the modernized term for the godhead condition, is available to anyone and everyone plays well into Satan's end game. We are told in Isaiah

14:13–14 that Satan himself seeks to someday exalt his throne above all the stars (angels in biblical typology) of God and be like the most high, alluding to God. Furthermore, we are informed in Daniel 11:36 that Satan's seed, the Antichrist, will ultimately attempt to magnify himself above every god.

It is obvious that Satan is the primary source of inspiration for paganism and that the old "you will be like God" garden lie is resurfacing again in a New Age format. A quick query on the Internet searching for "New Age religions" coupled with "Christ consciousness" yields pages of evidence that the predominant New Age belief is that humanity can strive to obtain the utopian mental state of godhead.

Humanity's quest for spiritual satisfaction is summed up by Jesus' statement, "I am the way, the truth, and the life; no man cometh unto the Father, but by me" (John 14:6).

The monotheistic religion of Christianity clearly teaches that there is a distinct difference between sinful humanity and its righteous Creator. According to the Bible, Adam and Eve and their offspring of humanity were created to worship God, not to become God. Jesus Christ declares that only through His personage, not His consciousness, can one even come to the heavenly Father, let alone worship Him. Thus there are foundational differences between Christianity and paganism.

Part and parcel of the revival of paganism are the concerns that numerous end-times Bible prophecies allude to a strong, deluding deception that overtakes humanity, causing it to believe in what Scripture calls "the lie."[326] According to 2 Thessalonians 2:9–11, powerful signs and lying wonders serve to convince mankind to believe in this deceptive lie. Since Satan is a liar, these lying wonders should have his fingerprints all over them. Some writers and researchers, including Tom Horn, I.D.E. Thomas, Patrick Heron, L.A. Marzulli, Terry James, David Flynn, and a host of others have connected the UFO phenomena to this coming great deception.

The coming Rapture and the harlot prophecy of Revelation 17 further complicate all of the above. The Rapture will be a powerful, world-changing event removing millions of born-again evangelical Christians from the earth. In the aftermath, the world will demand prompt and logical answers about what will have happened. This should open the door for the pagan perspective to be powerfully delivered. Many New Age channelers are already suggesting that the earth is about to be purged of the Christians by the gods and/or the aliens.

A common teaching about the harlot of Revelation 17 says the harlot represents a one-world religious system that emerges onto the international scene overlapping into the lifetime of the Antichrist. This system either ecumenically embraces and/or simply converts all religions into one universalistic format. With all true born-again Christians being previously raptured, this suggests that a pagan free-for-all will manifest about the time the world is deluded into believing "the lie" previously discussed.

Summary

This century appears to be the final one, and it will be filled with powerful, prophetic, world-changing events. The Rapture will likely occur, removing millions of Christians—and in the aftermath, a pagan revival could easily overtake humanity. Remaining world religions such as Islam, Hinduism, Buddhism, New Ageism, and "lukewarm" Christianity will be invited to ecumenically embrace a similar spiritual vision. About that time, the dreaded Antichrist will emerge upon the world scene.

Signs and lying wonders will accompany his beastly rise to power; ultimately, mankind will be overtaken by some great deceptive "lie." Meanwhile, powerful Middle East wars will be occurring prior to this or simultaneously, and humanity will be swept into the eye of the last-days storm.

Currently, the world appears to be going through a preparatory period for the above events. Christians should be watchful of the prophetic signs, and utilize them to witness to a world that is about to be overwhelmed by pagan deception. God issued prophecy for this important purpose. By accurately foretelling the future, God has equipped humanity with invaluable information. Twenty-first century Christians should be on the alert for the return of Christ in the Rapture, the rise of paganism on the horizon, and every opportunity to preach the Good News gospel to anyone who will listen in these days.

Time is of the essence and is running out. These are the last days, and the harvest field is increasingly bountiful. Christians can be certain that souls are searching for spiritual answers in these troubling times, and that Satan is lifting up pagan systems with deceitful theologies to satiate their growing appetites.

Mankind tends to prefer the possibility that its individuals can obtain godhead over the reality that it is a collection of sinners in need of a Savior. Thus, Christianity has to know thoroughly, and deliver powerfully, the Good News of Christ. These are the days of Laodicea, and the tendency to simmer the gospel message down to a lukewarm temperature must be resisted. The world is filled with itching ears seeking pleasing, socially spun, spiritual answers; however, Christians must rise to the occasion and take sinners back to the cross of crucifixion where they can repent and receive forgiveness through the shed blood of Christ.

Maranatha

Bill Salus

—

Bill Salus, host of Prophecy Update Radio Program, wrote the best-selling book ISRALESTINE: The Ancient Blueprints of the Future Middle East. *An expert at explaining prophetic relevance of current Mideast and world events, Salus has appeared on several television shows and regularly writes featured articles for WorldNetDaily, magazines, and various Internet websites. Visit his website at www.prophecydepot.com.*

chapter ten

Panspermia: What It Is and Why It Matters

by Dr. Michael Heiser

Description of Panspermia

The term "panspermia" comes from two Greek words: *pan*, which means "all" and *sperma*, which means "seed."[327] Panspermia is actually an umbrella term that describes any scientific theory that posits that all life as we know it on earth began in outer space.[328] The idea therefore assumes that life exists elsewhere in the universe, perhaps even abundantly, and that such life was a catalyst to life on earth. Positing that life began in outer space, though, says little.

Broadly defined panspermia can actually be thought of in two ways by scientists. An "extreme" view of panspermia, also known as cosmic ancestry, contends life has always existed everywhere in the universe. In this view, life was not transported to earth and has no single origin. As the earth was formed in the wake of the Big Bang, living microbes themselves formed after they took up residence on the new planet. The same process was repeated throughout the universe in countless places.

The second view is more common, that earth at one time did not have life, and so the ingredients for life came from elsewhere in space.

How living microbes from space came to the earth to spawn terrestrial life as we know it is debated by panspermia theorists. Options once again are categorized in two ways: undirected or non-intelligent panspermia, and directed or intelligent panspermia. Undirected panspermia presumes that the ingredients of life came to earth apart from any sort of intelligence, divine or extraterrestrial. The process was completely random. Directed or intelligent panspermia conjectures that a non-terrestrial intelligence, either divine or extraterrestrial, served as catalyst for the seeding of life.

Undirected and directed panspermia can be further nuanced by how proponents imagine the seeding of life indeed occurred. Undirected panspermia theorists often appeal to meteor and asteroid impact or radiation pressure for the interplanetary transfer of the basic elements of life to earth.[329] More recently, the so-called "red rain" phenomenon of Kerala, India, which began in 2001, has garnered much attention from panspermia scientists.[330]

Undirected panspermia has a long history in science, antedating the invention of space travel by over one hundred years. As one source notes:

> Panspermia began to assume a more scientific form through the proposals of Berzelius (1834), Richter (1865), Thomson (Lord Kelvin) (1871), and Helmholtz (1871), finally reaching the level of a detailed, widely-discussed hypothesis through the efforts of the Swedish chemist Svante Arrhenius. Originally in 1903, but then to a wider audience through a popular book in 1908, Arrhenius urged that life in the form of spores could survive in space and be spread from one planetary system to another by means of radiation pressure.[331]

Directed panspermia proponents are few in number, as this mechanistic option calls for intelligent intention of the seeding of life on earth.

Once again, this idea can be further refined into two variants. The first propounds that the intelligent agents behind the deliberate seeding of life on earth and other planets are intelligent extraterrestrials.[332] This theory was first seriously put forth in 1973 by Nobel Prize winner Dr. Francis Crick, along with Dr. Leslie Orgel of the Salk Institute. Crick and Orgel suggested that the seeds of life may have been purposely dispersed by an advanced extraterrestrial civilization, possibly on space craft. Crick, whose Nobel Prize was earned (with Dr. James D. Watson) for the discovery of the double helix structure of DNA, further posited that small "grains" containing DNA may have been fired randomly by extraterrestrials throughout space, perhaps by a civilization facing annihilation, or hoping to terraform planets for later colonization.[333] The second directed panspermia variant proposes that life was seeded from space under the providential direction of God. Several scientists intellectually aligned with the Intelligent Design theory of origins have written in defense of directed panspermia as part of God's grand design of the universe and for life within it. Much like theistic evolutionists see evolution as a tool in God's hand for creating life on earth, theistic scientists see in directed panspermia the intentional seeding of the ingredients for evolution on earth.[334]

These brief definitions call for some summary conclusions:

- Panspermia concerns the extraterrestrial origin of the fundamental building blocks of life or the primordial life forms that mark the commencement of the evolutionary process.
- Panspermia is therefore not about the process of evolution so much as it is about an explanation for how evolution became possible, on earth or anywhere else.
- One cannot embrace panspermia and reject evolution. The idea of mature advanced life forms being transported through space is an absurdity. Panspermia presumes the evolution of whatever was seeded on earth from space.
- Creation is not incompatible with panspermia if creation is conceived as a divine act that brought all matter into

existence. Such a creationist is then free to speculate how the ingredients for life were formed, and, with respect to panspermia, distributed throughout the universe and to earth so that life could evolve. Creationism that rejects evolution completely cannot accommodate panspermia and has no use for the theory.

Significance of the Idea

The notion of panspermia, mainly of the undirected variety, is firmly entrenched in the scientific community and the wider popular culture. This is easily demonstrated by tracking the dissemination of the idea through published material.

With respect to the technical literature produced by the scientific community, extensive databases such as Science Direct™, which indexes over twenty-five hundred peer-reviewed journals in all areas of the sciences, are quite useful.

The chart below illustrates how many articles that included various search terms (with Boolean operators) in the introduction to this essay were published in the last five years (2005–2009) in the technical literature.

SEARCH TERM(S)	ARTICLES
"panspermia"	60
"extraterrestrial" AND "life" AND "origin"	757
"exobiology" OR "astrobiology" AND "earth" AND "origin"	897

Moving to popular media, Lexis-Nexus is the premier research database of major U.S. and world publications and newswire services.

The chart on the following page illustrates how many articles that included various search terms (with Boolean operators) in the introduction to this essay were published in the last five years (2005–2009).

Search Term(s)	Articles appearing in U.S. and World Newspapers and Newswires	Articles appearing in U.S. and World Newspapers, Newswires plus Internet Publications, Television and Radio Transcripts
"panspermia"	87	113
"extraterrestrial" AND "life" AND "origin"	455	563
"exobiology" OR "astrobiology" AND "earth" AND "origin"	221	339

Taking the largest of these search results (563 articles) over the course of the last five years, the general public is exposed to the idea of life being seeded from space once every three days. This influence is actually multiplied with the advent of blogging.

Evaluation of the Panspermia Hypothesis

Framing the Issue

Although many scientists will say the odds that intelligent extraterrestrial life exists in the universe are reasonable, due mostly to the sheer number of places where life could evolve, the mainstream scientific community has not brought forth any evidence that intelligent extraterrestrial life actually exists.[335] Projects such as SETI (the Search for Extraterrestrial Intelligence) are seeking evidence through radio signal contact; such efforts have to this point been a failure. This means that serious discussion of panspermia focuses on models that posit the random distribution and presence of microbial life in the universe and its journey to earth.

The validity of panspermia as an explanation for the presence of life on earth depends on several questions:

(1) Is there evidence for microbial life in space?

(2) Is there evidence that microbial life from space made its way to earth?

(3) Is there any way to be sure that the primordial life on earth from which more advanced life forms are thought to have evolved could not have been on earth all along, never having been in space?

Is There Extraterrestrial Microbial Life?

To date there is no conclusive proof for the extraterrestrial microbial life that is critical to panspermia hypothesis. As such, the dominant paradigm in the modern scientific community is that life on earth evolved on earth. Despite the lack of firm proof for the hypothesis as a whole, there is evidence of at least some possible extraterrestrial contribution to terrestrial biology.

Pre-biotic chemicals of the type that most modern scientists presume to have been present at the beginning of evolution have been detected in interstellar clouds, comets, and meteorites. This gives panspermia theorists hope that some of the chemical raw ingredients for life may have come from space in addition to being manufactured on earth. The presence of these elements, though, falls short of actual microbial life forms.

A 2008 analysis of isotopic ratios of organic compounds found in the Murchison meteorite indicated non-terrestrial origin and not terrestrial contamination—but these are only isotopes, not life forms. The Red Rain of Kerala, initially thought to have been colored by fallout from a hypothetical meteor burst, has failed to provide evidence for extraterrestrial life. A study by the government of India found the coloration was likely caused by terrestrial alga. A subsequent study showed that the micro-organisms in the red rain had unusual properties (e.g., the ability to grow at 300 degrees C) and that, historically, red rain could be associated with meteorite falls. However, the same study also indicated other terrestrial possibilities, and so the evidence for extraterrestrial origin is uncertain.[336] In 2001 geologist Bruno D'Argenio and molecular biologist Giuseppe Geraci from the University of Naples claimed they had found live extraterrestrial bacteria inside a meteorite. The researchers claimed extraterrestrial origin for the bacteria since the sample was sterilized at high temperatures and washed with alcohol and yet survived. Other scientists argued that "Earth bacteria could have invaded the rock to depths that were not affected by the heat or alcohol."[337]

The most promising option for interstellar travel has been the discovery of meteorites on earth that have almost certainly come from the surface of Mars. These meteorites have been dubbed the "SNC" meteorites, named after the initials of the places where the first three were found: Shergotty, India in 1865, Chassigny, France in 1815, and Nahkla, Egypt in 1911.[338] There are more SNC meteorites than these three, however. The term encompasses meteorites that share the characteristics of their namesakes. The most compelling evidence for Martian origins for these meteorites comes from EETA 79001, an SNC meteorite found in Antarctica in 1980. When scientists examined tiny samples of gas trapped in EETA 79001, its composition was an exact match to the Martian atmosphere as analyzed by the Viking landers.[339]

The most famous Martian meteorite, ALH84001, which received global attention in 1996 when it was put forth as containing fossilized bacterial life, is still not accepted as credible evidence for extraterrestrial life.

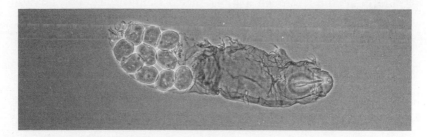

The presumed bacteria are considered by most scientists to have been possibly formed abiotically from organic molecules. This uncertainty in how these fossils were formed means ALH840001 is not proof of extraterrestrial life. Whether the organic molecules were created by non-biological extraterrestrial processes or are the result of contamination by Antarctic ice is still hotly debated.[340]

More recently, the survival of tiny tardigrades has renewed optimism in panspermia. As summarized on Space.com, "Tardigrades are speck-sized things, less than 1.5 millimeters long. They live on wet lichens and mosses, but when their environment dries out, they just wait for a return of water. They also resist heat, cold and radiation."[341]

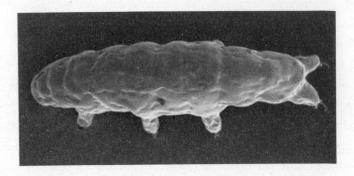

An analogy with sea monkeys (brine shrimp) is often drawn to illustrate the ability of tardigrades to survive without water. Tests conducted in space that involved exposing the tardigrades to ten days of exposure to solar radiation supports the idea that simple life forms could survive such radiation in space, since it demonstrates that animals such as tardigrades could travel through space on meteors and survive. This survival is key to the theory of panspermia.

Lastly, recent discoveries on Mars have served to keep panspermia alive as a theory. The Phoenix Mars Lander directly sampled ice in Martian soil in 2008.[342] NASA reports elsewhere that, "Recent high-resolution imagery from the *Mars Global Surveyor* Mars Orbiter Camera and the *Mars Odyssey* THEMIS reveals numerous examples of branched valleys that form tightly-packed, integrated drainage systems."[343] This evidence and similar points of analysis strongly suggest that water was at one time abundant on Mars and smaller unfrozen amounts may still be found on the planet's surface. Water, of course, is necessary for life as we know it. Even if there is currently water on Mars, the ultraviolet light currently bombarding is an impediment to living organisms being present therein. This circumstance does not rule out life on Mars in the distant past, however.

The Importance of Panspermia

It has already been noted that panspermia is not inherently incompatible with a theistic view of creation, given that view of creation not insist on a traditional, literal creation week of six solar days. But if panspermia would not alter the stand-off between those who believe in a Creator and those who do not, of what importance is it? The answer lies in understanding what many people would do with panspermia were it validated by scientific discovery.

Before describing how the public might respond to proof of panspermia, it is useful to be reminded of how difficult it would be to prove the theory. Even if life in space is found and is indisputable, that would not prove panspermia as a hypothesis. Recall the other elements involved:

(1) Is there evidence for microbial life in space?
(2) Is there evidence that microbial life from space made its way to earth?
(3) Is there any way to be sure that the primordial life on earth from which more advanced life forms are thought to have evolved could not have been on earth all along, never having been in space?

Discovering extraterrestrial life forms only affirms the first question. To be sure, an affirmative answer to the first question improves the odds of affirmative answers to the next two issues, but they are far from being considered likely. The second and third items *must* be demonstrated for the panspermia hypothesis to be proven, and this is no easy task.

But let's assume that someday panspermia transitions from a

hypothesis to an indisputable scientific reality. How would such valida-
tion influence thinking and worldview? What kinds of things would we
hear people say after scientists offer evidence to the public that extraterrestrial microbial life made the journey through space and had something to do with life here?

"Panspermia Renders a Belief in Creation Passé"

This is arguably the most weak-minded conclusion that could be drawn
in the wake of proof for panspermia. Frankly, this conclusion could
only be drawn by someone completely unacquainted with the academic
discussion on the interface of science and religion. Unfortunately, there
are many people who would fall into that category. Since many Christians, even those whose approach to theology is quite conservative, take
non-literalist or non-traditional views of Genesis, it would be false to
assume that Christianity and belief in divine creation rises or falls with
respect to panspermia.[344]

But what would be the fate of a more literal reading of Genesis if
panspermia is proven?

It may surprise readers that it is not difficult to take most of
Genesis at face value and come out with a theistic evolutionary view.
Most traditional literalist approaches to Genesis proceed along certain
assumptions:

> Genesis 1:1–3 is linked to the first day of Genesis, so that
> Genesis 1:1–5 must be seen as day one.
> Since the Hebrew word for "day" (*yom*) with a numerical
> adjective refers to a solar day, the days of Genesis must be
> a series of twenty-four-hour solar days *and* the entirety of
> creation as it occurred in real time must be accounted for
> in that series of six days.
> A consistently literal interpretation of Genesis 1–2 rules out
> any view of creation other than the traditional six-solar-
> day view.

> There is no language in Genesis that could possibly account
> for the production of life in any way other than special
> creation.

All of these assumptions are flawed. That does not mean, however, that the traditional view of six-solar-day creation is wrong. It simply means it is not the only view that can be held by taking the text at face value.

The first assumption is easily challenged (but not undone) by Hebrew syntax. In fact, the Hebrew syntax (sentence structure) of the first three verses is the real key to understanding what the biblical account can sustain in terms of creation viewpoints. I have written on this topic for the non-specialist elsewhere, so it is sufficient here to merely point out that the syntax of the first three verses demonstrates decisively that Genesis 1:1–3 can indeed be separated from 1:4–5 (and so the Genesis 1:1–5 unit is not at all certain).[345] Syntax also allows an indefinite period of time to *precede* Genesis 1:1, meaning that Genesis 1:1–3 describes a return by God to material he had created earlier. Genesis 1 may therefore describe a fashioning of already existent material. This would allow millions of years to pass before we even get to Genesis 1:1. This is not an allegorical interpretation; it is an interpretation that would be borne out of a face-value exegesis of the text according to the rules of Hebrew syntax.

The issue of the days is complicated, especially since it requires solar days before the sun is created (Day 4). Others have written much on this problem, so there is no need to rehearse the issue here.[346] Rather, I want to address the second proposition along with the third. Since the third proposition above is problematic, readers may do well to re-examine which parts of Genesis to take literally (including "day") and which to take less than (or more than) literally. What do I mean? Simply that the traditional literalist view of creation assumes its approach is consistent, but it is not. A truly consistently literal reading of Genesis 1–2 would result in a flat round earth, over which a solid dome rests, upon which the stars are fixed.[347] In other words, a completely literal view of Genesis 1–2 would result in the same sort of cosmology as the rest of the ancient Near East, particularly Mesopotamia and Egypt. The reality is that *everyone* who claims to be a literalist makes exceptions. The only question is why one person's exceptions are more "faithful" to the text than someone else's. Two people may be "90 percent literal" in their interpretation, but the one person who does not attribute a literal meaning to "day" (*yom*) is roundly criticized by the one who does. And yet who is more faithfully literal? Neither, especially when compared to the person who takes it all literally, as described above. By what litmus test is your 90 percent literal spiritually or hermeneutically superior to the other person's? The traditional view does not own literalism, and should stop pretending it does.

Lastly, the fourth proposition fails to take verses like Genesis 1:24 *literally*: "And God said, Let the earth bring forth the living creature after its kind, cattle, and creeping thing, and beast of the earth after its kind: and it was so."

A literal, face-value reading of this verse has the earth (not animals) producing living creatures. The text does not say God created these creatures out of nothing, or by the spoken word alone. It says the earth brought forth these life forms. It would be easy for a theistic evolutionist or a Christian scientist who has factored a proven panspermia theory into his worldview to say that this language in Scripture, taken literally, suggests that God had designed the earth itself to somehow contain the "ingredients" for life. There is nothing non-literal about this reading; it simply filters a literal reading through the filter of a particular scientific conclusion. This is the sort of hermeneutical tactic that one could employ in the wake of panspermia as fact without surrendering a face value reading of Genesis.

The point here is not to pontificate on how Genesis 1–2 should be interpreted. Rather, it is to say that those who favor literal interpretation of Genesis need to be honest about the fact that many interpreters often criticized by literalists really interpret the Bible with the same method: taking some things literal and others not. Instead of insisting that their use of literalism is the only way to do literal interpretation, traditional six-solar-day creationists ought to take comfort in the fact that one can still do literal interpretation while taking some things non-literally. This will be quite helpful to traditionalists should panspermia become a factual reality. Christians who insist on only one version of literalism risk trapping themselves in a fallacious either-or decision in the wake of proof for panspermia. If there only acceptable literalism of the type articulated by so many apologists and creationist organizations, that view will have no way to accommodate a genuine panspermia reality. In the either-or trap, some Christians may think the choice would come down to either rejecting the reality of panspermia science or rejecting the Bible as something untrustworthy since it cannot conform to their particular pre-conception of what "literal interpretation" entails. This is a needless tension.

"Random, Darwinistic Evolution is Supported or Proven by Panspermia"

The key word here is "random," as it betrays a position that has no place for a divine Creator. Simply put, if panspermia were declared fact tomorrow, thousands of Christian scientists would simply add it their theistic evolutionary model as a divine mechanism.[348] It would do absolutely nothing to eradicate a Creator. But I speak here of people who have genuinely thought through the issue of how evolution and biblical theology might intersect. On a popular level, the picture is quite different.

Consider the analogy of evolution without panspermia. Although Darwin's theory of evolution is no actual threat to a multitude of Christians, millions of people from all walks of life and educational levels believe erroneously that evolution proves there is no God. By analogy, even though panspermia would do little to convince a theistic scientist to dismiss his or her belief in God, millions will be led to conclude that panspermia adds to the evidence that there is no God since it will be perceived as lending credence to random evolutionary forces. This application of a certified panspermia theory, however illogical, would nonetheless be as common as the specious extrapolations made in regard to evolution.

"Panspermia Removes and Usurps the Arguments of Intelligent Design Theorists"

This outcome appears more serious, though upon close inspection, it need not be considered problematic. Many intelligent design theorists and traditional creation apologists frequently use the "anthropic principle" to defend creationism. Briefly stated, the anthropic principle suggests that that the fundamental constants of physics, astronomy, biology, and chemistry are *fine-tuned* to allow life as we know it to exist, and perhaps only to exist on earth.

If panspermia were proven, this principle is, to some extent, undermined, since circumstances for life formerly considered utterly unique would in fact not be unique at all, and they may in fact be common. This could have the effect of making the universe and life appear "less designed," but it would be any easy turn to just say that panspermia indicates *more* design to the universe. If the former is the focus, someone might assume that there is less need of intelligence for understanding how everything came to be. If the latter, one must admit that humanity may not be unique, and earth's simpler life forms are certainly not unique.

Another way the anthropic principle might be undermined is for someone to point out that nothing in the presumed design of the universe and earth *requires* intelligent human life to be a result. The universe and earth would still be ideally suited to sustain carbon-based life as we know it even if there were no humans. Further, if human life were never found elsewhere in the universe, then we would know that humanity was not the designed destiny of all the so-called "anthropic" parameters. The reader should know that this cuts both ways: just because life can sprout somewhere else in space does not require the conclusion that intelligent life will be part of what results *anywhere*. To dismiss the anthropic principle on such a basis, one would have to prove that panspermia and its ensuing evolutionary processes unfailingly lead to intelligent life.

The suitability of other locations in the universe for life that would be part of a validated panspermia hypothesis might then be used to argue that "design for life" does not require one to believe there is a personal creator-designer that planned panspermia and evolution for the sake of humankind. This objection over-reaches the data and logically implodes. It relies on analyzing and confounding the intent of a Creator to prove there is no Creator!

"If Panspermia is Real, then Intelligent Extraterrestrial Life Must Exist Elsewhere, and so the Image of God Teaching in the Bible is False"

The first part of this objection is related to the alleged undermining of the anthropic principle noted above. I will not repeat the refutation here.

It is of course an extrapolation that proof of panspermia at a microbial level invariably means that intelligent extraterrestrial life would be extant, but people will be more than willing to make such a leap. Indeed, they have been conditioned to do so by science fiction writing and major media. The extrapolation would simply be based on analogy with how panspermia presumably worked on earth. Given this leap in logic, humankind would not be unique. Would that mean the biblical teaching that humankind was created in God's image is false?

The answer to this question would be "yes"—given the traditional, ubiquitous definition for the image of God in most of Christian theology. The problem is that definition is terribly flawed, and so it is a straw man to this panspermia objection. Many Christians, however, would not realize this, and so the discovery of intelligent extraterrestrial life would be problematic to them. The solution is not to jettison the Bible; it is to have an accurate understanding of what the image of God means. Once that is the case, this objection is completely hollow. I have written on this topic elsewhere, and so I will only sketch the outlines of what the image really means here.[349]

To begin, it will be necessary to alert readers to why the traditional definitions of the image of God ought to be discarded. The image of God doctrine comes from Genesis 1:26–27, where we are told that God created humankind "in his image." Readers who have been studying the Bible for any length of time have likely heard or read definitions of what exactly the image means. The definition that is typically offered is something along the lines of the image of God being intelligence, rationality, emotions, the ability to commune with God, self-awareness, language capability, the presence of a soul, a conscience, or free will.

These are poor definitions that inadvertently disallow Christians to be consistently pro-life in their ethics, much less provide a defense against the panspermia argument we are presently engaging. The reason is simple. None of those definition candidates apply to simple-celled human life or of life in the womb in the early stages of development. The conceived contents of a woman's womb, when composed of little more than cells or tissue prior to brain development, has *none* of these capabilities. One might object that some or all of these are potentially present in life from the moment of fertilization. All this objection accomplishes is the flawed idea that the contents of the womb are therefore *potentially* in God's image, but not actually so until one or more of these abilities are resident. Why defend the unborn, for example, in the first trimester, until they are *actual* imagers? Since the image of God is the basis for the Christian idea of human personhood and this the sanctity of life, if the life in a woman's womb remains only potential and not actual in terms of the image, then the argument for the personhood of what is in the womb evaporates. The deficiency of these proposals undercuts a sanctity of life ethical foundation.

Genesis teaches us several things about the image of God, and *all* of what we learn from the text must be accounted for in any discussion of what "the image" means. First, both men and women are equally included in what I'll call for now "divine image bearing." Second, divine image bearing is what makes humankind distinct from the rest of the

Genesis creation (i.e., plants and animals and, for our purposes, intelligent extraterrestrials). Third, there is something about the image that makes mankind "like" God in some way. Fourth, there is nothing in the text to suggest that the image has been or can be bestowed incrementally or partially. This alone undermines any definition of the image that is not immediately possessed by all humans from the moment of their conception. You're either created as God's image bearer or you aren't. One cannot speak of being "partly" created in God's image or "potentially" bearing the image.

There are still other problems with the traditional view. Among the list of proposed answers to what the image is are a number of *abilities* or *properties*: intelligence, rationality, emotions, communing with God, self-awareness, language capability, and free will. It is a fact of biology and psychology (specifically the field of animal cognition) that animals possess *some* of these abilities, albeit not as fully. This means that these abilities are not unique to humans.[350] It matters not that humans possess them more fully, since animals have been shown to score higher on intelligence tests than very young humans, such as toddlers. Moreover, humans who suffer from various forms of retardation would score less than certain animals on intelligence tests.[351] Animals can learn to do things contrary to their nature, they can show emotion, and they have language (we have no reason to assume language must be *across* species to be real, as opposed to *within* species).[352]

Even the statement that human God was breathed into by God and thus became a "living soul" (Hebrew, *nephesh*; Genesis 2:7) fails these tests. The former doesn't work because animals also possess the *nephesh*, the Hebrew word translated "soul" in Genesis 2:7 ("and the man became a living *soul*"). For example, in Genesis 1:20 when we read that God made swarms of "living creatures," the Hebrew text underlying "creatures" is *nephesh*. The term means "conscious life" or "animate life" as opposed to something like plant life, and there are other clear examples where animals are described with the same word.[353] The objection that humankind also has a spirit, not just a *nephesh* fails, since the terms are used interchangeably in the Bible to describe the same properties, behaviors, and emotions.[354] There are also the general difficulties with the trichotomous (three parts: body, soul, spirit) view of man.[355] My point here is not that humans don't have a soul. They certainly do, and it is linked to personhood in biblical theology. My point is only that the soul isn't the image.

The correct view of what the image means is based on a point of Hebrew grammar, specifically a special function of the preposition "in" with respect to the phrase "*in* the image of God." In our own English language—and we don't often think about our own language in such detail—we use the preposition "in" to denote many different ideas. That is, "in" doesn't always mean the same thing when we use that word. For example, if I say, "put the dishes *in* the sink," I am using the preposition to denote *location*. If I say, "I broke the mirror *in* pieces," I am using "in" to denote the *result* of some action or accident. If I say, "I work *in* education," I am using the preposition to denote that I was *as* a teacher or principal, or some other administrative capacity.

This last example is the key to understanding what the Hebrew preposition usually translated "in" means in Genesis 1:26—and that will in turn unlock the meaning of image bearing. The idea I want to put forth is that humankind was created *as* God's image. In other words, the preposition tells us that humans work *as* God's imagers—that they work *in the capacity of* God's representatives. The image is therefore not a thing put in us; it is something we *are*. It is not a thing; it is a divinely-ordained or status. Don't think of it as a noun; think of it as a *verb*. Being created as God's imagers means we are God's representatives on earth. Humans were created to rule and care for the earth as God would if he were physically present. It is as though *we are Him* when it comes to overseeing His earth. If you are human, then, you are an imager of God, regardless of your abilities. Nothing else—including intelligent extraterrestrials—has been given this status on earth. Humankind is the unique imager of God on earth, and so it matters not if there are other intelligent beings in the universe.

"If We Discover That Panspermia is Real, and That There Are Intelligent Extraterrestrials, Then It Is Possible That God Used Highly-Evolved Extraterrestrials (Who May Be What Religions Call Angels) To Put Us Here"

This is, in my view, the most significant response to the hypothetical scenario put forth in this essay, where panspermia is eventually proven true. The chain of thought would proceed as follows. Once panspermia moves from hypothesis to scientific fact (or is perceived to have made that transition), the idea that the universe is teeming with life will move from a statistical probability to scientific truth. If life is floating around in the vast reaches of space, and we know that some of it was the catalyst for our own evolution, the existence of intelligent life forms elsewhere in space will seem almost self-evident. And from this idea it is but a short intellectual distance to the notion that these other evolved intelligent life forms could have reached our level of intelligence long before we did. Perhaps, the extrapolation may go, these highly evolved beings had something to do with our own evolution or even our existence.

At this point there would be a divergence. Some would stop the extrapolation and have a Creator God using extraterrestrials (angels) as creative agents. This would be the easiest way for people of faith to align intelligent panspermia to their faith, especially if they are members of the "book religions" (Christianity, Judaism, and Islam). Others will want to press for a naturalistic God, himself the product of evolution, but still the subsequent spreader of life elsewhere in the universe.

While many scientists and thinkers would see through the leaps in logic driving this string of ideas and conclusions, multitudes on the "popular" level will not. It is also fair to say that some scientists, certainly not immune to illogic, would want to draw the same conclusion. This is not slippery-slope paranoia. Proof of the plausibility of this concern is abundant in popular media, particular television and feature films. The most recent example, complete with compelling special effects, is the movie, *Knowing* (2009), starring Nicolas Cage.[356] This thinking and its presumed implications have been fodder for the entertainment industry for decades.[357]

The first perspective produces a viewpoint of origins to which our culture is well-suited. In the post-Christian world in which we are now living, assuming the extrapolation of panspermia described here, this view will be cast as a reasoned, scientifically-possible understanding not only of who we are and how we got here, but also why religion must have a place at the intellectual table. It will redefine God and faith while allowing people to retain God and faith in both literal and more imaginative terms. It paves the way for a true merging of science and religion. It will be the paradigm that allows the atheist to tolerate religion, and allows literalist Bible-readers, the eastern Buddhist, and the pagan to simultaneously parse the new science the same way. This might in turn be useful fodder for a global religion.

How is this possible?

The atheist and agnostic will have to admit that vastly superior beings to humanity very likely exist and that it is certainly possible they visited earth in the past. The stories in the Bible and other ancient documents that speak of God or gods fashioning humanity from the dust of the ground and other human material may be primitive ways of describing what is known as fact after panspermia becomes a reality. While not believing in the God of the Bible, who is certainly set apart from creation, atheist scientists could see how traditional religions somehow had the knowledge of intelligent panspermia first, though ancient people lacked the vocabulary to express it the way science does. They may seek to prod the religious toward seeing the God behind the extraterrestrials as an extraterrestrial himself, but even without that point everyone is talking the same language: there is now an intelligence behind how life got here. Indeed, this is precisely the angle the famous atheist scientist Richard Dawkins was blithely suggesting in the movie "Expelled!"[358]

Buddhists and pagans already have no trouble with evolution or the idea of an ultimate intelligence in the universe. Panspermia augments these ideas. Both of these belief systems, though having definite distinctions, nevertheless have already married the natural and the spiritual, so that there is no need to distinguish one from the other. Naturalistic deities that are the product of evolution, and presumably having command over natural forces, would be welcome.

Those who take the Bible seriously and literally would also be able to accommodate intelligent panspermia. Since there is more than one approach to literalism, this requires a bit of explanation. For example, Christians and Jews who embrace theistic evolution could see intelligent extraterrestrials as agents of God in the grand divine design for life on earth. Perhaps angels, since they are created beings and therefore made of *something*, are in fact extraterrestrials. If angels cannot be described this way, then they are merely their own category—and that does nothing to undermine God's use of extraterrestrials in the creation of life if He deemed that desirable.

More traditional creationists might be influenced to look for extraterrestrials in face-value statements of the Bible such as the plurals of Genesis 1:26 ("let *us* make man in *our* image"). True, the verbs of creation in the Bible are always singular, but that may be the writer's way of giving God all the credit. God could still have used other agents to do his bidding.[359] Perhaps, someone will propose, the use of extraterrestrials by God is the answer to the question of why the Hebrew plural noun *elohim* is singularized in the Hebrew Bible and frequently made to stand for the God of Israel. Maybe the singular means the plural, as in the Qur'an's habit of using "we" to refer to Allah. For Muslims this is a very easy transition to make. Ideas such as this will make it easier for literalist Jewish and Christian Bible-believers to embrace intelligent panspermia and keep their faith in the same stroke.

Conclusion

Readers need to recall that I am parsing an extrapolation of panspermia that lacks logical coherence and scientific basis, even if undirected panspermia is indeed valid. I expect that in the near future, science will propound some version of undirected panspermia and the kind of intellectual ripple effect I've outlined here. How far will the ripples extend? Since so many people now are willing to entertain the idea of ancient astronauts, it seems quite reasonable to suggest many more will join that bandwagon in the wake of a panspermia declaration.

In such a hypothetical extrapolation, it is worth asking, with the fundamentalist-literalist believer of book religions in the panspermia fold, whether there is any discernible obstacle to articulating a global religion that honors the cosmologies of all faiths, united as they are under the reality of panspermia and extraterrestrial influence. This intellectual scenario, of course, is presently the stuff of imagination.[360] But even now it should be easy for the reader to see how encompassing, persuasive, and powerful this set of ideas would be. Panspermia is without question a critical issue facing the Church of today—and tomorrow.

—

Mike Heiser earned a Ph.D. in Hebrew Bible and Semitic Languages at the University of Wisconsin-Madison. He is currently the academic editor at Logos Bible Software. He is best known to popular audiences for his numerous appearances on "Coast to Coast AM" and his novel, The Façade.

chapter eleven

The "Sneak" Business

by Dr. Gianni DeVincenti Hayes

Can you feel the piercing eyes on you when you wake, shower, make love to your spouse, drive your car, kiss your kids, meet with friends, go to your job, give a presentation, teach a class, have lunch at work or chat with friends? Do you hear the silent breathing while talking on your cell phone, using your blackberry, on your home landlines? If you don't, *beware!* "They" are watching, listening, monitoring and recording our every move, our dialogue, our interactions.

Many people know and feel that something isn't right in the world today, that people have strangely disappeared or been found dead or "suicided." Whistleblowers and writers are faced with harassment, threats, injury, and even death if they attempt to expose the plan. With today's super surveillance techniques, none of us can hide anywhere, and free speech no longer exists.

We are tracked and under surveillance in everything we do. "They" have taken away our dignity, our love for others, our love for ourselves, and our love for God, and made us objects in a camera lens that are to act and react in a designated manner. "They" have destroyed our self-security, our culture, and our values, and now have us where they want us to complete their sadistic plan. And we let "them" do it to us with vigor. Look at how technology captures us live:

> In the world detailed by George Orwell in the novel *1984,* surveillance cameras follow every move a person makes, and the slightest misstep, or apparent misstep, summons the authorities. Now, similarly, police departments, government agencies, banks, merchants, amusement parks, sports arenas, nanny-watching homeowners, swimming-pool operators, and employers are deploying cameras, pattern recognition algo- rithms, databases of information, and biometric tools that when taken as a whole can be combined into automated sur- veillance networks able to track just about anyone, just about anywhere…. "The technology is developing at the speed of light, but the privacy laws to protect us are back in the Stone Age," says Barry Steinhardt, associate director of the American Civil Liberties Union, which is among several groups that have tried, so far almost universally unsuccessfully, to introduce leg- islation aimed at protecting privacy."[361]

"They" have us right where they want us: Watched and controlled, and unequivocally reliant on "them." And who are "they"? And what is "The Plan"?

The Controllers

"They" are the Power Elite—the hand full of high-level world rulers who oversee the secret societies, advance the Illuminati, and infiltrate our minds, our businesses, and our lives. "They" are the ones who dic- tate what the economy will be, how we will worship, how low our mor- als will continue to drop, how elections will be run, and who the victors of those elections will be. "They" invade our Internet activities and use high technology against us. "They" teach our children that Christianity

is bad, homosexuality is good, and abortion is great (for their population control), and they posit untruths and rewritten histories in our
children's curricula. "They" hurdle us to a New World Order (NWO)
or one-world government—The Plan—and they have us just about
fully there. They are the "elites" of the world, members of Illuminati
and other secret societies. Some are central bankers, others are in high-
powered positions; all have the same goal: A one-world government.

Most of all, "they" are the very ones who snoop on us anytime
they desire. We are like fish in a bowl, bacteria under a microscope. Big
Brother *is* watching. There are more surveillance techniques today than
ever, and they're all being used on us innocent citizens to make sure we
obey and not give them a rough time. We are witnessing—and, unfortunately, accepting—government and elitists' intrusions in to almost every
facet of our lives, from tracking our landlines and wireless connections,
our locations through GPS and chips, through the internet, CCTV, via
tests, genetics, through our Social Security numbers, advanced biometrics, RFID, and even by monitoring our bank accounts.

We are being watched all the time. Yet this is exactly what the authors
of the Constitution wanted to avoid. If the globalists feel they don't know
what we're doing at all times, they don't trust us, and they get nervous,
feel their authority threatened, and, hence, go after us. Their only and
biggest fear is that one day we *all* will catch on and do something—perhaps rebel. Already there is much prattle on the internet about American troops being stationed in cities across the nation in preparation for
martial law and the capture of innocent citizens who would be thrown
into one of the three hundred detention camps on our land, supposedly
equipped with gas chambers and other extermination means.[362]

All one has to do is listen to alternative radio shows and microbroad-
casts, watch unbiased television news, read respected publications that
feature both sides of a story, and get online to type in a few key words
provided in this chapter to gather volumes of information. It leaves you
wondering how so many people know more than you, and yet no one
is able to stop the momentum of the NWO. Research and documentation should affirm who says what, and who's doing what. Just be wary

of everything that is written or said. You cannot trust the mainstream media because they are owned by the Elite. You also have to be careful of what's on the Net, as many regular ol' people, along with the NWO promoters, outright fabricate information. Disinformation is part of their agenda. People also use the Internet in self-serving ways.

How does the United States fare in this?

London-based [American Civil Liberties Union] ACLU partner Privacy International (PI) has issued its most recent ranking of the world's leading surveillance societies…examining national policies in fourteen categories such as constitutional protection, privacy enforcement, and workplace monitoring…. The United States ranked with Russia, China and the U.K. at the bottom among the worst surveillance societies. With the advent of powerful cameras, sensors, satellites, and other technologies, we have begun to see the reality of a surveillance society George Orwell fictionalized in his novel *1984*.[363]

The Catalyst

Since the September 11, 2001 tragedy, surveillance has gained steam and teeth. This heart-wrenching calamity warned us that our once seemingly ideal and eternally safe America no longer is shielded from the lunacy of the world. Since then, all types of security measures and tracking agents have been installed: Defense Advanced Research Projects Agency (DARPA), Homeland Security, alert levels, identification systems, and the abandonment of our beloved Constitution—a document that set us apart from all the other nations' citizen restrictions and platforms of socialism. Enforcement of the loss of our rights will likely result in detainment camps for those who protest the NWO.

Add to this the tattlers who are part of the major ongoing shadowing system who have children turning in parents, neighbors turning in neighbors, school personnel having parents arrested, and co-workers gossiping about fellow employees; yet, it has been shown that many of their accusations were unfounded and even contrived in some cases. *E-magazine* clarifies: "Martin Anderson reports that only those whistleblowers who win celebrity status…enjoy real protection from reprisal."[364] A *Daily Times* article offers a report released by the American Civil Liberties Union warning that the United States is evolving into a Big Brother system fueled by technology advances and legal standards loosened after the 9/11/01 terrorist attacks.[365]

Superiority

The invasion of our privacy has reached high-tech supremacy, allowing the globalists to keep tabs on us to throw off any threat we might be to them, or to punish us when we fail to follow their mandates or violate their rules and dissent. They can put an instant stop on any of our actions. Their methods include palm recognition, bar codes, license images, retinal scanners, face monitors, biochips for remote control, high-powered cameras and binoculars, human and vehicular global positioning systems (GPS), night vision devices, miniature eavesdropping devices, cell phones, the Internet, land phones, DNA samples of everyone, cameras at stoplights, and, of course, Social Security numbers and drivers' licenses. The BBC News announced that "retinal scanners will be used at the new…Venerable Bede Church of England Aided School… [and] will be used on pupils buying meals…[and] in the library."[366]

The Elite powers behind this plan are serious, evil, purposeful, intimidating, and dangerous, and they will stop at nothing to get what they want. They have made us feel as though we are terrorists in our own land.

Through the melee of bombed buildings and other frightening actions imposed by radical sects or the Elite, we are willingly ceding our rights in the name of "protections" when in reality they are the very ones against whom we need protection. So over a period of decades, the planners behind this strategy have mounted a scheme that is far reaching, extremely well designed, and heavily implemented—and it's now being accelerated the way they had hoped.

Also, many invisible elements work silently, continuously, method-ically, calculatingly, and unboundedly behind our backs. Like snakes crawling up water pipes in the dark recesses of a home, so it goes with the serpentine Elite, particularly within the parameters of religion and family values, where they are forcing us to bow to them. Surveillance, tracking, control, and consequences are their major approaches, work-ing in concert. They use their tools of power, networking, and pull-ing out wads of money for their party, their personal interests, and for extortion and blackmailing witnesses.

The exciting part of this plan is that it parallels biblical prophecy, and when we see the charismatic world leader emerge as the king of ten kings (a panel of ten world leaders) we will know the great dictator has arisen; the end has come.

Computerized Machinations

The Power Elite—Illuminati—crush us with a variety of methods to get us to accept the NWO,[367] but employing spying mechanics is one of their major tools.

High-tech and still-developing mechanisms for watching us rapidly hit the market in such forms as a national identity card, biometrics, cen-tral databases, data-sharing of information for secondary purposes, camera scrutiny in the public and private sectors, unlawful police shadowing and action, unauthorized investigations, performing unlawful telecommunica-tions "intercept capabilities," satellite spying, hovering helicopters/planes seeing right into a person's home, chipping, neurological synthesis tech-nology, and scanning detection machines. As Dave Eberhart confirms:

The federal government has already deployed new detection machines that can scan citizens without their knowledge from as far as fifty feet away and "read" their personal documents such as passports or driver's licenses...reads one's personal information right through a wallet or purse...without consent or a warrant and may set a worrisome precedent. The device [is] called Radio Frequency Identification machines.[368]

And the FBI in *Revelation Files*:

[There is] ongoing development of the Next Generation Identification System...evolution of our current Integrated Automated Fingerprint Identification System...includes not only enhanced fingerprints capabilities but also other forms of biometric identification like palm prints, scans, facial imaging, scars, marks, tattoos—in one searchable system...will increase the capacity of our fingerprint storage...[369]

The Elite are even on the threshold of creating massive nanotechnical, titanium-tipped robots such as "flying insects" that can be released in swarms to attack enemies—i.e., soldiers in a field or unhappy Americans protesting. An article on RaidersNewsUpdate states:

Consider these scenarios from *Popular Mechanics*: Alan H. Epstein, of Massachusetts Institute of Technology (MIT), recently described...GPS-guided MVAs [Mioro air vehicles] landing on structurally critical points along bridges deep in enemy territory. Each MVA would carry a small piece of shaped-charge plastique. Responding to a command transmitted from half a world away, the MVAs would explode in sequence, bringing down the bridge with only one hundredth of the amount of explosives required by a pinpoint-accurate bomb.... Some military strategists envision swarms of robot flies fluttering onto battlefields. Scout flies, equipped with miniature cameras, would do the work of reconnaissance teams by eavesdropping or tactical communications and sending back real-time videos of enemy positions...the MVAs of Revelation 9 torment those who receive the Mark of the Beast.[370]

But who's to say these methods won't be used on Americans for whatever reason the Power Elite deems necessary? Blurbs of various surveillance efforts are found on websites including www.youarebeing watched.us, where visitors see the following:

- Police officers zoomed the lenses of surveillance cameras in on nude models, took pictures of them, showed the photographs to pub mates, and tried to sell the snapshots.
- Demonstrators in Washington protesting everything from U.S. Middle East policy to globalization were seen and photographed not just by the media cameras they hoped to attract, but by the District of Columbia police, who watched every move they made.
- Officials using surveillance cameras identified twenty-six thousand, five hundred Maryland motorists using I-95, and then sent those people letters asking where they were going that day, why, and with whom.
- Thirty-four Tennessee middle school students sued various officials of the Overton County, Tennessee, public school system, alleging that the defendant school authorities had violated the students' constitutional right to privacy by installing and operating video surveillance equipment in the boys' and girls' locker rooms in Livingston Middle School, and by viewing and retaining the recorded images.
- A suicide in a Bronx housing project was filmed by surveillance cameras in the building's lobby; the footage was then leaked and circulated on the Internet.

Nigeria is already establishing twenty-four-hour surveillance of its citizens through the use of "ten thousand cameras that would feed the centre with data via wireless communications network"[371] over its eighteen million citizens, and…this is only one step in the whole platform."[372] If a third-world country can do this, one can only imagine what the superpowers are capable of. The United States is one of the most advanced nations in spying, as seen in surveillance companies like Law Enforcement Associates Corporation—the largest U.S. developer and manufacturer of electronic surveillance equipment. The company announced on January 13, 2009, that "its Surveillance Vehicle Division has received an order from a division of the federal government for two specialized surveillance vehicles, costing over one hundred thousand dollars."[373]

Our country has the hugely flawed E-Verify system, an Internet-based system operated by the Department of Homeland Security and the Social Security Administration that helps employers determine the employment eligibility of new hires. Tom DeWeese of American Policy Center (APC) states that this system will have "devastating effects on both naturalized U.S. citizens, as well as those who were native-born." He points out that this massive database will "not safeguard the United States from terrorists, will not preserve what's left of our Rule of Law, and will further decimate our liberty."[374]

New Reich

Society's acceptance of surveillance and of being tracked, even through strokes on keyboards, and its willingness to accept ID chips, smartcards and other marks along with Big Brotherism is the hallmark of a marxist, socialist, totalitarianism nation. Adolf Hitler said, "This New Reich will give its youth to no one but will take youth and give to youth its own education and upbringing."[375] Isn't a similar program being initiated by President Obama?

> Our children become no more than slave labor for the "group" who run us. Their tentacles stretch far, and their senses even farther...consider that these people can track us through our phones, faxes, cell phones, e-mails, Internet choices; that they

have such highly developed surveillance equipment that they can be flying overhead in a plane and look right into our homes; that they can hear conversations miles away from specialized "bugs," that they demand proof of our identity through palm or eye recognition, through smartcards, through palm-touch, through biometric identifiers; DNA samples; through ID-chips under our skin. "A Boca Raton newspaper headlines the interest in biochips: 'Family May Get Medical Info Chips Implanted.'"[376]

Big Brotherism is accomplished through both major and minor means, such as e-mail, online shopping, travel booking, automated teller machines, electronic toll-collection systems, credit-card payment terminals, and airline terminals. Say Markoff and Schwartz: "In essence, the Pentagon's main job would be to spin strands of software technology that would weave these sources of data into a vast electronic dragnet."[377] They go on to explain that all of this is falling under the program of TIA (Total Information Awareness, name changed to Terrorism Information Awareness) as headed then (circa 2003) by John Poindexter (an Iran-Contra felon), that falls under DARPA (see section below titled "Snoop Agencies"). This began in the 1960s when the government created the Internet:

> The first generation of the Internet…consisted of electronic mail and file transfer software that connected people to people. The second generation connected people to databases and… the World Wide Web. Now a new generation of software connects computers directly to computers.[378]

How high-tech are we even beyond TIA and surveillance? High-tech enough to complete the development of a microwave bomb that would neutralize biochemical warfare stockpiles and wipe out entire electronic systems. Imagine what that would do to our defense spying if the enemy could use this on us.[379]

The Beast

You say you won't let "them" spy on you, that you don't want the computer chip in your debit and credit cards, and—hey!—you won't ever
let them microchip you; you'd rather starve or be beheaded than fulfill the prophecy of Revelation. But chipping humans won't be these
Elite controllers' first step. They insidiously have been working towards
human chipping for decades; consider Microsoft as an example. The
Elite have been chipping us gradually and are moving on to our driver's
licenses, our passports, our GPS devices and others. And, finally they'll
demand that we get chipped in order to be eligible for medical treatment, to acquire insurance, to buy groceries, to put gas in our cars, to
get a loan, and on and on and on.

A Boca Raton newspaper [380] headlines advancements in biochips.
An article entitled, "Family May Get Medical Info Chips Implanted,"
reports that in 2002, the Jeff Jacobs family volunteered to be implanted
so that in an emergency, any of them could be located and treated.
Jacobs, his wife Leslie, and their son Derek, then fourteen years old,
were the nation's first family to receive the VeriChip made by Applied
Digital Solutions in Palm Beach County.

Steve Aftergood of *Secrecy* noted in his article at least seven years
ago: "In the Pentagon research effort to detect terrorism by electroni-
cally monitoring the civilian population, the most remarkable detail
may be this: Most of the pieces of the system are already in place."[381]

Additionally, a Cincinnati-based company was the first to require
two employees to get chipped:

> CityWatcher.com, a provider of surveillance equipment,
> attracted little notice itself—until a year ago—when two of its
> employees had glass-encapsulated microchips with miniature
> antennas embedded in their forearms. The "chipping" of two
> workers with RFIDs—radio frequency identification tags as
> long as two grains of rice, as thick as a toothpick—was merely
> a way of restricting access to vaults that held sensitive data and

images for police departments, a layer of security beyond key cards and clearance codes, the company said.... Sean Darks, chief executive of the...company...compared chip implants to retina scans or fingerprinting. "There's a reader outside the door; you walk up to the reader, put your arm under it, and it opens the door." ...To some, the microchip was a wondrous invention.... To others, [it]...was Orwellian, a departure from centuries of history and tradition in which people had the right to go and do as they pleased without being tracked, unless they were harming someone else.[382]

In some ways, surveillance is a vanguard idea that could help many physically and emotionally ill people, could help locate stolen or lost children, and could even serve as security badges for access into very private and secured entrances such as airplane cockpits, nuclear power plants, and research labs.

The Mark

But in reality, it's the stain of the fiend—either on our foreheads, in our palms, or on the back of our hands—and it's likely to be a microchip with the 666 barcode implanted in us. It has been said that all store barcodes have the beast's prefix 666; likely, so will we. We will not be able to buy, sell, trade, or barter without it. If we hold to the Revelation account, we, our children, our loved ones, our grandchildren, our pets, and even our enemies will starve and thirst to death; our possessions will be ripped from us (home, car, property, house contents); our jobs will be removed from us; and our families will be divided...unless an intricate private, underground system is developed for those needing to acquire the necessities to survive without giving in to Satan's mark.

This would be disastrous. Where does one draw the line? Will every child become registered and marked under the guise of "protection" when in reality the government is amassing records on our health, our medicines, where we go, what we do, what groups we belong to, how we spend our money, and what we purchase? Combine this with the Internet and you can see how this mark of the beast will be abused.

And speaking of beast, some countries, supposedly including Belgium, have concealed a massive computer system that keeps records on every American in the world; perhaps by now it has expanded to include every person in the universe. That is the goal of the Illuminati. We see tracking processes ongoing throughout the world, as though we are cattle needing to be branded and closely followed, with logs and manifestos on every move we make, everything we say, every item we send or receive, and every car we drive. GPS exemplifies this power. Connected to satellites, transportation systems can locate anyone anywhere; give directions on how to reach one's destination; or give data needed to locate someone trying to hide.

Do not be mistaken by believing that all this is science fiction. The Elite are way ahead of the game, and they are not about to let us know how developed they are in creating a twenty-first-century holocaust. They have no respect for our privacy and think nothing of watching us daily, keeping records on us, examining our banking habits, and using brainwashing techniques. They probably sit back and laugh at how they have made us jump through hoops to get a certificate for this, a license for that, authorization for everything…all the while, tracking every step we take. Our Social Security numbers serve, right now, as our ID marks, as do our debit and credit card numbers.

Through the mark of the Beast, the Elite will gauge the size of national and world populations, and then use the data and the chip to control the number of people in any section on the globe. Genocide is a favorite method, whether through military battles, invented disasters, imminent domain, force-fed drugs, limited health care, starvation, vaccinations, or bio and chemical warfare. They falsely believe the planet is already overpopulated, and thus want to protect the land, its natural resources, and bodies of water to insure that *they* are taken care of…never mind the rest of us whose lives will be ended to spare theirs. The decisions they make concerning who lives and who dies is akin to drawing names from a hat. Certainly the sick, the maimed, the elderly, the mentally challenged, the dependent on the government, and anyone else in society who isn't able to produce or who refuses to give up spiritual beliefs for the Elite's false religion—perhaps New Age tenets—will in some manner be terminated. And all of this is accomplished through tracking.

Just as lives will be destroyed, some births will be entirely prohibited and prevented, through schools handing out condoms and vaginal protective devices while wildly promoting birth control methods and abortions. President Barack Obama made his support of this quite clear in his platform during the 2008 presidential election; in fact, he wants Americans to pay for abortions in other nations. The Elite's means of preventing population growth also includes abortion drugs, encouragement of fetal mutilation by pregnant girls, the horrid partial birth abortion, and gene engineering (to ward off malformed babies who will be reliant on the state for help). "Lunch Break Abortions 383 are offered by a British Charity through Marie Stopes International, an organization like Planned Parenthood. Females less than twelve weeks pregnant can leave their workplace at lunch time, or teen girls could take an hour off from school, and have a three-to-four minute abortion. One critic, Josephine Quintavalle, wrote in the Religious News Today, 'I don't think a child's life should be disposed of in a lunch hour.'"[384]

Snoop Agencies

We are pawns on the chess board. Certain government and other agencies are master players, riding out on their dark horses with swords drawn, lopping off heads and stampeding over us, and, if we manage to escape instant death, they checkmate us by throwing us to into the lion's den, where we're finished off.

The U.S. Department of Homeland Security is one of those spy agencies. It goes to any extreme to build databases on presumed terrorists as well as on Americans. It has violated nearly all the rights guaranteed by our Constitution. In its so-called reach for the safety of Americans, Homeland Security and the Patriot Act confiscate our civil rights and liberties under the guise of protection. Much of the surveillance practice going on today against Americans came out of organizations such as this one, and there is no letting up. President Obama is front and center on this practice, too. He showed early favor with it in 2007, and renewed it the very first day he took office:

> We are here to do the work that ensures no other family members have to lose a loved one to a terrorist who turns a plane into a missile, a terrorist who straps a bomb around her waist and climbs aboard a bus, a terrorist who figures out how to set off a dirty bomb in one of our cities. This is why we are here: to make our country safer and make sure the nearly three thousand who were taken from us did not die in vain; that their legacy will be a more safe and secure Nation.[385]

Spying via Echelon, a government agency experimenting with advanced eavesdropping system capable of monitoring satellite communications, and the Total Information Awareness (TIA) program will be the primary way for the Elitists to determine if we're being obedient or making trouble for them in their stride for implementation of a finely designed master control plan. HB 1017 (2009–2010), as an example, could take more than $81 million to set up computerized tracking of child abuse cases through DARPA.[386] A current figure on computerized tracking of child abuse has not been made available.

The TIA program would use such software as Groove, Extended Markup Language (XML), and other esoteric means. In fact, many computers are used as part of this surveillance program that allows for tracking by the government and the Elite.[387] Some claim that TIA has folded; others counter that the group has only gone further underground.

The TIA provokes heated arguments between its proponents and the American public, which doesn't want to be tracked. The ACLU has proven weak in this regard:

> The Total Information Awareness program will be—by Poindexter's own public admission—the infrastructure for what

the government hopes will be the most extensive electronic surveillance system in history. That vision is encapsulated in the logo for Poindexter's office: the all-seeing eye and pyramid (prominent also on the one dollar bill) spying from above on the entire world. The office's motto is *Scientia Est Potentia*, Latin for "Knowledge is Power."[388]

The technology of today's surveillance methods is beyond description, as seen in Echelon and its equipment that will even enable the spies to smell us. Echelon first hit the news around 2000 as the all-seeing eye of Big Brother. In retrospect, it's dangerous—perhaps even as threatening as DARPA's TIA (the name was changed to Terrorist Information Awareness program after 9/11/01), which can track us every second of our lives and anywhere on earth. So dangerous is this to our privacy that Senators Patrick Leahy, Russell Feingold, and Maria Cantwell claim, "Reliance on data mining by law enforcement agencies may produce an increase in false leads and law enforcement mistakes. While the former is a waste of resources, the latter may result in mistaken arrests or surveillance."[389]

Key words spoken over the phone or generated on computer screen or faxes across the network alert the global Elitists about our thoughts and actions. McAlvaney offers the following: "A frightening possibility is that the government agency of Social Services could be given license to target and political intimidate or harass the conservative and 'religious right' populations, either as political retaliation or as a means of imposing a form of 'political correctness' defined in Colorado as a Hate Crime. H.B. #1017 has now become law."[390]

Over the last ten to fifteen years, global socialists have been pushing HR 1017. This bill encompasses all types of abuse—physical, emotional, spiritual, and mental—thus allowing the state to apply any negative accusation to an incident. The definition of emotional abuse forbids parents from indoctrinating their children with religious instructions. The exact wording goes: "emotional abuse shall mean an identifiable and substantial impairment of the child's intellectual or psychological function or development."[391]

The Trilateral Commission (TLC) is another agency of surveillance. It consists of a global network of plutocrats. Since surveillance of everyone's actions is this group's key goal, it has developed (and still is developing) the most high-tech surveillance equipment ever in existence, including "Big Brothership" of the Internet. This highly secretive organization is comprised of academicians, politicians, and various "Elites" around the world. Since the TLC was founded by David Rockefeller, it appears to be an offshoot or a front of the Council on Foreign Relations (CFR), which could gain control of the U.S. simply by consolidating banks. It has been stated over and over that whoever controls the country's money controls that nation. This is true for its influence on and expansion in other countries.

If the Elitists have their way, they will fingerprint every human on earth and create a massive database on everyone. In the *Privacy World* newsletter, proponents push for DNA databases: "Everybody in Europe and the US should have their genetic fingerprints entered into an international database to enable law enforcement agencies to fight crime and terrorism in an unstable world, according to James Watson, the co-discoverer of the DNA double helix and Nobel Prize winner."[392]

Spying on Americans raises potential legal, ethical, and religious issues. The occult—a religion of the dark side—has a long history in our government, from the likes of Helena Blavatsky, Annie Besant, Albert Pike, and Marxist Saul Alinsky, who presumably formed satanic cults, wrote books on paganism, infiltrated our government with sinister practices and socialism, and owned what has been called "satanic" businesses such as Lucis Trust, which at one time was Lucifer Trust. Worshiping the pentagram, drinking from skulls, climbing into coffins, having orgies in the Bohemian Grove, or practicing witchcraft are all part of the forces of darkness running rampant in our government and believed to be practiced by the Elite.

The people in the inner and outer circles know that weight is placed on the worship of demons to achieve what they want: more power, more fame, and more money, more control. There is a major faction of believers and practitioners of necromancy, and they make little attempt to hide it. If you doubt the existence of witches, demons, and warlocks—evil—then study history, research the Internet, look through the library stacks, and talk to members of covens. Ask young people about the satanic cults they belong to; check out the activities of the secret societies.

Those involved in the darkness are members of the Council on Foreign Relations, the Trilateral Commission, the Bilderbergers, the Illuminati, the Club of Rome, the Freemasons, and other secret organizations. Much of what is happening today is a result of nearly two hundred years of effort to work important people into the inner circle to do whatever the Elite have felt necessary for creating a one-world government. That group includes seemingly innocent people like Margaret Sanger, a member of the secret societies who founded Planned Parenthood—not to teach youngsters not to have sex before marriage, but to teach them how to be proactive in the battle toward population reduction. Yet, scientists have gone on record saying that we are not overpopulated, and that each person on the globe could all fit in the state of Texas. Depopulation is a false mantra, just as the global warming fraud.[393] We are overcrowded, not overpopulated, in certain areas—particularly urban centers. And, we're likely experiencing a transitory temperate period, not massive global warming; the earth naturally goes through heating and cooling cycles.

Just as disarming are the records amassing indicating how Christians are being treated because of their faith. In the Canadian military, for example, chaplains have been told to avoid all specific reference to Christianity, and to avoid saying the Lord's Prayer. We are now seeing in American public schools the restriction of referring to or practicing Christianity; yet, in many of those same schools, self-proclaimed witches and warlocks are invited to classrooms to speak, and stealthy handshakes and cryptic words shared among shadow cults and clubs are expressed by members. And although the ways of God and His Son are blasphemed, the worship of Satan and his trinity is encouraged. The last few years have seen the highest rise in satanism ever by both youth and adults.

Agape Newsletter states: "A federal judge has ordered Iowa's Woodbine High School Choir to stop rehearsing 'The Lord's Prayer' until he rules whether it can be sung at this year's graduation ceremony. The Iowa Civil Liberties Union filed suit on behalf of the two choir members whose parents are atheists."[394]

Wasn't it one voice who demanded that the Lord's Prayer be taken out of schools? One voice! What ever happened to majority rules?

Remote Control

For years, former CIA, FBI, and other government "alphabet" groups; many whistleblowers; and a number of research institutes (i.e., acclaimed universities such as Stanford Research Institute [SRI], the Air Force, and the American Society for Psychical Research) have been claiming the advancement of the surveillance technique called remote viewing: being able to see what's going on through a form of mind control with others who also have been taught this same technique.

> In 1995, the CIA hired the American Institutes for Research, a perennial intelligence-industry contractor, to perform a retrospective evaluation of the results generated by the remote-viewing program, the Stargate Project—a code name for the U.S. Federal Government's special psychically remote viewing project. These projects were active from the 1970s through 1995, and followed up early psychic research…[and] involved psychical research labs.[395]

So, by mere mental touching or ESP, a receiver can learn who is involved in what, and where. This is not only a form of mind control, but also a psychological invasive surveillance technique. Consider this:

In the early 1990s the Military Intelligence Board, chaired by DIA chief Soyster, appointed an Army Colonel, William Johnson, to manage the remote viewing unit and evaluate its objective usefulness. According to an account by former SRI-trained remote-viewer, Paul Smith (2005), Johnson spent several months running the remote viewing unit against military and DEA targets, and ended up a believer, not only in remote viewing's validity as a phenomenon but in its usefulness as an intelligence tool.[396]

Even more highly developed surveillance is "remote control" of citizens. Here is what a group of Chinese claim[397] (note that the following excerpt is reproduced exactly the way the wording and spelling appeared in the e-mail):

[We] have been cruelly harassed tortured and persecuted in a covert way by the means of secret remote control on human body & brain. Among us, there are corporate employees, teachers, students, retirees and other intellectual workers and physical workers. Our suffering period ranges from several months till over 30 years.... A group of secret criminals who abuse their powers, arbitrarily use [this technique to] illegally manipulate our bodies and brains covertly, and also cruelly torture and harass us psychologically and physically and persecute us days and nights so that a lot of victims live a very miserable and horrible life. Secret criminals utilize [these] weapons... to remotely influence us, and consequently our bodies suffer from "physiological diseases and physiological behaviors" caused artificially from their weapons such as aching, itching, coldness, hotness, trembling, unwell feeling and unhappiness, and so that our brains suffer harassments and tortures from "acoasm [sic] and hallucination." Besides, criminals do all they could to shamelessly steal and indecently spread our privacy in our brains in an abnormal psychology and crazily do all they could to intimidate and humiliate victims. All these vices do a great harm [sic] us psychologically and physically. Therefore, some innocent victims was [sic] forced to hospitals especially for being forced to accept mental treatment, some innocent victims were forced to suicide because of intolerable secret tortures and insults, and others died of "strange fatal diseases" yielded by criminals secretly in a special trap.[398]

Not only do they—the Elite—want to destroy life, but they also desire to create life. A plot line in my novel, *Lucifer's Legion*,[399] has the government managing to clone humans as soldiers and inset chips in them so that military chiefs can guide automaton clones to do their bidding. Although fictional, this,[400] scenario is not so far fetched, considering that we have been able to clone for over nine years, and now have the biochip. Several people—especially those who have been in the military—claim to have been chipped by our government, and long after, have said they suffer physically, psychologically,[401] and emotionally.

Where will all this lead?

Conclusion

High technology has allowed, and will continue to bring about, tracking, high-tech surveillance, and other technological advances that will be used against the people of the world (Revelation 13). The speed of computers today is unequaled, and they're only going to get faster and smarter, processing billions of operations in a blink of an eye. Just consider that without the invention of these high-tech machines, we could not have created computerized super-jets, ATMs, cell phones, DVDs, pacemakers/defibrillators, microwave ovens, surveillance systems, alarm systems, computerized cars, and especially, smart cards.

On the other hand, had we not become so technologically savvy, we would not be tracked or kept under surveillance, nor face the likelihood of having microchips—Satan's stain—implanted under our skin in order to travel, buy, sell, and trade just to survive.

We have wrought our own tribulations.

—

Dr. Gianni DeVincent-Hayes, a professional writer and an internationally recognized, highly published author, has appeared on numerous radio and television shows, including A & E's "Biography" series. She is a frequent speaker on topics related to her books. Visit her website at http://www.creative-services.biz/books.html or www.giannihayes.net

chapter twelve

Food and Fuel Shortages

---

by J. Michael Bennett, Ph.D.

"Control oil and you control nations;
control food and you control people."
HENRY KISSINGER, 1970

When considering the vast array of horrific hazards modern man might encounter in today's brutal and challenging world, and those further menaces man may devise through his own efforts and technology, as well as warfare and natural dangers feared in the "brave new world" of tomorrow, the commonplace topic of famine, or shortage of resources critical to societal life, might appear to be a relatively benign and "ho hum," low-priority issue of concern. In our comfortable and secure Western lifestyles, famine can appear to be a distant and foreign concept, limited to those pitiful images of children with bloated bellies dwelling in the mires of the ghettos and villages in Africa and the subcontinent.

The closest images we can relate to in our culture are those refugees of the Midwestern Dust Bowl of the 1930s, who relocated en masse out West to escape the unrelenting winds, soil erosion, and period of arid drought, or the soup lines, hobos, and impoverished lifestyle of the entire country during the Great Depression. Some of our elderly experienced those days of want as young people, and remembered the improvising, community cooperation, and humility required to survive those days. They as a generation have been known for their frugality, thrift, hesitation to waste, and distrust of banks and other civil institutions—traits that have lasted throughout their lifetimes as a result of the indelible imprint of their earlier deprivation. They were succeeded by a wartime generation that endured loss of working men due to the draft, Liberty Gardens, and rationing of key products such as gasoline, nylon stockings, and rubber tires. The post-War baby boomers, in comparison, have lived a rather idyllic life as far as access to the resources of societal living, with the exception of the short-lived fuel shortages and long gas lines of the early 1970s due to the rise of the OPEC (Organization of the Petroleum Exporting Companies) oil cartel, with such indignities being limited to being seen driving the "econo" Chevy Vegas and Ford Pintos on the highway.

Since the excesses of the 1980s, a generation has been raised that has been pampered with fast food, processed groceries, and an abundance of excess to any essential resources, such as the proliferation of supermarket chains and malls in every community, resulting in prices that permitted preference for exotic commodities (such as the four-dollar cup of coffee), gas-guzzling sport utility vehicles, and any desire that a full wallet (or more likely, a portfolio of credit cards) could secure. This lifestyle is so detached from the realities of famine, deprivation, and want that the return of such conditions in the West will likely result in major societal upheaval, rampant crime, and the rise in suicide and divorce rates, although such conditions still persist today in much of the world. Indeed, recent reports of massive economic collapse, fuel shortages, and food shortages that are now causing riots in major parts of the world at the time of this writing might well test this generation as a "reality check" of the ever-present threat of shortage and famine;

and if these days are indeed the dawn of the last days, these threats may particularly be applied to those who follow Christ, as well as to the rest of the awestruck world.

Famine and the associated prospect of starvation lead peoples and communities to take a number of desperate measures, with accelerating and destabilizing consequences. These include the sacrifice of long-term prosperity and security for short-term survival by taking actions such as killing draught animals (leading to lower production later) and eating the "seed corn," hence sacrificing the next year's crop in the vain hope that more seed can be found in the future. Next steps typically include migrations in search of remote areas for food, often into nearby cities in search of greater supplies and distribution, where crime often follows and increases as many peasants and refugees resort to banditry to secure scarce resources. Long-term effects of such periods on society include the widespread proliferation of disease and reduced birth rates, and often upheavals in civil governments and social orders.

Approximately 70 million people have died due to famine and starvation during the twentieth century—roughly equal to both the military and civilian fatalities during World Wars I and II combined (although a significant number of such civilian casualties may be attributed to malnutrition and intentional starvation). Famines don't always occur because of a local shortage of food; the Great Famine of Ireland, beginning in 1845 (which led to mass migrations of people to the U.S. and elsewhere), occurred as food was being shipped from Ireland to England because the English could pay higher prices, as an example of merely an economic stratagem. A strict free-market approach, enforced by the British Army guarding Irish ports and food depots from the starving crowds, ensured food exports continued as before, and even increased during the famine period. The largest famine ever, the Chinese famine of 1958–61, was due to the "Great Leap Forward" political ideological program led by Chairman Mao Tse-tung. That government policy led to a decrease in food production and ambivalence toward preventing the famine. In Mao's China, the political need to report only good news resulted in suppression of data about the escalating disaster, and the public did not realize the scale of the disaster until twenty years later, when censorship was lifted after 30 million lives were lost. Other governments in the future might yet again attempt similar maneuvers in the control of media, at least in its earlier stages, or under martial law, government-controlled media conditions.

Overpopulation is also pointed out as a primary source of food and other resource limitations. David Pimental, professor of ecology and agriculture at Cornell University, and Mario Giampietro, senior researcher at the National Research Institute of Food and Nutrition (INRAN), propose in their study, *Food, Land, Population and the U.S. Economy*, a maximum U.S. population for a sustainable economy at 200 million.[437] To support a sustainable economy and avert disaster, the United States must reduce its population by at least one-third, and world population will have to be reduced by two-thirds, according to this study. They also believe that the suggested agricultural crisis will only begin to impact us after 2020, and will not become critical until 2050. These dates presume no other global factors such as war or pandemics aggravate the situation; for example, a potential oncoming peaking of global oil production (and subsequent decline of production), along with the peak of North American natural gas production, will very likely accelerate the inevitable occurrence of this agricultural crisis much sooner than forecast. Recent increases in the use of bio-fuels in developing countries are also diverting precious foodstuffs, fertilizers, and arable land away from consumption purposes. Geologist Dale Allen Pfeiffer expects the coming decades to bring spiraling food prices without relief and massive starvation on a global level such as never experienced before.[438]

Just recently, the years 2007 and 2008 brought a dramatic increase in world food prices, ushering in a state of global crisis and fostering instability and social unrest in both poor and developed nations—including riots in Asia, South America, and Europe. The price rises affected parts of Asia and Africa particularly severely, with Burkina Faso,[439] Cameroon, Senegal, Mauritania, Cote d'Ivoire,[440] Egypt,[441] and Morocco seeing protests and riots in late 2007 and early 2008 over the unavailability of basic food staples. Other countries that have seen food riots or are facing related unrest are Mexico, Bolivia, Yemen, Uzbekistan, Bangladesh,[442] Pakistan,[443] Sri Lanka,[444] and South Africa.[445] Ten thousand workers rioted close to the Bangladeshi capital Dhaka, smashing cars and buses and vandalizing factories in anger at high food prices and low wages. (Ironically, the country achieved food self-sufficiency in 2002, but food prices have increased dramatically due to the reliance of agriculture on oil and fossil fuels.) Economists estimate 30 million of the country's 150 million people could go hungry.[446] Between the start of 2006 and 2008, the average world price for rice rose by 217 percent, wheat by 136 percent, maize by 125 percent, and soybeans by 107 percent.[447] In late April, 2008, rice prices hit twenty-four cents a pound, twice the price that it was seven months earlier.[448] Among the reasons given for this sudden shortage of local food supplies (and/or associated food price increases beyond the reach of the masses) worldwide were recent actions by the U.S. Federal Reserve in decreasing interest rates so that money is no longer a means to preserve wealth over the long term (i.e., people alternatively invest in food commodities, which causes an increase in demand and therefore price), as well as other changes to the world economy.[449] More recently, Gerald Celente, chief executive officer of The Trends Research Institute, the source of trends data for major media such as CNN and *The Wall Street Journal* (and who successfully predicted events such as the 1987 stock market crash, the 1997 Asian currency crisis, the fall of the Soviet Union, and the subprime mortgage collapse), told Fox News during the week of November 13, 2008, that by 2012 America will be an undeveloped nation, and that there will be a revolution marked by food riots, squatter rebellions, tax revolts, and job marches.[450] Internal memos from Citigroup bank obtained by *The London Telegraph* newspaper also suggest a similar fate due to dire government actions to mitigate the current financial crises, which may result in "depression, civil disorder, and possibly wars."[451] Similarly, a recent report by the U.S. Army War College's Strategic Institute, entitled *Known Unknowns: Unconventional Strategic Shocks in Defense Strategy Development*, acknowledges that the United States may soon experience massive civil unrest in the wake of a series of crises it termed "strategic shock," requiring the military to intervene to maintain order. The reasons for such unrest included "unforeseen economic collapse," "pervasive public health emergencies," and "catastrophic…human disasters," and claims that such events could occur early in the Obama administration.[452]

Much more could be said in this discussion concerning this crisis (even if further destabilizing, accelerating forces are not considered), and the unique (and possibly more daunting) perils due to the rapidly disappearing supplies of fresh water available to growing populations worldwide has not even been addressed. However, the information cited herein is sufficient to grasp the reality of the inevitable (and imminent) dawn of days of worldwide want and struggle to compete for resources, often under violent and devastating circumstances, with no long-term answers in sight. Fortunately, the Bible addresses this ever-present threat to the people of the world, anticipates the rise of its impact at its acme at the end of days, and offers hope for those whose fate leads them to experience it.

What the Bible Reveals about Famine

A large measure of the history of the world has been defined by the ramifications of particular famines and similar shortages, with the resultant wars, mass migrations, and societal changes that have accompanied them. Therefore, it should be no surprise that the greatest piece of literature in world history, the Holy Bible, has a good bit to say about such famines and shortages—describing the actual historical events and their outcomes, their significance in societal living and spiritual implications (even indirect blessings in some cases), their causes and cures, and the lessons and realities that can be learned through observing them and experiencing them.

In considering just a few historical examples recorded in the Bible, let's investigate the first such incident discussed in depth in God's Word—the Middle East famine at the time of Joseph, the patriarch.

Now, the first time that such a famine is mentioned earlier in the Bible is in Genesis chapter 12, shortly after Abraham's party entered the land of Canaan, where the "grievous famine" there led them to proceed further to Egypt. This began a cycle of God's children fleeing to Egypt to escape hard times in their own country (as a symbol of leaving God's direct will and purpose while under trial), resulting in troubles for the local leadership in Egypt (because Israel's God was prone to let them know they did not belong there), and their eventual departure (sometimes by force, and often loaded with Pharaoh's goods). Abraham's son Isaac experienced a second famine in the land, and did not retreat to Egypt due to a direct warning from God, but did interact with a Philistine king at Gerar. Ironically, both Abraham and his son passed off their wives as sisters to the Philistine king there at different times (as Abram did with Pharaoh as well); soon thereafter, Isaac had more serious water disputes with these peoples. Thus, these early famines resulted in hard decisions being made relative to societal displacement, association, and often deceit, setting a pattern to come. However, we see further detail in a later famine in the region involving Jacob and his family, in which his son Joseph plays a key role. Joseph has been previously carried off to slavery in Egypt, yet in time is placed second in command only to Pharoah after interpreting a dream related to impending famine and proposing a prudent response, and then later impacting his entire people. All these events are noted in the following passages in Genesis chapter 41, starting with Joseph's interpretation of Pharaoh's dream:

> "Behold, there come seven years of great plenty throughout all the land of Egypt: And there shall arise after them seven years of famine; and all the plenty shall be forgotten in the land of Egypt; and the famine shall consume the land; And the plenty shall not be known in the land by reason of that famine following; for it [shall be] very grievous." (Genesis 41:29–31)

> "Now therefore let Pharaoh look out a man discreet and wise, and set him over the land of Egypt. Let Pharaoh do [this], and

let him appoint officers over the land, and take up the fifth part of the land of Egypt in the seven plenteous years. And let them gather all the food of those good years that come, and lay up corn under the hand of Pharaoh, and let them keep food in the cities. And that food shall be for store to the land against the seven years of famine, which shall be in the land of Egypt; that the land perish not through the famine." (Genesis 41: 33–36)

"And Pharaoh said unto Joseph, Forasmuch as God hath shewed thee all this, [there is] none so discreet and wise as thou [art]: Thou shalt be over my house, and according unto thy word shall all my people be ruled: only in the throne will I be greater than thou." (Genesis 41:39–40)

"And the seven years of plenteousness, that was in the land of Egypt, were ended.... And the famine was over all the face of the earth: And Joseph opened all the storehouses, and sold unto the Egyptians; and the famine waxed sore in the land of Egypt. And all countries came into Egypt to Joseph for to buy [corn]; because that the famine was [so] sore in all lands." (Genesis 41: 53,56–57)

In this biblical narrative, God foretells the famine through Joseph so that these foreigners, and eventually even Hebrews, can be spared if they make prudent plans. (In fact, verse 32 of the narrative even states that God himself sends the famine.) We see here the lesson that a godly man (Joseph) who listens to a warning from God, believes it, and faithfully delivers the warning to others, has an opportunity to be a blessing to the pagan king and his people—as well as eventually to his own people. The blessing also requires that the people take action to store up provisions during times of plenty, acting in faith even when the dark days are nowhere in sight; obviously, waiting for proof of the impending famine would have been much too late. God created special opportunities for His man, in a foreign land, to fulfill a unique and special mission. It is interesting to observe how the New American Standard Bible translation of Genesis 41:35 notes that Joseph suggested to Pharaoh that he place guards over this strategic reserve, much like the British in Ireland and other countries in recent years.

In time, due to the prudence of Egypt under Joseph's guidance to store up blessings during times of plenty, not only Egyptian citizens, but peoples from the surrounding countries, begin to arrive to buy grain at a price of Egypt's asking (a point of "maximum leverage," in today's vernacular). In microcosm, God used this to guide Jacob (with God's blessing)—and before that, the rest of Joseph's family and the entire Hebrew people—to be provided for by God through Joseph, again using the wealth God gave Egypt. However, due to the leverage wielded by the party who has prepared, the Scripture shows that Joseph is able to manipulate whomever he wishes in his family, detaining them or dismissing them at his leisure, since the Hebrews and other starving peoples simply had no other choices. Thankfully, his motives were virtuous and redemptive in nature, albeit nerve-wracking to experience. This is largely because of Joseph's character, and the fact that he recognizes God's hand in placing him in a position of redemption—a position where we may occasionally find ourselves during the days ahead, if we seek it: "And God sent me before you to preserve you a posterity in the earth, and to save your lives by a great deliverance. So now [it was] not you [that] sent me hither, but God" (Genesis 45:7–8).

However, a later passage reveals that other significant, unfortunate developments occur as by-products of this event, which have had long-term ramifications as a template for similar future events:

> And Joseph gathered up all the money that was found in the land of Egypt, and in the land of Canaan, for the corn which they bought: and Joseph brought the money into Pharaoh's house. And when money failed in the land of Egypt, and in the land of Canaan, all the Egyptians came unto Joseph, and said, Give us bread: for why should we die in thy presence? for

the money faileth. And Joseph said, Give your cattle; and I will give you for your cattle, if money fail. And they brought their cattle unto Joseph: and Joseph gave them bread [in exchange] for horses, and for the flocks, and for the cattle of the herds, and for the asses: and he fed them with bread for all their cattle for that year. When that year was ended, they came unto him the second year, and said unto him, We will not hide [it] from my lord, how that our money is spent; my lord also hath our herds of cattle; there is not ought left in the sight of my lord, but our bodies, and our lands: Wherefore shall we die before thine eyes, both we and our land? buy us and our land for bread, and we and our land will be servants unto Pharaoh: and give [us] seed, that we may live, and not die, that the land be not desolate. And Joseph bought all the land of Egypt for Pharaoh; for the Egyptians sold every man his field, because the famine prevailed over them: so the land became Pharaoh's. And as for the people, he removed them to cities from [one] end of the borders of Egypt even to the [other] end thereof. Only the land of the priests bought he not; for the priests had a portion [assigned them] of Pharaoh, and did eat their portion which Pharaoh gave them: wherefore they sold not their lands. Then Joseph said unto the people, Behold, I have bought you this day and your land for Pharaoh: lo, [here is] seed for you, and ye shall sow the land. And it shall come to pass in the increase, that ye shall give the fifth [part] unto Pharaoh, and four parts shall be your own, for seed of the field, and for your food, and for them of your households, and for food for your little ones. And they said, Thou hast saved our lives: let us find grace in the sight of my lord, and we will be Pharaoh's servants. And Joseph made it a law over the land of Egypt unto this day, [that] Pharaoh should have the fifth [part]; except the land of the priests only, [which] became not Pharaoh's. (Genesis 47:14–26)

In this amazing passage, we see a chain of events that many such historical resource shortage crises have emulated, and that will be repeated in the days ahead. First, we see that through Joseph's actions, the government had a corner on the one asset with any value under those extreme conditions. They were then able to name their price in terms of money or coin in exchange for the essential asset. In the process, they accumulate the bulk of the nation's coinage, and thus the ability to purchase the other now-devalued assets still owned by the populace. The verse says then that the money "failed" in the economy (some alternative translations say that all the money was spent)—presumably a collapse of the currency of some form (as we anticipate soon in our world economy today), not only in Egypt, but in Canaan as well. Therefore, the people came again to their government for solutions, in essence a "bailout" of free food and necessities in a welfare-type program, since they felt that the only alternative was to simply perish, and doing that "in the presence" of the government served no one's purpose since the government needed them as well. However, the government officials themselves determined that there were indeed assets that were of value to the government (at least that they could secure to exchange for assets of value to the government later, even if they couldn't use them now). Those assets were their cattle, which also included their flocks, horses, and burden animals such as asses, in exchange for one year's supply of bread.

We can see a vicious cycle further developing in which the people were now giving up the equivalent of their future "seed corn" by "hocking" the very tools they would use to generate income and produce further food, and by sacrificing their sources of meat, milk, and "horsepower" to pull plows, tread grain, and transport crops to the market. Inevitably, the people would return needy again the second year. It is ironic that the government supplied them only a single year's food, even though their data suggested the famine would be far longer. This is an ancient practice of governments hiding or ignoring important information and setting up a welfare cycle whereby the citizens must repeatedly bow for mercy before their governments to "get a fish," as opposed to "learning how to fish" by getting resources that would inevitably lead to their independence. Remember that in Genesis chapter 41, Joseph took a fifth of the bumper crop produced during the bounty years on behalf of Pharaoh, as he earlier recommended; the passage does not clarify if this was mere confiscation or if the government made some compensation for its imminent domain over it. However, since current market value would have been greatly reduced at the time due to the ample supply, the government would have procured it at token prices, if any. So, as a practical matter, the difference is trivial. However, the resource-depleted people must then sacrifice their very land and their own freedom as a last attempt to obtain one more year's worth of food. (Note that a citizen's forfeiture of private property is in essence the equivalent of indentured servitude anyway.) It is cruelly ironic that the government then supplied seed for planting—the very asset that could have preserved the citizens' long-term security and independence earlier—but this time, to be used on recently government-confiscated land, using government-confiscated tools and work animals, to be produced by government-owned people! Presumably, the famine must have stabilized to a point that the proper seed, land, and tools could produce new crops, but the real damage to the citizens had already been done.

The government then flexed its totalitarian muscles by forcibly relocating people to the teeming, overcrowded cities, where they could be better controlled, and presumably placed in austere communal housing with a minimal real estate "footprint." Thus, the government minimized the resource usage per person, as did Joseph Stalin with the sea of utilitarian high-rise apartments to which he relocated the masses from the rural communities, to more efficiently dominate and control. The most tragic portion of the Genesis narrative is the response of the government, via Joseph, which acknowledged and announced its role as savior of the people, while "generously" letting the people keep 80 percent of the product of their hard work, although the government acknowledged their right to 100 percent of "their" assets. In turn, the broken, disillusioned, and brainwashed citizenry thanked the benevolent government for "saving their lives" and letting them keep any portion of their labors, even though such governmental rights were obtained by exploiting and manipulating their own people under the guise of protecting them. This transfer of wealth and property to the state, and the precedents of heavy taxation, lasted for generations—long after the crisis had subsided. It is amusing to note that God has the "last laugh" on worldly kingdoms eventually when they flaunt their powers: Many years later, much of this wealth must have been purloined and pillaged by Hebrews as they left Egypt in the days of Moses, as one of many examples in biblical history where God takes the resources of the proud to lift up the humble.

It should be noted that the pattern of crisis-based, state usurpation of power, authority, and property has happened again and again in subsequent resource shortages and famines around the world, when the people have been, regularly over time, relinquishing the assets that are essential to life. These assets retain or increase in value in times of crisis and bare necessity, and the people do not store up sufficient supplies to ride out extended times of want to prevent the destructive cycle of "selling the farm." In fact, this scenario is largely being played out at the time of this writing as trillions of dollars in financial instruments and risky credit-based investments are being made worthless overnight. Not only individual investors, but insurance companies and even large investment banks have had their assets and very worth erased, or have immediate debt obligations that cannot be met with readily available credit. As a result, the government has decided which institutions, including large investment banks, are dissolved overnight, and which receive government bailouts and credit to remain in business for limited additional time. However, such arrangements often have come with significant strings attached: The institutions have sacrificed their own independence of operations, and often direct control and ownership of their companies, as the U.S. government has taken on the unique role of managing and owning such entities (or at least a controlling interest) on behalf of the public. Due to these ownership arrangements or debt obligations now provided directly by the federal government, the tenuous status of these companies in a sustained period of economic downturn will likely result in most of these companies being ultimately owned in full by the government as they fall into receivership. The range of massive corporate entities now—or soon to be—owned to some degree by the government includes the largest insurance company (AIG), investment banks, and even auto makers, the backbone of American industry. (However, it should be noted that many of these assets will become virtually worthless, or even liabilities, in exchange for valuable taxpayer money, which will have to be paid back to the government by the taxpayer, with interest, at a later date.)

This usurpation of assets by the government is also being extended to the private property of individual citizens, as the government now backs a large portion of mortgages and the banks that issue them, and will also come to possess many of these homes later. The government may choose to rent these properties to citizens later (to produce cash flow, mitigate maintenance costs, and reduce vandalism), but the citizens who rent those homes will reside in homes their government owns, much as the Egyptians millennia earlier. It should be reiterated that the destructive collapses of these entities, both large and small, resulted from victims retaining their assets in commodities that can quickly become near worthless in times of crisis, such as paper money and financial instruments that depend upon a stable and mutually trustworthy economic environment, rather than crisis-proof commodities of timeless and robust value such as gold, and even more so, food, water, and fuel. These latter commodities should be particularly stored in sufficient levels to support families for extended periods when normal trade conditions are disrupted—and possibly additional amounts should be stored for later trading and ministering to others.

A final but key component of this historical narrative in Scripture is that one group in society was shown to actually prosper during this time of crisis: the priest class. The priests' prosperity was evidently due to the fact that their earlier "contract" with Pharaoh contained a clause that they were to be paid in an asset found to retain its value—the very food that later was in short supply. The increase in the cost of food later was irrelevant, since payment was in the denomination of the appreciating asset and it met basic needs without any further trading needed, even if the land they were uniquely able to retain sat temporarily idle during the famine. This startling insight should inspire us to seriously consider the various turns of events that could occur in resource shortages, the drastic change in fortunes that could subsequently occur in different portions of the citizenry, and the wisdom of planning all asset exchange, accumulation, and preservation for our families with an eye toward a range of possible long-term scenarios that could threaten its value and utility—to thus develop a strategic asset preservation plan to best protect the family during days of extreme need.

The Scriptures are replete with further examples of historical famine events, the reasons they occurred, and the ramifications and legacy they left behind. For brevity's sake, we'll mention just two other examples in Scripture that reveal lessons to be learned from these events. First, 2 Samuel 21 reports that a famine resided in Israel for three years; when King David sought the Lord for answers, the Lord responded that the famine was due to Saul's killing of the Gibeonites in breach of an earlier oath that had been taken by the Israelites. While the famine in Egypt discussed previously was said to have been sent by God himself as a vehicle to reunite Jacob and his family, and provide a prosperous place for them to dwell (and even a source of funds and a place of remembrance for the Hebrews after their centuries of suffering), in this case it is clearly a judgment. The famine was lifted when David took painful steps to provide justice to the offended Gibeonites.

Another such famine reported in 2 Kings 6 occurred because of a military siege of the land, a common cause of such shortages:

> And there was a great famine in Samaria: and, behold, they
> besieged it, until an ass's head was [sold] for fourscore [pieces]
> of silver, and the fourth part of a cab of dove's dung for five
> [pieces] of silver. And as the king of Israel was passing by upon
> the wall, there cried a woman unto him, saying, Help, my lord,
> O king. And he said, If the LORD do not help thee, whence

shall I help thee? out of the barn floor, or out of the wine-press? And the king said unto her, What aileth thee? And she answered, This woman said unto me, Give thy son, that we may eat him to day, and we will eat my son to morrow. So we boiled my son, and did eat him: and I said unto her on the next day, Give thy son, that we may eat him: and she hath hid her son. And it came to pass, when the king heard the words of the woman, that he rent his clothes; and he passed by upon the wall, and the people looked, and, behold, [he had] sackcloth within upon his flesh. (2 Kings 6:25–30)

In this shocking passage, we see the levels of depravity that occur when resources run out under war-time siege conditions. In this instance, the King of Syria surrounded Samaria and the kingdom of Israel, cutting off all external supplies until the inhabitants were no longer supportable, in a grinding waiting game of suffering and agony. We see how delectable treats like an ass' head becomes a valuable commodity (and money, even coinage, becomes ever more worthless, like Thurston Howell's stock certificates offered to the head hunters on "Gilligan's Island"). It should be noted the "dove's dung" may in fact be a very modest form of vegetables, such as with similar herbs known in the Arab world today as "sparrow's dung" (according to Strong's entry H02755), although it is feasible that it actually was the "real McCoy," and there is historical precedent for its consumption as well under crisis conditions. We see later in the story the horrific tale of familial cannibalism, a state that is hard to accept, but it not uncommon under the most severe famine and siege conditions. Most disturbing is the broken emotional state of the mother, who is no longer shocked by this taboo act, but laments the broken vow of the other mother to share in the ghoulish sacrifice. These types of desperate acts are commonly reported in history during the longest and most severe siege incidents, even in modern history. Similar acts were reported in Stalingrad during its multi-year siege by the German Army in World War II (they were also experienced in similar siege events in Judah, such as just before the Babylonian Exile, and during the Roman sacking of Jerusalem). The initial forecasts of food shortages earlier in this chapter did not include the multiplicative effects of war and its disruption of food and supply distribution, confiscation, and destruction, as well as seaport and city blockades that can starve out entrenched populations and lead to violent, depraved living conditions as the supplies start to dwindle. If the days we face soon are to be filled with widespread warfare and unrest, particularly if these days will turn out to be the last days, then the accelerating effects of intentional shortages created by conflict must be accounted for and planned for in the days ahead.

Expected Future Deprivations and Shortages Revealed from the Biblical Prophetic Record

The key passage in the New Testament that sheds light on the nature of how resource shortages will influence humanity in the last days is in Revelation chapter 6, in which the Lamb unseals the third seal of the scroll. John witnessed the following scene: "And when he had opened the third seal, I heard the third beast say, Come and see. And I beheld, and lo a black horse; and he that sat on him had a pair of balances in his hand. And I heard a voice in the midst of the four beasts say, A measure of wheat for a penny, and three measures of barley for a penny; and [see] thou hurt not the oil and the wine" (Revelation 6:5–6).

Sincere, Bible-believing scholars have debated for millennia the actual meaning and significance of the seals in this enigmatic book of prophetic revelation, such as whether it describes events that have happened historically during the church age (similar to theories regarding the deeper historical allegories attributed to the letters to the seven churches just beforehand), events just prior to the Rapture, during the Tribulation period, or as having multiple eras of fulfillment (interested readers are advised to review the recent unique and provocative theories proposed by Goodgame [453] and Lowe [454, 455] in their publications regarding these seals). Such a debate is beyond the scope of this treatise, and not essential to considering its relevance to our topic. However, if the events described in this passage are relevant to a period we or our descendants will yet experience, then this description reveals a time when we shall be exposed to blatant manipulation and exploitation by the control of our access to essential resources by earthly rulers, and likely their supernatural guiding entities.

What has just been discovered by the author are the unique implications in the original language (Greek) of key words in these passages, which have been largely masked by the various English translations. First, please note the key word translated as "scales" in verse 5, which has been the most identifiable symbol associated with this passage. Through the years, countless pictures illustrating this passage have depicted a scale/balance-wielding horseman. However, a brief review of the Greek word *zygos*, from which the English translation "pair of balances" is normally employed, is revealed in Strong's reference (entry G2218) to primarily refer to a "yoke," such as "is put on draught cattle," "used of any burden or burden," or "as that of slavery." A secondary reference is to a "balance" or "pair of scales." In fact, every other use of this word in the Bible is translated as a "yoke." The consideration of this device as a "yoke" is a much more enlightening translation, since it implies an economic "yoke" of slavery to debt and limited access to essential economic and other resources controlled by the evil entity who places the yoke. This picture is reminiscent of the scenario in Egypt where the citizens took the yoke of servitude to Pharaoh, using their own yokes that were then the property of the state in order to receive sustenance, since they had no other assets by which to otherwise obtain essential goods. We see in the modern era these same activities by globalist groups like the International Monetary Fund, which burdens entire third world countries with deep levels of debt in exchange for bare essentials in a vicious cycle from which they cannot escape, even if their era of crisis was initially only temporary. In fact, John Perkins, in his shocking, best-selling 2004 book, *Confessions of An Economic Hitman,* [456] describes his duties on behalf of the IMF in such a role. The following excerpt of his concise description of this role exhibits disturbing parallels to the aforementioned passage in Revelation: "Economic hit men (EHMs) are highly paid professionals who cheat countries around the globe out of trillions of dollars. They funnel money from the World Bank, the U.S. Agency for International Development (USAID), and other foreign "aid" organizations into the coffers of huge corporations and the pockets of a few wealthy families who *control the planet's natural resources...* They *play a game as old as empire,* but one that has taken on *new and terrifying dimensions during this time of globalization"* [italics added].

This is a hauntingly plausible description of how the black horse (as in the black ink of economics—in fact, the Greek word *melas* used for "black" here was commonly used by the Greeks to particularly denote "black ink") can realistically control the fate of millions of humans, without guns or other coercion. One last comment regarding this verse is directed to the last Greek word *cheir* (Strong's 5495), translated as the word "hand," as the instrument of holding and controlling the yoke. One of the more intriguing historical definitions of this Greek word by Strong's is the phrase "symbolizing...might, power, activity, in determining and controlling the destinies of men." Many times in Scripture, it is apparent this word is used to describe the actions and ability of God himself, dependent upon the context present in the passage. But, in this passage in question, it is clear that it is used by malevolent forces for diabolical purposes.

One might presume that the "balance" or "scales" translation might be more appropriate for this passage, given the further elaboration in verse 6, which states: "And I heard a voice in the midst of the four beasts say, A measure of wheat for a penny, and three measures of barley for a penny; and [see] thou hurt not the oil and the wine" (Revelation 6:6).

This can illustrate a picture of one "balancing" money and commodities in the pans of a scale, as one possibility, and that may indeed be the intended metaphor. However, the device known as a "yoke" in Scripture and in the ancient world was a device to join two entities together, such as two oxen. This understanding of their ancient procedures better illustrates the possible relationship Christ has to His followers when He says, "take My yoke upon you." Many have seen this as our installing the yoke of labor and servitude upon ourselves, with

Christ behind the reins as the master directing from behind. However, it can also be envisioned as Christ applying the yoke on us, with himself in the other side of the yoke, pulling as the lead ox. Because of this leadership role, He bears the brunt of the burden; thus, our burden is light in comparison. In fact, the previously discussed Greek word *zygos* for "yoke" is described by Strong's as "to join, especially by a yoke." Therefore, the "yoke" analogy can also be perceived as the joining of the value of money to precise quantities of critical resources such as food, under the control and whims of the "hand" wielding it, much like world bankers sometimes peg the value of currency to fixed assets such as gold, or in setting price controls, which can wreak havoc on the entire economies of countries and make large people groups rich or poor overnight at the determination of remote and dispassionate forces. In the case of this passage, a "measure" (Greek *choinix*: an amount of food sufficient to sustain a man for a day [Strong's G5518]) of wheat for a "penny" (Greek *denarion*: understood to be equivalent to a day's wages) and three measures of barley for a penny show that members of the populace will only be given a day's food for a day's work, with no other compensation for other needs implied. This illustrates the ultimate in irredeemable, irreversible dependency and servitude (no explanation is implied for the reason that three measures of barley are given; possibly it is less nutritious and requires more, or perhaps people are given weekends off after "Barley Friday"!). Other basic needs may be met in government housing, or even internment camps, to meet catastrophic needs or merely for population control, albeit with the need for detainees to supply a full day's work to receive their essential food needs. This scenario is eerily akin to the Egyptians, who lived in government-owned housing in the cities as they worked for the state in exchange for their minimal food needs.

The last portion of this verse exhibits a number of unremarkable words (in English); however, they yield a wide range of possible scenarios when considering the range of definitions of the original Greek words used. (This author is not a Greek scholar, or even a linguist, so any assertions submitted here should be verified by diligent students of the

Word.) First, the phrase "[see] thou hurt" is a translation of the Greek word *adikeo*, which Strong's (G91) lists as having a range of meanings, such as "to act unjustly or wickedly, to sin," "to be a criminal," "to do wrong," "to do hurt." In Revelation 22:11, for example, the word is translated as one being "unjust." Even more curious is the range of meanings possible for the Greek word *me* (Strong's G3361), translated in English as simply "not." It suggests possible translations such as "lest" or "God forbid"; it suggests "qualified negation" as opposed to "absolute negation," such as when the Greek word *ou* is translated as "no" or "not." Other meanings such as "unless" and "if not," among others, are also listed. Since this simple word has so many complex meanings, one must use extreme caution in committing to a single interpretation of this phrase, and it is prudent to consider a range of possible interpretations of how this passage could possibly be fulfilled. In modern vernacular, phrases such as, "God forbid they act unjustly with the oil and the wine," or "...unless they act criminally regarding the oil and the wine," are a few of a wide range of possible interpretations in the mind of this untrained linguist. The key point here is that one cannot confirm that the "wine" and "oil" will not be harmed or exploited in any case with absolute certainty, when considering only the range of interpretations of the Greek words used in this verse, regardless of the common English words chosen by modern translators.

Speaking of the "oil" and "wine," the Greek word used here (*oinos*, Strong's G3631) for the English word "wine" can pertain to the simple beverage known as wine, or as a metaphor of God's wrath, as it is used elsewhere in the book of Revelation. It is uncertain why this substance is chosen as a commodity in this reference, although it has been speculated upon by many. For example, maybe the totalitarian state will allow a form of "Victory Gin," as was available to the masses in the seminal book *1984* as a means of keeping the populace pacified, and their senses dulled. However, the findings are even more intriguing for the companion commodity translated in English as "oil," known in the Greek as *elaion* (Strong's G1637). This word is shown as representing a form of olive oil used for fuel oil for lamps, for healing the sick, and for anointing, but not for consumption. This particular word for oil is only used in Scripture for representing a fuel oil or as a medicine (as used by the Good Samaritan). This might imply that the substance is indeed heating oil, representing energy resources in general. If this is true, then determining the proper interpretation of the preceding phrase is paramount; it would hence reveal whether energy supplies might also be restricted and controlled alongside foodstuffs, or alternatively prevented from such manipulation, and thus might influence the priorities one makes to prepare for such days (if "those days" will be indeed be experienced by the reader).

These same diabolical characters are described in Revelation chapter 18, and are known as "Babylon, the Great City." I personally believe (at this time) that this passage describes the judgment and eventual, sudden downfall of the tyrannical economic institution that is described in the third seal (an unsealed indictment of sins, if you will), and which has been operating since the days of the Tower and the great kingdom of Babylon, being made manifest thence in numerous forms.

Let's consider a number of the verses from this passage:

And he cried mightily with a strong voice, saying, Babylon the great is fallen, is fallen, and is become the habitation of devils, and the hold of every foul spirit, and a cage of every unclean and hateful bird. For all nations have drunk of the wine of the wrath of her fornication, and the kings of the earth have committed fornication with her, and the merchants of the earth are waxed rich through the abundance of her delicacies. And I heard another voice from heaven, saying, Come out of her, my people, that ye be not partakers of her sins, and that ye receive not of her plagues. For her sins have reached unto heaven, and God hath remembered her iniquities...Therefore shall her plagues come in one day, death, and mourning, and famine; and she shall be utterly burned with fire: for strong [is] the Lord God who judgeth her. And the kings of the earth, who have committed fornication and lived deliciously with her, shall bewail her, and lament for her, when they shall see the smoke of her burning, Standing afar off for the fear of her torment, saying, Alas, alas, that great city Babylon, that mighty city! for in one hour is thy judgment come. And the merchants of the earth shall weep and mourn over her; for no man buyeth their merchandise any more…and cinnamon, and odours, and ointments, and frankincense, and wine, and oil, and fine flour, and wheat, and beasts, and sheep, and horses, and chariots, and slaves, and souls of men. And the fruits that thy soul lusted after are departed from thee, and all things which were dainty and goodly are departed from thee, and thou shalt find them no more at all. The merchants of these things, which were made rich by her, shall stand afar off for the fear of her torment, weeping and wailing…For in one hour so great riches is come to nought. And every shipmaster, and all the company in ships, and sailors, and as many as trade by sea, stood afar off… saying, Alas, alas, that great city, wherein were made rich all that had ships in the sea by reason of her costliness! for in one hour is she made desolate. Rejoice over her, [thou] heaven, and [ye] holy apostles and prophets; for God hath avenged you on her. And a mighty angel took up a stone like a great millstone, and cast [it] into the sea, saying, Thus with violence shall that great city Babylon be thrown down, and shall be found no more at all…. And the light of a candle shall shine no more at all in thee; and the voice of the bridegroom and of the bride shall be heard no more at all in thee: for thy merchants were the great men of the earth; for by thy sorceries were all nations deceived. And in her was found the blood of prophets, and of saints, and of all that were slain upon the earth. (Revelation 18:2–5, 8–11, 13–15, 17, 19–21, 23–24)

We see in the first verse that (a) the institution is known as "Babylon the Great"; (b) "devils" and "foul" spirits are behind its operations; (c) all nations, as well as individual world leaders ("kings") and merchants, have participated in her sins; and (d) the nations will also share in the wrath poured out on her. We see next a very important admonition: God's children should "come out of her" and "not be partakers of her sins" so they would "receive not of her plagues." The biggest question is this: How do we do this in a manner that God intends from this passage? This matter is worthy of all our prayer, meditation, contemplation, and discussion over the days ahead. If we are truly entering the last days, then we need to know how to recognize when and how this Babylon body forms to a degree, so that we can flee, if not earlier, like Lot did before Sodom and Gomorrah were destroyed within hours. Furthermore, one could interpret that we should consider leaving "Babylon" right now, and the command is for the reader of the book right now, and not just one found to be living in the "last" of the "last days."

We also need to consider how to accomplish this, as well as the scope and intent of this admonition. Does it mean that we get out of the world's financial, investment, and credit systems? If so, how do we do it? These things are the questions groups of Christians need to be discussing over coffee in homes and other venues. Are you affiliated with economic and financial groups that exploit other people by taking advantage of the poor or the third world, or by employing predatory credit practices? Would God consider these things the "sins" Babylon will be judged about? Pray about this issue—you may decide not to participate in the Federal-Reserve-controlled, fractional reserve credit and finance system, instead keeping your investments "honorable" endeavors such as local food production and crafts, as in your own efforts of labor. One can see the wisdom that taking such a position would have in the future days of food control by world powers—direct access to the basic assets of life could make the difference between life and death for members of your family, your church, and your community, as opportunities arise for you to bless others out of your excess, as the Lord provides. Activities and investments that do not involve bankers, and that do not exploit workers in far-away lands are honorable, and will be prudent when those days arrive—even though you may not make much money while others are making windfalls via the Babylon financial system in the meantime, and even though you may be subject to taunts from many, including even your Christian brethren. When operations are justified of a scale of capital that individuals cannot practically save for sufficiently (such as even procuring modest farms), then Christian groups need to start thinking about starting financial co-ops to provide honest investments "within the body" to support such honest and healthy commerce "out of Babylon," but such positive ideas will be discussed in a later section.

Further in this passage, it is clear that God sees these exploitative economic practices as sins that are important and grievous to the Lord. We also see that "the shoe will be on the other foot" as God issues a judgment of famine upon those who have artificially created local famines to control others in the past. Notice here that the kings of the earth stand "afar off, for fear of her torment," yet they mourn over her destruction; they had "good times" with her and used her while it lasted (like a prostitute), but when she meets her end, they want to be far enough away that the sulfur and brimstone don't land on them. (Don't worry, their just desserts will be meted out soon in a valley in Israel.) Men of evil are like this: They join together to pillage, exploit, and enjoy their plunder, but when the hard times come, they are nowhere to be found. (Heaven forbid when we treat other Christians like this!) Notice that the products Babylon was known to sell in the past included the "wine and oil" of Revelation chapter 6, and a host of nonessential but extravagant delicacies for the wealthy, as well as "the souls of men." That is what these wealthy cartels—particularly the ultra-wealthy, Rockefeller types who have no need for more money—really want to control. As the ultimate "power trip," they want to manipulate people as they like, including their very basics of survival, as the third seal of Revelation 6, the indentured servitude of the citizens of Egypt in Genesis 47, and the generations of people in between imply.

The writings we have from these types of people today confirm this very agenda (the content of which is beyond the scope of this chapter). All the merchants, including the international traders in ships, stand afar off, noting (a) how she had made them so wealthy, and (b) how rapidly she was destroyed ("within an hour"). I believe this destruction will be supernatural, physical, and clearly from God himself, but the way our current economic system is leveraged, with fractional reserve lending, one can see that even if it shakes financially, the whole system comes crashing down instantly, particularly if confidence in the artificial system is lost. While they are mourning, "heaven, the apostles and prophets" are told to "rejoice over her," because "God has avenged you on her." Later, this is explained because "in her was found the blood of prophets, and saints, and all that were slain upon the earth." I think this suggests that the Scripture here makes a point that the traditional "conspiracy theorists" make: that the wars of the world are typically fought for economic reasons and interests, and not for the reasons that kings tell their people to inspire patriotic fervor. The United States is not immune to this: We killed the Indians to get their valuable land for the railroads and settlers (and the British before that due to high taxes!), killed the Confederates to keep access to cheap raw materials, killed the Spanish to obtain imperialistic lands far away for their economic and strategic value, and the list goes on and on. Even the children of God have been killed for related reasons: They removed spirits from mediums who made money for their handlers, they did not provide money for the coffers of the institutionalized church, or they did not cooperate with state power structures when their consciences forbade them, and exhibited an air of even quiet rebellion that threatened the system (such as by merely refusing to briefly mention that "Caesar is Lord"), from Rome to the modern day, that "kings" felt might "catch on" with others, and threaten their lucrative positions at the government treasuries. These latter concerns were the kinds of reasons the Pharisees arrived at with Roman leaders to squash Christ and His followers to maintain the "status quo" in the religious, political, and economic realms. (I'm sure they never forgave Jesus for turning over the money changers' tables—where the presence of "Babylon" temporarily occupied and "conquered" the Temple in its own way, and by which Jesus displayed the need for followers to separate themselves from it, by chasing them out from this area.) The end of this passage also says that "thy merchants were the great men of the earth," which we understand and have established are the true power brokers of this age, as opposed to kings—be it the Rockefellers, Rothchilds, Morgans, etc., who have kept the nations and their kings on a leash for centuries. The passage also says that "for by thy sorceries were all nations deceived." God says that their seduction had a spiritual component, and was a "sorcery" of some sort—who knows what types of spirit communications these mysterious, powerful families conduct? In any case, entire nations in history were "deceived" by these economic power brokers, their motives, and how they had planned to enslave them, and possibly they had spiritual help in their deceptions.

Let's briefly look at Jesus' direct words regarding the role of famines in the last days: "For nation shall rise against nation, and kingdom against kingdom: and there shall be famines, and pestilences, and earthquakes, in divers places. All these [are] the beginning of sorrows. Then shall they deliver you up to be afflicted, and shall kill you: and ye shall be hated of all nations for my name's sake" (Matthew 24: 7–9).

In this brief passage, Jesus warns that part of the tribulations falling upon the earth, even during the "birth pangs" prior to the seventieth week of Daniel, will include famines and pestilences. Certainly the widespread outbreak of wars (possibly originating over limited critical resources), and natural disasters like earthquakes (which is why I don't go scuba diving, because of this threat in the last days of earthquakes "in divers places"—wink!) will compound the problem by curtailing food distribution, farming, and harvesting.

Here is another admonition from the Lord about those days: "And take heed to yourselves, lest at any time your hearts be overcharged with surfeiting, and drunkenness, and cares of this life, and [so] that day come upon you unawares. For as a snare shall it come on all them that dwell on the face of the whole earth. Watch ye therefore, and pray always, that ye may be accounted worthy to escape all these things that shall come to pass, and to stand before the Son of man" (Luke 21:34–36).

Our Lord Jesus warns here about "riotous living" in terms of exploiting and wasting the resources God gives us. He also warns about focusing ("hearts being 'overcharged' with…cares of this life") either on (a) your enjoyment and more accumulation of these resources and extravagant trinkets and delicacies, or (b) becoming obsessed with issues of this life (versus the things of heaven), even if well-intentioned in terms of trying to be prepared. If this is done at the expense of other duties the Lord gives us, our ability to spiritually be prepared and watch for His coming will be inhibited. He says these things will be a "snare" for everyone, possibly even Christians (hence the need to get out of "Babylon," even if only "in between the ears"!), and alternatively focus on watching and praying.

How do we "watch"? That is a good question! I submit that some activities that could possibly comprise watching, from what Scripture suggests, include:

(a) studying diligently to understand what the Bible says about the signs leading up to the last days;

(b) purposefully studying what is going on in the world, and even within the church that reveals evidence of the things prophesied in Scripture;

(c) listening to the Holy Spirit's suggestions and enlightenment (while confirming its origin from Him by comparing the understanding with the immutable Word of God); and

(d) listening to mature Christian teachers on the topic, etc., for a good start!

The interesting thing about the conclusion of this passage is that the Lord says that if we do these things, we may be accounted worthy to "escape all these things that shall come to pass." I know that Scripture is clear that we cannot be worthy of righteousness and salvation in our own strength (as opposed to the Lord's, through His atoning sacrifice), because the Bible is clear that "our righteousness is as filthy rags" and that "all have sinned, and fallen short of the glory of God." Therefore, I presume that the Lord may choose to spare, to some partial or full degree, some believers who are found "with their lamps lit" as an expression of their faith and belief, from at least some of the tribulation to come. I do not know if this refers to a Rapture prior to days of such suffering, or whether God will spare His faithful servants of the ongoing suffering to some degree. In any case, it is yet another reward Christ promises to those who are diligent and obey Scripture in faith, coming from the One whose nature is to richly reward His servants!

Admonitions

Here are a few more of the many admonitions in the Bible regarding "famines" and "drought":

> If there be in the land famine, if there be pestilence, blasting, mildew, locust, [or] if there be caterpiller; if their enemy besiege them in the land of their cities; whatsoever plague, whatsoever sickness [there be]; What prayer and supplication soever be [made] by any man, [or] by all thy people Israel, which shall know every man the plague of his own heart, and spread forth his hands toward this house: Then hear thou in heaven thy dwelling place, and forgive, and do, and give to every man according to his ways, whose heart thou knowest; (for thou, [even] thou only, knowest the hearts of all the children of men). (1 Kings 8:37–39)

This wonderful passage may be most relevant to events of pestilence or famine over history, particularly within Israel, whose origins of such events were due to sin. It reveals that sincere repentance may reduce or eliminate the impact of such afflictions. Since the last-days plagues are certain to occur ("it is written," in effect), such events at that time may be unstoppable, but possibly the impact on believers could be lessened, or localized protection received, if one or more choose to follow this biblical admonition. In the meantime, we might experience many other such pestilences, droughts, famines, and plagues, large and small; therefore, this instruction may prove valuable many times before those days arrive!

> "Son of man, when the land sinneth against me by trespassing grievously, then will I stretch out mine hand upon it, and will break the staff of the bread thereof, and will send famine upon it, and will cut off man and beast from it: For thus saith the Lord GOD; How much more when I send my four sore judgments upon Jerusalem, the sword, and the famine, and the noisome beast, and the pestilence, to cut off from it man and beast?" (Ezekiel 14:13, 21)

The Lord further elaborates very clearly in this passage that He can be the source of famine or other calamities when His children have sinned.

> "Who shall separate us from the love of Christ? [shall] tribulation, or distress, or persecution, or famine, or nakedness, or peril, or sword? As it is written, For thy sake we are killed all the day long; we are accounted as sheep for the slaughter. Nay, in all these things we are more than conquerors through him that loved us. For I am persuaded, that neither death, nor life, nor angels, nor principalities, nor powers, nor things present, nor things to come, Nor height, nor depth, nor any other creature, shall be able to separate us from the love of God, which is in Christ Jesus our Lord." (Romans 8:35–39)

This well-known passage offers a myriad of wonderful promises to believers under duress, including those who are enduring famine. Succinctly, this passage promises that even under such tribulation, (a) we shall not be separated from the love of Christ; (b) our persecution, its meaning, and its ultimate purpose was understood long ago (and thus everything is well under control); and (c) we will be "more than conquerers" in the midst of all this suffering—not by removing it, but by prevailing in spite of it!

God offers more promises for His children in the midst of famine:

"Behold, the eye of the LORD [is] upon them that fear him, upon them that hope in his mercy; To deliver their soul from death, and to keep them alive in famine." (Psalm 33:18–19)

"The LORD knoweth the days of the upright: and their inheritance shall be for ever. They shall not be ashamed in the evil time: and in the days of famine they shall be satisfied. But the wicked shall perish, and the enemies of the LORD [shall be] as the fat of lambs: they shall consume; into smoke shall they consume away. The wicked borroweth, and payeth not again: but the righteous sheweth mercy, and giveth. For [such as be] blessed of him shall inherit the earth; and [they that be] cursed of him shall be cut off. The steps of a [good] man are ordered by the LORD: and he delighteth in his way. Though he fall, he shall not be utterly cast down: for the LORD upholdeth [him with] his hand. I have been young, and [now] am old; yet have I not seen the righteous forsaken, nor his seed begging bread." (Psalm 37:18–25)

This amazing passage not only shows that the Lord will preserve the "upright," even in the "evil time," and shall be "satisfied" in the days of "famine," but that the "wicked" shall, by economic means or by more direct and personal methods, "borrow" when in need and not give back, whereas the "righteous" will be known by "showing mercy" and "giving." Is that what you will do in the days of need? Will you store up provisions not only for you and your family, but so that you can give and show mercy to others? The Lord promises that the steps of a "good" man are "ordered" (implying being well under God's control), and even when falling at times, he will not be cast down for good (note that we are not promised that we will not "fall" occasionally). The psalmist closes with his observation that, over his lifetime, he has not seen the righteous forsaken—this may be one of the best promises of all for this topic!

"Now concerning the collection for the saints, as I have given order to the churches of Galatia, even so do ye. Upon the first [day] of the week let every one of you lay by him in store, as [God] hath prospered him, that there be no gatherings when I come. And when I come, whomsoever ye shall approve by [your] letters, them will I send to bring your liberality unto Jerusalem" (1 Corinthians 16:1–3).

In the early days, the church at Jerusalem experienced a severe famine. Paul and the other apostles set a precedent within the body of using our cumulative resources to take care of everyone within the fellowship, everywhere around the world, "as God has prospered him" (and believe me, those deemed "prosperous" in those days were much more austere in their living than those of us in the West today!). Are you setting aside some of your "prosperity" (even when it doesn't "feel" like you are "prosperous," and you are not even "keeping up with the Joneses") to meet the needs of those in your church, your community, your country, and the world? In the days of famine, this network will be very important for ministering to those both within and outside the fellowship of Christ.

Practical Provisions

Some may have thought, when beginning to read (or considering to read) this chapter, that it would be chock-full of information and suggestions on where to buy food and supplies, go "off grid" and be independent, and even "hole up" away from the dangers and demands of the rest of civilization. To be honest, that type of information can become so quickly dated and somewhat obsolete (in terms of sources, and the best alternatives), that it is best to focus on general suggestions, to initiate a more detailed, personal search by the reader. I should note that I am not a doctor, nutritionist, electrician, safety inspector, professional, state-certified engineer (although I have a Ph.D. in engineering, my expertise is more in line with blowing things up, as opposed to constructing them!), and as such, I should not be considered an expert resource to advise in these areas, at least in detail. However, the Internet (a blessing in our age, if used appropriately) is a good initial source for such expertise, if suitable caution and discretion is used.

First of all, regarding food, I would distinguish between "short-term" and "long-term" food needs. Our own government (the Federal Emergency Management Agency [FEMA] and other agencies) recommends stockpiling up to three to six months of food and water supplies for possible outbreaks of avian bird flu and other emergencies. This recommendation was reiterated by Dr. Melissa Riley, a local county FEMA specialist, on my radio show; for example, she says that bird flu outbreaks may require citizens to stay in their own homes, away from the rest of the public, for up to three to six months until it runs its course (with a high degree of fatalities expected). She also stated that even if you "chance it" and make a run to the grocery store, food shipments into the "infected areas" are expected to be curtailed, and food at the grocery stores will run out within days. If you have a spouse (or parents, in-laws, kids, friends, neighbors, church folk, etc.) who is very reluctant to stockpile food and water supplies, and is concerned you are becoming a "conspiracy theorist" or the next "Unabomber," the government recommendations posted online might give you the credible reference you can cite to them to justify proceeding. These governmental guidelines should be an authoritative source of information for you, and any advice herein should be verified there, or by other credible resources. For example, before the "Y2K" scare a few years ago, various sites recommended making do-it-yourself storable water supplies using clean two-liter bottles, and some sites even recommended using one or two drops of bleach in the water to prevent growth of bacteria. (Health-related information like this should particularly be verified with reputable resources.) In any case, these supplies should be placed in a dry place, secured against vermin infiltration as well as moisture, dampness, and mildew or mold. If supplies can be placed in sealed bags—better yet, in plastic tubs with good, sealable lids—that might protect and preserve them better. Be sure to store them in a place where they can be periodically inspected. Pay particular attention to the shelf life date of food, and be aware that those dates are usually only valid under ideal storage conditions.

Regarding short-term food needs (for three to six months), make sure you:

(a) plan for a sufficient caloric intake for every member of your family;

(b) provide some variety of food—for psychological reasons if no other;

(c) can safely store and use the food both before the crisis and during the length of the event; and

(d) can prepare the food (if needed) using available sources of heating or other means of preparation.

In our family, we plan to have access to a significant stockpile of containers of a powdered, Ensure-type drink mix (designed to be mixed with water—not a dieting variety) as part of our supplies, because it is designed to provide a high-caloric source that is nutritionally rich; it can be stored compactly and easily; it uses water already stored and on hand; it has a long shelf life; and it requires no special heating or preparation. Other sources (including my radio show co-host, "Tom Bionic") recommend storing large quantities of rice and beans, because they have many of the same advantages and are low cost (plus they offer the luxury of chewing!). Further suggestions include adding a little oil (like olive oil) due to its calories, fat, and palatability. Other sources of food are military MREs (Meals Ready to Eat), C-Rations and K-Rations, many of which can be procured from military surplus stores, or other online sources.

Always keep in mind the storage and preparation needs of any particular food. Remember that in days of crisis (both natural and man-made), electricity might be in short supply, so freezing or refrigerating food might be a short-term luxury. If you have these types of foods on hand when a crisis hits, be sure to consume them first, and only as long as you are confident that they are safe to eat. Only keep any food stockpiled as long as you have good evidence to believe that it safe for the food type and storage method used.

As far as cooking options, many campers use a simple Coleman or similar camping stove, at least until their gas runs out (unless they have stockpiled it safely—see the bottle suppliers for recommendations). Similarly, food can be cooked on gas grills (particularly quickly, which can help speed up the preparation and subsequent consumption of the refrigerated and frozen food if electricity is unavailable) until the fuel is gone, but a simple charcoal grill might be more practical, with the ease of storage of charcoal briquettes. In our household, we like a "newspaper grill"—a simple, collapsible, metal tube with a handled grill on top, which is designed to burn wadded-up newspapers and similar material. It is a marvel of invention. The grease drippings from any meat used (or vegetables coated with vegetable oil) keep the fire going, allowing us to cook hamburgers within four or so minutes with a just few sheets of newspaper. This device doesn't need lighter fluid or other starter means, and is handy at home, camping, or tailgating in the meantime. You would be surprised how long an old telephone book, junk mail (finally, a good use for that), newspapers, and other scrap papers last for fuel. (Just don't use "slick" papers, such as some ads, because of the chemicals in them.) These devices, all the rage in the seventies, are listed under names such as "Kwik-Grill," "Safari," and "Arctic Portable Table Top Newspaper Grill." (We purchased ours at www.cajunoutdoorcooking.com.)

Water supply is a subject that should dictate consultation with specialists in this field (and information may be available online or at government resources). One decision you'll need to make is whether to store your water in multiple small containers or large reservoirs. In either case, you should be concerned about bacteria contamination and growth as well as chemical, dirt, or foreign matter contamination. Techniques that address one hazard often do not address the other. Water decontamination filter devices, which use manual hand pumping or other means, are very effective and available from a number of suppliers. Some manufacturers even report that they can make drinking water from sewage water (although I don't recommend trying that!). Remember the old adage—man can go without air for three minutes, water for three days, and food for three weeks. Therefore, don't scrimp on the amount of water you keep on hand! In days of crisis, water shortages may well become a bigger threat than food shortages (certainly on a world geopolitical level). Remember that you should also keep enough water for cooking, bathing, cleaning, and taking care of other sanitary needs. If you suspect that supplies may be imminently shut off (even due to natural disasters such as tornados, hurricanes, or earthquakes), fill any safe containers you have with water until the tap runs dry; you can also fill bathtubs and sinks with water for other uses.

Some energy and heating supplies have already been mentioned, such as kerosene, propane, wood, and even paper debris. The generation of carbon monoxide from these sources is a significant cause of home deaths in wintertime. Be sure to have a carbon dioxide detector in your home, with a battery backup that is tested regularly. Noncombustible sources of heat are best in homes or shelters under the most austere conditions (it's hard to beat body heat from one or more people under a pile of blankets—it worked wonders for the Willy Wonka family!). If you can generate electricity by some means, even by placing a gas-powered electricity generator outside (secured against theft and weather damage), and run electric heaters indoors, that may be a safer solution (if, of course, you follow the safety precautions provided by manufacturers). A well-designed, installed, and maintained wood-burning (or even corn-burning) stove is also obviously a good choice. Any means of generating electricity, such as geothermal, photocells (solar), or wind are excellent options that can save money for you now, and that can save your "neck" later. We might eventually go back to the days of heating stones or "bed warmers" in an outdoor fire and using them to heat our beds. Some of those techniques might be quite nice!

Regarding long-term food supplies (for periods greater than six months), more significant (or draconian) efforts are needed. The obvious solution is to start your own garden if you don't already have one. If you have land, use as much of it as you can, including your front yard, when times get really bad! If you are an apartment dweller or one of many who now have "McMansions" on postage-stamp-sized lots, then you may need to resort to community gardens (a proposed approach is in the next section). This might also be good even for those with their own, ample lots. In these emergencies, choose plants not based on taste or other factors, but on (a) nutritional value, (b) output per given plot of land, (c) resistance to drought, weather, and pests, and (d) ability to grow for multiple seasons without abusing the soil. This supply will be useful if wars, calamities, or other causes curtail the distribution network, but if it stops raining, then drought-resistant foods should be a priority (it is probably a good idea to practice growing such foods now). One should not tarry in at least getting seeds for later use, because widespread proliferation of questionable "genetically modified" food strains and their seeds are tainting our current food supply, and the supply of natural, healthy seeds might even disappear. In addition, the spread of currently manufactured "terminator" seeds, which will not regenerate (and thus require repurchasing seeds from the supplier each year, at their terms), would result in the same predicament as the Egyptian people in Genesis found themselves. Lastly, the use of community gardens, or swapping food with neighbors and friends, permits everyone to share more of a variety of food, possibly grown on plots more conducive to certain types of food. This helps take advantage of the "green thumbs" of the occupants, and is a neighborly, healthy, and wholesome way to enrich each other's lives. (Working the garden will also give many of us some much-needed exercise, as well!)

Regarding long-term water sources, the choices are few: using water from a well, or from natural water streams, rivers, or lakes. In both cases, a considerable issue is the safe use of such water. Numerous resources are available to provide guidance on how to safely use such supplies. If rainfall is still present, captured rainwater (secured by placing and then draining sheets on the roof or the ground) is an option, but the same issues regarding safe usage still apply. New technology is now available to capture water from the humidity in air (at least in small quantities); however, there's still research to be done as far as amount of water it can be reasonably expected to produce, and the possible need for electricity to power the devices.

Long-term energy supplies are most likely to come from solar cells, geothermal devices, or wind. This technology is now available, and government tax credits are often also available to defray some costs. I recommend beginning to tinker with some of these options now, and expand as you gain experience and skill in using them effectively. That way, you can learn what works for you and what doesn't, as new, more efficient, and user-friendly technologies become available. Then, when the crisis really hits, you will have at least some rudimentary capability (which will probably be at least better than your neighbors!), and your level of expertise will grow in the meantime.

Regardless of your food, water, or energy supplies, be aware that if your neighbors or others see you with these provisions, in desperate times you may become a target—even by people you would have otherwise trusted. You may already intend to share your provisions where possible (in fact, as we have seen, the Lord desires that you do), but if you are not careful in how you handle your provisions, your "sharing" might not be on your terms—and your family might suffer as a result. Therefore, I recommend that if the Lord lays on your heart to share your provisions with particular people at that time, do it in a discreet manner, and in a way that does not belie the resources you have wisely prepared in advance—all the while being as generous as the Lord would have you to be. If the Lord prompts you to do something bolder, then be aware of the consequences and trust that He will protect you and provide for you as you obey.

A good website for securing such supplies is the "Survivor Mall" at www.survivormall.com. Operated by Christians, the company offers food supplies, energy, shelter, communications resources, and anything else you might need. The world-famous Deyo family also published a landmark book (telephone-book sized, with everything from "soup" to "nuts") called *Dare to Prepare*, an invaluable resource for virtually every aspect of preparation for emergencies (available at www.standeyo.com). A number of companies that specialize in storable foods, communications, and energy supplies typically advertise on independent radio shows and networks (including web-based)— particularly those with an interest in Bible prophecy. As you shop, just be sure use discernment and ask around for product reviews and feedback from independent sources before you buy. Another excellent source for food, fuel, and even cooking supplies are military surplus stores (for MREs, emergency shelters, and cooking supplies), or camping or outdoor stores.

Positive Opportunities

For all of the discussion in the preceding pages about negative subjects such as crises, tribulation, and suffering, these events can also pose opportunities for the Lord's body to shine and reflect God's glory and love. It has always struck me that the Chinese symbol for "crisis" is the combination of the symbols for "danger" and "opportunity." In days of crisis, as we have discussed, we will have people's attention if we can minister to their basic needs while sharing with them the message God has given us to pronounce.

For example, I don't see why churches of any notable size don't attempt to design and install modern wind turbines, solar panels, or other similar energy generators for their property and facilities. Using such technologies makes sense for a number of reasons:

- Churches of even modest budgets can potentially fund reasonable equipment installation projects, with a return on investment of a few years. (This could be enhanced with special deals on equipment—including purchasing older generations of technology—and installation labor from the suppliers, and even by having such assets donated in whole or in part from companies.)
- The power is only usually needed intermittently for days and hours of worship and daily office use, and could be stored in battery banks or by other means.

- Some of the design, and particularly routine maintenance, could be provided by a team of people at the church who might actually enjoy working with and getting familiar with the technology. (They might even learn enough about it to try out their own systems at home.)
- Churches typically have ample property on their grounds or on their roofs for wind turbines or solar cells.
- Not only could the church defray or eliminate ever-increasing energy costs, it could sell back excess energy to the power company to further assist their budget.
- The church could have emergency power available for parishioners or other community citizens on their grounds in emergency shelter situations.
- This approach would send a message to those outside the church that Christians want to be good caretakers of the earth, and responsible citizens. In fact, publicizing these initiatives in local media, and even offering services such as electric plug stations for hybrid vehicles in church parking areas could cast a positive spotlight on the church. It might help persuade environmentally conscious citizens in the community to overcome any bias or misconceptions they may have about the church and its members and create new ministry opportunities for the church.

This might also open opportunities for Christian entrepreneurs to develop sophisticated design services for churches, a somewhat organized body worldwide. I have learned that secular activists outside the church envy our resources and latent, untapped ability to organize; this would give Christians a chance to take a leadership role in implementing renewable energy technologies.

In a similar vein, churches could use their typically ample grounds to develop congregation and/or community gardens. Such gardens could provide:

- Food for needy families in the church and community anytime
- Food for the entire church family
- A place for youth, those receiving assistance, or others to serve the body in tending the gardens (even those in poor health could shell beans, can or package food, etc.)
- A healthy reason for church members to spend time outdoors, and to help each other
- Access to healthy food
- A testimony of the caring and custodial nature of the local church (and Christ himself) in the community.

Even food co-ops could be established between church members and between churches themselves. They could not only exchange food items, but they could also take the opportunity to mass process food, where prudent. This process could be expanded to other "mini-economies" developed between churches, including the exchange of skilled labor and other assets. Furthermore, Christian investors could invest and manage such projects in a biblical, honorable way, without being muddied by the materialism and low morality of Wall Street and the financial world.

These possibilities get us back to developing an internal support structure within the body and communities that could circumvent the state (where possible) and the Babylon financial system—coming back full circle to the focus of our discussion. Much of this capability is in our hands, if we choose to grasp it. It will create a long-lost freedom and a dependence on God that we have lost as a society over the last few generations. (We are the weaker and less spiritual because of it.) To make the point that the Lord intended us to be free, let's look at just a few of the biblical passages that discuss our freedom:

"[Is] not this the fast that I have chosen? to loose the bands of wickedness, to undo the heavy burdens, and to let the oppressed go free, and that ye break every yoke?" (Isaiah 58:6)

"Therefore the word of the LORD came to Jeremiah from the LORD, saying, Thus saith the LORD, the God of Israel; I made a covenant with your fathers in the day that I brought them forth out of the land of Egypt, out of the house of bond-men, saying, At the end of seven years let ye go every man his brother an Hebrew, which hath been sold unto thee; and when he hath served thee six years, thou shalt let him go free from thee: but your fathers hearkened not unto me, neither inclined their ear. And ye were now turned, and had done right in my sight, in proclaiming liberty every man to his neighbour; and ye had made a covenant before me in the house which is called by my name: But ye turned and polluted my name, and caused every man his servant, and every man his handmaid, whom ye had set at liberty at their pleasure, to return, and brought them into subjection, to be unto you for servants and for handmaids. Therefore thus saith the LORD; Ye have not hearkened unto me, in proclaiming liberty, every one to his brother, and every man to his neighbour: behold, I proclaim a liberty for you, saith the LORD, to the sword, to the pestilence, and to the famine; and I will make you to be removed into all the king-doms of the earth." (Jeremiah 34:12–17)

"And ye shall know the truth, and the truth shall make you free." (John 8:32)

"If the Son therefore shall make you free, ye shall be free indeed." (John 8:36)

"Being then made free from sin, ye became the servants of righteousness. For when ye were the servants of sin, ye were free from righteousness. But now being made free from sin, and become servants to God, ye have your fruit unto holiness, and the end everlasting life." (Romans 6:18, 20, 22)

"For the law of the Spirit of life in Christ Jesus hath made me free from the law of sin and death." (Romans 8:2)

"Art thou called [being] a servant? care not for it: but if thou mayest be made free, use [it] rather. For he that is called in the Lord, [being] a servant, is the Lord's freeman: likewise also he that is called, [being] free, is Christ's servant. Ye are bought with a price; be not ye the servants of men." (1 Corinthians 7:21–23)

"For though I be free from all [men], yet have I made myself servant unto all, that I might gain the more." (1 Corinthians 9:19)

"Stand fast therefore in the liberty wherewith Christ hath made us free, and be not entangled again with the yoke of bondage." (Galations 5:1)

"For so is the will of God, that with well doing ye may put to silence the ignorance of foolish men: As free, and not using [your] liberty for a cloak of maliciousness, but as the servants of God." (1 Peter 2:15, 16)

Conclusion

This study has shown the current, real-world developments now underway that will create dire shortages in food, water, and energy, and even more so in the near future. The historical causes and outcomes of such famines and shortages, including major shifts in society and world demographics, were discussed. The impact that famines and shortages had in historical Bible times was explored, including the very important example in Egypt with Joseph in some detail, and how it set the precedent for the enslaving effects of food and other critical resource shortages, for millennia to come. The potential prophetic implications of such developments, in facilitating an imminent end-times scenario as expressed in the Bible, was discussed in depth, including an examination of detailed passages regarding the nature of the exploitation of the world's resources by evil powers and their earthly institutions, as well as their eventual destruction, with lessons learned from these narratives. A number of various admonitions from Scripture regarding famines, God's economy in using them, and the proper response of God's people, were briefly examined. Practical provisions concerning food, water, and energy sources, for both short-term and long-term needs, and the issues at play in making proper preparations were briefly investigated, as well as positive opportunities for such crises to enable God's people to be a blessing to others. All of these aspects point to our need to prepare, but ultimately to rely upon our Heavenly Father and live as free men, dependent only upon His matchless care.

—

J. Michael Bennett, Ph.D., is a successful entrepreneur and researcher in aerospace safety and fire protection technology development, with a doctorate in mechanical engineering. His analyses are heard worldwide on the "Future Quake" radio program he produces and hosts. Dr. Bennett recently served as a keynote speaker at a United Nations-sponsored conference on religion and spirituality.

Collapse of Financial Institutions

---

by Wilfred Hahn

The title of this chapter will immediately resonate with any reader living in the Western world. During the great systemic financial crisis of 2007 through 2009—one that may well yet continue for some time—many financial institutions around the world had already either collapsed, disappeared, or required a government bailout. Shockingly, some of these were very large and recognizable companies with global franchises, such as Lehman Brothers, Bear Stearns, and AIG. Other troubled entities were swallowed up or merged, including such major well-known firms as Merrill Lynch—bought by Bank of America—or Wachovia Bank, which was snapped up by Wells Fargo.

Many other financial institutions were threatened with collapse, or indeed did collapse. Such venerable companies as Morgan Stanley, UBS, and Salomon Brothers ran hat in hand to various sovereign wealth funds (SWFs) or governments for emergency funding. But the very largest financial companies—those deemed too big to fail—were propped up by governments. Here, such global juggernauts as Citigroup, ING, the insurance colossus AIG, the United Kingdom-based Fortis, and the Royal Bank of Scotland (once the king of British banks) required government investment to keep afloat.

As never before, a virtual financial storm ripped through the world's financial securities and credit markets, shaking the infrastructure of mankind's money systems to the very foundation. Every type of financial institution was touched, from banks to insurers, brokers, hedge funds, pensions, central banks, and SWFs. We can hardly attempt to completely recount the many rescued or folded financial institutions during this period. Without a doubt, it was an unprecedented financial debacle; it was more complex and potentially lethal than even the disastrous financial conditions of the 1930s.

Yet, despite the epic scale of the crisis, as of yet, the world's financial system still stands. This is a significant point, though it may be obvious. While the global financial edifice may still be quivering and parts of it greatly weakened or collapsed, these international systems remain operative. This system is not yet at an end, but rather is experiencing a transition. But a transition to what? It is critical to understand the answer to this question, whether or not you are a Christian. However, crucially for Christians, there are added and urgent perspectives to understand: where these worldly developments intersect with faith, affections of the soul, and eternal hopes. This saga and its challenges to Christians, as we will explain, are much different than popularly thought. It is not the collapse of global financial institutions, but rather their continued enmeshing of human affairs that is the greater threat. The challenge does not primarily center upon financial gains and losses or the basic task of stewardship, but instead upon the vulnerability to materialistic entrapment and idolatry, especially during these last days. Without such a perspective on end-time global financial developments, one is at great risk of falling for the "cares of this world" (Mark 4:19) and being weighed "down with dissipation, drunkenness and the anxieties of life, and that day will close on you unexpectedly like a trap" (Luke 21:34).

Still a Future Global Role for Financial Institutions

The final chapter on global financial collapse has yet to be written. As the Bible reveals, the great final demise—this likely being a series of events, but definitely ending in total collapse—is yet future. The complete and final collapse of global commercial systems occurs in the latter half of the Tribulation period, most likely spanning periods of the sixth and seventh seal judgments described in Revelation Chapters 6–16. Until that fated time, the role of financial institutions—arrayed as they are in their global networked architecture—plays a significant and necessary role in end-time processes. Not only are these developments utilized for the capture and materialistic enslavement of unsuspecting mankind, but also to provide a facilitating foundation to humanism. With such global solidarity and prosperity possible through mankind's global economic and financial systems, who would search for a heaven anywhere else than on earth, or think that God still sits on His throne? That said, financial and economic crises such as have occurred in recent years should surely cause people to think twice before putting their full faith and hope in mankind's systems.

Looking behind the rather formidable complexity of financial markets and systems, we realize that the real essence behind global financial trends are essentially spiritual issues (what is not seen) and the affections of the human heart. The financial systems themselves cannot be blamed for disaster or hardships. After all, this must be the case as systems and machinery are amoral. They are incapable of either moral or immoral behavior. It is people who infuse them with intent and application. As the saying goes, it is people who kill people—not machines and oppressive systems. It is the affections of gain, comfort, and convenience, the emotions of greed and fear, that help build this monstrous, world-controlling edifice of financial tentacles.

Given that the topic of financial institutions cannot really be disentangled from matters of the human heart concerning issues of faith and confidence—we must not lose ourselves in the technical detail of this global siege machinery of financial systems. As such, in our discussions of the roles of financial institutions, we must emphasize the human heart and not inanimate systems and dry financial theory. The reader will be pleased to know that we will not delve into complex financial terminology—monetarism, fractional reserve banking systems[457] of international trade law and policy, and so on. At their very core, financial markets and their participants, whether individuals or institutions, are driven by human impulses, as we will examine.

Global financial systems are made up of financial institutions, both privately owned or sponsored by individual countries or groups. These would certainly include central banks. Almost all countries today have one these days, all of them based on the same corrupting doctrine of fractional-reserve banking. Also included in this list of institutions would be such global organizations as the International Monetary Fund (IMF) or the Bank of International Settlements (BIS), which either coordinate financial activities globally or determine policy, not to mention a myriad of private companies that are involved in various types of financial services or activities. This latter group is made up of small and large companies, some perhaps only one-city credit unions while the operations of others can span one hundred countries and more. They may be active in insurance, banking, investments, or leasing—anything to do with trading or claims on money and credit. All of these entities are interconnected through trading markets, making up the totality of the global financial system. Uppermost, one must not forget that these systems are devised and commandeered by humans, from enterprising business executives to experts in greed.

Taken together, the involvement of these financial institutions in the everyday activities of humans has continued to grow leaps and bounds. The invasion of modern money has been rapid, if not near complete. It is a perspective that few in our modern age can fully fathom. Living inside the fishbowl, most people don't realize it is full of water. We are so accustomed to conditions and conveniences of our times that we do not realize how different they are from the past—how institutionalized materialism and idolatry have become in our times. According to this author's calculations, total global financial obligations at the end of 2007 were at a level fifteen times the annual economic output of the entire world ($818 trillion measured in U.S. dollar equivalents).[458] Here, we are tabulating figures that necessarily involve financial institutions. If that were not so, these statistics would neither be available nor possible. What we see, reviewing this data, is a virtual explosion in financial position values in recent years and decades, catapulting upwards by a factor of sixty-five times from twenty-five years earlier (adjusted for population growth during that period).[459]

Twenty-five years earlier, financialization (the process of expressing human activities into forms of money)[460] was at a much lower level. We could employ a number of statistical definitions to track this trend. Suffice it to say that financialization then was less than a third of today's intensity. Even earlier, the intrusion of financial institutions and their services was much lower still. Viewed differently, today probably as much as 80 percent of human activity in the Western world is already counted or logged through a financial transaction (this being a different component than the financialization trend of the previous twenty-five years). Seen over the course of the past two centuries, that represents at least a tripling of the role of money in the lives of humans, not to mention the cumulative piling up of financial obligations.

It therefore goes without saying that the financial institutions have been a growth industry. This sector in recent decades, before recent reversals, became the largest industry in the world by market value— larger even than the energy sector. At one point, financial industries accounted for greater than 40 percent of total corporate profits (2002) in the United States and other countries. Imagine! How is it that the business of money changing could make so much money? It really did not make sense as this industry was not making a commensurate contribution to world's productivity and quality of life. Much of the profits were illusory, as became painfully evident during the later crisis period. But such is the power and potential alchemy of this industry viewed collectively.

While profits will surely have declined significantly during the financial downturn of recent years, we can be reasonably sure that the role of financial institutions in world affairs will not diminish. It might be more regulated following recent financial catastrophes, but it will remain the most powerful industry in the world. If anything, its global grip upon human affairs will only tighten and consolidate as a result of recent events.

Hallmarks of the Recent Global Financial Crisis

Of what purpose is the recent booming development of a great globalized network of financial institutions that we see today? As we already reviewed, its invasiveness to all of human life, to the entire globe, is without precedent. But why? No other system on earth could be constructed with such capabilities of control that transcend peoples, cultures, and nations. Without a doubt, it must have a very important end-time role. But before we describe this function, it will help to first review the forces and issues that were (and still are) at play in the most recent world financial crises.

Looking back, the catastrophic financial crisis of 2007–2009 was clearly a global phenomenon; most certainly, it was the biggest globally interconnected crisis ever. It would be impossible to provide an accurate tally of the market losses and costs of government interventions, whether to undergird financial institutions, protect private depositors, or provide stimulus to credit-shocked economies. However, the scale of these costs is instructive. The bill for the world's latest financial crisis could yet amount to the equivalent of 20–30 percent and more of annual world economic output—perhaps $15 trillion and greater. Most probably, the battle against global systemic collapse will end up costing in excess of any known world war in history.

To illustrate in the case of the United States—still the world's largest economy—consider that its involvement in World War II is estimated to have cost $3.6 trillion (inflation-adjusted to 2008 dollars). By comparison, total U.S. financial interventions of all types had already risen to a total exceeding $5 trillion by the end of 2008. This is equivalent to approximately 35 percent of recent annualized U.S. economic output. While it is expected that significant portions of these government guarantees and expenditures will be recovered, America's financial crisis is far from over. Its full economic fallout has yet to be fully determined. Some of the more extreme doomsayers predict that America alone will require the equivalent of $8 to $10 million in interventions. No doubt, the scale of these figures are stupendous.

The Psychology of Crisis

As we have already mentioned, despite the savagery of the financial storm of recent years, the world's financial system has not collapsed. Though the scale and rapidity of the crisis was unprecedented in history, to date the interventions of the world's leaders and authorities have managed to prevent total demise. Actually, it is partly because of the great government interventions around the world that global economic collapse has not occurred. It is these reactions on the part of policymakers and their role in establishing the nature of global financial systems that we wish to examine further.

The severity of the financial collapses prompted the interventions of policymakers in the first place. At this point, it might begin to seem somewhat circuitous that the crises themselves prompt interventions to further prevent them. But it's actually not. This is precisely how mankind has propelled itself up the slope of globalism. It is the fears and irrational expectations of emotional humans that push up globalism's slope. This is an important process to understand, beginning with the individual.

The carnal Homo sapien, driven by his or her basic impulses—"the lust of the flesh, and the lust of the eyes, and the pride of life" (1 John 2:16)—is to an extent facilitated by prewired neurological programming. In other words, it is the innate sinful nature of man that responds behaviorally to expectations and wants. At this level, the goals of natural man are quite basic—namely, the pursuit of pleasure and the avoidance of displeasure. Viewed in the great arena of monetary finance and economies, unsustainable economic excesses driven by unbridled greed and wants lead to conditions where threatening economic downturns generate avoidance behavior. This process is evident both at the individual and societal levels.

But, it is the "official" interventions that we want to focus upon in our examination of the role of financial institutions. Today, we live in an age when government intervention is considered a developed science. Policymakers and voters alike have come to believe that prosperity is an inviolable right and that it can be fabricated without any accountability to morality or behavior. No matter what might have occurred in the past—whether excesses, corruption, manias, organized deceptions, or national sins—a new period of prosperity can always be coaxed out of the magician's hat by its policy-making wizards. Prosperity is always ahead, never to be restrained by past sins, whether or not past wrongs have been righted or restitution paid.

When Global Policymakers Know Best

A recent comment by Paul Volcker captures the times: "Fortunately, there is also good reason to believe that the means are now available to turn the tide. Financial authorities, in the United States and elsewhere, are now in a position to take needed and convincing action to stabilize markets and to restore trust...the point is the needed tools to restore and maintain functioning markets are there." [461] The octogenarian Mr. Volcker is highly respected, given his firm stewardship of America's monetary affairs as chairman of the Federal Reserve Board between 1979 and 1987. While he certainly does not ignore the fact that it will take time to clean up the financial mess of recent years, his comments reflect the consensus of policymakers that governments today can fix any problem.

Few politicians are elected on the promise of delivering tough times to their constituents. Therefore, the fear of a very large, horrible financial meltdown or economic travails will trigger a very large intervention on the part of authorities. A smaller threat, on the other hand, may generate no response at all. The point being made here is that a crisis must be threatening enough to prompt an official government response and to be more easily accepted by the populace, especially when interventions may infringe upon freedoms.

Following a crisis, when the memories of previous fears and the sting of losses are still very fresh, policymakers collaborate to institute changes that will forevermore ensure that their country—or indeed, the entire world—will never again experience such a crisis. These may include new government spending programs, new laws or financial regulations, and new agencies with responsibilities as deemed necessary. Once these changes are made, society takes comfort from these changes, soon thinking that financial systems and economies will be invulnerable to similar disasters in the future.

However, in time, greed, unrealistic expectations, and complacency born of new confidence lead to another crisis. The important aspect of this repetitive and rotating cycle between human hubris and insecurity is that each new crisis must by definition be seen as greater and more unprecedented. If this were not the case, new interventions likely would not be seen as necessary. On balance, each round brings intervention and policy to new levels. Seen in the big picture, a progressive process is at work leading to ever more organized control and intervention. In the global arena, these same trends lead to heightened globalism and globalization.

The complacency and confidence born of past changes to "crisis-proof" financial markets and economies themselves often lead to the greater excesses. To illustrate, consider the great changes that took place as a result of the Great Depression of the 1930s. The hardships experienced during that time were the catalysts to deficit spending by governments, new central banking practices, and government-sponsored mortgage agencies. In time, the confidence put into these actions and new institutions led to even greater excesses. Mortgage debt over the following decades began to grow relative to household incomes (eventually exploding upwards in 2001 to 2005), central bankers were seen to become gods of wealth who reputedly could spin riches from nothing, and the large role of government spending came to be thought of as the shock-absorbing bedrock of continued economic prosperity.

Most of the twists and turns of modern financial history can be explained in this way. Human confidence builds, leading to a boom, only to falter due to the unsustainable dynamics of a false prosperity, which then leads to a panic stage. National governments and global agencies bring in restorative changes and central bankers steer a new, supposedly better course. In time, confidence again begins to build. The cycle repeats. In fact, to this point in history, countless financial and economic crises have occurred. Some have been local affairs limited to one country. Others have engulfed many nations or the entire world. According to the authors of one report from the IMF, as many as 124 systemic banking crises alone occurred between 1970 and 2007.[462]

Evidently then, crises play a regular role in the affairs of mankind and should not be viewed as a surprise when they do occur. Most people, of course, have no idea that this is the case, thinking them complete accidents. It is therefore no wonder that the world's wealth skew continues to widen. The rich become wealthier and the poor less wealthy in relative terms. The average person has little chance to keep abreast of these macro, global developments, and are not wise to the dynamics of fear and greed. As such, many become unwitting casualties.

The point is that crises are catalysts to organized changes, in fact, to a progression of changes. Nowhere do we see this more clearly than on a global level. The world's path to greater globalism and globalization has been driven forward by crises. These have usually, but not exclusively, been of financial origin. The aftermath of major wars, for example, has quickened mankind's resolve to coordinate global peace. Mostly, these initiatives (consider the formation of the League of Nations—the forerunner to the United Nations—the World Bank, the International Monetary Fund, etc.) sought to further peace by promoting global prosperity. Sometimes, two steps back have occurred, but generally two steps forward have unfolded for every one step back. Nevertheless, over time, mankind has proceeded to a greater, more centralized network of global financial institutions.

No Global Change without Sufficient Pain

The scale of crisis must be world threatening before a global consensus will be sufficient to enact changes. Consider some of the ideas that were proposed to address world financial instabilities following the Asian crisis of 1997–1998. It proved to be a major crisis that had destabilizing knock-on effects on all financial markets around the world. At the time, a number of Asian countries succumbed to some steep financial and economic declines. Russia's markets also collapsed. The World Bank and the International Monetary Fund were called upon to extend enormous bailout and emergency financing programs at that time. All in all, the crisis was chilling enough that many new initiatives were suggested to "fix the global financial architecture." A United Nations (UN) report[463] on this subject listed the following proposals:

The creation of a world financial authority. This institution would set policies for all financial institutions in the world;

An establishment of an international credit insurance corporation;

Exchange rate system reform, the most radical initiative proposed here being the adoption adopt of a single world currency, issued by a world monetary authority.

Other initiatives were also mentioned. Virtually all pointed in the same direction—towards an increasingly centralized, global financial system. What then happened? Actually, nothing. None of these remedies was further pursued by either regulators or global organizations. Why? The previous crisis subsided too quickly. Before the global architecture of financial systems could be amended and ostensibly improved, a new world financial bubble was underway. Soaring financial markets soon rendered these solutions no longer urgent or necessary. In any case, it is not easy to develop global consensus on such changes when some large countries or a superpower wishes to scuttle such efforts out of self interest.

Clearly the severity of the threat of breakdown to the financial system and world trade structures must be great enough. Why? It produces the urgency for action and the imperative for global cooperation.

But, even more, a serious crisis provides license for more urgent and inventive responses on the part of governments and authorities. It creates the moral imperative to break previous conventions, regulations and laws. These must be brushed aside (sometimes illegally or without proper constitutional process) in the name of the higher objective—the perceived common good of preventing total economic collapse and to seek the benefits of a greater ship—the global economy and its financial system.

This was evident during the American financial meltdowns of 2007 to 2009. The U.S. Treasury and the central bank needed to respond quickly and imaginatively. Facing the harrowing time pressures of financial firefighting, decisions needed to be made quickly. There was little time for debate. In fact, if anything, time delays due to the congressional or Senate reviews of major new rescue initiatives only seemed to trigger further financial market declines. As such, many groundbreaking and unprecedented actions took place, legitimized by nothing more than perceived urgency. The U.S. taxpayer and future generations were involuntarily conscripted to take on enormous risks and crippling government debt levels.

Behind the cover of crisis, arbitrary decisions were made as to which financial institutions to save and which to let collapse. Not surprisingly, decision-makers chose to prop up the financial institutions that were the most "systemically" significant. In other words, the financial institutions that were the largest and the most globally intertwined attracted the greatest priorities of policymakers. Firms that were key cornerstones to global financial structures such as the hyper-growth derivatives markets could not be allowed to collapse. For example, to have allowed Royal Bank of Scotland or Citigroup to fail would surely have brought the world to the brink of an even greater economic disaster. Both of these companies had considerable global operations. Smaller financial companies, on the other hand, were allowed to founder on the rocks, to be snapped up by larger companies or be closed.

Without a doubt, the global landscape of major financial institutions has changed radically in the Western world over recent decades, and much of this change has been driven by the rotating imperatives of greed and the staving off of crisis. By either means, a nefarious bias can be seen working behind these actions. The world's web of financial institutions continues to consolidate, giving more power to an ever smaller group of institutions and their executives. The structure of a global financial system is shifting to one of ever greater centralization and global interconnectedness. Financial institutions therefore are becoming consolidated into a smaller group of globally significant entities.

A similar trend has already occurred in other industries, particularly producers of commodities such as hydrocarbon fuels (think of the five sisters: Shell, Exxon Mobil, Chevron, Saudi Aramco, and National Iranian Oil) or the global news business where fewer than three agencies are the source of more than 80 percent of news feeds. Financial conglomerates are becoming ever larger and financial systems ever more invasive. Today, the fifty largest financial corporations in the world represent well over one third of total world banking assets. Interestingly, as a group they are the most internationalized of the world's transnational corporations (TNCs), thirty-four of these fifty largest companies being headquartered in Europe.[464]

Increasing Global Snare of Global Financial Institutions

Our brief review of the forces at work, both before and throughout the previous global financial crises, reveal a longer-running trend. Though financial consolidation is certainly occurring more rapidly than ever before in recent times, the major financial institutions of the world had already been marching to a similar drummer for a long, long time. The traces of these trends of convergence were already observable hundreds of years ago. Recent financial troubles are merely the latest chapter in a saga towards increasing globalization and worldwide commercial interconnectedness. What is different is that these processes are gaining greater speed in recent times.

Globalization and globalism are old ideas though these words were only invented in the last century. Actually, these developments and their connections to money and commercialism are clearly prophesied in the Bible. To no surprise, many secular thinkers have long theorized that the road to peace and salvation for mankind is through the stomach and the pocketbook. Give everyone a warm bowl of soup and earthly economic security, and mankind will then prove to be agreeable, accepting peace, convergence, and contentment with prosperity.

Some Christian writers saw globalization developing hundreds of years ago, clearly connecting it with Bible prophecy. For example, consider the writings of Benjamin Wills Newton in 1841:

> When the ruin of one involves the danger of all, men in such circumstances become wonderfully careful of each other's interests. This is the kind of dependence into which nations are being brought, one on the other. Inhabitants of the commercial nations are interested in the maintenance of order and tranquility in their own countries (for commerce diffuses wealth, and gives to millions an interest in the prosperity of the common weal, which they never had before). But when the wealth of one nation becomes closely tied to the undertakings of another, or when one nation lives by selling to another, they become dependent on each other, and soon becoming aware of their mutual dependency, they understand that common interests involve common prosperity or common ruin.[465]

Other secular philosophers waxed prophetically in their own right, anticipating that a day would arrive in the distant future where financial and economic systems would prove the common basis to unite all mankind. Philosopher Jean Baptiste Say thought that "...the theory of markets will necessarily scatter the seeds of concord and peace."[466] Richard Cobden, who was behind the famous Corn Laws of the 1800s in Britain, was reported to have said: "The progress of freedom depends more upon the maintenance of peace, the spread of commerce, and the diffusion of education, than upon the labors of cabinets and foreign offices." These observers clearly saw that global commerce would be the common platform and interest that would draw all nations together. Of course, for global commerce to work, it must have a global financial system comprised of financial institutions.

Many other voices proclaimed commerce and trade as the sinecure to mankind's ails much earlier. Perhaps most eloquent was Alfred Tennyson's call for a global "parliament of man" in his famous poem published in 1846, Locksley Hall.

> For I dipt into the future, far as human eye could see,
> Saw the Vision of the world, and all the wonder that
> would be:
> Saw the heavens fill with commerce, argosies of magic
> sails,
> Pilots of the purple twilight, dropping down with costly
> bales...
> Till the war-drum throb'd no longer, and the battle flags
> were furl'd
> In the parliament of man, the Federation of the World.
> There the common sense of most shall hold a fretful
> realm in awe,
> And the kindly earth shall slumber, lapt in universal law.

Though the details of recent financial debacles are fresh and new, we can recognize the impulses of old history lurking in the background. Crises born of mankind's actions must be seen as part of an ancient progression—mankind's ostensible assent to self-determination and humanism. The emotional firestorms of crises act as catalysts for change and the construction of mankind's one common argosy—the global vessel of globalized commerce, mankind's general path to global collectivism. In this connection, worldwide financial systems and economic globalization play an essential role. While the innate human impulses of fear and greed play facilitating roles, it is crisis that breaks inertia and hastens new solutions.

What Role Financial Institutions

But just what do the financial institutions have to do with mankind's destiny? Of what significance are these financial trends to Christians, if at all? We have already concluded how ideally suited financial systems are to controlling all peoples of the world. We can further assert that it would not be possible for the conspirator against the glory of the Creator and Savior—the Antichrist spirit, Satan—to apply his earthly deceptions and human captivity to his plans without such commercial structures. It simply could not be accomplished by a being that cannot be omnipresent—everywhere simultaneously, as only God. There is no better and effective means on earth to control and coordinate the actions of all human beings than through a common financial and global trade systems. Can you think of one?

Indeed, the invasion of modern-day money has been rapid. The state long ago took over control of money and credit, determining their value and operation by virtual fiat. Money has become a controlled (or more aptly, a manipulated) medium, not only nationally but also globally within a very short space of human history. Through means of central and fractional-reserve banking,[467] the money has become the world's most controlling and invasive medium. We are surely only offering a very abbreviated perspective on the devices and structures of world money systems. Other resources written by the author provide a detailed explanation of the underlying processes and mechanisms. Suffice it to conclude that in the man-created order, there can be nothing else as powerful, as ubiquitous, as omnipresent, as manipulative, and as controlling as the system of modern monetarism. It is not without reason that the Bible contrasts God and money, as it is only the systematic idolatry of money (mammon) that can approach the omnipresence and power of God on earth. However, the former, of course, doesn't lead to heaven. As Jesus Christ clearly warned: "No man can serve two masters; for either he will hate the one, and love the other; or else he will hold to the one, and despise the other. Ye cannot serve God and mammon" (Matthew 6:24). Sadly, the big lie being perpetrated in much of organized Christianity today is that one can serve both. It is not possible and therefore explains why the major religion in the world today is mammonism.

Cosmic Significance: Elements Behind an End-Time Economic Snare

Why is it that after many millennia of human existence, world finan cial developments have exponentially boomed so suddenly? We could seek to document all of the contributing streams to the financial flood of recent history—perhaps examine the impact of fractional reserve banking begun in Holland in the fifteenth century, the critical and necessary technological inventions at various times, the philosophical and religious groundswells that gave foment to capitalism, or Anglo-balization.[468] Doing so, we would find many contributing tributaries. More financial wealth was created (whether representing real wealth or not) in the twentieth century than in the previous nineteen centuries combined. Yet, the questions remain mostly unanswered: Why after thousands of years of glacial change should such a materialistic phe-nomenon erupt upon the world stage in such a short space of time of only several centuries? Why didn't it happen earlier...or later? Could it be part of the plan of the cosmos?

Scripture provides some answers. For those living in the West—in the United States, Canada, in Europe, or Australia, for example—who have been born into this post-modern era, they are likely so thoroughly inculcated into the corrupt and idolatrous values and philosophies of our times that they will not recognize the dangerous foundations upon which our societies rest, nor identify the spiritual and cosmic signifi-cance of the trends discussed here.

Bible readers who understand things of the end (eschatology) know that an economic and financial control structure takes form on earth (pictured in great detail in Revelation 13 and 18); a boom in (false) wealth takes place (James 5:3); and an elite group of wealthy complici-tors emerges (Daniel 11:39)—even as a greater part of humanity become entrapped slaves. All these processes, though perhaps not yet complete, are clearly observable today. Much worse manifestations occur in the Tribulation period itself.

Consider that the global trend of financialization is the bedrock—the very seedbed—of the end-time power structure that underpins the last-day ecumenicism and rulership of the final false prophet and Antichrist, respectively. Remember that it is the false prophet who brings in the commercial initiative so that no one could buy or sell without the mark (Revelation 13:17). It is the trends of globalization, globalism, financialization, corporatization, etc.—all of which are interrelated—that provide the sinew and connectedness of a last-day world that has staked its hopes and faith upon the common commercialism of mankind. It is a structure that can only be strung together with financial institutions.

The main constructs of the cosmos that begin to answer our question were already foreshadowed in the opening chapters of the Bible. The account of Adam and Eve in Eden found in Genesis forewarns how mankind could be deceived by three main temptations. It foreshadows how at the end of days, humanity could be duped into receiving a ruler that comes in the name of the world—a false Christ—settling for a cheapened heaven on earth and willingly opening themselves to economic ensnarement.

At that time, the majority of people on earth—the *modus operandi* of the world—would do exactly what the apostle John counseled against: "Love not the world, neither the things that are in the world. If any man love the world, the love of the Father is not in him. For all that is in the world, the lust of the flesh, and the lust of the eyes, and the pride of life, is not of the Father, but is of the world [mammon]" (1 John 2:15–16). Mentioned here are the three main temptations of the world: lust of the flesh, lust of the eyes, and boasting of what we have and do. Mankind's fall into sin in the Garden of Eden involved all three. The forbidden fruit was good for food (the lust of the flesh); Adam and Eve wanted dominion over the tree (the lust of the eyes)— the very thing they were not to covet; and they fell for "knowledge," the key to self-determination (boasting).

Preying on Three Human Weaknesses

Prophetically, the three temptations reviewed can be seen at work in the world globally today as never before. Satan himself is working these human weaknesses to maximum advantage. Tactically, he targeted the same three innate vulnerabilities when testing Christ in the wilderness. In Matthew 4 and Luke 4 we find the accounts of how Jesus was led by the Holy Spirit into the wilderness, where He fasted for forty days. At the end of the fast, Satan, sensing an opportune moment, approached Christ with three proposals. As Christ was both man and God, sharing in all of the sufferings and temptations known to mankind, Satan targeted these three greatest vulnerabilities of Jesus' humanity.

In a sense, Christ's trial was prophetic. While He resisted all three proposals, He would know that Satan would target these same three vulnerabilities in order to mislead an end-time, apostate world. Through these worldly affections—harbored in the hearts of every human—mankind would be ensnared into a diabolical end-time plan as complicitors, unwitting pawns, captives or the suppressed. The world continues its headlong run into financialization, a process that assigns a monetary value or transaction to an ever greater share of human activities.

Headlong into a Spreading Money Snare

Now that the contagion of financial crisis has again deeply rocked the entire world, the calls for greater global coordination are becoming shrill. That governments must step in and that intervention is required stimulates hardly any debate. Says an economist on a prominent policy site, "It is now commonly agreed that the global financial system and its architecture require major improvements in the designing of regulation, in the assessment of systemic risk and in the global coordination of action before and during crisis."[469]

Not only are changes to be organized around the globe, some high-profile voices argue that there is less risk making large shifts than too little. Says Lawrence Summers (head of the White House National Economic

Council), "In this crisis, doing too little poses a greater threat than doing too much."[470]

With that prior mindset, many politicians are prescribing ground-breaking actions. For example, Miguel Angel Ordonez, Bank of Spain's governor, said, "We've got to get together on both sides of the Atlantic. It is absolutely essential to co-ordinate everything, including monetary policy."[471]

According to a global financial analyst, "A global conference along the lines of Bretton Woods under a respected chairman must be convened. It would bring together all the major players including the vital creditor nations—China, Japan...etc.—to develop a framework for the major economic reforms to work towards a resolution of the crisis."[472]

To that end, new world meeting forums have been planned. The heads of state for Britain and France organized support for their global plans at a special European Union summit. G20 (Group of 20) meetings first scheduled to take place in Washington will be followed by a second one scheduled in Paris. Some geopolitical analysts are encouraged by the spirit of multipolarism that is apparently galvanizing a new participative spirit for these meetings.

All in all, what appeared as global disorder at times of near-fatal financial collapse actually is a catalyst in the rapid metamorphosis to further global integration of financial systems and its institutions. Roger Altman, former U.S. deputy Treasury secretary, said, "Much of the world is turning a historic corner and heading into a period in which the role of the state will be larger and that of the private sector will be smaller."[473]

There assuredly is a broad consensus now that a group of nations needs to come together to find economic and financial solutions for the world. How many nations? Some argue that twenty is too many and others that the G7 (Group of 7) is not enough. Could a group of ten emerge? Without a doubt, a group of ten kings (leaders or heads of state) will come together. In Daniel 2:41–42, we see that an end-time "power coalition" of ten kings that is portrayed as ten toes. In that chapter we read the account of Nebuchadnezzar's famous vision, in which he saw a tall statue made of various materials, from a head of gold down to ten toes of iron and clay. This vision outlined the future kingdoms and power structures of the Gentiles, right to the time of the return of Jesus Christ, when He establishes his millennial reign upon earth. These ten kings are shown at least four other times in the Bible: Daniel 7, Revelation 12, 13, and 17. This group is referenced as ten horns, ten toes or ten kings, exactly ten times.

At present, radical reforms have been recommended by the G20, touching upon virtually all global agencies from the Bank of International Settlements to the International Monetary Fund and many others. But will any of these reforms actually be carried out this time? We think yes, since the degree of crisis this time around has been so severe and debilitating. A second reason is that the world is moving to a multipolar state, meaning an arrangement in which groups of countries—rather than one or two superpowers—determine global policy. Says Roger Altman, quoted earlier, "The economic collapse of 2008, the worst in seventy-five years, is a major geopolitical setback for the West. It has stripped Washington and European governments of the resources and credibility they need to maintain their roles in global affairs."[474]

Indeed, seventy-five years have seen much change already in this direction, certainly with respect to the distribution of global power. For one, the collective influence of the United States and other major high-income countries has diminished. For the first time in history, such countries as China and Brazil have been invited to G20 meetings.

One More Last-Day Boom?

If the Lord tarries, it is likely the world will yet see at least one more economic recovery—or at least a manipulated image of recovery. Conceivably, many more cycles may be yet ahead. Frankly, we cannot know the future with precise certainty. However, there must at least be one more global economic recovery to bring about the prophesied end-time conditions that the Bible outlines. But could a recovery really rise out the economic ashes of 2009? Viewed with the recent specter of financial wreckage fresh in our minds, this seems so implausible, even bordering on the ridiculous. But, in fact, a global economic boom could yet occur. Monetary authorities and government policymakers do indeed have the means to create a temporary recovery, though not a lasting, stable prosperity. We do not need to anticipate anything more than another monetarily induced, bubble-type prosperity.

Bible prophecy indicates that a time is ahead when the world will feel much more complacent than we see today. If past trends are any guide, we should expect the next economic boom to be world scale, enveloping all nations and ever more firmly entrenching mankind in the last-day money snare—the systemic Babylonian colossus of Bible prophecy. It could be argued that more than 60 percent of the world's population is yet only marginally participating in the world's emerging commercial structure. While there have been great strides to date in this respect, much more globalization could lie ahead.

At the time that the final end-time troubles come upon the world, they will occur suddenly, like a trap. Says the Bible, "And take heed to yourselves, lest at any time your hearts be overcharged with surfeiting, and drunkenness, and care of this life, and so that day come upon you unawares. For like a snare shall it come on all them that dwell on the face of the whole earth" (Luke 21:34–35). In this verse, we see that people will be more preoccupied with indulgence and the cares of this world than with great global crises. Moreover, Jesus told the disciples that the world will be generally unaware of what's going on in the last days. "But as the days of Noah were, so shall also the coming of the Son of man be. For as in the days that were before the flood they were eating and drinking, marrying and giving in marriage, until the day that Noah entered into the ark, And knew not until the flood came, and took them all away" (Matthew 24:37–39). For all of these conditions to occur, a recovery, repair, or reform of world financial systems and economies must first unfold.

An End-Time Economic Snare: A Prophetic View

To this writer's understanding, Scripture reveals much more information about the monetary and economic condition of the world in the end times than has already been mentioned. To be sure, Scripture doesn't use the financial jargon we are familiar with today. Yet, the foreshadowings of such end-time conditions are clear.

There are numerous biblical indications that the people of the last days will be smitten with enormous, unsatiated greed—rampant materialism, in other words. The most direct prophecy comes from the apostle Paul. In 2 Timothy 3:2, he clearly states that in the last days, people will be lovers of money. This single statement reveals much about that future society. It indicates a time when money and commerce are the primacy of everything. That certainly already is the case in many societies today.

Other passages in the Bible indicate that materialism will be the ultimate focus of mankind. A prominent financial characteristic of the last days is clearly revealed in the book of James. "Ye have heaped treasure together for the last days," he charges in his prophecy to rich people in James 5:3. "Ye have lived in pleasure on the earth, and been wanton; ye have nourished your hearts, as in a day of slaughter," he goes on to say in verse 5. It's a development that is already well underway today. As already documented briefly, financial wealth has virtually exploded this past century.

It is instructive to note that the last of the seven churches addressed by the apostle John in the book of Revelation is one that has become fat, wealthy, and content...one that has fallen asleep. The attitude of this Laodicean church is complacent and smug. This church says, "I am rich, and increased with goods, and have need of nothing" (Revelation 3:17). If this church is intended to be an allegory of the church in the end time—the last church—it certainly parallels the explosion of wealth foretold of the last days.

Particularly the account of Babylon the Great found in Revelation 17–18 indicates just how pervasive will be an end-time fixation with trade, wealth, and luxury around the world. The attitude of this Babylon is very similar to the church. While the Laodiceans' church had become wealthy and had "need of nothing," Babylon the Great, mother of prostitutes, also regards herself complacently. She boasts, "I sit a queen, and am no widow, and shall see no sorrow" (Revelation 18:7).

Evident from the Revelation 18 account is that Babylon the Great is an end-time commercial regime that will be global in nature. Its reign over the entire earth parallels the global reach of the fourth future kingdom that the prophet Daniel foresaw in his four separate visions. The three previous kingdoms or kings Daniel saw were indeed the leading powers of the known world in their day, yet they were not global as we know today. Only the last one is stated to have a worldwide reach, spanning the earth. "All nations" (Revelation 14:8, 18:3, 23) and "kings of the earth" (verses 3, 9) "merchants of the earth" (verse 3, 11) "great men of the earth" (verse 23) and "all...on earth" are part of it.

Represented in this case is the hub of a coordinated international trading system that serves as part of a reigning world kingdom that will "devour the whole earth, and shall tread it down, and break it in pieces" (Daniel 7:23). Here we see the all-controlling aspect of this commercial regime operating under the sweet guise of prosperity. In order for a system such as described to overcome and devour the whole earth, global interconnection and worldwide mechanisms of coordination and influence are required. It cannot be done without a global financial system—a network of powerful, coordinated, interconnected financial institutions. As we have briefly outlined, this is happening in many ways, along numerous conduits, rapidly converging towards the point where one man will take power at its apex, who "shall destroy many" in their prosperity (Daniel 8.25).

Significance to Christians

The world's systems are certainly and indelibly proceeding to an endpoint. In that sense, many of the trends we are witnessing today (globalism and globalization, for example) should be viewed as prophetic preparation in that they play a role in the continuing process towards the ultimate and literal events yet to come.

Overall, world financial systems will not "melt down" before their time. They may suffer tremors, hair-raising crises, temporary panics, and so on, but not incapacitating meltdown. Why? It stands to reason that they must remain operational for at least the early stages of the Tribulation period.

The thought that at least one financial and economic recovery might yet be ahead for the world could possibly elate some readers. However, it would be important to test one's perspective on this prospect. There may be many Christians today who take delight in the belief that they will not suffer in any troubles of the Tribulation period...particularly financial losses. Why? Because their hearts and affections are entirely ensnared in materialism and the comforts of life right now. Doing so, they show themselves to be "earth dwellers."[475] We would do well to remind ourselves of the three points we outline next.

Above all, the Lord's return is imminent. Whatever the theories or speculations, we could be with Him at any time and our sojourn upon earth completed. We would have no more chance to set things right, to shed our idolatries and worldliness. The bema seat lies ahead.

Secondly, certainty about the specific time of future events in this present dispensation has not been given to man. We can know the general season and such things as the destination point of the path upon which the world is traveling, but we are not given the hour or the day. That means that even though we may theorize that another global economic cycle may be underway at some point, and that the final "big financial meltdown" need wait until the Tribulation, these give no assurances of anything near-term.

Scripture clearly states that a time of wrath will come when God says that He will bring down the pride of mankind. Literal Bible readers understand that this will unfold in the Tribulation period for the entirety of mankind. Isaiah sheds light on some of the different manifestations of the "day of the Lord" (referring to the Tribulation period or possibly just the second half):

For the day of the Lord of hosts shall be upon every one who is proud and lofty, and upon every one who is lifted up, and he shall be brought low; And upon all the cedars of Lebanon, that are high and lifted up, and upon all the oaks of Bashan, And upon all the high mountains, and upon all the hills that are lifted up, And upon every high tower, and upon every fortified wall, And upon all the ships of Tarshish, and upon all pleasant pictures. And the loftiness of man shall be bowed down, and the haughtiness of men shall be made low; and the Lord alone shall be exalted in that day. And the idols he shall utterly abolish. (Isaiah 2:12–18)

We can be sure that it will not be until the second half of the Tribulation—"the terrible day of the Lord" (Joel 2:31)—when global systems begin to totally break down. Until that time, systemic or geopolitical troubles of a lesser type—though surely disastrous and frightening for those involved as they are today—will continue to unfold. In fact, it is these types of crises that continue to drive the world into higher states of globalism and globalization, and likely will yet play a role in cementing the Antichrist as a global problem solver at that future time.

This brings us to the third and final point. Deception and corruption remain the primary mode of the world's developing systems. The successive economic booms of the world…the temptations of the rising end-time apparition of great wealth or the "deceitfulness of riches" (Matthew 13:22)…the greater material comforts or the "cares of this life" (Luke 21:34)…the ever ensnaring end-time money trap…they all play upon the affections of Christians. Who then can sustain such an assault on the affections and still stand ready at all times for His coming?

Challenges to Christians

With respect to the world's headlong rush into the last-day super-religion—the ecumenical attempt to merge the masters of God and mammon—we can be sure of its occurrence. The world is on a path to destruction—morally, economically, and spiritually. We have the more sure word of prophecy on that point.

On this road, there are serious, scary financial tremors (also wars, pestilences, earthquakes, etc.) through which many people (greedy, naïve, or otherwise) will suffer or profit greatly. However, it is not the financial crises or collapses of financial institutions that represent the greatest threats to Christians, at least in terms of things that can contribute to the killing of the soul. It is the idolatries and affections that could cause people's faith to be abandoned that is the greater danger.

Not only does an end-time, global regime as partly reflected by Babylon the Great entrap a great many people, it is also inherently inhospitable to believers. "Rejoice over her, thou heaven, and ye holy apostles and prophets; for God hath avenged you on her," says Revelation 18:20. "In her was found the blood of prophets, and of the saints, and of *all* that were slain upon the earth" (verse 24, emphasis added). The idolatries, humanism, and love of money underlying the advance of this global commercial/financial system are potentially deadly to Christians.

How well is this world system treating Christians? Are you comfortable living in it? Revelation 18:4 implores us to not have any complicity with it: "Come out of her, my people, that ye be not partakers of her sins, and that receive not of her plagues."

Yet, despite it all, there is hope: Though conditions may seem difficult, and falsehood and traps press in from every side, Jeremiah, with all his scare-mongering, provides a comforting promise: "Blessed is the man who trusteth in the Lord, and whose hope the Lord is. For he shall be like a tree planted by the waters, and that spreadeth out her roots by the river, and shall not see when heat cometh, but her leaf shall be green; and shall not be anxious in the year of drought, neither shall cease from yielding fruit" (Jeremiah 17:7–8).

How should we respond to these crises while we remain upon earth? Living our lives in the "Age of Global Capital," we can strive to stay mindful of David's exhortation: "If riches increase, set not your heart upon them" (Psalm 62:10).

We are encouraged to "let your manner of life be without covetousness, and be content with such things as ye have; for he hath said, I will never leave thee, nor forsake thee. So that we may boldly say, The Lord is my helper, and I will not fear what man shall do unto me" (Hebrews 13:5–6).

—

Wilfred Hahn, who has worked on the frontlines of global money for almost three decades, is the founder of The Mulberry Ministry, which produces Eternal Value Review, a periodical for "thinking Christians seeking to understand the times." He has written forty books and booklets. His latest—Global Financial Apocalypse Prophesied—*updates his outlook on the dangerous times ahead.*

Prophecies of Doom

---

by Terry James

Non-Christian media produce and broadcast hour after hour of programming on the end of days, as they term doomsday prophecy. Paradoxically, the church that names the name of Jesus Christ for the most part either maintains a strange silence on the subject or scoffs at prophecy as having any literal relevance to our time. It seems the very people who should be aware of the portentous days in which we live better fit the description given by the apostle Peter than do unbelievers: "Knowing this first, that there shall come in the last days scoffers, walking after their own lusts, And saying, Where is the promise of his coming? for since the fathers fell asleep, all things continue as they were from the beginning of the creation" (2 Peter 3:3–4).

Despite the fact that the secular news media views any deity there might be as existential at best, it increasingly demonstrates through programming that it senses an almost supernatural cataclysm looming in the gloomy murkiness of things to come. The Christian church (those who have accepted Christ as their Savior through His sacrifice for the sins of man upon the cross at Calvary) sadly, on the other hand, doesn't give much indication that its members worry, or even care about, what might lurk around the next corner of human history. This, even though their Lord Jesus Christ, the very Word of God (John 1:1), knows the end from the beginning and has given through Bible prophecy much about what will unfold while His second coming draws near.

Jesus tells the believer what to do in response to witnessing the end-times signals He and the Old and New Testament prophets gave through the spoken and written Word. He said, after giving many signs of the times for the generation alive at the time of His second coming, "And what I say unto you I say unto all, Watch" (Mark 13:37). Again, Jesus gave a profound commandment to believers: "And when these things begin to come to pass, then look up, and lift up your heads; for your redemption draweth nigh" (Luke 21:28).

So many things of biblically prophetic significance are convulsing today's world that it requires book-length examination to look at all matters involved. We will, with this chapter, however, attempt to cover—at least in summary—the most relevant prophecies from God's Word and apply these to the examination of the more pertinent issues and events that we see unfolding.

Setting the Prophetic Stage

No prophecies are currently being fulfilled, in my view. The one possible exception is the reality that Israel is back in the center of the land God promised to Abraham, Isaac, and Jacob. That said, I cannot emphasize strongly enough that God's mighty hand can be seen moving prophetically in virtually every facet of the human condition at this present moment.

The Lord of heaven, who alone knows the end from the beginning—and who has revealed much about future things in His written Word—can be likened to a producer and director setting the stage for a great production. He is letting us look behind the curtain to see the setting of the stage for the end-times play that is about to begin.

The ominous title chosen here for the play that is written by the awesome finger of God—"Prophecies of Doom"—is ours, the producers of this volume. The title is intended to provide a to-the-point description of the phenomenally dramatic theme that this earth is passing away in preparation for the coming thousand-year reign of the King of kings and Lord of Lords. God himself promises that there will be nothing gloomy or frightening about that future glorious era of the planet called earth. Getting to that time of Christ's reign, however, will require billions of this fallen sphere's inhabitants having to go through hell on earth.

We will look at God's end-times play, for the sake of making matters involved more easily understood, in three acts. Act 1 will examine the church age, or age of grace; Act 2 will unveil the Tribulation; and Act 3 will give a brief overview of the millennial, or one-thousand-year, reign of Christ upon earth.

Act 1
Age of Grace

Christ's death, burial, and resurrection somewhere around 33–36 A.D. initiated the age of grace, also known as the church age. This is the era in which you and I are living today. The age of grace designation revolves around the fact that God sent His only Son, Jesus the Christ, to die for the sin of fallen man. It is the grace of God—the giving of God's Son, the only sinless person ever to have been born in the flesh, as the sacrificial Lamb who takes away the sin of the world—that can bring each and every person into reconciliation with God the Father. God did this unfathomable act of supreme love without any of His creation called man having any worthiness whatever to be saved from sin that brings eternal death. Redemption through God's grace is the only way to go to heaven.

Jesus made this clear. "I am the way, the truth, and the life; no [person] cometh to the father but by me" (John 14:6).

The Church Age

This age of grace is also known as the church age. This is the era when Jesus' words to Peter and His other disciples began to be fulfilled: "And I say also unto thee, That thou art Peter, and upon this rock I will build my church; and the gates of hell shall not prevail against it" (Matthew 16:18).

From the moment God's grace plan was implemented, Christ's church began building. This means that one individual human being at a time is being added to the church through his or her individual acceptance of Christ as Savior. This is done through God's grace gift, as described above. The process of being added to Christ's church is wrapped up in the following words from the Bible: "If thou shalt confess with thy mouth the Lord Jesus, and shalt believe in thine heart that God hath raised him from the dead, thou shalt be saved" (Romans 10:9).

Many pretribulation prophetic indicators are given in the Bible that will be prevalent in the age of grace. However, there is only one prophecy that God's Word tells us for sure will be fulfilled during this dispensation (distinct era on God's timeline). Other prophecies yet future might be fulfilled in this present church age, but the possibility of those instances is very limited, as we will see.

Church Age Indicators Pointing to Coming Tribulation Era

Jesus forewarned of indicators to look for in the times leading up to His second advent. I'm aware that some Bible prophecy students will argue the point, and there isn't sufficient space to confute those arguments that Jesus prophesied in the Olivet Discourse (see Matthew 24; Mark 13; and Luke 21) only about the Tribulation dispensation, Daniel's seventieth week, the last seven years of human history before Christ's return. I will simply say that I'm of the conviction that the Lord spoke partly about the church age, partly about the Tribulation, and, in some instances, about both dispensations at the same time while discoursing with His disciples atop Mt. Moriah that day.

False Christs/False Prophets /False Teachers

And as he sat upon the mount of Olives, the disciples came unto him privately, saying, Tell us, when shall these things be? and what shall be the sign of thy coming, and of the end of the world? And Jesus answered and said unto them, Take heed that no man deceive you. For many shall come in my name, saying, I am Christ; and shall deceive many. And many false prophets shall rise, and shall deceive many. (Matthew 24:3–5, 11)

Prophecies of doom begin with the Lord, the Creator of all things, the very Word of God (John 1:1). Jesus forewarned that the doom of fallen mankind begins with being deceived by the claims of those who falsely say that they come in His name, or who claim to actually be Him. All such claims are wrapped up in the denial that Jesus has come in the flesh as the only payment for sin God the Father recognizes. The spirit of Antichrist is at the heart of denial that Jesus came for the purpose described above in this chapter.

John the apostle and prophet wrote: "Little children, it is the last time: and as ye have heard that antichrist shall come, even now are there many antichrists; whereby we know that it is the last time" (1 John 2:18).

The prophet wrote further: "And every spirit that confesseth not that Jesus Christ is come in the flesh is not of God: and this is that spirit of antichrist, whereof ye have heard that it should come; and even now already is it in the world" (1 John 4:3).

Today's Christ-Deniers

Twenty-first century religiosity has brought about an onslaught of the deceivers about whom Jesus and the old apostle forewarned. While the first decade of the third millennium since Christ's birth moves swiftly towards its end, the Antichrist spirit is alive and well–and gathering millions of the deluded within its deadly cloud of deception.

The insidious methodologies Satan has used to bring about the delusion is amazing. And most of Christianity—those people who should be alert to the serpent's ways—has been lulled into spiritual lethargy that sedates them to what is unfolding around them and to what is bringing on those prophecies of doom that we consider at the moment.

Prosperity Preaching Paves the Way to Perdition

It only takes a quick click through the channels with the TV remote to discover that most of Christian television today is about the prosperity gospel, which some call the name-it-and-claim-it gospel.

The preachers and the promoters ministries sometimes hire to act as hucksters to bring in contributions dwell almost exclusively on encouraging an inward turning of the people in their audiences.

Their message is, rather than the all-important truth that Jesus is the only way to salvation, the lie that God wants all of His people to be financially prosperous. The way to get this prosperity is to give money—preferably to them. When the TV viewers "plant a seed" with the particular ministry doing the huckstering, they are promised great, overflowing abundance in return.

While there is a God-prescribed way to give to the Lord's work, the give-to-get inward turning is egregiously detrimental to the cause of Christ and the salvation message. These are teachers of a gospel other than the gospel of Jesus Christ, as Paul forewarned: "But though we, or an angel from heaven, preach any other gospel unto you than that which we have preached unto you, let him be accursed. As we said before, so say I now again, If any [man] preach any other gospel unto you than that ye have received, let him be accursed" (Galatians 1:8–9).

This false teaching has within the past few decades brought about a falling away from the very heart of God's Word—the redemption and reconciliation of mankind to the Heavenly Father, who is not willing that any should perish, but that all should receive everlasting life (read John 3:16).

Antichrist Spirit Rampant

Name-it-and-claim-it prosperity purveyors have opened the floodgates for another gospel and for the Antichrist spirit about which the apostle John forewarned. Christians who are now desensitized to this false teaching and preaching have become dull to truth about the very heart of Jesus' purpose for coming in the flesh as the perfect God-man—the Lamb slain from the foundation of the world.

Millions, in large part due to false teaching and preaching, will go into that last seven years of horror on earth, the Tribulation. They will take the mark of the Beast of Revelation 13:16–18 because they believe the lie that there are many ways, not one way (John 14:6), to salvation: "And all that dwell upon the earth shall worship him, whose names are not written in the book of life of the Lamb slain from the foundation of the world" (Revelation 13:8).

The deluded, dulled-down church has to a considerable extent been responsible for the sin that separates lost men, women, and children from salvation, which can come only through the Lord Jesus Christ. The church has gone, without giving much prayer or thought to matters involved, into the fold of false shepherds who teach and preach that there must be unity in the world to save it.

The "intolerant" message that there is only one way to God and heaven, these sheep in wolves clothing incessantly put forth, is the holdup to true world peace. One pastor even has his own "PEACE" plan—a social gospel of inclusiveness of all religious belief systems. Salvation will come, his theology basically implies, once the social ills are cured and people are able to then concentrate on receiving salvation, their various appetites having been satisfied.

Jesus went about offering salvation precisely the opposite way. He sought out and saved the souls of the poorest of the people. He never promised prosperity, or even unity, on this earth. As a matter of fact, Jesus said that He came to divide believers from unbelievers. He said He was hated by the world, not loved by it, for His message. The gurus of the present ecumenical effort to bring all to unity and love through another gospel indeed hate the "intolerant" message that Jesus Christ is the Way—the only Way—to God the Father and heaven.

Jesus said to His followers—including those who would be His disciples down through the centuries to this present day—"If the world hate you, ye know that it hated me before it hated you. If ye were of the world, the world would love his own: but because ye are not of the world, but I have chosen you out of the world, therefore the world hateth you" (John 15:18–19).

Church Age Rage

So, there is world rage during this dispensation called the church age, or age of grace. Satan is at the heart of the rage against Christ and all who are His disciples. From this luciferian, insane, white-hot anger flows and spins all of the prophecies of doom found in God's Word.

The world of rebellious earth-dwellers who hate Jesus Christ and reject God's only way of redemption and reconciliation for lost mankind is creating the perilous times of the present hour. They follow their father, the devil, down the broad way that leads to outer darkness and separation from God and heaven for eternity.

Jesus said: "Enter ye in at the strait gate: for wide is the gate, and broad is the way, that leadeth to destruction, and many there be which go in thereat: Because strait is the gate, and narrow is the way, which leadeth unto life, and few there be that find it" (Matthew 7:13–14).

To those who reject Him for salvation, the Lord puts it bluntly: "Ye are of [your] father the devil, and the lusts of your father ye will do. He was a murderer from the beginning, and abode not in the truth, because there is no truth in him. When he speaketh a lie, he speaketh of his own: for he is a liar, and the father of it" (John 8:44).

Perilous Times the Result

Act 1—this age of grace—is a specific dispensation on God's timeline. It is an era in which God's grace plan is in place to save from their sins all who will believe in Christ for redemption and reconciliation. At the same time, Satan, who is the father of lies, is doing all he can to keep men, women, and children from accepting God's grace gift, Jesus Christ.

Paul the apostle and prophet foretold that Satan's evil work will also be in force during this dispensation, fomenting perilous times through rebellious activities and characteristics of sin-saturated mankind. These end-times human beings' actions in rebellion to their Creator will ultimately bring prophecies of doom to fruition. Read these "perilous times" characteristics of end-times mankind in 2 Timothy 3:1–5. For now, we will go to Act 2 and the dispensation of Tribulation. We will look at specific prophecies that are scheduled for that last seven years immediately preceding Christ's second coming to earth. Jesus said about that time: "For then shall be great tribulation, such as was not since the beginning of the world to this time, no, nor ever shall be" (Matthew 24:21).

Act 2
The Tribulation

Most every signal of that future seven-year period that will be so horrendous that Jesus said it will be the worst time of all human history thunders on the prophetic horizon in this generation. The student of Bible prophecy who adheres to the literalist point of view receives ever-increasing verification that indeed we are on the very cusp of end-times prophetic fulfillment. Let's look at specifics to see if anything seems familiar.

Precursor Prophecy

Stage-setting for prophecies of future fulfillment leading to the Second Advent (the moment when Christ's foot will touch down on the Mount of Olives after breaking through the clouds above Armageddon—see Revelation 19:11) can be seen in every direction the diligent student of Bible prophecy looks. Today's newspaper headlines and news broadcast lead stories invariably include Israel, its neighbor antagonists, and the potential for war in the Middle East.

Jesus said this would be a key prophetic indicator of His soon return to this fallen planet. As a matter of fact, His forewarning of this precise situation was given right after His forewarning of false teachers, false Christs, and great deception, as we looked at above: "And ye shall hear of wars and rumours of wars: see that ye be not troubled: for all these things must come to pass, but the end is not yet" (Matthew 24:6).

Certainly, wars are breaking out involving Israel on a consistent basis.

This has been the case since its rebirth as a modern nation on May 14, 1948. War involving Israel and its terroristic enemies is raging even while I'm writing this chapter. Let us examine some of the specifics of things to come, according to God's Word.

Damascus Doomed

I, as many who study Bible prophecy, find one of the most profoundly interesting prophecies that likely awaits fulfillment just ahead to be that involving Damascus, Syria: "The burden of Damascus. Behold, Damascus is taken away from being a city, and it shall be a ruinous heap" (Isaiah 17:1).

The fascination stems from the fact that every major Middle East Islamic terroristic organization is headquartered in Damascus. The Syrian government of Bashar Al-Assad looks the other way. He even gives perks to these fanatics, who in the name of Allah are blood-vowed to obliterate Israel, to sweep it and all Jews from the face of the earth. It is Damascus where the murderous plots to destroy God's chosen nation are hatched. One prophecy of doom most easily observed in preparation for fulfillment is the doom of Damascus. Damascus' destruction will happen; make no mistake.

Covenant with Death and Hell

The cry for peace in the world, and most specifically for peace in the Middle East, is growing by the hour. Iran's nuclear program, which everyone knows is not in place for the peaceful development of energy to produce electricity in the area of ancient Persia, has diplomat councils in a collective dither. All focus, it seems to me at least, is not on forcing Iran to give up its nuclear weapons development, but on pressuring Israel to give up any idea of attacking those weapons development facilities. Israel is expected to let Iranian President Mahmoud Ahmadinejad's many-times-stated intention to eradicate Israel just pass through one Israeli Defense Force ear and out the other without doing anything to eliminate those threats.

The Roadmap for Peace continues to circulate, with the Quartet (the United States, the United Nations, the European Union, and Russia) pressuring Israel in particular to accept the international community's prescription for peace. That prescription, of course, calls for Israel to give up even more land, and for a two-state solution to the Palestinian question.

Daniel the prophet foretold a peace that would be approved and guaranteed by the one who will become Antichrist: "And he shall confirm the covenant with many for one week: and in the midst of the week he shall cause the sacrifice and the oblation to cease, and for the overspreading of abominations he shall make it desolate, even until the consummation, and that determined shall be poured upon the desolate" (Daniel 9:27).

The peace the "prince that shall come"—Antichrist—will make between Israel and its enemies will affect the entire world. It will be for the worse, not for the better. Isaiah the prophet tells of this prophecy of doom in quite frightening terminology: "Wherefore hear the word of the LORD, ye scornful men, that rule this people which is in Jerusalem. Because ye have said, We have made a covenant with death, and with hell are we at agreement; when the overflowing scourge shall pass through, it shall not come unto us: for we have made lies our refuge, and under falsehood have we hid ourselves.... And your covenant with death shall be disannulled, and your agreement with hell shall not stand; when the overflowing scourge shall pass through, then ye shall be trodden down by it" (Isaiah 28:14–15, 18).

Watching the "peace" process in the Middle East is vital for the student of Bible prophecy in these troubling though exciting times.

Gog-Magog

No prophecy yet future is more observably in the stage-setting process at present than the Gog-Magog foretelling of Ezekiel chapters 38 and 39. And, it is a prophecy of utter doom for those who plan and initiate the attack against God's chosen nation, Israel.

Here's the bottom line for that coalition that storms southward, determined to destroy Israel and take great spoils of war from the oil-rich Middle East:

Therefore, thou son of man, prophesy against Gog, and say, Thus saith the Lord GOD; Behold, I am against thee, O Gog, the chief prince of Meshech and Tubal:

And I will turn thee back, and leave but the sixth part of thee, and will cause thee to come up from the north parts, and will bring thee upon the mountains of Israel: And I will smite thy bow out of thy left hand, and will cause thine arrows to fall out of thy right hand.

Thou shalt fall upon the mountains of Israel, thou, and all thy bands, and the people that is with thee: I will give thee unto the ravenous birds of every sort, and to the beasts of the field to be devoured.

Thou shalt fall upon the open field: for I have spoken it, saith the Lord GOD. (Ezekiel 39:1–5)

Even to those who believe in and study Bible prophecy as destined to be literally fulfilled in most minute detail, it is astonishing to watch this prophecy shaping up in the headlines today.

Russia (Rosh) and Iran (Persia) are becoming closer by the hour in an alliance that portends trouble for Israel and the world. Other national entities and regions are also beginning to coalesce against God's chosen people.

For example, Turkey and regions surrounding that country—representing the Gog-Magog coalition member Togarmah—are as of this writing sending threatening diplomatic protests Israel's way for Israel's military action into the Gaza because of the thousands of rocket attacks by Hamas.

This force from the north of Israel will be completely routed, and will have five sixth of its armies completely destroyed. This is a prophecy of doom for a Russian leader the Bible calls "Gog" and all who follow him against God's chosen nation. The rapidity with which this prophecy is setting up for fulfillment is phenomenal.

Global World Order

God's Word predicts a time when all of the world will have but one government that controls. It will be ruled over by the worst tyrant of all time. This man is called many names in the Bible: the son of perdition, the prince that shall come, the Assyrian, the beast, the man of sin, the king of fierce countenance, and Antichrist.

His ultimate control over the world, through satanically indwelt power, is prophesied in the following verses: "And he causeth all, both small and great, rich and poor, free and bond, to receive a mark in their right hand, or in their foreheads: And that no man might buy or sell, save he that had the mark, or the name of the beast, or the number of his name. Here is wisdom. Let him that hath understanding count the number of the beast: for it is the number of a man; and his number is Six hundred threescore and six" (Revelation 13:16–18).

There must be a coming together of nations to agree to one world government. The nations might still be separate in some sense in the ultimate arrangement, but they will all have to agree that global government—under one auspice—is the only way to govern the masses of the world.

In fact, this very global coming together of rulers of the earth is prophesied in God's Word, with the Lord giving His opinion of the effort to return to the Babel-like time of Nimrod's day (see Genesis 11): "Why do the heathen rage, and the people imagine a vain thing? The kings of the earth set themselves, and the rulers take counsel together, against the LORD, and against his anointed, saying, Let us break their bands asunder, and cast away their cords from us. He that sitteth in the heavens shall laugh: the Lord shall have them in derision. Then shall he speak unto them in his wrath, and vex them in his sore displeasure. Yet have I set my king upon my holy hill of Zion" (Psalm 2:1–6).

God says that Jesus Christ will be established upon Zion (the reconfigured and lifted-up Mt. Moriah). His throne will overthrow all of these attempts by fallen man and their governors—like Lucifer—to try to usurp the very throne of God.

A prophecy that precisely puts God's finger on our generation concerning those determined to put together a world empire—through world trading blocs such as the North American Union, along the lines of the European Union—is found in this Scripture, I believe: "And the ten horns which thou sawest are ten kings, which have received no kingdom as yet; but receive power as kings one hour with the beast. These have one mind, and shall give their power and strength unto the beast" (Revelation 17:12–13).

This is another profound stage-setting for fulfillment in our time.

The recent economic earthquake has set all the globalist elitists on a course of bringing the world under one economic order. The American currency—the dollar—is under assault, with the intention of bringing down its power to control the other monetary institutions of the earth's nations.

The things we see happening financially on a global scale, I'm convinced, will eventuate in all currencies melding into one. That one will be in the form of electronic funds drawing rights. Money will, eventually, be all electronic units, an electronic funds transfer system of buying and selling. This is, in my view, how the Antichrist will be able to control all buying and selling.

The Internet—the World Wide Web—in some hybrid form will be the vehicle through which all buying and selling is accomplished.

Words by Dr. Henry Kissinger, thrilling to most geopoliticians but chilling to those of us who know what God's prophetic Word has to say about things to come, frame the globalist elite's vision as of this writing.

Not since the inauguration of President John F. Kennedy half a century ago has a new administration come into office with such a reservoir of expectations. It is unprecedented that all the principal actors on the world stage are avowing their desire to undertake the transformations imposed on them by the world crisis in collaboration with the United States.

The extraordinary impact of the president-elect on the imagination of humanity is an important element in shaping a new world order...

An international order can be permanent only if its participants have a share not only in building but also in securing it. In this manner, America and its potential partners have a unique opportunity to transform a moment of crisis into a vision of hope.[476]

As optimistic as Dr. Kissinger's words are, such a system is doomed, according to God's Holy Word. And, the ultimate coming to fruition of a one-world order will absolutely come to pass. All who accept Antichrist's system by agreeing to accept a coded number designation that includes Antichrist's number of required worship—666—are doomed to eternity apart from God and heaven.

Seals, Trumpets, and Vials of Wrath

All who refuse to accept God's grace gift and who live to go into the Tribulation dispensation are facing a time of unprecedented trouble for planet earth. Jesus himself said it would be the worst time of human history (Matthew 24:21–22).

There is coming the development of the Antichrist system as just described. Millions of people who accept Christ after the Rapture and Jews will be persecuted and will die under this monster's genocidal command. That period and that government will make Adolf Hitler and his Nazi regime look like good times by comparison. You don't want to go through the time of Jacob's trouble (Jeremiah 30:7), another name for the Tribulation or Daniel's seventieth week—the last seven years of history leading up to Christ's Second Advent.

But the worst is yet to come, even more horrendous than anything Antichrist can do. God's wrathful judgment will pour out upon all rebellious earth-dwellers, beginning at the midpoint of the seven-year Tribulation.

To understand the things that will judge the rebels who refuse God's offer of redemption, read the book of Revelation—particularly chapters 6 through 19. There you will read of twenty-one specific judgments in a series of seven seals, seven trumpets, and seven vials of God's wrath. As many as two-thirds of all peoples on earth will die by the plagues of these judgments.

Judgment of Wickedness, the False System of Worship, and the Coming of Armageddon

God's judgment and wrath will fall upon the evil people and system of wicked commercialism. A mighty city called Babylon representing all of this evil will be destroyed in a single hour at that judgment (read Revelation 18).

The false system of worship, much of which we see in rapid development at this present hour, will suffer total decimation. Just as the church is the pure bride of Jesus Christ, this will be the filthy mistress of Antichrist. This system is termed "Mystery Babylon." It is likened to a prostitute who has served the kingmakers of the world, the rich, and those who have ruled wickedly (read this judgment in Revelation 17).

God says He will bring all armies of earth to Armageddon, man's final military conflict of history before Christ's return.

John the apostle and prophet was given the Word on what is coming:

And he gathered them together into a place called in the Hebrew tongue Armageddon. And the seventh angel poured out his vial into the air; and there came a great voice out of the temple of heaven, from the throne, saying, It is done. And there were voices, and thunders, and lightnings; and there was a great earthquake, such as was not since men were upon the earth, so mighty an earthquake, and so great. And the great city was divided into three parts, and the cities of the nations fell: and great Babylon came in remembrance before God, to give unto her the cup of the wine of the fierceness of his wrath. And every island fled away, and the mountains were not found. And there fell upon men a great hail out of heaven, every stone about the weight of a talent: and men blasphemed God because of the plague of the hail; for the plague thereof was exceeding great. (Revelation 16:16–21)

Blood will flow as high as the horse bridle, the prophecy says, and that will be for two hundred miles or so! The vultures and other scavengers will dine on the flesh of kings and captains, the Word of God says. All at Armageddon are doomed.

The Great Escape

Though we are looking at prophecies of doom, doom is not God's desire for you, or for anyone else. There is one hope for lost mankind and one hope of escape of the horrors to come during the time the Lord must judge sin.

God is love. He wants all to come to repentance and reconciliation with himself. He has literally moved heaven and hell to bring all to redemption so they won't have to fade His judgment on sin. He must judge sin because it is the vile thing that separates man from His Creator.

The Lord of heaven sent His son Jesus, the Christ, to take away the sin of the world. All who believe in Him, as we looked at earlier, will be saved, redeemed, and reconciled to God the Father. (Read again Romans 10:9.)

The person who accepts Christ for salvation will, if alive when

God's way of escape intervenes into the affairs of mankind, move instantaneously from this fallen sphere and into the presence of Christ. This is the Rapture of the church—all born again—those who have accepted Christ for salvation. (Read 1 Corinthians 15–55 and 1 Thessalonians 4:13–18.)

Jesus talked about this moment, I'm convinced, when He said:

"Let not your heart be troubled: ye believe in God, believe also in me. In my Father's house are many mansions: if it were not so, I would have told you. I go to prepare a place for you.

"And if I go and prepare a place for you, I will come again, and receive you unto myself; that where I am, there ye may be also." (John 14:1–3)

The Rapture will be a stupendous moment when all who are believers will vanish. This moment will come without any sign or signal. It will throw the world into instant chaos and panic. Rearrangements of the sort we've looked at above will begin to take place as the world's leaders try to find answers to what has happened and attempt to figure out how to quell the fears of the panicked masses.

Those who have disappeared will be in heaven in the places Jesus has prepared for them while planet earth experiences the worst time in history.

All seems in place for that time of Tribulation. There is nothing that must be fulfilled before the Rapture of Christians will take place. Rapture is imminent!

Act 3
The Millennium and Final Judgments

All who live through the seven years of Tribulation will face Christ just outside Jerusalem for judgment. The lost will be placed in what is described as "goat nations." The saved—all who have accepted Christ during the Tribulation—will be placed in the "sheep nations."

The goat nations will be cast into everlasting darkness; the sheep nations will go into Christ's millennial kingdom and will, as flesh and blood people, enjoy His reign upon a refurbished, pristine planet earth for a thousand years.

The saints in heaven who went in the Rapture will return with Jesus as He puts an end to rebellion at Armageddon (see Revelation 19:11), then sets up the sheep/goat judgment before beginning the Millennium.

The precursor events in heaven to the saints' return with Christ will be as follows:

While God's seven seals, seven trumpets, and seven vials of wrath are taking place, the church enjoys a royal wedding banquet—the wedding supper of the Lamb, as God's prophetic Word calls it. Christians will have been given their wedding garments based upon rewards for how they lived for Christ while on earth. This will take place at the bema, or judgment seat of Christ.

All who stand for this judgment are saved. They will spend eternity with Christ in heaven, living an ever-upward movement into exultant, creative, indescribably magnificent everlasting life.

Those who are lost—tragically, sadly—because of their rejection of God's way of redemption and reconciliation, will face quite another judgment. The Great White Throne Judgment—the final judgment as given in God's Word—will be only for the lost, those who will spend eternity apart from God and heaven. Theirs will be an ever-spiraling descent into indescribably horrendous terrors. They will be constantly dying, but never reaching the point of death. This is the prophecy of ultimate doom.

This doesn't have to be the fate of anyone. The verse many of us learned, or at least heard, as children tells of God's unfathomable love for each and every person ever born. It is the one and only way of escaping the doom that lies ahead for all who reject God's Son: "For God so loved the world, that he gave his only begotten Son, that whosoever believeth in him should not perish, but have everlasting life" (John 3:16).

—

Terry James, author of numerous books on Bible prophecy, is a frequent lecturer who interviews often with national and international media on world issues and events. He is partner and general editor in www.raptureready.com, which was recently rated as the #1 Bible prophecy website on the Internet. He writes a weekly column, "Nearing Midnight," for the site.

chapter fifteen

Is a Brave New World Upon Us?

---

by Thomas Glessner

In his famous novel *Brave New World*, twentieth-century writer Aldous Huxley wrote of a future society where human life is disposable and can be manipulated, abused, and even destroyed for what is perceived as the greater societal good. Perhaps Huxley accurately foresaw the future of America.

The Pandora's box opened by *Roe v. Wade* has led American society and culture into areas once written about only by science fiction writers. We must ask: "Is Huxley's 'brave new world' upon us?"

Wrongful Life and Wrongful Birth Lawsuits

While the decision in *Roe* directly affected the enforcement of criminal prohibitions against abortion, it also paved the way for new frontiers in the civil law. It ruled that abortion, an act that was a felony in all fifty states at the time, was a fundamental constitutional right. Such a decision was previously unheard of in the history of constitutional jurisprudence. Imagine, if you will, that in the near future the Supreme Court rules that car theft, a felony in all fifty states, is a protected constitutional right and cannot be prohibited by law. Such a ruling would have serious ramifications in the civil law concerning property rights. In the same manner, *Roe* had serious implications for the civil law regarding childbirth and medical practice.

Prior to *Roe*, abortion was illegal and a felony in all fifty states. (Four states—California, New York, Oregon, and Washington—had liberalized their abortion laws in the mid-sixties and early seventies, but none of these legislative revisions came close to the radical changes in abortion law accomplished by the *Roe* decision.) Now, however, because of *Roe*, it is a fundamental constitutional right. Accordingly, women now have a right to receive information during their pregnancies so they can exercise this right in an informed manner. Hence, failure of a medical healthcare professional to provide relevant information to the pregnant woman regarding the physical condition of her child *in utero* could render him or her civilly liable under what are now known as wrongful birth and wrongful life lawsuits.

In a wrongful birth lawsuit, a mother who gives birth to a child who is handicapped is given a legal right to sue the physician who provided prenatal care for the wrongful birth, provided that she can show that during her pregnancy she was deprived of information that would have informed her of the child's handicapped condition. The mother's legal claim, in this instance, is to assert that had she known of her child's handicapped condition while pregnant, she would have chosen abortion instead of delivery to term. Hence, the child's birth is deemed wrongful and should have never happened. Accordingly, the physician handling the prenatal care is liable for damages for the cost of raising the child throughout his or her life.

In a wrongful life lawsuit, the child born with the handicapped condition is given the right to sue the doctor for his or her wrongful life. In essence, the child has a legal claim that says if her mother had been given the proper information regarding the handicap, her mother would have chosen abortion. Since this information was not given to the mother during prenatal care, the child alleges that she was wrongfully born and, thus, should have been aborted. Hence, the child's life is wrongful. Accordingly, the physician who failed to give the mother the proper information regarding the fetal anomalies must pay damages to the child for her wrongful life.

Seven years after *Roe*—for the first time in the nation—a state appeals court upheld the right of a child to claim damages for wrongful life. An infant girl was born with Tay-Sachs disease and alleged that genetic tests performed on her mother during pregnancy were negligently performed and interpreted. In a lengthy and impassioned decision, a California appellate court stated:

> The appeal presents an issue of first impression in California: What remedy, if any, is available in this state to a severely impaired child—genetically defective—born as a result of defendants' negligence in conducting certain genetic tests of the child's parents—tests which, if properly done, would have disclosed the high probability that the actual, catastrophic result would occur?
>
> Plaintiff, in essence, was seeking damages for negligence which resulted in her birth; the action was thus termed one for wrongful life, a cause of action which, when brought by the infant so born, has almost universally been barred in various factual contexts by courts in jurisdictions other than California.... The term wrongful life will be confined to those causes of action brought by the infant alleging that, due to the negligence of the defendant, birth occurred.... Of some significance with respect to this question is the fact that in 1973, Roe v. Wade was decided by the United States Supreme Court. The nation's high court determined that parents have a constitutionally protected right to obtain an abortion during the first trimester of pregnancy, free of state interference. We deem this decision to be of considerable importance in defining the parameters of "wrongful-life" litigation...

[Previous courts have] explained that one of the most deeply held beliefs of our society is that life—whether experienced with or without a major physical handicap—is more precious than non-life. [The child], by virtue of its birth, will be able to love and be loved and to experience happiness and pleasure—emotions which are truly the essence of life and which are far more valuable than the suffering the child may endure.... Whether it is better to have never been born at all rather than to have been born with serious mental defects is a mystery more properly left to the philosophers and theologians, a mystery that would lead us to the field of metaphysics, beyond the realm of our understanding or ability to solve....

[There has been a] dramatic increase in the last few decades of the medical knowledge and skill needed to avoid genetic disaster.... Genetic defects represent an increasingly large part of the overall national health burden.... We have no difficulty in ascertaining and finding the existence of duty owed by medical laboratories engaged in genetic testing for parents and their as yet unborn children to use ordinary care in administration of available tests for the purpose of providing information concerning potential genetic defects in the unborn.... We find no bar to a holding that the defendants owed a duty to the child plaintiff before us and breached that duty.... The reality of the "wrongful-life" concept is that such a plaintiff both exists and suffers, due to the negligence of others. It is neither necessary nor just to retreat into meditation on the mysteries of life. The certainty of genetic impairment is no longer a mystery. In addition, reverent appreciation of life compels recognition that plaintiff, however impaired she may be, has come into existence as a living person with certain rights.

The "wrongful-life" cause of action with which we are concerned is based upon negligently caused failure by someone under a duty to do so to inform the prospective parents of facts needed by them to make a conscious choice not to become parents.... The complaint sought costs of care as an element of special damages, an appropriate item of recovery.[477]

Four years later, the Supreme Court of New Jersey for the first time held that a child could recover treatment and rehabilitation costs associated with handicaps resulting from his mother having had rubella during her first trimester of pregnancy. The child filed a malpractice lawsuit against three board-certified obstetricians for negligently failing to diagnose his mother's German measles during her pregnancy, thus depriving his parents of the choice of terminating the pregnancy.[478]

Not all jurisdictions have allowed wrongful birth and/or wrongful life lawsuits. With only three exceptions, state courts have rejected legal claims for wrongful life. In doing so, some of these courts reason that life burdened with defects is better than no life at all, and thus the plaintiff child suffers no legally cognizable injury by being born. In contrast, three states—California, New Jersey, and Washington—acknowledge wrongful life suits and have concluded that life is not always preferable to non-existence. Currently, twenty-eight states recognize wrongful birth, and nine prohibit it as a cause of action: Georgia, Michigan, Minnesota, Missouri, North Carolina, Ohio, Pennsylvania, South Dakota, and Utah.

The Supreme Court's ruling in *Roe* that life must be "meaningful" to be protected under the law has effectively opened the door to establish legal precedents that proclaim that there is such a thing as a life not worthy to be lived. With the recognition in the legal system of wrongful birth and wrongful life laws, there is a movement in society that proclaims that some human lives are meaningless.

Fetal Tissue and Stem Cell Research

During the 1980s, medical advances began to view the unborn child as a prime source of fresh, living cells to treat certain diseases such as diabetes, Parkinson's disease, Alzheimer's disease, nerve degeneration, bone marrow diseases, and even some skin disorders. Demand began to build for tissues and organs to use in research. Of course, such material is readily available from the remains of aborted children. The use of tissue from aborted children is intriguing to medical researchers because these cells are soft and pliable and easy to use in transplants. Fetal tissues also have strong regenerative abilities and develop rapidly in a recipient's body.

Medical research using the fetal tissue of animals for transplants into adult animals has been conducted since the 1800s. However, in 1985 two Denver researchers, Everett Spees and Kevin Lafferty, used pancreatic tissue from aborted human babies and transplanted them into an adult diabetic. By the end of 1987, fifteen other diabetics had received similar transplants. Others have reportedly received fetal liver cells as a treatment for a blood disorder.[479]

In September 1987, doctors in Mexico reported a successful treatment for Parkinson's disease by transplanting tissue from the brain and adrenal gland of a thirteen-week-old aborted baby into the brains of two patients.[480] The report set off a wave of controversy regarding the ethics of the research and the implications it holds for the future. The prospects for this technology make it apparent that marketing in fetal tissue and organs may become a lucrative business. It has also led to some bizarre reported incidents. For instance, in 1987 a Minnesota woman with diabetes said that she wanted to get pregnant, have an abortion, and then transplant insulin-producing islet cells from her baby into her own body in hopes of curing her disease.[481]

A California woman wanted to become pregnant by her father through artificial insemination, abort the baby, and transplant its brain cells into her father who is suffering from Alzheimer's disease.[482] In still another reported case from Rochester, New York, a woman searched among participants at an international conference on brain implants for a surgeon who would use fetal cells to treat her husband's severe Parkinson's disease. Since the woman was too old to conceive, her daughters were willing to produce a fetus to help.

For fetal tissue to be most useful, the cells must be sufficiently mature—at least sixteen to twenty-four weeks into the pregnancy. Since the vast majority of miscarriages occur within the first eight weeks of pregnancy, the pool of available fetal tissue must come from babies slated for late-term abortions. If fetal tissue transplants become routinely accepted, one can easily envision a black market for the tissue of aborted babies and the exploitation of women as fetal organ farms. Financial encouragement for women to abort late in their pregnancies or to become pregnant for the purpose of aborting will become commonplace under this new field of medicine.

Former abortionist Dr. Bernard Nathanson says: "And where would it end? Now it is proposed these organs be used for treatment of disease, but tomorrow these abhorrent practices will certainly be proposed for failing sexual function (transplantation of fetal testicular tissues, probably costing $10,000 or so) and the day after tomorrow for cosmetic purposes (fetal skin probably $20,000 an ounce)."[483]

The scientific breakthrough of using fetal tissue to cure disease failed to materialize during the 1980s and 1990s, so medical researchers began to place research efforts into the use of embryonic stem cells. Stem cells are primal cells found in all multi-cellular organisms. They retain the ability to renew themselves through mitotic cell division and can differentiate into a diverse range of specialized cell types. Three broad categories of stem cells exist: (1) embryonic stem cells, which are derived from the inner cell mass of a human embryo and have the potential to develop into all or nearly all of the tissues in the body; (2) adult stem cells, which are unspecialized cells found in adult tissue that can renew themselves and become specialized to yield all of the cell types of the tissue from which they originate; and (3) cord blood stem cells, which are found in the umbilical cord.

In a developing human embryo, stem cells can differentiate into all of the specialized embryonic tissues. Embryonic stem cells can be grown and transformed into specialized cells with characteristics consistent with the cells of various tissues such as muscles or nerves. In adult organisms, stem cells act as a repair system for the body, replenishing specialized cells.

Research using embryonic stem cells to improve medical therapies is now being undertaken. Some in the medical research community believe that embryonic stem cell research could lead to therapies to treat diseases that afflict up to 126 million Americans. Proposed treatments include replacing destroyed dopamine-secreting neurons in a Parkinson patient's brain, transplanting insulin-producing pancreatic beta cells in diabetic patients, and infusing cardiac muscle cells in a heart damaged by myocardial infarction. Embryonic stem cells may also be used to understand basic biology and to evaluate the safety and efficacy of new medicines.

An obvious controversy exists, however, when the stem cells used in such therapies are embryonic stem cells. In order for such cells to be available for this use they must be removed from the human embryo, thereby killing the embryonic human being. The current debate on this issue is centered upon this very uncomfortable fact for those who promote such research.

Who would have thought it possible a few years ago that we would be debating in the public arena the concept of creating embryonic life in a test tube for the sole purpose of destroying it—and then using its cells for the treatment of disease? If American society supports the destruction of embryonic human beings for the advancement of such medical therapies, we have crossed a moral line.

The use of adult stem cells for medical therapy is not controversial, since the removal of such cells does not destroy a developing human life. Adult stem cells can be collected from bone marrow, amniotic fluid, the placenta, testicular tissue, cord blood, and nasal tissue. The use of these cells in medical research indicates that they are flexible when used to treat a number of diseases and injuries, and success of such treatments is being reported in a number of cases.

This controversy prompted President George W. Bush to issue an executive order in 2001 banning the use of federal funds for the creation of new lines of embryonic stem cell cultures for medical research. This decision permits the federal funding of research that uses the more than sixty existing stem cell lines that had already been derived prior to the executive order. Further, such research is only allowed if the existing stem cell lines were derived: (1) with the informed consent of the donors, (2) from excess embryos created solely for reproductive purposes, and (3) without any financial inducements to the donors. The executive order specifically bans federal funds for: (1) the derivation or use of stem cell lines derived from newly destroyed embryos, (2) the creation of any human embryos for research purposes, or (3) the cloning of human embryos for any purpose.

Further efforts have been made in Congress to differentiate between embryonic stem cell research and adult stem cell research. The "Patients First Act of 2007" has been introduced in Congress to "intensify stem cell research showing evidence of substantial clinical benefit to patients." The bill, if enacted into law, would prohibit "the creation of a human embryo for research purposes," and would ban "the destruction of or discarding of, or risk of injury to, a living human embryo."[484]

This proposed legislation further states that its purpose is to: (1) intensify research that may result in improved understanding of treatments for diseases and other adverse health conditions, (2) promote research and human clinical trials using stem cells that are ethically obtained and show evidence of providing clinical benefit for human patients, and (3) promote the derivation of pluripotent stem cell lines (i.e., adult stem cell lines) without the creation of human embryos for research purposes and without the destruction or discarding of, or risk of injury to, a human embryo.

This bill has created intense debate on the topic of stem cell research, as candidates for federal public office at all levels are taking sides on which direction on this issue the nation should pursue. While the political arena is hotly debating this controversy, recent scientific research appears to be pointing the way to an acceptable solution. In November 2007, teams of research scientists reported that they succeeded in reprogramming human skin cells so that they behave like embryonic stem cells. Such cells are referred to as induced pluripotent stem cells. This work appeared online in two prestigious medical research journals, *Cell* and *Science*. The research reported in *Cell* comes from a group led by Shinya Yamanaka of Kyoto University in Japan. The *Science* research comes from a group led by Junying Yu and James Thompson at the University of Wisconsin-Madison.[485]

Dr. Thompson produced the first human embryonic stem cell lines, but concluded that induced pluripotent stem cells hold more promise for patients than embryonic stem cells. He further cited the promise of this new technique because induced pluripotent stem cells are derived from the person to receive the therapy and, thus, are genetically identical with said recipient.

The new technique uses retroviruses to make the skin cells act like stem cells. Retroviruses insert genetic material into the chromosome of the cells. One possible drawback, however, is that retroviruses have been linked to cancer.

It may take years to perfect this new technique to make it workable in the treatment of human diseases. However, this new research does provide promise that a morally acceptable answer to the stem cell research controversy is around the corner. Until it does come, the debate will continue.

It is a terrible irony that we can abort unborn children on the pretense that they are not human, but then turn around and extract their stem cells, brains, bone marrow, and other organs for research and transplants because they are, indeed, so very human. In *Roe v. Wade*, the Supreme Court said no one knows when human life begins and only "meaningful life" can be protected under the law. The advent of transplants using fetal tissue and the use of embryonic stem cells to treat disease exposes this nonsense from the Court. If the use of fetal tissues and embryonic stem cells to treat disease becomes acceptable, we are acknowledging that these little ones are human, that they are living and have value. However, if the only value we place on the unborn is in their utility as spare parts for other humans, we have indeed become an exploitative society that abuses its most vulnerable and helpless members—the unborn.

In February 2009, President Obama issued an executive order allowing for the federal funding of embryonic stem cell research, overturning the previous executive order of President George W. Bush. The order not only frees up federal funds for this research, but also opens wide the door for funding research into the cloning of human stem cells, thereby unleashing the probability that the cloning of human beings is around the corner.

Such steps of "scientific advancement" clearly place America on the slippery slope to a brave new world. And such steps have happened because society has, since the issuance of the Roe v. Wade decision, accepted the idea that not all human beings are "persons." Thus, because the Constitution only protects the lives of "persons," such human beings that fail to qualify as persons (i.e., the unborn) can be killed for the perceived overall good of society. Under this viewpoint, if society can benefit from the killing of human embryos because the stem cells of such tiny humans may serve a useful purpose in curing disease, then such research not only should be allowed but should be funded by federal tax dollars.

It is a serious tragedy that in Obama's refusal to accept the humanity of unborn human beings, he has opened the doors to scientific research that manipulates and kills embryonic human beings for a misconceived notion that the destruction of such lives will bring about great good in society.

Any nation and culture will ultimately be judged not by its military might or economic power. Rather, a nation will be judged by history according to how it treated its most vulnerable members. In America today, the most vulnerable members of our society are the unborn—subject to abortion, and now subject to killing for purposes of scientific research.

Obama's executive order on stem cell research has paved the way for further manipulation of humanity by science and the emergence of a brave new world where humanity is redefined, manipulated, and killed for the perceived betterment of society as a whole.

"Selective Reduction" of Multiple Fetuses

Roe has opened the door for another bizarre practice in the medical profession. Women who are unwillingly pregnant with more than one baby can now "reduce" their pregnancy by aborting some of the unborn children while allowing the rest to proceed to birth. This practice is described by an Orwellian euphemism: "selective reduction."

The practice is made possible by ultrasound techniques developed in the last few years that allow a doctor to guide a needle into the chest cavity of an unborn child. Injected into the child's heart is a potassium chloride solution, and the fetal heart is then monitored. If heart activity continues, a sterile saline solution is injected next to the heart to destroy it by extrinsic pressure. After the child's cardiac functions cease, the procedure is then repeated in one or more additional fetuses. The fetal material is generally reabsorbed into the woman's body. While the procedure typically reduces the overall risk level for the remaining unborn children, "reduction" does have its own risks, including the possibility that one or more of the remaining children will also die.

Before being discharged from the hospital, the mother undergoes a second ultrasound scanning. If cardiac activity is observed in a child that was to be killed, the mother is scheduled to undergo the procedure again.[486]

The practice is generally performed on women who have become pregnant with multiple fetuses through the use of fertility drugs. In some cases the practice is used in a multiple pregnancy to abort a fetus with a genetic handicap. In one case a test revealed that a woman gave birth to twin boys—one normal and one afflicted with Down's syndrome. The woman said she aborted both of the children so she would not have to raise a child with this disorder. But Dr. Thomas D. Kerenyi and Dr. Usha Chitkara at Mt. Sinai School of Medicine in New York successfully killed the handicapped child and later reported: "It was a very gratifying experience in such an endangered pregnancy to follow the normal fetus to full term and through vaginal delivery."[487]

Proponents of "selective reduction" defend the practice by arguing that it increases the chances of survival for the children that are left in the womb. Dr. Joseph Schulman, director of the Genetics and IVF Institute in Fairfax, Virginia, once observed another doctor reduce quadruplets to twins. "It was not a pleasant sight," he said. "No one's proud of doing it, but doctors see it as a medical necessity."[488]

Regardless, this practice should be uniformly condemned since it kills an innocent child to improve the chances of another child surviving. Such "selective execution" (as it should properly be called) allows a doctor to play God and determine who can and cannot be born.

Sex Selection Abortions

Modem technology now has provided us with tests that will indicate the gender of a child prior to birth. Through amniocentesis, ultrasound, and/or a test called chorionic villi sampling (CVS), a determination of the gender of the unborn child may be made *in utero*. Amniocentesis is performed when the pregnancy is at least sixteen weeks along, while CVS can determine the sex of a child in the first seven to nine weeks. Ultrasound can generally determine the gender of the child after nine weeks gestational age.

Some women from ethnic groups that value males above females may want to abort a female baby and try to get pregnant again with the hope of giving birth to a male, and there are doctors willing to perform the test to enable such sex selection abortions to occur. In a survey of 295 geneticists in the U.S., nearly two-thirds said they would perform prenatal diagnosis for the sole purpose of determining the sex of the child so the parents could choose to abort if the child is the undesired gender.[489] In 1973, the year of *Roe v. Wade,* only 1 percent of the medical geneticists surveyed approved of prenatal diagnosis for sex selection. In a similar survey conducted sixteen years later, nearly 20 percent approved of the practice.[490]

There is growing evidence that this is exactly what some parents are choosing to do. Dr. Laird Jackson, director of the medical genetics division at Thomas Jefferson University in Philadelphia, stated that about ten of the twenty-five hundred pregnant women tested have opted for an abortion solely because the baby was the undesired sex.[491] Officials of the Baylor University medical school in Houston have said that four of the 320 women who have undergone CVS procedures have had abortions for sex selection purposes, and officials at Michael Reese Medical Center in Chicago and the University of California at San Francisco each state that about one out of one thousand women in the testing programs abort for gender selection.[492]

Internationally, the idea of aborting for gender selection is not new. In India, some women undergo the test for the sole purpose of discovering whether the child is a girl.[493] If it is, the child is promptly aborted. The reasons given are painfully familiar—the expense of marrying a daughter off, the need for sons to help in the family business and to carry on the family name. In short—the age-old preference of boys over girls.

Following reports of sex selection abortions in Britain, some laboratories that test for fetal abnormalities are withholding information about the sex of the unborn child from the parents. Michael Ridler of the Kennedy Galton Center says: "I and my staff do not want to contribute to the killing of normal babies, so we have stopped routinely reporting sex and have reverted strictly to our contract, which is to screen for abnormalities."[494]

The growing practice of sex selection abortions is another indication of the collapse of the wall of protection. To their credit, even some feminists oppose this practice, correctly calling it an atrocity and "feticide."[495] However, such pious denunciations ring a bit hollow since these same feminists assert that abortion must be safeguarded so that women can control their own lives.

The Population Research Institute, a think tank located in Front Royal, Virginia, issued a briefing on sex selection abortions entitled "Feminism's Triumph: the Extermination of Women," dated January 19, 2007. The briefing states, in part:

In the last two years, international organizations and Asian nations have stepped up their efforts to eliminate sex-selection abortions, which have created a massive dearth of girls in many nations over the past twenty years.... The result of these efforts? The sex imbalance continues to worsen, not improve, thanks to the ever-increasing spread of cheap abortion...into more and more areas of China, India, and other countries.

One expert who spoke at the United Nations estimates that up to 200 million women and girls are missing worldwide because of sex-selective abortion and female infanticide.

By 2020, 30 million Chinese men of marriageable age are expected to be in that situation because of 30 million "missing" young women. Many historians warn that a large number of unmarried men in a society is a recipe for social unrest and war.

The great experiment of feminism...has produced this wonder: The ever-growing elimination of more and more girls worldwide. And so far, nothing can stop it. Indeed, from the feminist perspective, how or why should it be stopped? If women have a right to an abortion, why can they not exercise it on the basis of sex selection?[496]

Without denying in any sense the depravity of killing unborn baby girls, I submit that the feminist position is morally bankrupt. They cannot have it both ways. Once the abortion of any child for any reason is permitted, the abortion of all children becomes permissible. Once abortion-on-demand is accepted, as it is in modern-day America, all unborn children are subject to abortion for any reason—including gender selection. If society and feminists believe it is acceptable to kill a child because the child is handicapped, because the mother is unmarried, or because it is a third child in a family that only wanted two, that same faulty logic allows the killing of a child because she is a girl.

While the process of aborting little girls when little boys are wanted is termed "selective abortion," every abortion is a selective one and must be opposed with every ounce of energy we have. Only the values of the parents make one abortion different from another. Parents who value only physically and mentally normal children might reject a child who is physically or mentally handicapped. Parents who value education and want to provide their children with it might reject a third child if their resources can only educate two. Parents who value their time and freedom might reject any children they produce, and parents who value boys might well reject a girl.

The Abortion Pill—RU-486

The emergence of the abortion pill, RU-486, is a further example of the destruction of the wall of protection for the unborn and raises new questions in the abortion debate. Dr. Etienne Beaulieu, a researcher for Roussel-Uclaf laboratories in France, discovered the drug in 1982. The drug company reached an agreement with the World Health Organization to provide the abortion pill at low cost to developing nations.

During the 1980s, the Reagan and Bush Administrations prohibited the U.S. Food and Drug Administration (FDA) from approving the drug to be marketed in the United States. However, pro-abortion advocates continued to apply intense pressure upon government officials to allow the drug to come into this country. Finally, under the Clinton Administration in 2000, the FDA gave its approval to RU-486. Distribution began in October of that year.

The drug is taken orally and works on the lining of the uterus to prevent implantation of the human embryo. The maintenance of this lining is essential to human reproduction. Progesterone, a hormone produced by the ovaries, prepares the uterus for the implantation of the fertilized egg. RU-486 interacts with progesterone receptors in the woman to block the effects of the progesterone. The resulting chemistry makes the womb hostile to the implanted embryo and induces abortion.[497] A U.S. team of medical researchers reported that RU-486 induces abortion in nine out of ten women who are less than seven weeks pregnant.[498] Dr. Beaulieu suggests that a complementary dosage of prostaglandin given early after the dose of RU-486 could push the effectiveness rate to 95 percent.[499]

Dr. David Elia, a Paris gynecologist, has organized clinical tests of

RU-486 and claims that its use has significant advantages over surgical abortions. Elia states: "We imagine there will be less infection, less injuries for the uterus and the cervix." Another advantage, according to Elia, is that "a lot of women prefer the methodology because they don't want the physician to touch their bodies. A lot of women prefer to do it like a natural spontaneous abortion, or miscarriage, and they don't want to have anesthesia and to be hospitalized or in a private clinic. It seems to them it's less offensive to their bodies."[500]

Elia's patients understand that using RU-486 is an abortion procedure; avoiding a surgical abortion does not cover over this reality. "To my patients it felt the same in their minds and in their hearts. This is always an abortion. They don't experience it like some natural bleedings. When they want this compound, it is not because they want to hide from the abortion, but because they prefer the method. They experience it like an abortion. There is no ambiguity on that point."[501]

A pregnant woman wanting to use RU-486 must obtain the drug early in her pregnancy, since after the first few weeks she produces too much of her own progesterone for it to be neutralized by the drug. Two days after taking the pill the woman may receive a dosage of prostaglandin, either in the form of a vaginal suppository or injection. Within three hours abdominal cramps begin and she may be given a painkiller. In the next one to three days, the unborn child will be expelled. Another visit to the clinic is required to verify that the abortion has been successful. If it has not been successful, the woman has a choice of other abortion methods.[502]

RU-486 is trumpeted as an alternative to surgical abortion. An article appearing in the *New England Journal of Medicine,* coauthored by Dr. Beaulieu, states: "RU-486 offers a reasonable alternative to surgical abortion, which carries the risks of anesthesia, surgical complications, infertility, and psychological sequelae."[503] In response, the late Dr. Joseph R. Stanton, a prominent Boston physician, stated:

> The American populace has been told that "surgical" abortion is a medical procedure, safe, easy, without significant complications. How often have we not heard preached from impeccable

medical auspices that abortion is safer than having a baby? Those who have raised caution or caveat have been imperiously swept aside by the purveyors of abortion as the safe new freedom. One wonders, did the editorial board of the *New England Journal of Medicine* perhaps give the game away when it printed on its pristine paper that surgical abortion has "complications," "infertility," and "psychological" sequelae?[504]

The availability of RU-486 on the market has created new concerns for the Food and Drug Administration. Laboratories received reports of serious bacterial infection, bleeding, ectopic pregnancies that have ruptured, and death from the use of RU-486. Because of this, on November 15, 2004, the FDA announced safety changes to the Danco Laboratories, LLC's labeling of mifepristone (RU-486). The warnings add information on the risk of serious bacterial infections, sepsis, bleeding, and death that may occur following any termination of pregnancy.

The information reminds healthcare providers that serious bacterial infection and sepsis may occur without the usual signs of infection, such as fever and tenderness on examination. Healthcare providers are further informed that prolonged, heavy bleeding may warrant surgical interventions. The label also warns that healthcare providers should be vigilant for patients with undiagnosed ectopic pregnancies (tubal pregnancies), as this condition may be missed by physical examination and ultrasound. Some of the symptoms of an ectopic pregnancy may mimic the expected symptoms of a medical termination of pregnancy.

For consumers, the medication guide that goes with the drug states that they should contact their healthcare provider right away for fever, abdominal pain, and heavy bleeding. Also, consumers are advised to take their medication guide to the emergency room or any healthcare provider they visit for problems. This allows healthcare providers to understand that the patient is undergoing a termination of pregnancy, and assess risks associated with that condition.

The Internet has now become a source to obtain RU-486. One

can conveniently order the drug at www.abortion-pill-online.com. The Web site proclaims the following: "Abortion At Home: The right to choose."[505] The site goes on to give information on how it may be obtained with a simple purchase through the Internet.

The development of RU-486 is a step towards a longtime goal of the abortion industry—to reduce abortion to a private act, and making it as easy as taking a pill at home. Pro-abortionists argue that since American society accepts contraception, there should be no significant moral problems in accepting abortifacients and early induced abortions through RU-486. They argue further that until the human embryo "looks like a human," its evident biological humanity is not of moral significance. Hence, abortion advocates are arguing strenuously that abortion in the early stages of pregnancy should be a free fire zone, and the abortion pill will be a tool to accomplish this.

Human Cloning

Science fiction has long written of the ability of science to one day perfect the cloning of humans. Cloning of a human being means that an exact genetic copy of such human is reproduced by using the DNA from a cell in the donor's body. Over the years such thoughts were dismissed as science fiction fantasy. However, such a fantasy became a real scientific possibility in 1997.

The reality of future human cloning was raised when Scottish scientists at Roslin Institute created a cloned sheep—the much-celebrated "Dolly."[506] This feat aroused worldwide interest and concern because of its scientific and ethical implications. Thus, the cloning of a human being, an act once thought unattainable and even unthinkable, was now being touted as a likely occurrence in the very near future.

For human cloning (the terms "recombinant DNA technology," "DNA cloning," "molecular cloning, "or "gene cloning" all refer to the same process) to be successful, there must be a transfer of a DNA fragment of interest from one cell to a self-replicating genetic element such as a bacterial plasmid. The DNA of interest can then be propagated in a foreign host cell. Theoretically, what is produced is an exact genetic carbon copy of the human who donated the DNA.

There are three kinds of human cloning. They are:

1) Embryo cloning: This medical technique produces identical twins or triplets. It duplicates the process that nature uses to produce twins or triplets. One or more cells are removed from a fertilized embryo and are encouraged to develop into one or more duplicate embryos. Twins or triplets are thus formed, with identical DNA.

2) Adult DNA cloning (also known as reproductive cloning): This technique is intended to produce a duplicate of an existing animal. The DNA from an ovum is removed and replaced with the DNA from a cell removed from an adult animal. The fertilized ovum is then implanted in a womb and allowed to develop into a new animal. It has the potential of producing a twin of an existing person. Based on previous animal studies, it also has the potential of producing severe genetic defects. There are currently no documented cases of this being successfully performed on humans. However, Congress, to date, has failed to pass a federal ban on the practice. It has the potential of producing a twin of an existing person.

3) "Therapeutic cloning" (also known as biomedical cloning): This procedure is identical to adult DNA cloning. In these cases embryonic stem cells are removed from the embryo with the intent of producing tissue or a whole organ for transplant back into the person who supplied the DNA. The embryo dies in the process. The goal of "therapeutic cloning" is to produce a healthy copy of a sick person's tissue or organ for transplant. Proponents of this argue that this technique is vastly superior to relying on organ transplants from other people, because the supply would be unlimited and there would be no waiting lists. Further, they argue the tissue or organ would have the sick person's original DNA and the patient would not have to take immuno suppressant drugs for the rest of his life, as is now required after transplants.

The current public debate about cloning is intense. Most parties in this debate, although not all, agree that attempts to clone another human being should be banned. However, this passionate public debate centers around "therapeutic cloning," which is directly related to embryonic stem cell research. Human cloning advocates assert that such a practice is an opportunity to remake mankind in an image of health, prosperity, and nobility and, thus, is the ultimate expression of man's unlimited potential.

However, those who believe in the sanctity-of-life ethic must reject the premises upon which proponents of "therapeutic cloning" rely to support their assertions. Regardless of the emergence of any medical breakthroughs using stem cells from human embryos through the cloning process, it must be understood that such a process is the intentional breeding of human beings for the sole purpose of killing them to harvest their tissues and organs. Further, so-called "therapeutic cloning" creates a new life without a father, and reduces a mother to the provider of an egg. The determination to destroy this new human life for scientific research in finding new medical therapies reduces the most vulnerable of the human family to medical research tissue to be used for the cure of ailments in adults. As such, cloning embryonic human life under any circumstances crosses an ethical line and takes an irrevocable step towards Huxley's *Brave New World*. If crossed, this is a step from which science can never turn back.

Partial Birth Abortion

Most people refuse to believe that, under *Roe*, abortion is allowable for all nine months of pregnancy. However, in the later stages of pregnancy, even up to the time of birth, the Supreme Court said that abortion could not be prohibited if it is necessary to preserve the "health" of the mother.[507] Of course, the broad definition of "health" adopted by the court allows for abortion for virtually any reason at all. This reality of the scope of *Roe* became very clear during the mid-1990s when intense political debate ensued over what is referred to as partial birth abortion.

What exactly is partial birth abortion? According to online ency-clopedia Wikipedia:

> This procedure has four main elements. First, the cervix is
> dilated. Second, the fetus is positioned for a footling breech.
> Third, the fetus is extracted except for the head. Fourth, the
> brain of the fetus is evacuated so that a dead but otherwise
> intact fetus is delivered via the vagina.
>
> Usually, preliminary procedures are performed over
> a period of two to three days, to gradually dilate the cervix
> using laminaria tents (sticks of seaweed which absorb fluid and
> swell). Sometimes drugs such as synthetic pitocin are used to
> induce labor. Once the cervix is sufficiently dilated, the doctor
> uses an ultrasound and forceps to grasp the fetus' leg. The fetus
> is turned to a breech position, if necessary, and the doctor pulls
> one or both legs out of the birth canal, causing what is referred
> to by some people as the "partial birth" of the fetus. The doctor
> subsequently extracts the rest of the fetus, usually without the
> aid of forceps, leaving only the head still inside the birth canal.
> An incision is made at the base of the skull, scissors are inserted
> into the incision and opened to widen the opening, and then
> a suction catheter is inserted into the opening. The brain is
> suctioned out, which causes the skull to collapse and allows the
> fetus to pass more easily through the birth canal. The placenta
> is removed and the uterine wall is vacuum aspirated using a
> suction curette.[508]

This description is quite clinical, so perhaps a better way to describe it is to see it through the eyes of an eyewitness. In September 1993, Brenda Pratt Shafer, a registered nurse with thirteen years of experience, was assigned by her nursing agency to work at an abortion clinic. At the time Shafer considered herself "very pro-choice."[509] However, what she saw changed her viewpoint and her life forever. Nurse Shafer states:

I stood at the doctor's side and watched him perform a partial-birth abortion on a woman who was six months pregnant. The baby's heartbeat was clearly visible on the ultrasound screen. The doctor delivered the baby's body and arms, everything but his little head. The baby's body was moving. His little fingers were clasping together. He was kicking his feet. The doctor took a pair of scissors and inserted them into the back of the baby's head, and the baby's arms jerked out in a flinch, a startle reaction, like a baby does when he thinks that he might fall. Then the doctor opened the scissors up. Then he stuck the high-powered suction tube into the hole and sucked the baby's brains out. Now the baby was completely limp. I never went back to the clinic. But I am still haunted by the face of that little boy. It was the most perfect, angelic face I have ever seen.[510]

Congress attempted to pass federal legislation to ban partial birth abortion in the 1990s, only to have such legislation vetoed by President Bill Clinton. Further, a state ban on the procedure in Nebraska was found by the Supreme Court to be unconstitutional in a 5–4 ruling.[511]

In 2003 Congress tried to ban the procedure again by revising its ban in an attempt to satisfy the decision of the Supreme Court. President George W. Bush signed this ban into law, and it was immediately challenged in federal court. This legislation, known as the "Partial-Birth Abortion Ban Act of 2003," made the following initial findings: "A moral, medical, and ethical consensus exists that the practice of performing a partial-birth abortion—an abortion in which a physician delivers an unborn child's body until only the head remains inside the womb, punctures the back of the child's skull with a sharp instrument, and sucks the child's brains out before completing delivery of the dead infant—is a gruesome and inhumane procedure that is never medically necessary and should be prohibited."

Rather than being an abortion procedure that is embraced by the medical community, particularly among physicians who routinely perform other abortion procedures, partial-birth abortion remains a disfavored procedure that is not only unnecessary to preserve the health of the mother, but in fact, possesses serious risk to the long-term health of women and in some circumstances, their lives. As a result, twenty-seven states banned the procedure as did the United States Congress, which voted to ban the procedure during the 104th, 105th, and 106th Congresses.[512] The law was immediately challenged and found to be unconstitutional by a lower federal court. This time, however, the United States Supreme Court upheld the ban in another 5–4 ruling.[513] The difference in the voting on the Court came from the fact that an opponent of the ban, Justice Sandra Day O'Connor, had been replaced with a supporter of the ban, Justice Samuel Alito.

Transhumanism and the Redefining of Humanity

The central holding of *Roe* says that some human beings, (i.e., unborn babies) are not *persons* under the Constitution and, thus, are not afforded legal protection. This was a judicial proclamation that changed the common understanding of what it means to be human. By divorcing humanity from *personhood* the Supreme Court established a precedent that changes the understanding as to what is the very meaning of being a human. With the meaning of a human being now subject to cultural changes via judicial fiat, doors have been opened to very bizarre attempts to further redefine the definition of a human being. Such an attempt is being aggressively pursued today through a movement known as "transhumanism."

According to Wikipedia, transhumanism is "an international, intellectual and cultural movement supporting the use of new sciences and technologies to enhance human mental and physical abilities and aptitudes, and ameliorate what it regards as undesirable and unnecessary aspects of the human condition, such as stupidity, suffering, disease, aging and involuntary death."

Transhumanist thinkers predict that human beings will eventually be transformed by scientific advances into beings with expanded abilities so as to merit the label "post-human." (In actuality, the transhumanist movement is no more than the old eugenics movement that was launched by Adolf Hitler and his Nazi henchmen who attempted to purify humanity with a new Aryan race.)

Transhumanists, according to Wikipedia, support the use of both current and future technologies so that humans can "become more than human. They support the recognition and/or protection of cognitive liberty, morphological freedom, and procreative liberty as civil liberties, so as to guarantee individuals the choice of using human enhancement technologies on themselves and their children."[514]

Cultural observer Wesley J. Smith, in commenting on the transhumanist movement, says this: "In recent years, scientists have mixed the DNA of a jellyfish with that of a monkey, creating a 'transgenic' animal that glows in the dark. ('Transgenic' means possessing the genes of more than one type of organism.) Scientists have also inserted spider DNA into the genes of goats, creating ewes that produce milk containing spider-web silk. The goal of the project is to extract sufficient web silk—one of the strongest and lightest substances known—to create an industry in spider-silk products."[515]

Smith goes on to say that while it is currently unknown whether any biotech companies are at the present doing such transgenic research mixing animal DNA into human embryos, some transhumanist bioethicists and philosophers explicitly endorse such genetic engineering as one method of producing the "post-human race." Indeed, Smith discusses how transhumanists claim that human beings should be allowed to "metamorphose themselves" with cybertechnology and, in so doing, control the "destiny of their genes," including using artificial chromosomes to replace nature chromosomes and "mixing species boundaries through transgenic technologies."[516]

Will it be possible in the future to use scientific advances to produce a race and higher class of "post-human" beings or "super humans" that are superior in intellect, talent, and physical prowess to the average human? If so, will the future society that accepts such genetic manipulation proclaim such beings to be superior in the enjoyment of legal rights and protection as opposed to the lower class of humans? If this frightening scenario happens, the emergence of Huxley's "brave new world" will have come upon us.

Is a "Brave New World" Inevitable?

In *Brave New World*, Huxley wrote about developments in reproductive technology, biological engineering, and sleep-learning that combine together to change society. The novel describes a "utopian" world where humanity is carefree, healthy, and technologically advanced. Poverty and warfare are eliminated and happiness pervades the culture. Ironically, however, these things are achieved by eliminating what is essential to the very identity of humanity—family, culture, art, literature, science, religion, and philosophy. It is also a pleasure-seeking society that is obsessed with promiscuous sex and drugs, especially the use of "soma," a powerful drug taken to escape pain and bad memories through hallucinatory fantasies. While there is apparent stability in this world, it is maintained through deliberately engineered and strictly enforced social stratification. Abortion-on-demand, selective reduction, fetal and stem cell research, sex-selection abortion, and human cloning would all fit in nicely in this "utopia."

In this "brave new world" human beings are not made in the image of God, but rather are pawns to be manipulated to conform to the notions of an elite as to what is most beneficial for society. Individual rights, indeed, individual lives, are valueless in such a society. What only matters is the "quality" of life (defined by the ruling elite) that is achieved for the public as a whole. In such a world the very essence of what constitutes a human being is changed so that some human beings are not regarded as truly humans, while others who have qualities deemed superior are considered a new breed of humanity that is protected in the law. It is this new breed of humanity that controls and determines the fate of others whose lives are seen as expendable for the good of society as a whole.

The only way to combat the onslaught of this "brave new world" is for American society to restore the traditional and foundational belief in the sanctity of every human life. A human life made in the image of God can never be manipulated and destroyed for what is perceived to be the advancement of medical therapies for the betterment of others.

While it appears that the momentum in American culture today is moving us rapidly towards Huxley's nightmare vision of the future, there is one sleeping force that has the power and ability to turn the tide—the community of faith and the body of Christ. The efforts to restore the sanctity-of-life ethic in America must go far beyond efforts to change the law and public policy regarding innocent human life. It must reach the very hearts and minds of the American people to be successful.

—

Thomas A. Glessner is president of the National Institute of Family and Life Advocates (NIFLA), a public-interest law firm founded in 1993. A graduate of the University of Washington School of Law in Seattle, he is the author of Destiny's Team: A Story about Love, Choices and Eternity *(Anamalos, 2007) and* The Emerging Brave New World *(Anamalos, 2008).*

The Coming Persecution
of Christians

---

by Phillip Goodman

A Non-Issue

Right up front this must be said: The persecution of Christians is a non-issue if you do not believe in Jesus. If you have not received Jesus Christ as your Savior, then there are bigger issues, such as the reality of hell. This might sound harsh, but this is a "reality" book. Jesus put it simply, but it hits like a fire-forged hammer: "I said therefore to you, that you shall die in your sins; for unless you believe that I am He, you shall die in your sins" (John 8:24).

The earthly persecution of a Christian pales against the alternative to becoming a Christian. So, my friend, as the Bible puts it, examine yourself to be certain of your salvation in Christ—that is the utmost priority.[517] The verse above is what might be called the negative side of the gospel (good news). There are consequences to sin. But Jesus paid the price for the sins of the entire human race when He laid down His life for us at the cross. That brings us to the positive part of the gospel: You do not have to die in your sins and spend eternity in hell. That is good news, indeed! Make certain you are a Christian by believing this promise: "For God so loved the world, that He gave His only begotten Son, that whosoever believeth in Him should not perish, but have everlasting life" (John 3:16).

Now, if you have a relationship with God through His only begotten Son, Jesus Christ, then yes, there are still other issues you must confront while dwelling on earth. The Bible teaches that a true Christian will act like a Christian; every Christian will walk through life as if swimming "upstream." Why? Because the ways of the world are diametrically opposed to the ways of Christianity. The values, practices, and methods of the world "flow" in one direction while the values, practices, and methods of every sincere Christian "flow" in quite another. And naturally, when "going against the flow," we meet resistance. The "flow" of the world, at best, offers Christians the resistance of a steady stream, but more often it requires us to struggle against a raging torrent. We read:

"Love not the world, neither the things that are in the world. If any man love the world, the love of the Father is not in him. For all that is in the world, the lust of the flesh, and the lust of the eyes, and the pride of life, is not of the Father, but is of the world. And the world passeth away, and the lust thereof: but he that doeth the will of God abideth for ever." (1 John 2:15–17)

This sounds like a litmus test for determining followers of Jesus. The loves, likes, and passions of the world run counter to the character of Jesus. Thus, those who are born again[518] in Christ and as a consequence live in conformity with the character of Christ find their loves, likes, and passions a direct contradiction to those of the world. This sounds a bit black and white. But the Bible draws such a clear distinction between the ways of God and the ways of the world that indeed the distinction *is* black and white—and surely one's attitude toward the ways of the world reveals whether one is truly a Christian. Here is that litmus test:

"Ye adulterers and adulteresses, know ye not that the friendship of the world is enmity with God? whosoever therefore will be a friend of the world is the enemy of God" (James 4:4).

The testimony of the Bible is abundant: Christians who are living the life of Christians will find life in this world at times uncomfortable, hurtful, or even dangerous. When Jesus Christ identified himself with us, He did so totally. He laid down His life so that we can have eternal life when we accept His gift of salvation. Being identified with Christ is a two-way street. The Bible says that Christians will be persecuted by the world in Christ's name. As a result, Christians have always been persecuted by an un-Christian world. However, the scope and depth of the persecution of Christians in the days to come is predicted by Bible prophecy to surpass anything the world has yet seen.

The Writing on the Marquee

Take a drive with me through the buckle of the Bible belt. That would be Tulsa, Oklahoma. More than six hundred churches—or I should say, church buildings—can be found in the Tulsa metropolitan area. Of those churches, the few that are Bible-based stand out like lights on a hill at midnight. They vividly illustrate the following passage, "Ye are the light of the world. A city that is set on an hill cannot be hid.... Let your light so shine before men, that they may see your good works, and glorify your Father which is in heaven" (Matthew 5:14, 16) because of what they say on their signs.

Let me explain. Almost every church in Tulsa features a marquee with words that express what that church is about. The churches with ministry leaders who preach and teach from the Bible usually post Bible verses on their signs. The Word of God is like a torchlight cutting through the blackness: "We have also a more sure word of prophecy; whereunto ye do well that ye take heed, as unto a light that shineth in a dark place, until the day dawn, and the day star arise in your hearts" (2 Peter 1:19).

What a contrast to the monotonous signboard minutia when

drivers-by catch the piercing power of a Bible citation on a well placed church sign! These signboard verses can prick the heart of many a lost passerby who needs direction or hurting person who needs hope. The verses are beacons and invitations for anyone to enter those churches to hear more about the only One who can provide that direction and hope. They do what no social, medical, or psychological program ever devised by man can possibly do: penetrate the darkest soul with the Word of God and provide the ultimate reality, a Savior: "For the word of God is quick, and powerful, and sharper than any twoedged sword, piercing even to the dividing asunder of soul and spirit, and of the joints and marrow, and is a discerner of the thoughts and intents of the heart" (Hebrews 4:12).

But friends, churches such as these are but a few among many in the Tulsa metro vicinity. The majority of the church marquees carry worldly words and platitudes that sound no different than the words offered in every social service club, benevolent organization, education center, or recreation hall. The frills-centered gibberish announcing dance lessons, art classes, twelve-step programs, relational psychology, and education-based nonsense junk up the billboards of these Chamber of Commerce-friendly, world-centric, spiritually vacuous bricks-and-mortar, steeple-topped pieces of real estate called "churches."

Jesus had a definition for these "churches":

"I know thy works, that thou art neither cold nor hot: I would thou wert cold or hot. So then because thou art lukewarm, and neither cold nor hot, I will spue thee out of my mouth. Because thou sayest, I am rich, and increased with goods, and have need of nothing; and knowest not that thou art wretched, and miserable, and poor, and blind, and naked." (Revelation 3:15–7)

This particular type of church, the church of Laodicea, is foreseen by the writer of the book of Revelation to dominate the religious landscape of end-time Christianity. This church makes the prideful and boisterous claim that "I am rich, and have become wealthy, and have need of nothing," then it sets out to prove that claim by consorting with the world, fleecing the flock of billions of dollars, and sinking the money into monstrously lavish buildings and shamelessly degenerate feel-good programs. It substitutes human wisdom for biblical teaching—thus, the blind lead the blind, and both fall into a pit.[519]

The church of Laodicea will never see persecution, but it will see divine judgment. In its magnitude and wealth, its members have their reward—now. What the church of Laodicea reflects on its sign, it preaches from its pulpit. And from its pulpit and its programs, this church mimics the world. No, this church will not experience persecution because the world loves its own: "Love not the world, neither the things that are in the world. If any man love the world, the love of the Father is not in him" (1 John 2:15).

But the leadership and congregations of churches that let the Bible verse shine forth week after week from their marquees invariably preach, teach, and practice the same from inside their buildings. Unlike the members of the church of Laodicea, they *will* see persecution because they oppose the degeneracy of the world, which in response will hate them. The persecution will in fact serve as a test of the true nature of the church and its members. Those who are not undergoing some degree of persecution need to take a closer look at their "light." If they are not allowing it to shine forth, and if they are essentially practicing "closet Christianity," then persecution will not be their fate because the world only persecutes light-bearers. Again, we read, "Love not the world, neither the things that are in the world. If any man love the world, the love of the Father is not in him. For all that is in the world, the lust of the flesh, and the lust of the eyes, and the pride of life, is not of the Father, but is of the world. And the world passeth away, and the lust thereof: but he that doeth the will of God abideth for ever" (1 John 2:15–17).

Interestingly, persecution of people for their Christian faith usually begins inside the professing church. Jesus said that believers and unbelievers would be mixed together within an entity that proclaimed the kingdom of heaven. This, of course, would be the organized church.

He compared it to a field of wheat and tares.[520] These two plants bear a superficial resemblance, but are essentially different because of the fruit that they bear. Christians and christianizers have superficial resemblance. They both belong to a religious organization and they both appear religious. The difference is that one is truly indwelt through faith by the Holy Spirit (the Spirit of the living Christ—Romans 8:9) and the other is preoccupied with the spirit of the world. The latter will persecute the former. The church with the spirit of worldly banter reflected on its marquee will break fellowship with and malign the reputation of those within the structural church who proclaim the gospel of Jesus Christ.

The Persecution of Christians in America

Church signs are, of course, only symptomatic of the worldly chit chat billowing forth from the so-called Christian platforms of televangelists, religious media, and psycho-spiritual programs. Scripturally bankrupt, they torment the biblical spirit of Christians. Biblically-minded believers are persecuted in the same way Abraham's nephew, Lot, was persecuted.

Lot was repulsed by the behavior of the unbelievers in the wicked cities of Sodom and Gomorrah. His righteous spirit was tormented by the worldly debauchery he saw. Lot was persecuted without bloodshed. As the apostle Peter stated, "...just Lot, vexed with the filthy conversation of the wicked: (For that righteous man dwelling among them, in seeing and hearing, vexed his righteous soul from day to day with their unlawful deeds)" (2 Peter 2:7–8).

True, Bible-believing Christians in Tulsa, Oklahoma are also oppressed, not only by the mockery of church buildings bearing worldly platitudes on their marquees, but by the cavorting of these religious bodies with the agendas of the world, such as the approval of abortion on demand, the acceptance of the homosexual lifestyle, the promotion of evolution in the classroom, the effort to "remove" Christ from

Christmas, the displacement of the Bible by the new tolerance, and the co-opting of Christ-like values to the service of humanistic programs. The persecution of Christians begins in the church. But in America, it is still persecution without bloodshed.

Christian persecution, before reaching its full orb of bloodshed, begins with psychological, economic, and social persecution, and even before that, the derisive torture of the righteous conscience of believers. The expulsion of God and every mention of biblical righteousness from the public square is also a mockery directed specifically at Christians and the Judeo-Christian heritage upon which this nation was founded. The list of the public policy and judicial mandates against Christians is startling! Jesus said these abominations are directed at Him personally (see John 15:15–18).

One Nation under God

Our founding fathers framed the Declaration of Independence around this statement: "We hold these truths to be self-evident, that all men are created equal, that they are endowed by their Creator with certain unalienable Rights…among these are Life, Liberty and the pursuit of happiness…That to secure these rights, Governments are instituted…"

In this brief statement, the founders affirmed the **Creator**, the **creature**, and **moral absolutes**. One can easily see the biblical chain of authority woven into the rationale of the Declaration and of the United States Constitution. These documents clearly assert the following:

1. The nation relies on a Judeo-Christian Creator-God.
2. People are created beings, personally reliant on God.
3. There exists an absolute moral code from which people derive "unalienable rights" (life, liberty, and the pursuit of happiness).
4. The purpose of government is to secure these God-given, moral absolutes.

The Preamble to the Constitution picks it up from there, affirming its purpose of setting up a government that would secure this God-given liberty.

From that time until relatively recently, America was a "nation under God" in its national conscientiousness. In fact, our country formed its three branches of government around the biblical model of Isaiah 33:22: "For the Lord is our **Judge** [Supreme Court], the Lord is our **Law giver** [Congress], the Lord is our **King** [President]" (emphasis added).

The founders made prayer an official part of the deliberations of these branches. Even the Ten Commandments are carved into the stone and wood of the Supreme Court buildings to this day!

Attempts to Expel God from the Public Square

But then, ever so slightly at first, came the groundwork for the efforts to remove God from our public squares and schoolrooms. By 1962, the trend was clear. Here is the shameful list:

1840 Horace Mann, the humanist-Unitarian, took philosophical control of the U.S. educational system.

1930 John Dewey, the father of modern secular humanism, instituted the modern U.S. educational framework.

1962 Praying was outlawed in U.S. schools.

1963 Reading the Bible was outlawed in U.S. schools.

1987 The Creator's name was outlawed in U.S. school science classes.

1991 The name of "God" was outlawed at graduation ceremonies in U.S. schools.

2000 Vermont began offering civil unions after a ruling by the state's Supreme Court.

2002 The Pledge of Allegiance with the phrase "under God" in it was outlawed in U.S. schools.

2003 Massachusetts' highest court ruled that the state constitution guarantees same-sex couples the right to marry.

2005 Connecticut became the first state to approve civil unions without being forced by the courts.

2005 California lawmakers became the first in the country to approve a bill allowing same-sex marriages. This trend has continued through the New England states.

And it continues…

Persecution in the U. S. Military

The tormenting of the spirit of "just Lot" (2 Peter 2:7–9) is also prevalent in America's armed forces. Because of the "conduct of unprincipled men" who reign as the civilian leaders of the military, the name of Jesus Christ is rapidly being marginalized. Here is what Larry Johnston, Major USAF (retired), writes. I quote him at length because of his association, as a Christian, with the military that spans almost half a century.

> …based on what I was taught growing up and what exposure I have had with the US Armed Forces since 1964, I have noticed a very disturbing trend.
>
> History verifies that use of Christ's name by US Presidents, US Governmental employees, Generals and all other military ranks was very common. Prayer in "Jesus name" was vital for those men and women that stood in harms way to defend liberty.
>
> Considering the overwhelming sacrifices expected of military personnel, exclusion of Christ's name would have been deemed unimaginable by our "one nation under God" founding fathers.
>
> Unfortunately, beginning in the late '80s until the present, the separation of church and state debate has eroded the formal acknowledgment by our "leaders" of the US Armed Forces and "leaders" in the US Armed Forces that Jesus Christ is our Lord. In fact, use of Christ's name at formal military functions by military personnel can result in disciplinary action.

Traditional annual military "Christmas Parties" are now referred to as "Holiday Parties." Use of Christ's name in the US Armed Forces has become a "use at your own risk" term. You can get away with "God" but use of the Lord, Christ or Jesus is not encouraged in some units and strictly prohibited in others.

I have family members, friends, associates and fellow military members that have been called upon to make disabling sacrifices or the ultimate sacrifice for our nation. I have placed the remains of a USAF pilot that had two young sons in a body bag, informed a mother that her young son was killed on his way to his first duty station and commanded the funeral detail of a WWII fighter pilot. I have counseled with an addicted and mentally ill homeless veteran that never recovered from his part in killing large numbers of children that were "attaching" his emplacement with grenades tied to their bodies. I assisted another veteran that was called upon to kill twelve enemy soldiers with his bare hands while defending his fellow soldiers. I counseled with US Army Ranger "POW" Lt Col Nick Roe that survived confinement in a bamboo cage for over 5 years in North Viet Nam living off of a diet of raw rats and prayer. In my life long association with POWs (family and in-service), I have never been with a POW that did not give Jesus the glory for their return home. While counseling addicts since the early '70s I have found that the best "counselor" and source of "healing" is Jesus Christ...period!!

The consequences of denying Christ in the US Armed Forces, in our lives and the life of our nation will be "death." As Christians, we have hope. We need to pray in Jesus' name for ourselves, our nation and our men and women [in] uniform. Duty, Honor, Country in Jesus' name...Amen! Larry A Johnston, Major USAF (Retired).[521]

Our military men, asked to endure hardship and risks of injury or death, must now do so under the same spiritual torment and persecution that Lot endured.

One Nation—Under God

The framers of our government believed in God, but He was a specific God. He had an identity: He was the God of Abraham, Isaac, and Jacob, and, for most of the founding fathers, of Jesus Christ. It is this acknowledgment of the biblical God in the fabric of American life that has compelled this country to stand by Israel as God's chosen people. When Israel returned to its ancient land and grew into the state of Israel in 1948, and then recaptured Jerusalem in 1967, there was still a persuasion in the halls of government and among the American electorate that God was bringing His prophetic Word to fulfillment:

"And I will bless them that bless thee, and curse him that curseth thee: [Why? Because of the next statement. It is through Israel that the Messiah Jesus would come and make it possible for the rest of humanity to be saved from sin] and in thee shall all families of the earth be blessed" (Genesis 12:3).

"For I will take you from among the heathen, and gather you out of all countries, and will bring you into your own land" (Ezekiel 36:24 [fulfilled in 1948]).

"…and Jerusalem shall be trodden down of the Gentiles, until the times of the Gentiles be fulfilled" (Luke 21:24 [fulfilled in 1967 and continuing]).

The United States supported Israel through all of these stages of prophetic fulfillment.

God's Chosen People Given to the Nations

But, just as America began to erase from its national consciousness the memory of God by trying to deport Him from its public places, our country began the next logical step: withdrawing—albeit ever so slightly—support for God's chosen people. That brings us face to face with the following prophecies, all set in the context of the last days:

"…[Arabs], which *have appointed my land* into their possession…" (Ezekiel 36:5).

"...he [Antichrist]...shall divide the land..." (Daniel 11:39).

"...and will plead with them there for my people...they have... parted my land" (Joel 3:2).

Because it is God who is bringing the Jews back to His land (and it is His land—see below), then America is going against God to divide His land and give it away!

"The land shall not be sold for ever: for the land is mine, for ye are strangers and sojourners with me" (Leviticus 25:23).

"And they shall dwell in the land that I have given unto Jacob [Israel] my servant, wherein your fathers have dwelt; and they shall dwell therein, even they, and their children, and their children's children for ever..." (Ezekiel 37:25).

The policy of the United States since the early 1990s has been to divide up the land of Israel and apportion it out to Israel's enemies. All of these policies—the rejection of God in our public life and the compromising of our support for Israel—have brought both persecution and judgment. America's Christians are persecuted and tormented by what they see and hear. But America is under judgment for aligning itself with the enemies of Israel and for rewriting its foundational history to reflect the godlessness of our age.

America's Parallel Rejection of God

In summary, here is what we see in America's history: We began as a publicly God-fearing nation. Our forefathers made this plain in our foundational documents. Our schools made it plain in its McGuffey readers. Our policymakers made it manifest in their support of Israel. Then, in the 1960s, God was asked to leave our public places and our public consciousness. By the 1990s, America, in the name of tolerance, had welcomed all of the gods of the various cultures to fill up the vacuum left by the attempted expulsion of the God of Abraham, Isaac, and Jacob. And in the same decade came the drift toward "partitioning" away the state of Israel. Today, we have come to two parallel paths of godlessness—America's rejection of God and America's rejection of God's plan for Israel.

At the crossroads is the ratcheting up of the persecution of Christians in the United States, with the parallel persecution of Israel by the United States.

Worlds-away Persecution and Worldwide Persecution

The headlines typically are only printed in Christian publications. The news is hard to read; it is frightening. The events seem—as they almost are, geographically—a world away: Chinese underground churches, marginalized Russian believers, martyred Egyptian Christians, butchered African pastors. What seems worlds away is foreseen in Bible prophecy to become worldwide. In America, from the oxymoron of secularist church marquees to public square God-rejections, the persecution of western Christians is on a fast track to playing catch up with the violent persecution of Christians in far-away places! The final war against the saints has already begun, and it is becoming global: "I beheld, and the same horn made war with the saints, and prevailed against them..." (Daniel 7:21).

This prophecy by Daniel is scheduled for the last days. Every indication is that our generation is currently on the edge of entering those days. Often called the end time, this period will be a relatively short but intensely cruel period under the iron fist of the Antichrist. His primary purpose will be to link the nations of the world into a one-world planet with the singular purpose of destroying Jews and Christians. As we've seen, this type of wholesale persecution begins with seemingly innocuous occurrences such as biblically vacuous church signs in tranquil communities, but then proceeds steadily toward full-scale "war with the saints." "Worlds away" is happening now. Here are some examples:

1. **India:** Two native missionaries were beaten by an angry mob in the northeastern state of Manipur after showing the *Jesus* film. It is only one in a series of attacks against evangelists in the Asian nation.

2. **England:** A major British health trust suspended a nurse for offering to pray for an elderly patient. The nurse reported that "it was around lunchtime and I had spent about twenty to twenty-five minutes

with her. I had applied dressings to her legs and shortly before I left I said to her: 'Would you like me to pray for you?' She [the patient] said, 'No, thank you.' And I said: 'OK.' I only offered to pray for her because I was concerned about her welfare and wanted her to get better," the nurse said.

3. Saudi Arabia: The Saudi government instituted a country-wide crackdown on Christian converts and church activities. A Saudi national was arrested after writing on his Web site about his decision to follow Jesus instead of Islam. He had already been held for nine months in 2004 and for one month in 2008 for similar witnessing attempts in the name of Jesus. Saudi Christians expressed concern that the Internet writer might be executed for apostasy under the country's strict interpretation of Islamic law that states a Muslim who abandons Islam is seen as someone who offends his family, his country, and his religion.

4. Iran: Christians with a Muslim background are routinely detained and tortured—this is a country that is on the verge of introducing a law forcing judges to impose the death penalty on those abandoning Islam.

5. Afghanistan: Pressure is exerted by the Taliban and other Muslim extremist groups against Christian minorities, despite the presence of an international peacekeeping force.

6. India: Witnesses have seen an explosion of violence since Christians were blamed for the death of a Hindu nationalist leader in the state of Orissa, although Maoist rebels claim responsibility for the attack.

7. Eritrea: More than three thousand Christians are imprisoned for their faith in such places as cellars, containers, and military prison camps. Several believers have died from torture and the lack of medical attention.

8. Iraq: After years of violence and intimidation from al-Qaida and other Islamic extremist groups, life is a constant struggle for the embattled Christian minority. Christians in northern Iraq are shaken by a string of murders, and find themselves in the middle of a power struggle between Kurds and Sunni Arabs.

9. Pakistan: Two Christian teenage girls are rescued after being kidnapped, sold to other men as sex slaves, and forced into Islam by radical Muslims.

10. Washington, D. C.: Visitors entering the Capitol Visitor Center in Washington, D.C., are told in a prominent display that America's national motto is "*E pluribus unum*," or "Out of Many One." The real motto, "In God We Trust," is nowhere to be found in the sprawling five-hundred-eighty-eight-thousand-square-foot-square-foot exhibition space.[522]

The Rest of the Story—Relief for the Persecuted

Earlier, we read about the inevitable persecution of Jews and Christians predicted by the prophet Daniel. But, praise God, that is not the whole story, for the passage goes on to say that the saints will be rescued by the only one who could possibly rescue them from this worldwide holocaust: "...until the Ancient of Days came, and judgment was passed in favor of the saints of the Highest One, and the time arrived when the saints took possession of the kingdom" (Daniel 7:22).

Jesus Christ, returning as the Son of the Ancient of Days (God the Father) will defeat Antichrist and put an eternal stop to the war against the saints. This same prophecy was reiterated by Jesus himself when He said about the last days, "For then shall be great tribulation, such as was not since the beginning of the world to this time, no, nor ever shall be. And except those days should be shortened, there should no flesh be saved: but for the elect's sake those days shall be shortened" (Matthew 24:21–22).

Here again are the advance headlines of the coming global tribulation against Jews and Christians—a tribulation so far surpassing any that the world has ever seen that the entire world, not just the saints, will be on a path to destruction. But this passage also says that there is more to the story. We read, "...but for the elect's sake those days shall be shortened" (Matthew 24:22).

The Bible assures believers in Christ that there will be justice. There will come a reckoning. There will be divine recompense for the sake of those who trust in Christ. The prophecies of the rescue of Christians and the judgment of those who persecute Christians are as clear and certain as prophecies of the persecution of believers. We find the rest of the story again in 2 Thessalonians: "For after all it is only just for God to repay with affliction those who afflict you, and to give relief to you who are afflicted and to us as well when the Lord Jesus shall be revealed from heaven with His mighty angels in flaming fire, dealing out retribution to those who do not know God and to those who do not obey the gospel of our Lord Jesus" (2 Thessalonians 1:6–8).

This is another way of stating the prediction of our Lord that "...except those days should be shortened, there should no flesh be saved: but for the elect's sake those days shall be shortened" (Matthew 24:22).

Persecution of believers is here. It will increase to global proportions in the coming days. But the rest of the story is that justice will prevail in favor of believers in Jesus Christ, and it will last forever!

The Reward: Free But Costly

The price for becoming a Christian is absolutely free. But the price for being a Christian is costly.

The New Testament is full of the teaching that eternal life is a free gift. The apostles of Christ emphasized this gospel truth over and over in their letters. But the gospel is the great enemy of Satan, who wants to destroy people by leading them away from the true gospel. And Satan is a "religious" worker. His aim is to lead people captive through religion into a false gospel—one that imprisons them in their sin and one that even preaches another "Christ" who can't deliver them to eternal life. The apostle Paul warned of Satan's evil schemes to deceive people straight into hell: "But I fear, lest by any means, as the serpent beguiled Eve through his subtilty, so your minds should be corrupted from the simplicity that is in Christ. For if he that cometh preacheth another Jesus, whom we have not preached, or if ye receive another spirit, which ye have not received, or another gospel, which ye have not accepted..." (2 Corinthians 11:3–4).

In warning of this false gospel, Paul went on in the same passage to warn that it will be taught by Satan through churches, by religious teachers and preachers. Satan uses the "trust factor" at the core of his deception: "For such are false apostles, deceitful workers, transforming themselves into the apostles of Christ. And no marvel; for Satan himself is transformed into an angel of light" (2 Corinthians 11:13–14).

These religious preachers teach that though Paul (who wrote most of the New Testament) and the other apostles might seem to claim that eternal life is a free gift from God, Jesus actually never made such a claim. Therefore, the apostolic letters of the New Testament, and their gospel claims, must be reinterpreted in the light of what Jesus actually said. Even many Christians wish Jesus had been clearer about the gospel of the free gift of eternal life. But this could not possibly be farther from the truth, which is exactly where one would expect Satan to place his "gospel" on the truth scale.

The good news is that Jesus was perfectly clear. Salvation is free; Jesus spoke of the free gift of eternal life many times. But I want to focus on just one statement Jesus made about the good news (gospel) of eternal life—a free gift from God. I will use this statement for three reasons. First, it is so clear it cannot be misinterpreted. Second, Jesus used it twice. Third, He said it on earth, and He said it again in heaven. Here is the version He used while on the earth, when He was thirsty after a long and dusty trip, and He asked the Samaritan woman at the well for a drink of water: "Jesus answered and said unto her, If thou knewest the **gift of God**, and **who it is** that saith to thee, Give me to drink; thou wouldest **have asked of him**, and he would have **given thee living water**...But whosoever drinketh of the water that I **shall give him** shall never thirst; but the water that I **shall give him** shall be in him a well of water springing up into **everlasting life**" (John 4:10,14, emphasis added).

Let's take a close look at this one and only true gospel, straight from the lips of Jesus, emphasizing the words in bold. Jesus said that salvation is a **gift of God**, and the giving of this gift centers on **who is** speaking. The one speaking was Jesus, the promised divine Messiah of the Old Testament, the prophesied Savior of the world. The only key to receiving the gift is to **ask Him** for it—by definition, a gift is free to the recipient, but not to the giver. Jesus paid for the gift by His death and resurrection. To anyone who asks, Jesus will **give** the gift of **living water**, that is, **eternal life**.

Sixty-five years after Jesus articulated the gospel to the Samaritan woman at the well, He restated it again from heaven, using the same word pictures to make it understandable to the simplest person: "And the Spirit and the bride say, Come. And let him that heareth say, Come. And let him that is athirst come. And whosoever will, let him take the water of life freely" (Revelation 22:17).

Jesus said it while on the earth. He said it again while exalted to the throne of God in heaven: To the one who simply asks, believing, Jesus shall give the gift of "living water," that is, eternal life. To *become* a Christian, then, is without cost and everlasting. But as we noted earlier, *being* a Christian is costly, often troublesome, and sometimes lethal.

Jesus said that there is a cost to bearing His name. He referred to it as "bearing His cross." This is the essence of Christian persecution: "And he that taketh not his cross, and followeth after me, is not worthy of me" (Matthew 10:38).

Even the apostles at first did not fully understand the cost of following Jesus. The mother of James and John asked Jesus to let her two sons occupy the place of honor beside His throne in the coming kingdom—one on the left, one on the right. Hear Jesus' answer to her request: "But Jesus answered and said, Ye know not what ye ask. [turning to James and John] Are ye able to drink of the cup that I shall drink of, and to be baptized with the baptism that I am baptized with? They say unto him, We are able. And he saith unto them, Ye shall drink indeed of my cup, and be baptized with the baptism that I am baptized with: but to sit on my right hand, and on my left, is not mine to give, but it shall be given to them for whom it is prepared of my Father" (Matthew 20:22–23).

Jesus warned that following Him would be costly. James was in fact the first apostle to be martyred (see Acts 12:2). Jesus has given the same forewarning to all Christians. Love for the world versus love for God is a litmus test. If professing Christians hide their faith in the closet and keep quiet, the world is friendly to them. But the hostile reaction of the world to Christians who "walk the talk" identifies those Christians with Christ. "If the world hate you, ye know that it hated me before it hated you. If ye were of the world, the world would love his own: but because ye are not of the world, but I have chosen you out of the world, therefore the world hateth you. Remember the word that I said unto you, The servant is not greater than his lord. If they have persecuted me, they will also persecute you; if they have kept my saying, they will keep yours also. But all these things will they do unto you for my name's sake, because they know not him that sent me" (John 15:18–21).

Three days earlier, Jesus had foretold of the rise of Christian and Jewish persecution to a global scale and a genocidal intensity just before His return. Indeed, every indication from the prophetic Scriptures is that we are now living on the edge of that Great Tribulation.

War and the Weapons of Spiritual Destruction

Everyone has heard of weapons of mass destruction. Then comes the question, "Where did they go?" But few have heard of weapons of spiritual destruction, yet they are warring against us every day! This war began at the dawn of creation and will climax during the Great Tribulation.

Just as we can trace the scarlet thread of redemption (God's salvation plan for mankind) through the entire Bible, we can also track the plan of spiritual destruction instituted by Satan. Satan launched his plan to destroy man's life and relationship with God in the Garden of Eden. But God had a plan of redemption in place from all eternity past for every person in the future who would want restoration of relationship with the loving Creator.

God promised that through the "seed of the woman" a Savior would come.[373] While Satan pursued his evil plan, God's foreordained plan was already in action. God called a man named Abraham and promised that the seed of the Messiah (Jesus Christ) would come from the nation that would be named through Abraham's offspring.[524] These were the Jews. God set His name on the Jews, and through these chosen people, Jesus was born, ministered, was crucified and resurrected. But before He went to the cross, Jesus told His followers that they would not only suffer tribulation in this world, but that a Great Tribulation—one unequalled in the history of mankind—would climax this current age just before He returns. He put it starkly and simply: "Then shall they deliver you up to be afflicted, and shall kill you: and ye shall be hated of all nations for my name's sake" (Matthew 24:9).

In these last days, there is the prediction that the persecution of Christians (and Jews) will increase. The world will hate Christians and Christianity. There will no longer be any safe-haven countries for believers. Christ said His followers would be hated by "all nations." Though this is true today in many parts of the world (for example, the vitriolic hatred of the Muslim world toward Christians), the time is drawing nigh when this hatred of believers will become global. And the hatred will become routinely violent to the point of mass martyrdom. This is the prophecy that Jesus himself gave to prepare believers for the reality of the world of the coming Antichrist. The book of Revelation says of this world of the Antichrist, "And it was given unto him to make war with the saints, and to overcome them: and power was given him over all kindreds, and tongues, and nations" (Revelation 13:7).

Jesus went on to warn that the persecution of Christian believers would be so fierce that false Christians would fall away from their supposed Christianity and turn against each other as well as against true Christians: "And then shall many be offended, and shall betray one another, and shall hate one another" (Matthew 24:10).

In His prophecy of those coming days, Jesus said true believers would suffer the onslaught of intense religious deception accompanied by intense religious cruelty. (Keep in mind that true Christianity identifies with Christ, while religion identifies with the world, over which Satan rules during this present age—John 12:31.) This will be the apex of Satan's age-long plan to destroy the people of Jesus Christ, whom he failed to destroy at the cross.

"And many false prophets shall rise, and shall deceive many. And because iniquity shall abound, the love of many shall wax cold" (Matthew 24:11–12). The greatest false prophet who ever lived was Mohammad. By today's count, his followers have misled more than a billion people now living as Muslims. A particularly foreboding passage gives evidence that the current wave of Islamic terrorism (slicing off the heads of victims in the name of the false god Allah) is not a passing wave at all, but rather a growing tsunami of bloodletting that will peak just prior to the return of Christ. Revelation chapter 20 speaks of the victims of Antichrist as having been "beheaded":"And I saw thrones, and they sat upon them, and judgment was given unto them: and I saw the souls of them that were beheaded for the witness of Jesus, and for the word of God, and which had not worshipped the beast, neither his image, neither had received his mark upon their foreheads, or in their hands; and they lived and reigned with Christ a thousand years" (Revelation 20:4).

This is where Christian persecution is going on a planetary scope. These are people who are beheaded (the mode often used by Allah-fanatics) because of the word of God.

All of this will occur during the Great Tribulation Jesus spoke of in Matthew 24:21.[525] But let us be forewarned—Bible prophecy fulfillment is preceded by Bible prophecy foreshadows. The early signs of these "birth pangs" of great trouble are upon this generation. Yet there is victory for the true Christian, for Jesus goes on to say that "he that shall endure unto the end, the same shall be saved" (Matthew 24:13).

But let us not get this scene—the Great Tribulation—backwards. The mass holocaust against believers is without a doubt massive in its physical atrocities. Believers will die by the gross. But the warfare is first and foremost Satan's attempt at weapons of spiritual destruction. Satan has no more authority after he has killed the body, but God does: "And fear not them which kill the body, but are not able to kill the soul: but rather fear him which is able to destroy both soul and body in hell" (Matthew 10:28).

Satan knows that believers who die in Christ will live in a blessed state forever and ever. Thus his war against believers is actually spiritual. He wants to scare the faith out of those who may be on the verge of coming to Christ, and he wants to do that by killing believers. This is actually what is meant by "weapons of spiritual destruction." But the weapons of mass destruction come from God. The effect of the God-sent seal and trumpet judgments that befall the followers of the Antichrist as they war against the saints amounts to the death of half of the world's population during the Tribulation. All of those killed by these judgments are persecutors of Christians and Jews.[526]

From Bad to Worse

The apostle Paul suffered many persecutions. Eventually he was martyred for his faith in Jesus Christ. Under the inspiration of the Holy Spirit, Paul made this statement: "[There were many] Persecutions, afflictions, which came unto me at Antioch, at Iconium, at Lystra; what persecutions I endured: but out of them all the Lord delivered me. Yea, and all that will live godly in Christ Jesus shall suffer persecution. But evil men and seducers shall wax worse and worse, deceiving, and being deceived" (2 Timothy 3:11–13).

Paul set forth the history of the persecution of Christians in three phases. First, the apostles, including Paul, suffered intense persecution. Paul was eventually martyred in Rome. All of the apostles except John met their deaths at the hands of those who were out to destroy the gospel of Christ.

Second, just as Jesus had said earlier in John 15:18–21, Paul said that the inevitability of persecution will indicate the reality of a true believer. That is, everyone who proves the claim of being in Christ by walking as Christ walked will suffer persecution.

Third, throughout church history, the persecution of true believers will increase, going from bad to worse. The "bad," as we've seen, begins with social, economic, and psychological persecution. The degeneracy and perversions of social mores are often directed specifically at biblical standards. This is the type of persecution that plagued the godly Lot when he resided in Sodom and Gomorrah, for he was "vexed with the filthy conversation of the wicked: (For that righteous man dwelling among them, in seeing and hearing, vexed his righteous soul from day to day with their unlawful deeds)" (2 Peter 2:7–8). Persecution at this level is bad enough. But it is not as bad as it can get: "For consider him that endured such contradiction of sinners against himself, lest ye be wearied and faint in your minds. Ye have not yet resisted unto blood, striving against sin" (Hebrews 12:3–4).

This is the "bad." But Paul prophesied that persecution will go from bad to worse. And it will happen at the hands of "evil men and impostors" whose satanic agenda is to deceive the world into a united front against God and His Anointed, Jesus Christ: "The kings of the earth set themselves, and the rulers take counsel together, against the LORD, and against his anointed" (Psalms 2:2).

The "worse" will eventuate in the Great Tribulation. Paul said that the progression of persecution against God's children is a process. It proceeds from "bad to worse." It doesn't reverse and go the other direction, say, from worse to bad to better. Persecution will proceed from social, economic, and psychological persecution, which has not yet reached "the point of shedding blood" (Hebrews 12:3–4), to physical bondage, torture and death, which will define the reign of the coming Antichrist and the Great Tribulation:

"...and there shall be a time of trouble, such as never was since there was a nation even to that same time: and at that time thy people shall be delivered, every one that shall be found written in the book." (Daniel 12:1)

"For in those days shall be affliction, such as was not from the beginning of the creation which God created unto this time, neither shall be." (Mark 13:19)

"And it was given unto him [the Antichrist] to make war with the saints, and to overcome them: and power was given him over all kindreds, and tongues, and nations." (Revelation 13:7)

Christians living today should expect to see this trend of persecution increase. The cost of following Christ will become even costlier. We are now entering that rapid downhill slide between the "bad" and the "worse." Bible prophecy always includes a leading foreshadow. This is a pre-fulfillment stage when events begin to build to their final climax. The stage for predicted events of the Great Tribulation and the ensuing imprisonment, torture, and martyrdom of believers is being set as we speak. But God will have the last word: "The kings of the earth set themselves, and the rulers take counsel together, against the LORD, and against his anointed…[But] He that sitteth in the heavens shall laugh: the LORD shall have them in derision" (Psalms 2:2–4).

God will bring victory out of the most depressing scenario. And it is victory for which He has destined Christians—victory without end!

Preparing for the Battle

Prepare your heart for the Rapture, the great rescue mission God will send in the last days. The only way to be ready for this rescue mission is to have your heart ready for Christ when He comes. He could come at any moment to rescue His saints from persecution, because we know that it will happen sometime before the Great Tribulation.[527] We do not know exactly when Jesus will come, but we do know that the more we see the buildup of signs pointing to His return after the Tribulation, the closer must be this rescue mission when we will be caught up to meet Him in the air to return to heaven before the Tribulation. And the signs of the approaching Tribulation and His coming at the end of that Tribulation are rapidly accumulating.[528] Here is how to make sure that your heart is right before the Lord so that you will be prepared both for the battle, and for that great rescue mission. Remember what we said at the beginning of this chapter: Christian persecution is a non-issue unless you are truly a Christian. But you can be certain, for "That if thou shalt confess with thy mouth the Lord Jesus, and shalt believe in thine heart that God hath raised him from the dead, thou shalt be saved. For with the heart man believeth unto righteousness; and with the mouth confession is made unto salvation" (Romans 10:9–10).

A true confession of Jesus as your Savior and Lord also prepares you for the Rapture, when Jesus will "...descend from heaven with a shout, with the voice of the archangel, and with the trump of God: and the dead in Christ shall rise first: Then we which are alive and remain shall be caught up together with them in the clouds, to meet the Lord in the air: and so shall we ever be with the Lord. Wherefore comfort one another with these words" (1 Thessalonians 4:16–18).

But, in the meantime, while we await His coming in the Rapture, we are here on the earth—prepared for the battle, and arming for the war.

Arming for the War

The satanic war of the persecution of Christians is upon us and is growing at an accelerated pace. As we have seen, this is predicted in Bible prophecy. The world will ratchet up the violence against Christians to a degree that will match its intolerance of Christians that already exists. As these end times mature into the full-blown onset of the final Tribulation, Christians will increasingly feel the heat. Yet God provides for us by arming us with the weapons of spiritual warfare. To be armed to face persecution is nowhere better summed up than in the famous "spiritual armor" passage in Ephesians chapter 6:

> For we wrestle not against flesh and blood, but against principalities, against powers, against the rulers of the darkness of this world, against spiritual wickedness in high places. Wherefore take unto you the whole armour of God, that ye may be able to withstand in the evil day, and having done all, to stand.

Stand therefore, having your loins girt about with truth, and having on the breastplate of righteousness; And your feet shod with the preparation of the gospel of peace; Above all, taking the shield of faith, wherewith ye shall be able to quench all the fiery darts of the wicked. And take the helmet of salvation, and the sword of the Spirit, which is the word of God: Praying always with all prayer and supplication in the Spirit, and watching thereunto with all perseverance and supplication for all saints. (Ephesians 6:12–18)

The persecution of Christians is a spiritual war; it is Satan's war against Jesus Christ. And every true Christian is a participant. The persecution, in all of its forms—from intolerance to ridicule to physical violence—is deeper than those human persecutors who precipitate the acts. Satan and his demonic emissaries are behind the scenes directing the hellish activity. Therefore, God has equipped every willing Christian with the necessary and adequate weapons of spiritual warfare. Ephesians 6:12–18 essentially says this: Be fully assured of your salvation in Christ, completely confident that He is the truth, and in faith study your Bible, walking in obedient righteousness to its words, and with prayer in the Spirit, always witnessing to the gospel of Christ, who overcomes persecution and makes peace between us and God. This is the key to living fearlessly as we face the coming persecution of Christians.

—

Phillip Goodman is president of Thy Kingdom Come Ministries, hosts Prophecy Watch television, seen throughout North America, and conducts the annual Tulsa International Prophecy Conference. The author of The Assyrian Connection *and several other prophecy books, he has taught Bible prophecy widely. His wife Mary is from Bethlehem, Israel.*

chapter seventeen

America and the Coming Day of the Lord

by John P. McTernan

"For the day of the LORD is near upon all the heathen:
as thou hast done (To Israel), it shall be done unto thee:
thy reward shall return upon thine own head."

OBADIAH 1:15

Modern Israel is completely unique among all the nations on earth. Israel cannot be viewed as a nation such a Great Britain or France, nor Jerusalem just as any other city. Both Israel and Jerusalem are rooted in Bible prophecy that gives them a spiritual dimension, making them so different.

The rebirth of the nation of Israel in 1948, after being dead for nineteen hurndred years, is without parallel in history. The entire nation was destroyed not once, but twice. Amazingly, after each devastation, Israel came back into existence. Not only was the nation destroyed twice, but each time, the vast majority of the people were taken captive into foreign countries. Yet the Jewish people always returned to the land. All this points to the uniqueness of Israel; this nation is not like other nations.

In 586 BC, the Babylonians totally destroyed Israel, Jerusalem, and the temple. This destruction resulted in nearly all the Jews being taken captive to Babylon. In ancient times, when a people were taken captive as the Jews were, they usually were lost to history. The Jewish people were different because they were not absorbed into Babylon. They remained in Babylon for seventy years, then returned to rebuild Jerusalem and their destroyed temple. The exile resulted in the elimination of Israel's kingdom. This occurred 2,540 years ago!

The Romans, some 650 years later, in 70 AD, again destroyed the nation, Jerusalem, and the temple. In 136 AD, the Jews once more revolted against Rome. They were totally defeated and suffered their final dispersion into the entire world. Very few Jews remained on the land after this war with Rome. The temple, which was at the center of the Jewish religion, was never rebuilt.

Israel should have ceased to exist as a nation—and probably as a people—in 586 BC, but it survived. Israel definitely should have ceased to be a nation in 70 AD, but just as the ancient Bible prophets wrote, the nation was literally reborn nearly nineteen hundred years later on May 14, 1948. In June 1967, Jerusalem once again became the unified capital of Israel. The Hebrew language was almost extinct, yet it was revived and today the Israelis speak Hebrew. They speak the same language as their ancient ancestors! Even without the temple, they kept the same religion while in exile. After two dispersions and losing the kingdom and base for their religion, Israel survived and once again is a nation. There is simply no other nation like Israel.

The Everlasting Covenant

The explanation for the uniqueness of Israel is found in the everlasting covenant God made with Abraham, the father of the Jewish people some four thousand years ago. The everlasting covenant is the reason the Jews and the nation of Israel exist today. This is why the Jewish people were able to survive two dispersions over twenty-six hundred years; and yet the nation of Israel came back into existence in 1948. The invisible hand of God, through this covenant, enabled the Jewish people to survive in the face of tremendous odds.

The covenant included the land of Canaan becoming an everlasting possession for the Jewish people. Today, the area of Canaan includes Jerusalem, Israel, Gaza, West Bank (Judea and Samaria in the Bible), Golan Heights, southern Lebanon, and a part of the nation of Jordan. The everlasting covenant God made with Abraham follows:

"And I will establish my covenant between me and thee and thy seed after thee in their generations for an **everlasting covenant**, to be a God unto thee, and to thy seed after thee. And I will give unto thee, and to thy seed after thee, the land wherein thou art a stranger, all the land of Canaan, for an **everlasting possession**; and I will be their God." (Genesis 17:7, 8)

"He hath remembered his covenant for ever, the word which he commanded to a thousand generations. Which covenant he made with Abraham, and his oath unto Isaac; And confirmed the same unto Jacob for a law, and to Israel for an **everlasting covenant**: Saying, Unto thee will I give the land of Canaan, the lot of your inheritance." (Psalm 105:8–11)

This covenant focused on the land now called the nation of Israel. God deals with nations according to this covenant. God's covenant relationship with the descendants of Abraham is still in effect. God has never cancelled the everlasting covenant concerning the land of Israel.

Moses and the prophets warned the Jewish people not to turn from God to worship pagan gods. Unfortunately, they rebelled against God. According to the law of Moses, one penalty for this rebellion was removal from the land and dispersion into all nations. This was literally fulfilled by the Babylonians and the Romans.

The prophet Ezekiel explained why the Jews were driven from the land and dispersed throughout the nations: "Wherefore I poured my fury upon them for the blood that they had shed upon the land, and for their idols wherewith they had polluted it: And I scattered them among the heathen, and they were dispersed through the countries: according to their way and according to their doings I judged them" (Ezekiel 36:18, 19).

The Bible is very clear that the dispersions were not permanent, but because of the everlasting covenant God made with Abraham, and later with Isaac and Jacob, Israel would once again become a nation. God promised that one day He would bring the Jews back into the land of Israel: "Then will I remember my covenant with Jacob, and also my covenant with Isaac, and also my covenant with Abraham will I remember; and I will remember the land" (Leviticus 26:42).

Prior to dying on the cross, the Lord Jesus also warned of the coming destruction of Israel. He said that Jerusalem would be destroyed and the people scattered into all the nations, but like the Old Testament prophets, He also stated one day the Jews would return. He identified the return of the Jews to Israel, to the time just prior to His Second Coming:

- "And they shall fall by the edge of the sword, and shall be led away captive into all nations: and Jerusalem shall be trodden down of the Gentiles, until the times of the Gentiles be fulfilled." (Luke 21:24)
- "And then shall they see the Son of man coming in a cloud with power and great glory." (Luke 21:27)

We are now living in the time that the Lord Jesus and the ancient Jewish prophets spoke about. The nation of Israel has been reborn and Jerusalem is once again its capital. The reality of God and the authority of the Bible can be validated through the fulfillment of what the Bible states about the nation of Israel. What a time we live in, as Bible prophecy is alive before our very eyes! God warned the nations that the land of Israel is not to be divided; God will judge the nation that attempts to divide Israel: "I will also gather all nations, and will bring them down into the valley of Jehoshaphat, and will plead with them there for my people and for my heritage Israel, whom they have scattered among the nations, and parted [divided] my land" (Joel 3:2).

Throughout its history, the United States has been a blessing to the Jewish people and was directly used by God to help in the rebirth of Israel. President George Washington set the stage for America to be a blessing to the Jewish people. In 1790, he wrote letters to the Jewish communities in America. He made amazing statements in these letters, but in his letter to the Hebrews in Savannah, Georgia, he linked the creation of the United States to the Holy God of Israel and actually made a direct reference to Psalm 144:15. A section of this letter follows:

"May the same wonder-working Deity, who long since delivered the Hebrews from their Egyptian oppressors, planted them in a promised land, whose providential agency has lately been conspicuous in establishing these United States as an independent nation, still continue to water them with the dews of heaven and make the inhabitants of every denomination participate in the temporal and spiritual blessings of that people whose God is Jehovah."[529]

The benevolence toward the Jewish people that started with George Washington continued throughout American history. President Harry Truman was a major player in the rebirth of Israel in 1948, and without his help, it is doubtful that Israel would exist today. The great blessings the American people enjoyed were a result of obeying God's Word regarding the Jewish people and the nation of Israel.

Unfortunately, starting with President George H.W. Bush, America began to interfere with God's prophetic plan by pressuring Israel to divide the covenant land and create a Palestinian state. This started in 1991 with the Madrid Peace Process and continues to this day through the administrations of Bill Clinton, George W. Bush and Barack Obama.

On the very day the U.S. government pressured Israel to divide the land, awesome disasters hit the nation. These disasters included hurricanes, earthquakes, massive tornado outbreaks, record flooding, and forest fires, along with the terrible stock market crashes. Since 1991, there have been over fifty such correlations. The greatest natural disasters to ever hit America occurred within twenty-four hours of the United States pressuring Israel to divide the land; these disasters include Hurricanes Katrina and Andrew, along with the Northridge Earthquake.

The following are a few examples of what happened when the United States pressured Israel to divide the covenant land.

October 30, 1991 - President Bush initiates the Madrid Peace Process. On the very day the president is speaking in Spain, what became known as "the Perfect Storm" sends thirty-foot waves against his home in Kennebunkport, Maine, destroying the house.

August 24, 1992—The Madrid Peace Process transfers to Washington and meets for the first time in America. On this day, Hurricane Andrew destroys southern Florida with category 5 winds. At this time, it is the greatest disaster in U.S. history.

January 17, 1994—A powerful 6.8 magnitude earthquake centered in Northridge, California, rocks the Los Angeles area. The result is widespread destruction and $25 billion in damages. This is the day after President Clinton met with Syrian dictator Hafez al-Assad and pressured Israel to withdraw from the Golan Heights.

March 1, 1997—Yasser Arafat arrives in the United States to discuss Jerusalem with President Clinton. On the very day Arafat lands, powerful tornadoes devastate huge sections of the nation. It is one of the worst tornado storms in the nation's history. The states of Texas, Arkansas, Tennessee, Kentucky, and Ohio suffer tremendous damage.

May 3, 1999—The most powerful tornado storms ever to hit the United States fall on Oklahoma and Kansas. The meteorologists officially measure the winds at 316 miles per hour, making it the fastest ever recorded. On this same day, President Clinton sent a letter to Arafat telling him to be patient for a Palestinian state and saying the Palestinians had a right to "determine their own future on their own land," and deserved "to live free, today, tomorrow and forever."[530]

August 27, 2005—On this day, Israel removes the last of the Jewish settlers from Gaza. This is done under pressure from President George W. Bush. On this day, Hurricane Katrina is named for the first time. Two days later, the massive hurricane slams into New Orleans, creating the greatest disaster in U.S. history.

January 9, 2008—President George W. Bush goes to Israel to assist in the implementation of dividing Israel with his two-state plan. On this day, a path of deadly tornadoes stretches from Alabama to Wisconsin. It is the worst January tornado storm in history. The stock market plunges at this time, causing the president to create a $165 billion economic stimulus to save the economy.

June 3, 2008—Secretary of State Condoleezza Rice and Israeli Prime Minister Ehud Olmert speak in Washington, DC. Once again, Rice promotes the creation of a Palestinian state by dividing the covenant land of Israel. While Olmert is in the U.S. about dividing Israel, the economy is melting down; plus, there are torrential rains in the Midwest that will result in one of the worst floods in U.S. history. A few of the news headlines include: "DOW Falls Nearly 400 on Oil Surge"; "Oil Surges $11 to Record 138"; "Foreclosures Reach Record High in First Quarter"; "Unemployment Rate Jumps Highest in 22 Years"; and "Dangerous Storms and Tornadoes Rake the Plains This Week."

September 2008—The economic situation becomes critical during this month. All during 2007 and 2008, the major downturns in the economy occur on the days America is involved in attempting to divide Israel. In September, the U.S. Consul General to Israel admits that the United States is directly involved in attempting to divide Jerusalem. At the height of the economic crisis, President George W. Bush invites Mahmoud Abbas, the leader of the Palestinians, to Washington. On September 30, the biblical feast of Passover, the stock market falls 777 points for the greatest one-day fall. Then on October 9, Yom Kippur (the Bible's day of judgment for sin), the market falls 679 for the third greatest one-day fall, and on October 15, the biblical feast called Tabernacles, the market falls 737 points for the second greatest one-day fall. The greatest stock market crash in history occurs on the three fall feasts of the Bible!

The Day of the Lord

A very large percent of Bible prophecy is about the Day of The Lord. The Day of the Lord is an expression referring to a long period that begins with God's judgment on the world for rejecting both Him and the everlasting covenant with Abraham, and continues through the one-thousand-year reign of Jesus Christ. It is the time when God interferes directly in the affairs of man. This is God's last attempt to reach man before the Second Coming of the Lord Jesus and the judgment of the nations.

· Israel and Jerusalem play a key role in the Day of the Lord. The key to the Day of the Lord is when Israel is once again a nation with Jerusalem its capital. These indicators are now in place and the world is racing towards the prophetic events with all the terrible judgments described in the Bible. The main judgment revolves around three terrible wars that focus against Israel and result in total destruction of entire nations. The wars get progressively greater, culminating in the final battle called Armageddon. The wars are so awesome that the book of Revelation reports that one third of mankind will be killed in one war. With today's population, that would amount to 2 billion people.

"Behold, the day of the LORD cometh, and thy spoil shall be divided in the midst of thee. For I will gather all nations against Jerusalem to battle…" (Zechariah 14:1).

The prophet Obadiah is one of the keys to understanding the Day of the Lord and the future of America. The first war involves the United States' policy toward Israel since 1991. The warnings God has given to America starting in 1991, and the Madrid Peace Plan, culminates in the war described by Obadiah.

Obadiah states that God is going to bless or curse nations directly as they deal with Israel. The prophet is very clear that what a nation does to Israel will in turn happen to that nation. If a nation tries to divide Israel or Jerusalem, that nation will suffer greatly. This is clearly shown in the Scriptures, but few believe and respect the authority of the Bible. Nevertheless, the warnings are there: "For the day of the LORD is near upon all the heathen: as thou hast done [to Israel], it shall be done unto thee: thy reward shall return upon thine own head" (Obadiah 1:15).

Obadiah states that there will be intense warfare between the Jews, the house of Jacob, and the Palestinians, the house of Esau. The warfare results in the total destruction of the Palestinians as they are driven from the land. The Palestinians refuse to accept the Jews and the nation of Israel. They do not want two states with one for Israel and the other Palestine. They want the destruction of Israel and only the Muslim state of Palestine. The United States' policy of the two-state solution is a complete failure, and directly interferes with God's prophetic plan for Israel: "And the house of Jacob shall be a fire, and the house of Joseph a flame, and the house of Esau for stubble, and they shall kindle in them, and devour them; and there shall not be any remaining of the house of Esau; for the LORD hath spoken it" (Obadiah 1:18).

When this war is over, Israel will possess Gaza, the plain of the Philistines, and all of the West Bank (Samaria). There will be no Palestinian areas. The war is not limited to the Palestinians, as it spreads into Lebanon and Jordan. The prophet writes that Israel will move north into Lebanon and take over the area that is controlled by Hezbullah. Israel will also extend into Jordan and control the area called Gilead. This area stretches from the top of the Dead Sea to the Sea of Galilee and about twenty miles eastward.

"And they of the south shall possess the mount of Esau; and they of the plain the Philistines [Gaza]: and they shall possess the fields of Ephraim, and the fields of Samaria [West Bank]: and Benjamin shall possess Gilead [Part of Jordan]. And the captivity of this host of the children of Israel shall possess that of the Canaanites, even unto Zarephath [Lebanon]..." (Obadiah 1:19–20)

This war described by Obadiah could explode at any moment. Israel is surrounded by enemies who exist to destroy the Jewish state. This includes Hamas, Hezbullah, and several other organizations. Syria and Iran are linked together in the destruction of Israel, while Iran is very close to building a nuclear weapon. Iran already has the missile capability to reach Israel, and its leaders have boasted that, when they obtain a nuclear weapon, they will use it against Israel.

Israel, on numerous occasions, has stated it will not let Iran obtain a nuclear weapon. The Jewish state has one of the finest armies in the world along with perhaps the best air force. If needed, Israel will attack Iran's nuclear facilities. This act could very easily trigger the war described by Obadiah and, through a domino effect, lead to the other wars described in the Bible.

The Bible is clear that entire nations will disappear during these wars. The world is going to be in convulsions. The Middle East is now on the verge of a horrific war that is going to shake the world to its core. It is highly likely that nuclear weapons will be used. A war of this nature would accelerate the meltdown of the world economy.

It appears that the confrontation between Israel and the Islamic nations cannot be stopped. Iran with its allies is committed to destroying Israel just as the Nazis were committed to World War II and the destruction of the Jews. The questions now are: What happens to the United States? And what does an individual do in face of these events?

What Happens to the United States?

From studying the Scriptures about the Day of the Lord, it is evident that the United States is not involved. Russia and Islamic nations are identified, along with a unified Asia (most likely under the control of China) as major players. When the wars take place, the United States cannot be a world power.

God has warned America through the many disasters that have

occurred on the very days U.S. leaders were pressuring Israel to divide the covenant land. It appears that God will remove America from its position as a world power. The economic meltdown that started in 2007 might directly lead to the downfall of America as a world power.

What Does an Individual Do in the Face of These Events?

"Now is the accepted time; behold, Now is the day of salvation" (2 Corinthians 6:2). The authority of God's Word can be seen today through the rebirth of Israel and all the events that are transpiring. Israel exists because of the everlasting covenant God made with Abraham four thousand years ago. God now wants to make a covenant with you for your eternal life with Him.

The very foundation of a person's relationship with God is assurance of the eternal life. A person can live now with the assurance of eternal life. This assurance is based upon knowing that God loves you and wants you to have eternal life through Jesus Christ. This is a promise from God directly to you: "For God so loved the world, that he gave his only begotten Son, that whosoever believeth in him should not perish, but have everlasting life" (John 3:16).

The way of believing in Jesus Christ as your Savior is to repent of sin and trust Him completely as your Lord and Savior. When you trust Jesus Christ in your heart as your Savior, all your sin is forgiven by God, because Jesus shed His blood and paid the penalty on the cross for you. Without repentance of sin and the confession of Jesus Christ as Lord and Savior, it is impossible to have eternal life with God.

"That if thou shalt confess with thy mouth the Lord Jesus, and shalt believe in thine heart that God hath raised him from the dead, thou shalt be saved. For with the heart man believeth unto righteousness; and with the mouth confession is made unto salvation" (Romans 10:9,10). When you confess Jesus as your Lord and Savior, you are to live with the expectation of His Second Coming in your heart. This is called "the blessed hope"—the expectation of the Second Coming of the Lord Jesus and the privilege of being with Him forever. Your confession of Jesus Christ and your expectation of His Second Coming are the evidence that you will be with the Lord Jesus forever: "Looking for that blessed hope, and the glorious appearing of the great God and our Saviour Jesus Christ" (Titus 2:13).

The Lord Jesus has paid the penalty for your sin by His shed blood on the cross. God has provided His way for you to have eternal life with Him. Right now, you can turn to God by prayer through faith in Jesus Christ as your Lord and Savior. Please do not put this off, because now is the day of salvation.

The Blessed Hope

God has not hidden His prophetic plan. It appears on page after page in the Bible. God is not hiding the coming Day of the Lord. It is visible to all who focus on the Second Coming and understand God's covenant nation Israel. To focus on Jesus' Second Coming is called the Blessed Hope. This hope is a living hope. It is not a theory, but a living reality in a person's life. The message of the hour is for the church to focus on the Second Coming of Jesus Christ and to live with the blessed hope: "Looking for that blessed hope, and the glorious appearing of the great God and our Saviour Jesus Christ" (Titus 2:13).

The blessed hope is an anchor for our souls. This is the hope that God has set before us. He requires that we keep the blessed hope with full assurance until He returns, or until we pass away. This hope steadies us during the storms of life. We are to hold onto this hope and let no one or anything take it from us.

The Bible also tells us to establish our hearts about His coming. When we establish the blessed hope in our hearts, holiness naturally flows. The Bible leaves no doubt that we are to focus on the blessed hope and live every day as if the Lord could return for His church. We are to live with patience, looking for His coming for the church:

"Be patient therefore, brethren, unto the coming of the Lord. Behold, the husbandman waiteth for the precious fruit of the earth, and hath long patience for it, until he receive the early and latter rain. Be ye also patient; stablish your hearts: for the coming of the Lord draweth nigh" (James 5:7, 8).

"I Will Bless Them That Bless Thee"

God told Abraham that He would bless the people who blessed Abraham and the Jewish people. It is most important to line our lives up with God's prophetic plan for Israel and the Jewish people. We are living in a time of prophecy.

God's prophetic plan is all laid out in the Bible. Events in the Middle East are now accelerating toward the Day of the Lord and Christ's return. Are you ready to face Jesus Christ? The nation of Israel was reborn just as the prophets predicted thousands of years ago. Jerusalem is once again its capital. More and more, Jerusalem is the focus of world attention. The prophecies about Israel and Jerusalem confirm that the Bible is truly the Word of God!

Now is the time to bless and support Israel. Now is the time to stand with the Jewish people as they are coming under attack all over the world. As time goes on, the attacks will become more vicious. America might even turn against Israel and the Jewish people. No matter what happens, as individuals we can stand and bless Israel and the Jewish people, and trust that God will bless us according to His Word. "And I will bless them that bless thee, and curse him that curseth thee: and in thee shall all families of the earth be blessed" (Genesis 12:3).

As the Day of The Lord approaches, God needs people who will not flinch, but who will stand strong in His word. He needs people who are a true witness to Israel and the Jewish people of the love of God through the Lord Jesus Christ. Please realize the hour we are now living in and the world events that are now accelerating towards the Day of the Lord. If you are not anchored in faith, you could be crushed by fear because the events are so earth-shaking. Those who are anchored in the Lord will not be shaken, but will do mighty exploits in the name of the Lord Jesus: "Wherefore take unto you the whole armour of God, that ye may be able to withstand in the evil day, and having done all, to stand" (Ephesians 6:13).

—

For further in-depth study of the information presented in this chapter, see John McTernan's book, As America Has Done To Israel. *For an analysis of current events in light of Bible prophecy, see John's blog at: johnmcternan. name. For additional teachings, see his website at: defendproclaimthefaith. org.*

chapter eighteen

The Coming Reign of Antichrist

by Patrick Heron

The vast majority of evangelical Christians living today believe that we are in what the Bible calls the last days or end times. That is, they recognize that the signs we were told would usher in this period are all occurring right now. Central to the topic of the end times and the beginning of the Apocalypse is the emergence of a political leader who is to rule the world during this horrific period. He is commonly known as the Antichrist.

Speculation about who this man might be is ongoing with the passage of time and events. Many evangelical Christians presently believe that Barack Obama fits the role as the one who will plunge the world into the bloody events of the Apocalypse, which will end in the last battle prophesied in the book of Revelation, the battle of Armageddon. Other men throughout history have also been thought to be the Antichrist—from Nero to Hitler, and from the early popes to Bill Clinton, with scores more in between. So, can we know for certain who the real Antichrist is? Or, is this information simply not available?

Antichrist's Identity Revealed in Scripture

Many of the commentators, writers, and end-times experts who are interested in this topic fail to look for answers about the identity of this coming evil ruler in the one place that can be trusted above all else: Holy Writ. I am about to make a solemn declaration here, one that may come as a surprise to many people: The name of the Antichrist, his present whereabouts, and the timing of his emergence onto the world stage are clearly given in the plain text of Scripture. That is correct. Commentators, and Bible scholars, and end-times experts have failed to see that the identity of the Antichrist and his present abode are provided for any who have eyes to see and ears to hear. The information is hidden in plain sight in the book of Revelation and elsewhere. When we go to the Word and accept what the Spirit has to say on this subject, there is no more need for loose speculation and the opinions of man.

Quite a lot of information is given in the Bible that allows us to paint a full picture of the coming Antichrist and the activities he and his accomplices will be involved in. The book of Daniel provides many parallel prophecies that back up and validate those given in the book of Revelation. Much other information regarding the Antichrist is written in the Gospels, as well as in some of the Epistles. By piecing together all the various pieces if the jigsaw, we can assemble a clear picture of this man and of the events that will take place during his reign. I will deal with just some of these issues in this essay.

Sticking to the Truth

But first things first. I shall not be engaging in mere speculation here. I will be going to the Scriptures and allowing them to interpret themselves so that the Word of truth may be magnified, and so that we do not stray from that narrow path. To illustrate the necessity for sticking with these simple truths, I would like to quote a lesson from the Master himself in a passage in Matthew 16:

[Jesus] asked his disciples, saying, "Who do men say that I, the Son of man, am?" And they said, "Some say that thou art John the Baptist; some, Elijah; and others, Jeremiah, or one of the prophets."

He saith unto them, "But who say ye that I am?"

And Simon Peter answered and said, "Thou are the Christ, the Son of the living God."

And Jesus answered and said unto him, "Blessed are thou Simon Barjona; for flesh and blood hath not revealed it unto thee, but my Father which is in heaven..."

...From that time forth began Jesus to show unto his disciples, how he must go unto Jerusalem, and suffer many things from the elders and chief priests and scribes, and be killed, and be raised again, the third day.

Then Peter took him, and began to rebuke him, saying, "Be it far from thee, Lord: this shall not be unto thee."

But he turned and said unto Peter: "Get thee behind me Satan, for thou art and offence unto me: for thou savourest not the things that be of God, but those that be of men." (Matthew 16:14–17, 21–23)

This passage contains some very important lessons that we must grasp before we continue. Jesus asked His disciples who they thought He was. Peter gave the correct answer, and Jesus praised him, telling him that it was by way of revelation from God himself that Peter had received this knowledge. Jesus then began to explain that He must fulfil prophecy by going to Jerusalem, suffering at the hands of the religious leaders, and dying before being raised from the dead.

At this, Peter lost the run of himself, and more or less said, "No way is this going to happen while I am around to protect you." Then Jesus looked Peter square in the eyes and said, "Get thee behind me Satan. Thou art an offense unto me; for thou savorest not the things that are of God, but those that are of men" (v. 23).

Whew! What a turnaround! One minute, Peter was the cock of the walk because Jesus had praised him for his spiritual insight and had given him the keys to the kingdom (verses 18,19). Next thing, He hit him right between the eyes with, "Satan is working through you; you are more interested in man's opinions than the Word of God," or words to that effect. So Peter went from hero to zero within a couple of minutes.

The lesson here is this: The way of truth is a very narrow path. Jesus was the Word made flesh. He spoke the Word of truth because he *was* truth. So when He began to explain to His disciples what had to come to pass in order that man's redemption could be attained, He was speaking God's truth. And the truth is a narrow path. But when Peter reacted as he did, he was using his five senses and going directly against the revealed Word of truth. Thus, he was in error.

As soon as we start to stray from the simple teaching of Scripture and begin to put forth our own opinions, we make the same mistake Peter made. Thus, the Lord's rebuke to us might be the same as it was to his disciple: "Get you behind me Satan." He can say that because when we stray off the narrow path of truth, the half-truths or speculation we perpetrate—if we are to take Jesus at face value—are satanic in nature. When we exit the path of truth, we are in error.

I say this because in this essay, I will be sticking to the plain teaching of Scripture. And although I am fully aware that the prophecies of the book of Revelation can be difficult to understand, some of them are quite simple when all the dots are joined in a reasoned fashion. I believe the Scriptures that point to the identity of the Antichrist and what his name is are relatively easy to decode when laid out in a logical sequence. That is what I shall attempt to do here.

Biblical References to Antichrist

Scripture provides various names for the person we call the Antichrist. In fact, the word "antichrist" only appears in the Bible four times, and these instances are found in John's epistles:

"Little children, it is the last time: and as ye have heard that antichrist shall come, even now are there many antichrists, by which we know that it is the last time.... Who is a liar but he that denieth that Jesus is the Christ? He is antichrist, that denieth the Father and the Son." (1 John 2:18, 22)

It is interesting to note that the words, "the Antichrist," appear only twice in the entire Scripture. But in the book of Revelation, he is never referred to as "the Antichrist." John the Revelator gives him another name that is totally different.

The epistle of Paul to the Thessalonians provides us with three other names given to this Antichrist: "Let no man deceive you by any means; for that day shall not come, except there come a falling away first, and that man of sin be revealed, the son of perdition, Who opposeth and exalteth himself above all that is called God, or that is worshiped, so that he, as God, sitteth in the Temple of God, shewing himself that he is God.... And then shall that wicked be revealed, whom the Lord shall consume with the spirit of his mouth, and shall destroy with the brightness of his coming" (2 Thessalonians 2:3, 4, 8).

Here the Antichrist is called the "man of sin," the "son of perdition," and "that wicked" (or lawless one). In the book of Daniel, he is referred to as "a little horn" (Daniel 7:8).

Now here is the rub: We talk of "the antichrist" even though these words are used only twice in the Bible in 1 John. These other terms are seldom used except in dissertations or books on this coming world leader. Yet in the book of Revelation, this same man is given a different name, and is called many times in nine separate chapters by that same title. Yet commentators seldom refer to him by the name the Spirit puts on him. Also, it is in this name that the person of the Antichrist is identified and his proper name is given. The present whereabouts of this character is also provided within the name appointed him in the book of Revelation.

Jesus' Interesting Activity

Before I present this name, I want to lay some enigmatic verses before you that are very pertinent to this study and to understanding who this Antichrist is. First, we examine a passage in 1 Peter that concerns something Christ Jesus did after His resurrection from the dead and before His ascension into heaven. Peter says: "By whom also he went and preached unto the spirits in prison, Who at one time were disobedient, when once the longsuffering of God waited in the days of Noah, while the ark was a preparing…" (2 Peter 3:19, 20).

This verse is sadly overlooked. It tells us that Jesus, in His supernatural risen body, went to the "spirits" in prison and "preached" to them! It also tells us that it was these same spirits that were disobedient in the days while Noah was building the ark. That is, they were active in the years preceding the Flood of Noah.

The Greek word for "preached" here is *kerusso*, which means "heralded." That is, Jesus heralded or announced His triumph over these spirits that were disobedient in the years before the Flood.

Also 2 Peter 2:4, 5 is linked and provides another couple of parts of the puzzle: "For if God spared not the angels that sinned, but cast them down to hell, and delivered them into chains of darkness, to be reserved unto the judgment; And spared not the old world, but saved Noah, the eighth person…bringing in the flood upon the world of the ungodly."

Here we are told that the angels who sinned are cast down to a place called Tartarus, which is the Greek word in the text given for "hell." This passage states that these angels are "reserved unto the judgment." Many times the Day of the Lord—or the time called Tribulation—is referred to as "the day of judgment." This also connects these angels with the time of the Flood.

These angels are the spirits to whom Jesus went and announced His triumph, for angels are spirit beings. ("But to which of the angels said he at any time, Sit on my right hand…Are they not all ministering spirits…" [Hebrews 1:13, 14].) Their sin is the same as the disobedience mentioned in 1 Peter. And the "Tartarus" and "chains of darkness" referred to here are the same as the prison mentioned earlier.

Where the Angels Are

Yet another part of the conundrum is found in Jude 6: "And the angels that kept not their first estate, but left their own habitation, he hath reserved in everlasting chains under darkness unto the judgment of the great day."

The extra piece of information we are given here regarding these same angels is that they "kept not their first estate, but left their own habitation." "Their first estate" and "their own habitation" is heaven, for heaven is the original abode of these angels.

This copper-fastens the previous two passages, which is a startling truth that few Christians are aware of and that most commentators gloss over or ignore. To summarize: There are angels locked up in a gloomy prison called Tartarus. They are imprisoned there because they left their "first estate," heaven, and were disobedient and sinned in the years before the Flood in the days of Noah.

Furthermore, and another amazing truth, Jesus himself, after He had been raised from the dead and while still on this earth, went to this place called Tartarus and announced His triumph to these spirits who are angels. My goodness! It must be an important truth for us to know, if Jesus himself went down to these spirit men and heralded His triumph over them in His new spiritual body. This truth is borne out in a verse from Ephesians. Again speaking of Jesus, it says: "Now that he ascended, what is it but that he also descended first into the lower parts of the earth?" (Ephesians 4:9). This is not referring to the burial of Jesus when He died, for His body was laid in a tomb that was on level ground. No, this is referring to Jesus travelling to this prison where the angels are kept, which we can deduce from this verse as being in "the lower parts of the earth." Jesus could go to this place only because He had a new, glorious body that He received after He was raised from death. We are to receive similar new spiritual bodies when He returns.

These verses Paul wrote explain it well: "Behold, I show you a mystery: We shall not all sleep, but we shall all be changed. In a moment, in the twinkling of an eye, at the last trump; for the trumpet shall sound, and the dead shall be raised incorruptible, and we shall be changed. For this corruptible must put on incorruption, and this mortal must put on immortality" (1 Corinthians 15:51–53).

That this prison holding these angels is called Tartarus is itself interesting, for it is so-called only once in Scripture. But the name gives us a hint as to its occupants, as Tartarus is a famous name used in early Greek mythology to refer to the place where the gods of legend are imprisoned. (We shall return to this later.)

So this gloomy prison called Tartarus is not out in space in some black hole somewhere, but is in the lower parts of the earth. That is, it is down below our feet somewhere in the bowels of this planet. What an amazing revelation, yet so few have ever gleaned these truths even though they have been right under our noses all these years.

The Abyss

I want to present one more passage before we reveal the name of the Antichrist. This is from Luke 8:26–39, and it concerns the time Jesus was confronted by a man who was possessed by many demons. The man was always cutting himself with stones and crying aloud, and he lived in the tombs. When bound with chains, he would even break the iron. When he met Jesus, the demons cried out: "'What have I to do with thee, Jesus, Son of God Most High? I beseech thee, torment me not.'… And Jesus asked him, saying, 'What is thy name?' And he said; 'Legion;' Because many demons were entered into him" (Luke 8:28, 30).

There were about six thousand men in a Roman legion. Note what the demons said when Jesus was casting out the unclean spirits: "And they besought him that he would not command them to go out into the deep" (v. 31).

The Greek word for "deep" here is *abussos*. This literally translates as "the abyss." So the demons did not want to be cast into the abyss. We will shortly see that this abyss is the same place the other spirits—those who left heaven and sinned in the years prior to the flood in the days of Noah—are imprisoned. And it was to this abyss that Jesus went in His risen body to herald His triumph to these same angels.

Antichrist's Identity

Now to the book of Revelation and just who the Antichrist is. As already stated, nine chapters in Revelation refer to the man we call the Antichrist. But in Revelation, he is given a different name. He is called "the beast that ascendeth out of the bottomless pit."

Revelation 11 foretells of the two witnesses who will evangelize on behalf of God during the coming Apocalypse. These prophets have the power to shut up heaven so there is no rain, and anyone who tries to harm them is devoured by fire from the prophets' mouths. For three and a half years, they prophesy on behalf of God and are a thorn in the side of the Antichrist and his one-world government. But the beast has the power to kill them: "And when they shall have finished their testimony, the beast that ascendeth out of the bottomless pit shall make war against them, and shall overcome them, and kill them" (Revelation 11:7).

Throughout nine chapters, the man we call the Antichrist is defined as "the beast," and in the above verse he is called "the beast that ascendeth out of the bottomless pit." In fact, the name "beast" is used thirty-five times in the book of Revelation. So what is the background of this beast, and why is he given this title? Let's go to Chapter 9 to assess the full picture: "The fifth angel sounded and I saw a star fall from heaven unto the earth: and to him was given the key to the bottomless pit. And he opened the bottomless pit, and there arose a smoke out of the pit, like the smoke of a great furnace; and the sun and the air were darkened by reason of the smoke of the pit. And there came out of the smoke locusts upon the earth, and unto them was given power, as the scorpions of the earth have power" (Revelation 9:1-3).

Let us examine these words more closely. The first thing to notice is that a "star" falls from heaven to earth. This is not a regular star, because stars do not originate in heaven, they do not carry keys, and they do not fall to earth. What we call a falling star is actually a small piece of matter burning up as it hurtles through earth's atmosphere from space. The word "star" here is used as a metaphor for an angel. This star has the key to the bottomless pit and unlocks it. This denotes a place of incarceration.

Then what happens?

Locusts come out of the smoke that arises from the bottomless pit. These locusts are given power "as the scorpions of the earth have power." Now what do these words mean? To unravel this mystery, we go back to Luke 10, to the story of Jesus sending out seventy of His disciples to teach and preach in His name. When they return, this is what they report: "And the seventy returned with joy, saying, 'Lord, even the demons are subject unto us through thy name.' And He said unto them, 'I beheld Satan as lightning fall from heaven. Behold, I give you power to thread on serpents and scorpions, and over all the power of the enemy…Notwithstanding, in this rejoice not, that *the spirits* are subject unto you…'" (Luke 10:17–20, emphasis added).

The context of this passage is that devils (demons), Satan, serpents, scorpions, and spirits were subject to the disciples through Jesus' name. Jesus replied with a prophetic utterance about Satan and told them they had power over "serpents and scorpions," whom He defined as the enemy. Then He further elaborated on these by stating that these scorpions and serpents were "spirits"—that is, "the spirits are subject unto you."

Now we know who the enemy is: Satan, his serpents, and scorpions, which are spirits. Angels are spirits. The main serpent is Satan himself, a fallen angel, for he is called that twice in Revelation. Here is one instance: "And the great dragon was cast out, that old serpent, called the Devil; and Satan…" (Revelation 12:9).

So, here we have the names of animals and insects, given as metaphors, to mean various beings. Dragon, serpent, scorpion, and locust. Near the beginning of Luke 10, Jesus said: "…behold, I send you forth as lambs among wolves" (Luke 10:3). Again we see the use of names of animals as metaphors for beings. The lambs are His disciples and the wolves are the demons, scorpions, and serpents that are spirits, or evil angels.

The Antichrist's Name Revealed

Thus returning to Revelation 9, we can now deduce that the locusts released from the bottomless pit are spirits that are now given power— just as the scorpions, or evil angels, presently have power on this earth. To prove that these locusts are indeed spirit beings or angels, let's jump down to verse 11 of this same chapter. Now study the words in this coming verse very closely. For not only does this verse verify that these locusts are evil fallen angels, but it gives the name of their leader: "And they had a *king* over them, who is the *angel* of the bottomless pit, whose name in the Hebrew tongue is Abaddon, but in the Greek tongue hath his name Apollyon" (Revelation 9:11, emphasis added).

Eureka! Can anything be plainer? We are told here that the king of the locusts is an angel. And we have concluded that the locusts also are angels that are evil spirit beings. But there's more: This king from the bottomless pit throughout Revelation is called "the beast" and "the beast who ascends out of the bottomless pit." This is the Antichrist and his name is…Barack Obama? No. Stalin? No. Hitler? No? Some rich Saudi prince? No. The leader of the European Union? No. Tony Blair? No. The Pope? Negative. All wrong!

The Spirit expressly states here that the man we commonly call the Antichrist is an angel and a king (ruler) who presently resides in the bottomless pit, but who will one day arise from this abyss. His name is Abaddon in Hebrew and Apollyon in Greek. This is the beast that ascends from the bottomless pit and overcomes and kills the two witnesses. That is why he is called the beast from the abyss or bottomless pit, because that is exactly what he is. He is the king or ruler of those angels who left their first estate and who are incarcerated in Tartarus because of their activities on earth in the thousand or so years before to the Flood of Noah. These are the same spirits whom Jesus presented himself to in His glorified body after His resurrection and before His ascension.

So these beings must be important. If Jesus saw fit to visit these evil angels and herald His triumph before them, then we cannot blow off these truths and ignore them because they interfere with our theology. These verses are telling us exactly who the Antichrist is and where he presently resides. We are told when he will emerge from this abyss, and we are given his two names. Can it be simpler? Can it be plainer? I think not. The Antichrist is not a flesh-and-blood politician. He is not a human who is alive as we speak and is being groomed to take his position as world leader when the Apocalypse begins.

Antichrist's Nature

The Antichrist is a spirit being, a supernatural, powerful angel who is locked up in the gloomy prison called Tartarus, or the bottomless pit, along with a band of other fallen angels. But remember: Angels are men. Everywhere in Scripture where angels appear, they are called "men." They look like ordinary humans. They eat, drink, and wear clothes just as we do. People have entertained angels unawares. When two angels went to visit Lot and his family in Sodom, all the men of that city wanted to gang-rape them. So they must have been regular-looking guys. But their nature is spirit, which allows them accomplish feats that we mere mortals cannot.

The fact that angels are men is borne out several times in Genesis and in the writings of Paul and others. We are told in Genesis, "Let us make man in our image, after our likeness...So God created man in his own image, in the image of God created he him; male and female created he them" (Genesis 1:26, 27). So we look like them, and they look like us. Except they are celestial beings and we are of this earth. When the beast from the abyss appears on the world stage, he will be the "man of sin" and the "son of perdition" just as Paul describes. But he will possess powers far beyond those of any human politician. Paul tells us, "Even him whose coming is after the working of Satan with all power and signs and lying wonders, And with all deceivableness of unrighteousness in them that perish..." (2 Thessalonians 2:9).

This beast is able to perform supernatural signs, miracles, and wonders. No human politician has exhibited these feats, and no human ever will. Some may argue that a human could be possessed by Satan to perform miracles. This might be so. But when these gods manifested on the earth in the years before Noah, it was they themselves who appeared and carried out their sinful doings.

When we read through the book of Revelation, we see another beast mentioned. This one is called the False Prophet, and he too performs signs and wonders on behalf of the Antichrist and by the power of the dragon. He even orders that an image of the beast from the abyss be erected, and then he has the power to make the image come alive and speak. Can anyone really believe a human politician or religious leader who is presently in existence could accomplish this? But these two are going to perform many spellbinding, fake miracles that will deceive almost all the population of the whole world. At one point, this beast receives a fatal wound. That possibly suggests he will be assassinated. But he will be raised from death by the power of the dragon before the eyes of the world. This is a counterfeit resurrection. Then all people of all the nations of the world will worship the beast and give their allegiance to him.

What you have just read is a unique truth. For I have pointed out to you from Scripture what very few Christians know or understand. By joining together the dots of some obscure and often-ignored passages in Scripture, and by linking these together in order to present a clear picture, we have seen what few have yet discovered. I understand that when new light is presented, sometimes it hurts the eyes at first, and can be hard to focus. But I am confident that those who take the time to ponder the passages covered and search the Scriptures for themselves will arrive at the same conclusions.

Fallen Angels before the Flood

Now to add some color to the sketch we've already drawn, it is necessary to go back to the time before the Flood, in the days of Noah, to see exactly what happened there and find out what the original angels did that caused them to be put into Tartarus. These are the angels who left heaven, their first estate, and fell to earth and sinned. This record is in Genesis 6: "And it came to pass, when men began to multiply on the face of the earth, and daughters were born unto them, That the sons of God saw the daughters of men that they were fair; and they took them wives of all which they chose.... There were giants [*nephilim*] in the earth in those days; and also after that, when the sons of God came in unto the daughters of men, and they bare children to them; the same became mighty men which were of old, men of renown" (Genesis 6:1–2, 4). I will paraphrase here because of space constraints. Basically, the "sons of God" are angels. This phrase appears eight times in the Old Testament, and it is clear from these references that the sons of God are angels. But they're not good angels. These sons of God were created spirit beings who rebelled with Satan and tried to overthrow the Most High God in a military coup in the distant past. These angels are called *nephilim*, a Hebrew word that the majority of Hebrew scholars agree literally means "the fallen ones." Hence, the *nephilim* were fallen angels, because they fell from grace, fell from heaven, and fell to earth. They took human women as wives who bore children for them. But these were no ordinary offspring; they were giants, and were extremely evil.

The next few verses in Genesis 6 report that the earth became filled with violence and bloodshed. According to my calculations, these angels fell to earth circa one thousand years before the Flood, which happened in 2348 BC. These *nephilim* so infected and affected the whole DNA of the human race at that time that there was in men's hearts "only evil continually." This so grieved God that He sent the Flood and wiped all life off the face of the earth except for Noah and his family.

But spirit men cannot be drowned. So these fallen angels were cast into prison to await a day of judgment in the far-distant future.

In this record of the *nephilim* coming to earth and mating with women, we have the origins of the so-called legends and mythologies of yore. Many, many legends from various cultures speak of gods coming to earth, taking humans as wives, and producing demigods as offspring. For instance, take the stories of Greek mythology, which are rife with the doings of their gods. These legends speak of the gods descending to earth from heaven and living on Mount Olympus and Delphi. Zeus took Alcmene, a mortal, as his wife and she almost died giving birth to Hercules.

Greek and Roman mythology also informs us that these same gods, because of their rebellion, were incarcerated in an underground prison called in Greek—wait for this—Tartarus. This place is mentioned many times in the writings of Homer. Egyptian writings such as the Pyramid Texts and the Egyptian Book of the Dead give a similar story. They tell of a place called the Underworld, which is a prison of the gods. Hades is the keeper of this prison, and one must cross the river Styx in order to gain entry to this horrid place.

The Book of Enoch fills in many of the blanks not found in the Bible. Enoch was the seventh-generation offspring of Adam, and we are told Enoch walked with God and was taken out of this life, but did not die. He was the great-grandfather of Noah. His writings are not included in the Bible now, but they were for five hundred years or so. Enoch describes these fallen angels coming to earth and details the evil they taught men and the violence they perpetrated against humankind. There is a direct quote from the book of Enoch in Jude's epistle. This gives this book credence and means we can trust it. Otherwise, it would not be included in the Word of God. In speaking of the details of these watchers from heaven, Enoch proved it was these evil angels themselves—in person—who committed the crimes. They did not possess humans and work through them. And neither shall the beast from the abyss possess; he will be clearly visible for all to see.

The fact that we are told in 1 Peter that Jesus visited the angels locked up in Tartarus makes a link between the truths of Holy Writ and the gods of Greece and Rome. For it is clear that the gods spoken of in these legends are none other than the same fallen angels or *nephilim* of Genesis 6 and elsewhere. Yet another clear link connects the fallen angels or sons of God with the gods of ancient lore, and ties them into the prophecies of the book of Revelation. This clue is found in the same verse that provided us with the two names given to the beast from the bottomless pit. Abaddon is his Hebrew name and his name in the Greek tongue is Apollyon. But we speak English—and the English for Apollyon is Apollo. Any student of Greek mythology will explain that Apollo was a leader of the original pantheon of Greek gods along with Mars, Saturn, Mercury, Jupiter, Venus, Orion, Zeus, Pluto, etc. Apollo was the god of prophecy, medicine, music, and was the epitome of the beauty of man. His most famous oracle was at Delphi in Greece, and many temples dedicated to Apollo are all over Greece, Turkey, and the Near East, all of which can be viewed today.

Even More Answers Found in Scripture

So now we have an even clearer picture of who the Antichrist, aka, the beast that ascends from the abyss, is. He is none other than the leader of the gods from the most ancient of times whom we know as Apollo. I very much doubt he will be going by this name when he emerges from the bottomless pit along with his other spirit friends in the near future. Nevertheless, this is the name given him by the Spirit in Revelation 9:11. So the name of the Antichrist, plus his present whereabouts, plus when he is going to be released, is all written in the plain text of Scripture. These secrets have been hidden in plain sight right before our eyes for centuries. Yet few have managed to piece together the pertinent strands of Scripture needed to unravel the mystery and make plain the sense of it. Thank you, Lord, for opening our eyes.

Many more passages in the book of Revelation speak of both the Beast from the abyss and the False Prophet. For instance, regarding the Beast that arises from the sea, we are told he has seven heads and ten horns. What does this mean, and does it pertain to the global scene in our day and time? The False Prophet, we are told, arises from the earth and is described as a beast with two horns. What does this signify, and can we understand these hard sayings?

Speaking again of the Antichrist, Scripture says he, "once was; now is not; and shall ascend out of the bottomless pit and go to his destruction." Can we decode this cryptic message? What is the mark of the Beast?

I have been working on a book that answers all these questions and many, many more. Its working title is "The Return of the Antichrist and the New World Order." I expect it to be published shortly (watch my website for news on this: www.neph.ie). In it, I expand on all the issues I have written about here and bring the reader behind the veil of the Apocalypse so that we may endeavour to seek out the hidden secrets of the book of Revelation not yet revealed. We do this work in order to inform the members of the body of Christ of the revelation of Jesus Christ so that their spirits may be quickened and they might, in turn, warn others of the impending cataclysm that is soon to fall on this sorry world. But we also do it to provide hope for those who seek hope, and as an anchor for those who are already saved Christians in the church of God. For there is good news for those who want it! Three times in Revelation, we are told we are blessed if we read its words and blessed if we hear them. It is the only book in the Bible where we are promised a double blessing if we read it or hear its words. Besides, this book is the direct revelation of Jesus Christ to His servants.

Conclusion

What we are seeing in the world today is what I call the shadows of the Apocalypse. The world is a time bomb whose fuse has long since been lit. The hoofbeats of the four horsemen of the Apocalypse are clearly to be heard by all those who have ears to hear. To make a metaphor: The bad news is that the Titanic is going down. The good news is that you don't have to be on board. There is a way out, an alternative, an escape route. And yes, there is hope. For we are assured by our Lord that we will be saved from the coming wrath. This is our blessed hope. I will leave you with a promise of our Messiah, Jesus who is the Christ. May God bless you.

"Let not your heart be troubled; ye believe in God, believe also in me. In my Father's house are many mansions; if it were not so, I would have told you. I go to prepare a place for you. And if I go and prepare a place for you, I will come again, and receive you unto myself, that where I am, there ye may be also" (John 14:1–4).

—

Patrick Heron, born in Dublin, Ireland, has written several books, including The Nephilim and the Pyramid of the Apocalypse *and* The Return of the Antichrist and the New World Order. *A frequent conference speaker, he has been featured on hundreds of radio and TV stations both in the U.S. and internationally. Contact him through his website at www. neph.ie.*

Going Off the Grid and Living Self-Sufficiently

---

by Carl and Althia Anderson

Driving along Coastal Highway 101 in Oregon, I remember seeing them everywhere: old farm houses that told a story all their own. These breathtaking landmarks of years gone by were reminiscent of a lifestyle nearly forgotten. They sparked memories of stories told by grandparents and made passersby dream of stepping into another life. There is no mistaking these beautiful homesteads; they are replete with the elements of a former lifestyle. The shade offered by grape arbors reminds us of a day when there was no air conditioning. Weathered but still-standing outhouses take us back to a time when indoor plumbing did not exist. Dilapidated barns draw us into their charm as they tell of horse-drawn buggies and farm equipment pulled by livestock instead of tractors.

For many of us, modern conveniences such as electricity have been readily available for as long as we can remember. We have come to rely on these amenities and can't imagine life without them. The chaos and inconvenience caused by one power outage due to a storm is enough to make us certain that it would not be possible to live without these things. How would we cook if there is no electricity? How would we keep cool or warm when the weather is extreme? And how could we live without a refrigerator? Where do people find food if not at the local grocery store? How do they get toiletries, medicines, or even shoes, if not from a local department store? And how would they manage all this while still paying off existing debts and medical bills, keeping transportation, and maintaining insurance on their cars and their homes?

But for a growing number of individuals and families, a new set of questions is surfacing: How do we continue to pay for these things with skyrocketing expenses and a faltering economy? And what would we do if these resources were to become unavailable? The fear of being at the mercy of the availability of such services and products is becoming a growing concern everywhere. In such politically, economically, and even domestically turbulent times, how do we prepare for the unexpected?

And, perhaps the biggest question of all: How do we just unplug from society and survive "off the grid"?

For some, "going off the grid" can be as simple as eliminating the need for paid utilities. But for others, the very term "grid" represents a silent enemy that has slowly taken over, enslaving them and all of those around them, and stripping them of their independence. The grid then becomes a system from which they must work to free themselves.

There are also many different perspectives between these two extremes. But while going off the grid can mean many things to many people, the common denominator for most is that the very idea can be so overwhelming that people often feel powerless and unsure of where to even begin.

Make the Switch Slowly and Sensibly

The decision to go off the grid—and the extent to which one does so—is something to be made on an individual basis. For many, the phrase "off the grid" automatically conjures up a picture of living without a car or truck, surviving off the land with no outside employment, keeping livestock for food, and working countless acres of land in order to make all of this happen. This extreme lifestyle can be possible—and even perhaps the best solution—for some people. But many give up on the idea because they realize these extreme measures are not an option. They either are too expensive, too impractical, or impossible to obtain and implement. So, it is important to remember that "off grid" and complete self-sufficiency are two different things. Reaching whatever point between the two that you envision is a change that can—and should—happen slowly. By honestly looking at your own situation, your finances, the local economy, and available resources, you can set goals a little a time. When you meet those goals and feel good about those successes, then you can make new ones to take your self-sufficiency even further. Just remember to tackle your goals calmly and with patience. Don't try to make dramatic changes overnight.

Many who aren't intimidated by what all is involved in becoming completely self-sufficient are often tempted to be too hasty in making the changes. For those who believe times are indeed very dire, the immediate need for all amenities they believe necessary might overshadow the need to be both practical and far-sighted. Some rush into debt to meet their off-grid needs full of momentum fueled by fear, adrenalin, and more debt. Certainly, desperate times sometimes call for desperate measures. However, as often as not, these people find themselves later with their fear subsided, adrenaline depleted, debt inflated, and momentum deflated. They are left holding half-baked, incomplete, and abandoned off-grid plans—plus a mountain of debt yet to be paid.

So the important thing to note is that attaining self-sufficiency requires skills as well as possessions. It would be better to acquire the skills over time as possessions are afforded. Having many systems in place without the knowledge or skill to operate those systems won't be nearly as successful as a maintaining a few simple-to-operate, tried-and-true systems.

Generating Electricity

The term "off the grid" refers to the "power grid," or the chart-like system that keeps energy and utilities flowing to the general population. As mentioned earlier, some people confuse the term "off the grid" with being completely self-sufficient. If you simply want to be off the grid, then generating your own supply of electricity is a good first step. There are many avenues for doing this, including using water, wind, or solar energy. Some of these methods are very expensive and others are not.

For those who can't live without electricity and who can afford to immediately set up an alternative power source, the options are increasing daily. The nice thing about many of these methods is that can you operate them right in the middle of town. For example, if you opt for solar energy, you can mount solar panels to the roof of your home. Or, if you choose to tap into the energy generated by the wind, you could erect a wind turbine, which requires a tower from 25 to 120 feet tall. Some people even combine two power sources; hybrid systems typically are the most dependable. Yet another option is to use water power for energy by installing a hydrogenerator if you live near a river or stream. (If you're considering this, check the laws in your area. Although highly restricted, most local inspectors can help you attain your goal and maintain compliance with local laws.)

If installing these types of energy manufacturing systems is out of your price range, you can always consider purchasing a small generator that runs on regular or diesel fuel, and simply limit electrical use to necessities. Storing your energy in batteries is another option that comes with an added expense.

Once You've Installed Your Energy System

After you have installed an alternative power source, you may choose to remain connected to your power company for the time being. If you do that, speak to a representative from your power company about selling back the extra power. Many digital meters do not record power added to the grid, but you can ask to have a meter installed that will. Keep in mind, however, that if you do remain connected to your power company in any way, you're not officially considered off the grid.

Another thing to consider once you've installed an alternative power source is the difference you'll experience in usage of power. When you're on the grid, you can run as many appliances at once as you choose. However, when you are manufacturing your own electricity, you will need to be more careful about your consumption. Appliances such as microwaves, washing machines, and hair dryers use a lot of electricity, so other things must be turned off when those are being operated. Some might consider this inconvenient, but when compared to rising energy costs, many consider it a worthy trade.

Once you're generating your own electricity, you'll definitely want to conserve it. Something that makes it easier to conserve your energy is to invest, if you have the money, in a green roof. A green roof is an insulating roof that will keep cool air and warm air either in or out, depending on the season.

Establishing a Water Supply

For obvious reasons, you will need to plan for a way to maintain an adequate water supply with plenty of safe, clean storage. Again, many options are available, depending on your resources. The best and easiest way to have a water supply is to live near a fresh running body of water nearby, such as a river or creek. Make sure to consider year round flow to ensure supply and cleanliness. Boiling the water you use to ensure sanitation is a must.

Or, if possible, you could install a well. Sub-surface water is a much safer source for potable water due to soil strata filtration. If you plan to run a well pump, you will need electricity to run it. However, it is also possible to attach a manual pump to a well, although it may be more difficult to set up. Some people use a cistern and others collect their water in rain barrels, although making sure it is clean for drinking is more of a challenge.

Setting Up a Sewage System

If you live in the city or are on a city sewer system, you will still be considered on the grid until you find a way to disconnect from that. Establishing a system for disposing of sewage can be more of a challenge and an expense than getting a water supply. Purchasing a compost toilet is one choice, although it doesn't address the issue of disposing of waste from the sink or the bathtub. Another alternative—albeit quite expensive—is to install an independent septic tank; however, the city might put limitations on this as well.

Disposing of Waste

If you find that you are no longer eligible for garbage services, or if you choose to discontinue using that service, you'll need to decide what to do with your household garbage. You can probably burn much of it. What you can't burn, you might be able to drop off at one of the many recycling centers offered in various communities.

Keeping Open Lines of Communication

Certainly there are times when not having a telephone can be inconvenient. But, as mentioned earlier, people lived without then for centuries. In fact, the uninterrupted peace and quiet that comes without having a phone can be a newfound freedom for those who are tired of listening to incessant ringing! Telephone service is much easier to disconnect from your dwelling than other utilities, such as electricity, water, and sewage systems. As an alternative means of communicating, you can simply switch to using a cell phone, borrow a neighbor's phone when necessary, or simply live without. Our personal preference, however—because there are times it is necessary to have some way to contact the outside world—is a prepaid cell phone. These are usually available near the checkout aisle or in the electronics department of a grocery store, home supply center, or super center.

Another communication concern, especially if you go off the grid in a very remote place, is mail service. You may find it necessary to get a post office box in the nearest town.

Once you have overcome these obstacles and have no more paid utilities attached to your residence, you are officially considered off the grid. Then you can enjoy the benefits of using your power without worrying about its cost or outages. It might take time, but you will eventually recoup your monetary investment as well. Plus, you can enjoy the peace of mind of being your own energy supplier.

Father Knows Best, But Grandpa Knew Even Better

One of the greatest, yet most commonly overlooked, resources available to many people is family stories. Many people today forget that there ever was a day without the grid, but it wasn't as long ago as they think. You and your parents may have been raised on the grid, but your grandparents and their parents probably were not—and their knowledge is something akin to "free college" on this subject. For example, when you were a child, you may have heard stories about your grandmother, as a little girl, churning butter or scrubbing the clothes clean on a washboard in a stream. Or perhaps your grandfather told you about splitting wood with an axe when he was twelve years old so that the family would be able to keep warm with fires during the winter. Of course, the best source for information is almost always the first-hand source, so if you are fortunate to have grandparents who are still living, ask them for more details about living self-sufficiently. If this isn't the case, try to find information about the subject in old books—remember, the older the source, the less "grid-integrated" the information will be.

For example, an antique book on raising vegetables will describe a variety of good ways to rid plants of pests by using such products as nicotine, vinegar, coffee, or even whiskey. A more modern book, however, will direct you to the pesticide aisle of the gardening center at your local home improvement store. Many of these modern products are very effective, but if part of your plan involves being prepared for a crisis that might interrupt supplies to your area, it is a good idea to have a more readily available solution—such as the ones described in the older book—at hand.

Another benefit of consulting older books is that they are often very inexpensive. Keep an eye out at garage sales, flea markets, or antique stores for reasonably priced books on any subject matter you think you might someday need "old" knowledge about. You can create a reference bookshelf you can always consult—even if you have no electricity or the internet is down.

"I Want To Be More Self-Sufficient, But Where Do I Start?"

A common misconception about people who live off the grid is that they don't have regular jobs, drive wherever they need to go, or shop at the grocery store. In fact, quite the opposite is often true. Many of these people are only living off of the power grid. While being free from worries of outages from storms or the rising costs of utility bills, they are not completely self-sufficient. They still rely on the grid as it pertains to the local businesses around them. They depend on the grid to power the local grocery store, for example, and they count on it to power local gas stations.

Don't misunderstand: These people have tackled and conquered a huge step toward becoming self-sufficient, and they reap the benefits monthly as they enjoy living without utility bills. But becoming truly self-sufficient in every aspect of life is a much larger project involving the sacrifice of many other conveniences. Whether this type of drastic change is right for you and your family is only for you to decide, based on your needs and goals. Getting off the power grid is enough of a step to make many people feel secure. But others need to feel they have taken more measures to obtain self-sufficiency. Where to start is as diverse and individual as each person's needs, goals, and available resources. The obstacles can seem insurmountable for those who try to take them on all at once, so it's best to start with the strongest need.

Location, Location, Location

Many factors are involved in choosing a location for setting up and maintaining a lifestyle of self-sufficiency. First, consider the size of your family and determine why you are making this change. If you are single and simply want to learn to live off the land, then you can get by with very little property. On the other hand, if you are retired, concerned about the economy, and want to create a place for your children and grandchildren as a back-up plan in case of financial crisis, more land may be necessary. Consider both your budget and the number of people you might be expected to feed and house. Be realistic when shopping for and purchasing land if you are considering preparing for economic crisis: It is better to house more people in tight living quarters on property with a low mortgage (or no mortgage) than to purchase a sprawling house on hundreds of acres with a large debt. In a case like this, the extra financial burden of added people eating with you or even living with you could be the undoing of even your own self-sufficiency.

Second, consider the local community. If you have or are expecting to have (or care for) children, how far away is the nearest school? (Or will you homeschool?) Are there neighbors nearby? Is the community a place where you feel safe? In case of a large-scale grid crisis, would the community easily transform into a barter-and-trade setting? Are your goals similar to those of others in this community? It would be less beneficial to live outside a large city if you were the only one growing your own food than it would be to face increasing difficulty in protecting your supplies during a large-scale crisis. Finding a community where you can become part of a network, where you can possibly participate in a barter-and-trade system, will add to your security as you embark on this journey. Becoming somewhat active in your community can help you meet and make vital connections with your neighbors as well.

Third, assess the location's natural resources. Is a water supply available? Is it available year-round? Does the land have good soil? Does it have good sun exposure? If you plan to raise livestock, is the land suitable for pasture? Planning in advance as many details as possible will help you put your systems into place later. Keep in mind where barns and outbuildings will need to be, what kind of animal predators live in the nearby area, what grows well in the climate and terrain, and anything else you think might help you later. For example, if you know you want to raise chickens, finding out what animal predators live in any nearby woods will help you decide where to place your chicken coop. Or, if you know that you eventually want to make a man-made pond, you can place your fence lines accordingly. Planning such as this will make transitions much easier later.

Food Supply

Once you have chosen your location, your next step should be to begin establishing your food supply. This might take some time if you buy bare property and are building a house on it, but even at this stage you can plant fruit trees. It is wise to go ahead and do that now anyway since it can take from two to nine years, depending on the species, for a tree to mature enough to bear fruit or nuts. The earlier the tree is planted, the sooner a food supply will begin to form. (If you're not building—if a home is already on the property—then this is the time to consider adding solar panels, wind towers, or whatever other energy generator you plan to use.)

Even though securing a food supply is one of the biggest tasks involved in becoming self-sufficient, it can also be one of the most rewarding, even fun, challenges you'll undertake. A good place to start is at your local conservation department, your city hall, or—if you would like to keep a lower profile—your local feed store. Find out what grows well in your area. You can add specialty fruits or vegetables, or even exotics, to the mix later, but at first try to keep establishing a food supply as easy as possible. Find out what plants yield fruits, nuts, and vegetables that are edible; look for those that absolutely thrive in your climate zone and then make up your mind to eat a lot of those things in the beginning. As you learn what plants are easy to grow where you live, you will become more skilled and can then take on raising plants that will be more difficult to grow, that are less pest-resistant, or that require more specialized soil conditions. (At this point, a greenhouse would be a good investment if finances allow.) Further, buying seeds from local seed harvesters, farmers, or even your local feed store can ensure that the seeds you are buying will be better suited to the soil in your area, making them more foolproof.

Ask neighbors or newfound friends about any weeds, pests, rodents, or even animal predators that you have questions about. Remember that the local, hands-on experience of a neighbor can sometimes be just as valuable as any advice or instructions you would find in a book.

As your gardening skills grow, you can begin to branch out into growing spices, pollinator-attracting flowers, and particularly herbs, for which there are many good medicinal uses. For example, many herbs—such as Echinacea and sage—are great natural antibiotics. Some are great for soothing nerves, and others are useful in curbing asthma. Harvested herbs are easily dried, preserved, and stored for off-season use. An exhaustive handbook detailing the uses of each type of herb can be a good resource for those who want to become completely self-sufficient.

If you don't plan to manufacture electricity and therefore won't have refrigeration, you will want to plan for dehydrating, canning, or even curing the food you raise and grow. Find out about these procedures from books, the Internet, neighbors, and experts in your community.

Taking Advantage of Natural Cycles

A beautiful harmony can be achieved between the farmer, the livestock and poultry, and the land. The farmer grows fruits and vegetables, then harvests them for canning or eating. Many of the discarded parts of the fruits and vegetables can be thrown into a compost pile and agitated into potting soil for the following year's planting. In the meantime, chickens will help keep snakes and insects away from the property—all the while providing eggs for the farmer's family. Further, a cow or goat can produce milk for drinking. Any vegetable or fruit trimmings that don't go into the compost pile, as well as extra chicken eggs, fat trimmings, plate scraps, and even excess cow or goat milk, can go into a bucket that is used to feed a pig. When the pig is slaughtered for food in the winter, when less fresh vegetation is available for food, the lard can be used to make soap.

Heating and Cooling

Yet another critical step toward becoming self-sufficient is heating and cooling your home. If you will manufacture your own electricity, these tasks will be a little easier. However, because heaters and air conditioners each require a lot of electricity, powering them might be more challenging than you expect. You might even think about buying a separate generator just to run these appliances.

Or, you might choose another route, such as wood heat. Heating your home with wood involves more work than running heating and cooling appliances with generated energy, but many people find it is a great alternative—especially since a wood-burning stove can both heat your home *and* cook your food.

If you take the wood-heating route, you will want to invest in a few tools like a good chainsaw and some splitting wedges. It also helps if you have some land where you can manage a wood lot. But if this isn't possible, you can easily find other ways to obtain wood. Often, winds from a strong storm will blow down trees. If you spot a tree that has fallen in someone's way—perhaps on a driveway or a road—you can offer to help clear away the tree in exchange for some or all of the wood. By keeping your eyes open and being ready to volunteer your services, you're likely to find yourself with more wood than you have time to harvest!

The options for cooling your home are a little more limited than for heating, but there are several ways to at least minimize the oppressive heat if you live in an area that gets unbearably hot in the summertime. If you're going to be designing and/or building your home yourself, you can install strategically placed windows to channel the evening breeze. If not, plant shade trees anywhere that the sunlight directly hits windows or doors. Another way to help keep the house cool in summer is to invest in a barbeque grill or use other outdoor cooking method. This keeps heat out of the house and eliminates the need for electricity to be carried to a stove. Charcoal or wood chips can be used to cook outdoors in a pit, and as long as you are not preparing for a large-scale crisis when it might not be available, propane can be very convenient for cooking as well. (Propane can also be a good way to solve your heating and cooling problems if you are not worried about availability. It is also a reliable way to make sure you have hot water on tap if you choose to have a hot water heater.)

Keeping Clean

A final—and quite critical—step toward self-sufficiency is providing a way to have clean laundry, a place for bathing, and a sanitary restroom.

Laundry. If you do not plan to have an electric washer and dryer, your method of keeping laundry clean will vary depending on your circumstances and plans. A washboard or even an old-fashioned, crank-style, wringer washing machine and a clothesline might be worthwhile investments. If this is what you choose to do, keep in mind that clothes won't dry on an outdoor clothesline during the winter; you'll need to come up with an alternate, indoor strategy during the cold months.

Bathing. As for bathing, this can be one of the hardest comforts of the modern world to give up if you don't plan to manufacture your own electricity. Depending how far off the grid you want to go and how rustic a lifestyle you choose, you will simply have to decide whether it is worth it to you to bathe in a river or if you would rather heat water (with propane, solar power, or wood) and bathe indoors.

Restroom. If you have a septic system and choose to have a running water supply inside the house, this will make the restroom issue easier to solve, because you can simply have a toilet in your house.

However, if you decide to go completely rustic, you can build an outhouse (if local laws allow). As for personal and feminine hygiene supplies, plenty of washable products are available. Again, it's important to remember that decisions such as this are to be made on an individual basis; regardless of what modern inconveniences you choose to go without, your grandparents did exactly the same thing, and they did just fine.

A Few Final Tips

We should stress one last time that whether you decide simply to go off the grid or to become completely self-sufficient, your options are limitless. While you strive to become independent, keep in mind that there are hundreds of trades that can be invaluable to you both for obtaining what you need and for helping others get what they need. Anything you can do with your hands, or any skill you have—i.e., sewing, mechanics, building, or knitting, to name a few examples—can be a tremendous asset.

Choose your own reasons for going off the grid or becoming self-sufficient, then set your goals accordingly. Remember to keep the follow-through at the same pace as your goals, and don't become overambitious. It bears repeating again: A small but well-worked system is a much better asset than overambitious plans that are beyond reach. You will not be alone. Soon you will find yourself making new contacts and networking with others who have been working toward the same goals. Most people are more than willing to take you under their wing and give you advice as you become more self-sufficient.

The point of going off the grid is to build your own stability and security, both financially and personally. Grasp the challenges and enjoy them, as each new obstacle overcome offers a new level of achievement and freedom. See the opportunities as fun and liberating. Don't be surprised when, as soon as you accomplish certain goals, you find yourself taking things a step further and making new goals. Someday, you will even wonder how you ever lived, paying those utility bills and relying on the local market for food!

—

Carl and Allie Anderson live with their two children in Missouri, where they have adopted an "off grid" plan and strive to preserve and share as much knowledge as possible about gardening, crafting, sewing, mechanics, soapmaking, candle making, home remedies, and much more. Keep an eye on their website, www.edensessentials.com, for free information, as knowledge is power!

chapter twenty

Does God Have an Emergency Preparedness Plan?

by Thomas Horn

Today, a strange paradox exists. What looks like the fulfillment of prophecy is everywhere: unrest in the Middle East, the rise of a European super state, the alignment of Gog and Magog, the formation of a national ID, and gateways through biotechnology that could unleash upon earth pestilence of biblical proportions. People from all three of the world's great religions see these developments as potential omens of an "end-times" scenario leading to the Apocalypse. Between now and when the Lord removes his own from earth, significant trials could develop for which all of us must be readied to survive.

Yet many believers in God, especially in America, are indifferent to the need to prepare for the unexpected.

An article by Mimi Hall in *USA Today* recently acknowledged, "Most Americans haven't taken steps to prepare for a natural disaster, terrorist attack or other emergency, according to a new study on preparedness, and only about a third have made plans with family members about how they would communicate with each other during a crisis."[531]

Part of the reason for this may be, until recent years, how well off we have been in the United States, and how we have trusted in our bank accounts to sustain us. Unfortunately, money sitting in savings accounts and investments are useless if we become stuck in a storm or other crisis.

Another disarming reason I witnessed during my twenty-five years of pastoring for why people of faith neglect preparedness has to do with an odd defeatism that says, "If current events are prophesied to happen, then there's nothing we can do about it anyway."

The notion that calamity is unavoidable if it is divinely predicted is even sanctioned by some expositors who miss the pattern for preparedness in the Bible. While it is true that famine was prophesied for Egypt, it is also a fact that God led Joseph to prepare for it, and, as a result, he saved his family and the nations around about.

Proverbs 22:3 tells us that a prudent person will foresee such difficulties and prepare for them, while a simpleton will go blindly on and suffer the consequences. This is good advice not only for religious folks, but also for people of any persuasion.

A third and perhaps the greatest reason some people, including religious people, never plan for disaster is that they view the need to prepare for the unexpected as too complicated and costly. They imagine the back yard being dug up for construction of a massive bomb shelter and the basement crammed with row after row of dry grains and large containers filled with backup water supplies.

The truth is, survival preparation is modestly affordable. Under most circumstances, the ability for individuals to remain mobile for a few days to a week or so by simply grabbing an inexpensive "survival bag" and heading out is more important than having silos filled with long-term storage foods.

Even when we envision a worst-case scenario—such as a terrorist nuke or an ICBM exchange—low-cost shelters that can be built at home, combined with the use of a minimal amount of potassium iodide, would help keep as much as 99 percent of the population alive, according to one synopsis by the Department of Homeland Security. Designs for building such family shelters are available free online at places like www.SurvivorMall.com.

While having to try to endure radioactive fallout is a growing possibility, the fact is that most people are more likely to face disaster as a result of things like nature. A few weeks ago, a journalist became lost in a snowstorm in Oregon and died from the exposure to freezing temperatures. If his car had been equipped with a simple survival kit, he would have had an excellent chance of survival.

During Hurricane Katrina, one woman had an emergency supplies kit in her attic that kept her and her two cats alive for days until help arrived. Another man, a doctor who had read a survival-tips book and followed its instructions, was prepared with equipment and supplies. His house became a gathering place for people displaced by the storm.

For reasons such as these, my wife and I recently provided each of our children with a "walk out" kit for the trunks of their cars. These emergency bags we got from SurvivorMall.com contain enough food, water, shelter, first aid, lighting, and communication supplies to keep them alive for days in the case of a vehicle malfunction or other situation in which they would need to abandon their cars.

Many of the items vital for a good survival kit can also be found at your local shopping center: an inexpensive poncho, a basic first aid assortment, nylon cord, canvas for temporary shelter, duck tape, and a whistle. Other items are a bit trickier to find, and may need to be acquired from an online emergency preparedness company like SurvivorMall.com. These include five-year-shelf-life food bars, five-year-shelf-life water boxes or pouches, paper-thin thermal blankets designed by NASA to retain body heat, special hand-crank combination flashlights with radios and emergency signals built in, and so on. My personal favorite is the "Transformer 3-in-1 Radio Flashlight," which requires no maintenance, no batteries, no bulb replacements, and can even power your cell phone.

Pre-made emergency kits containing items such as those above can be acquired online at costs from $30 and up, depending on the number of people and the number of days they are designed to sustain.

Why then, given how affordable disaster preparedness is, are so many people unprepared for an emergency?

Within "faith communities," part of the problem goes back to western dispensational fatalism that fails to see God's instructions about the future and the responsibility He gives concerning preparation. Church authorities may speak of the hidden shelter that God provides His followers during a storm, yet they often fail to see the believer's responsibility cast throughout the Bible where we are to care for our families and communities by readying for the unknown.

Some teachers also erroneously believe that emergency preparedness reflects a lack of faith in God. The opposite is true. The book of James measures faith by personal action, and Hebrews 11:7 describes true faith this way: "By faith Noah, being warned of God of things not seen as yet, moved with fear and prepared an ark to the saving of his house."

God told Noah that He would destroy the earth by a flood. He gave Noah instructions on how to be prepared so that he and his family could survive. Noah didn't know when the flood would come, only that it was prophesied; and he prepared for it. When the Flood arrived, he was ready. His faith in and obedience to God's word, his survival instincts, and ultimately his preparedness actions saved his family and preserved the human race.

The parallel between Noah's time and today is astounding. "As it was in the days of Noah," says Luke 17:26–27 concerning the last days. Noah's actions should define the modern believer's responsibility, including the need for spiritual and physical preparedness. Of course, there are other places in the Bible that provide lessons about preparedness, including principles in the books of Psalms and Proverbs, the parable of the faithful and evil servants (Matthew 24:45–51), and the parable of the ten virgins (Matthew 25:1–13). But 1 Timothy 5:8 goes even further, saying that a person who does not provide for the survival of relatives has denied the faith and is worse than an unbeliever.

Given these instructions and the belief held by many today that we are living in "the last days," or at a minimum, a time of unusual challenges, leaders of religious institutions urgently need to educate their followers about taking personal responsibility for preparedness in an age of growing uncertainty. Dramatic lessons over the last few years have proven that we should not depend on government agencies such as FEMA to save us if we need them. In fact, a report recently found that five years after the September 11, 2001, terror attacks, the government still isn't fully prepared to respond to a major public health emergency such as bioterrorism or a pandemic flu outbreak.

So what can one do to help people with disaster preparedness?

This is the good news. Hundreds of free pages from reports and booklets on how to perform first aid, prepare temporary shelters, build bomb shelters, defend against terrorism and chemical contamination, shield against nuclear fallout, survive earthquakes, storms, floods, and dozens of other emergency situations are available free at places like www.SurvivorMall.com. Spiritual leaders can download these booklets and reports, print them out, and place them on a table in a church foyer, hand them to neighbors, give them out during classes, or—better yet—teach a class on preparedness and tie it in with the mandates of Scripture. If nothing else, everybody can share this book with people they know with a recommendation that they do what is right to protect themselves as well as those God has placed under their care.

As a veteran of more than thirty years of church ministry, I call on pastors and other religious leaders to stand at the forefront of this issue and to make disaster preparedness some part of their ministry. This doesn't need to define what you or your fellowship is about, but this can and must be part of the wise counsel you offer those you have responsibility for. You could literally save a believer's life! Better yet, why not invite one of the authors of this book to speak at your church or convention on the subject of facing the future with confidence and preparedness? To discuss this possibility, contact the publisher through tomhorn@defenderpublishing.com.

Deuteronomy 30:19 says, "Today I have given you the choice

between life and death, between blessings and curses. I call on heaven and earth to witness the choice you make. Oh, that you would choose life, that you and your descendants might live!"

Together as people of faith, we should face the future with confidence and take the lead in future preparedness.

Notes

Chapter 3

1. Lisa Hopkins, *Memory at the End of History, Mary Shelley's "The Last Man,"* Romanticism on the Net 6, http://www.erudit.org/revue/ron/1997/v/n6/005746ar.html (April 7, 2009).

2. UN Millennium Project, "Millennium Project," http://www.unmillenniumproject.org (April 7, 2009).

3. The UN Millennium Project, "The UN Millennium Declaration and the MDGs: What They Are," http://www.unmillenniumproject.org/goals/index.htm (April 7, 2009).

4. The UN Millennium Project, "Goal 6," http://www.unmillenniumproject.org/ goals/gti.htm#goal6 (April 7, 2009).

5. Ban Ki-moon, UN Secretary General, The United Nations Millennium Development Goals, "High-level Event," http://www.un.org/millenniumgoals/2008highlevel/ (April 9, 2009).

6. Mike Leavitt, Secretary, U.S. Department of Health and Human Services, "Press Briefing: Pandemic Influenza Plan," November 2, 2005, http://www.hhs.gov/news/transcripts/ briefing20051102.html (April 9, 2009).

7. World Health Organization, "WHO Guidelines for Humanitarian Agencies," (2006) Background, 2.1, p. 9, http://whqlibdoc.who.int/hq/2006/WHO_CDS_NTD_DCE_2006.2_eng.pdf (April 9, 2009).

8. World Health Organization, "Avian Influenza, Assessing the Pandemic Threat," January 2005, p. 25. http://www.who.int/csr/disease/influenza/H5N1-9reduit.pdf. (April 7, 2009).

9. Victorian Health Management Plan for Pandemic Influenza, (July 2007)12, www.health.vic.gov.au/__data/assets/pdf_file/0017/54503/Victorian_health_management_plan_for_pandemic_influenza.pdf (April 2, 2009).

10. United States Department of Health and Human Services, "HHS Pandemic Influenza Implementation Plan," http://www.hhs.gov/pandemicflu/implementationplan/intro.htm (April 7, 2009).

11. U.S. Department of Homeland Security, *Guide for Critical Infrastructure and Key Resources,* Sec. 1.3, p. 6, (September 2006) http://www.pandemicflu.gov/plan/pdf/cikrpandemicinfluenzeguide.pdf (April 9, 2009).

12. World Health Organization, *Operational Procedures for Event Management*, 2008, http://www.who.int/csr/HSE_EPR_ARO_2008_1.pdf (April 7, 2009).

13. World Health Organization, International Health Regulations, http://www.who.int/ihr/en/ (April 2, 2009).

14. World Health Organization, International Health Regulations, http://www.who.int/csr/HSE_EPR_ARO_2008_1.pdf (April 7, 2009).

15. World Health Organization, "International Spread of Disease Threatens Public Health Security" (August 23, 2008) http://www.who.int/mediacentre/news/releases/2007/pr44/en/index.html.

16. Centers for Disease Control and Prevention, "H1N1 (Swine Flu) and You, Novel H1N1Flu," (May 8, 2009) http://www.cdc.gov/H1N1flu/qa.htm.

17. Emma Hitt, PhD., "WHO Maintains Level 5 Pandemic Level," *Medscape Today*, (April 29, 2009) http://www.medscape.com/viewarticle/702149 (April 30, 2009).

18. Pan American Health Organization, *International Health Regulations* (2005) http://new.paho.org/hq/ index.php?option=com_content&task=view&id=534&Itemid=259.

19. Physicians for Civil Defense, "21ˢᵗ Century Living Terrors," (November 2002) http://www.physiciansforcivildefense.org/cdp/nov2002.html.

20. Tom Mangold, Jeff Goldberg, *Plague Wars: A True Story of Biological Warfare* (New York: MacMillan, 2000), xi.

21. Ibid., 373.

22. Mark Wheelis, Lajos Rózsa, Malcolm Dando, *Deadly Cultures* (Cambridge, MA: Harvard University, 2006), 1.

23. Ibid., 355.

24. U.S. Department of Homeland Security, "Homeland Security Presidential Directive 9: Defense of United States Agriculture and Food," (January 30, 2004) http://www.dhs.gov/xabout/laws/gc_1217449547663.shtm (April 7, 2009).

25. U.S. Department of Energy, *NEST: Nuclear Emergency Support Team*, http://www.nv.doe.gov/nationalsecurity/homelandsecurity/nest.htm.

26. Jim Wilson, "When UFOs Arrive," *Popular Mechanics* (February 2004).

27. Thomas Beardon, Lt. Col. (ret.) U.S. Army, "Extraordinary Biology," *Aids, Biological Warfare*, (April 25, 2009) http://www.cheniere.org.

28. Ibid.

29. Ibid.

30. Ibid.

31. Ibid.

32. Ibid.
33. Thomas Bearden, Lt. Col. (ret.) U.S. Army, "Tom Talks Tesla," DVD (1990) http://www.cheniere.org.
34. Sharon K. Gilbert, *Peering Into Darkness*, "H1N1 Talks: Phase 6 Is Likely Next Announcement," May 19, 2009, http://peeringintodarkness.com/?p=1649 (May 19, 2009).
35. Stephen King, *The Stand* (New York: Doubleday, 1990). Author's note.
36. Special thanks for informational and organizational contributions to Steven DeNagy, M.D., Idaho Falls, ID and Eduardo Codina, M.D., Barcelona, Spain.

Chapter 4

37. Woodrow Wilson, *The New Freedom* (New York: Doubleday, 1918), 13–14.
38. Available from Radio Liberty, P.O. Box 969, Soquel, CA, 95073.
39. Barry Goldwater, *With No Apologies* (New York: William Morrow, 1979), 280.
40. Planned Police State Syllabus, Radio Liberty.
41. *Encyclopedia Americana*, International Edition, Vol. 26 (New York, 1966) 716.
42. Wilson.
43. Carroll Quigley, Tragedy and Hope: A History of the World in Our Time (New York: McMillan, 1966) 72.
44. "The Rockefeller Shadow Government," http://www.acsa2000.net/interlocks.htm.
45. Wilson, 184–186.
46. Oscar Callaway, *Congressional Record*: 2nd Session, 64th Congress of the United States of America, Vol. LIV, p. 2947.
47. Frederic Howe, *The Confessions of a Reformer* (New York: Scribner's, 1925), 295–296. See also, Stanley Monteith, *Brotherhood of Darkness* (Oklahoma City: Hearthstone, 2000) 113.
48. Letter from William Dodd to Col. Edward Mandell House, October 29, 1936, Sterling Library, Yale University. Copy available from Radio Liberty.
49. Antony Sutton, *Wall Street and the Rise of Hitler* (Seal Beach, CA: '76 Press, 1976), 213–220.
50. www.the7thfire.com/.
51. "The State Steps In: Setting the Anti-Communist Agenda," from Ellen Schrecker, *The Age of McCarthyism: A Brief History with*

Documents (Boston: St. Martin's Press, 1994), www.writing.upenn. edu/~afilreis/50s/state-agenda.html.

52. http://www.paranormality.com/napoleon_fate_book.shtml and http://napoleonsbookofffate.blogspot.com.

53. http://www.angelfire.com/weird2/obscure2/druid.html.

54. Quigley, 48.

55. http://www.astrologyguidance.com/financial/index.shtml.

56. Quigley, 952.

57. Monteith, 122–138.

58. Quigley, 325.

59. Ibid., 324.

60. Cecil Rhodes, *Confession of Faith*, available from Radio Liberty.

61. Barry Goldwater, 280, 284, 285.

62. http://www.augustreview.com/news_commentary/trilateral_commission/

63. https://www.augustreview.com/news_commentary/trilateral_commission/.

64. http://www.augustreview.com/knowledge_base/getting_started_with_globalism/.

65. For a list of the media outlets controlled by members of the CFR and the Bilderbergers, access: http://www.apfn.org/apfn/efr/cfr-members. htm.

66. www.augustreview.com/knowledge_base/.

67. For a list of the financial institutions controlled by members of the CFR and the Bilderbergers access: http://www.apfn.org/apfn/cfr-members.htm.

68. Henry Kissinger, "The Chance for a New World Order," *International Herald Tribune,* (January 12, 2009).

Chapter 5

69. Dennis Laurence Cuddy, Ph.D., *Secret Records Revealed: The Men, Money & the Methods Behind the New World Order* (Oklahoma City, OK: Hearthstone, 1999) 101.

70. James Rizzuti, "The Gods of Olympus," *Midnight Call* (April, May, June, July, 1998) 16–33.

71. Ibid., 33.

72. Ted Flynn, *Hope of the Wicked* (Sterling, VA: MaxKol Communications, 2000) 2.

73. United Nations, *Report on Human Development* (Oxford, United Kingdom: Oxford University, 1994) 81.

74. H.G. Wells, *The Open Conspiracy: Blue Prints for a World Revolution* (London: Book Tree, 1928) XVIII.

75. http://www.enterstageright.com/archive/articles/0800globalgov.htm.
76. These quotes come from a lecture at Harvard University given by Nelson Rockefeller in 1962. See also: Nelson Rockefeller, *The Future of Federalism* (Cambridge, MA: Harvard University, 1964).
77. Darwinism is the systematic, codified view of today's prevailing and politically correct theory of evolution. It explains the macro-evolutionary process through principles of natural and sexual selection.
78. Ethical naturalism contends that religious verities are illusionary, and everything is explicable only by means chance and natural law.
79. Empiricism is the philosophical belief that all knowledge is ultimately derived from sense experience.
80. Written primarily by Raymond Bragg, the first *Humanist Manifesto* with thirty-four signers was published in 1933. Unlike later manifestos, *Humanist Manifesto I* refers to humanism as a religious movement meant to transcend and replace previous, deity-based systems. With 120 signatories, *The Humanist Manifesto II* first appeared in *The Humanist* (September/ October, 1973) when Paul Kurtz and Edwin H. Wilson were editor and editor emeritus, respectively. *Humanism and Its Aspirations* (subtitled *Humanist Manifesto III*), is the most recent manifesto published by the American Humanist Association (AHA). The newest one is considerably shorter and lists these six primary beliefs:
    a. Knowledge of the world is derived by observation, experimentation, and rational analysis.
    b. Humans are an integral part of nature, the result of unguided evolutionary change.
    c. Ethical values are derived from human need and interest as tested by experience.
    d. Life's fulfillment emerges from individual participation in the service of humane ideals.
    e. Humans are social by nature and find meaning in relationships.
    f. Working to benefit society maximizes individual happiness.
81. A theocracy is a form of government in which a god or deity is recognized as the supreme civil ruler.
82. The book of Daniel is a prophetic book that includes four apocalyptic visions predicting the course of world history (Chapters 7–12 with Revelation 13:2, 17:15).
83. A latter-day visionary, Antichrist eventually will become the greatest dictator the world has ever known. He will rule but for "a short space" of time; and though his message will be one of peace, he will war mercilessly. The most fearful punishment found anywhere in Scripture

is related to the "mark of the Beast." Enforced by Antichrist's false prophet, this mark is a brand required by all in order to buy or sell in the world community this dictatorial administration forges (Daniel 7:25 with Revelation 12:14; 17:10; Daniel 8:25; Revelation 14:9–10).

84. 2 Thessalonians 2:7.

85. Daniel 7:8. In Scripture, the horn depicts power.

86. Antichrist can be interpreted "in place of Christ," or "a substitute for" Him. In general, the term "antichrist" refers to one who stands in opposition to all that Jesus Christ represents. He will not regard the God of his fathers, nor any god, for he'll magnify himself above all others (1 John 2:18, 22; 4:3; 2 John 7; Daniel 11:37).

87. Nelson Rockefeller referenced a powerful "free-world supra-national political being" (also, a single, benevolent world "Administrator") while lecturing at Harvard University in 1962. See also: Nelson Rockefeller, *The Future of Federalism* (Cambridge, MA: Harvard University, 1964).

88. Revelation 6:2–8.

89. Revelation 19:11.

90. The term, "Aquarian Conspiracy," was popularized in 1980. See: Marilyn Ferguson, *The Aquarian Conspiracy* (Los Angeles: Penguin, 1980).

91. Gary Allen, *The Rockefeller File* (Seal Beach, California: '76 Press, 1976) 77.

92. Arnold Toynbee, "The Trend of International Affairs Since the War" (Copenhagen, Denmark: The Institute for the Study of International Affairs, November 1931). See also: Dennis Laurence Cuddy, Ph.D., *Secret Records Revealed: The Men, Money & the Methods behind the New World Order* (Oklahoma City, OK: Hearthstone, 1999) 50–51.

93. United Nations Development Program, *Our Global Neighborhood: The Report of the Commission on Global Governance* (Oxford, United Kingdom: Oxford University, 1995) 35.

94. Mikhail Gorbachev exalts the *cosmos* (world order) as his God. See the transcription from the Charlie Rose television program on PBS television, aired October 23, 1996.

95. http://www.earthcharter.org. Note that the *Earth Charter* emphasizes our saving Mother Earth. Objectives include tolerance, united strength with armed forces under the UN banner, and involuntary redistribution of wealth. The charter redefines America's doctrine of original intent, the *U.S. Constitution*, which has served as the supreme law of the federal government since its adoption in 1789.

96. In 1977, the *Constitution for the Federation of Earth* was adopted by twenty-five countries at the second session of the World Constituent

Assembly. It's been said that its preamble reads like a New Age occult manual.

97. In Daniel 11:24, the Bible makes prophetic reference to distribution of wealth. A type of the Antichrist, whom he foreshadows, King Antiochus Epiphanes (known as "the Mad One") would likewise "scatter the prey and spoil and riches" among the peaceable league made with him.

98. Brzezinski believed that "Marxism represents a further vital and creative stage in the maturing of man's universal vision." See: Zbigniew Brzezinski, *In Between Two Ages: America's Role in the Technetronic Era* (New York: Viking, 1970).

99. 2 Thessalonians 3:10; Matthew 25:25–26, 29–30. In Proverbs 6:6, the root word for sluggard means "to lean." In contemporary America, those who indulge in welfare fraud qualify as "leaners." They likewise warrant the uncomely label *Adam belial,* or "worthless mankind." The root word for "wicked man" in verse 12 is "to pant"—that is, to expend energy without producing and, consequently, to facsimile a brute beast, prone to mischief and discord (verse 14).

100. UNESCO, *Operational Guidelines for the Implementation of the World Heritage Convention,* I (D) (45) (New York: The United Nations, February 1994) 15.

101. John Davis, "The Wildlands Project," *Wild Earth* Special Issue (Richmond, VT: Cenozoic Society, 1992) 3.

102. United Nations, *UN Conference on Desertification* (New York: The United Nations Environment Programme, or UNEP, 1992).

103. Genesis 1:31.

104. Maurice Strong, *Global Biodiversity Assessment, CBA* (Cambridge, MA: Cambridge University, 1995) 773.

105. Biblically, the earth as we know it is destined to pass away. God never intended for it to last forever. Instead, a new earth (not to be confused with Eckhart Tolle's "new earth") will take its place (Revelation 21:1). Until then, God will not fail to supply all material needs according to His riches in glory by Christ Jesus (Philippians 4:19).

106. Genesis 3:18 with 1:26–31.

107. John Tierney, "Recycling is Garbage," *New York Times,* June 30, 1996, 24–29, 44, 48, 51, 53.

108. 1 Timothy 6:20.

109. Henry Lamb, *The Environmental Movement* (Hollow Rock, TN: Sovereignty International, 2008) 41.

110. Senator James Inhofe, Chairman, Senate Committee on Environment and Public Works, *A Skeptic's Guide to Debunking Global Warming Alarmism, Hot & Cold Media Spin Cycle: A Challenge to Journalists*

who Cover Global Warming (Washington, D.C.: Senate Floor Speech Delivered September 25, 2006).

111. Known as the NGO Triumvirate, the International Union for the Conservation of Nature (IUCN), the World Wide Fund for Nature (WWF), and the World Resources Institute (WRI) have developed and promoted globalism since the 1970s.

112. Henry Lamb, "Excessive Rise of Global Government" (Hollow Rock, TN: Sovereignty International, 2008) 141.

113. Thomas Robert Malthus (1766–1834) was an English economist and cleric whose *Essay on the Principle of Population* (1798, revised 1803) advocated population control. Malthus first presented the flawed theory that earth's resources are limited and, with massive increase in human population, they face depletion. His philosophy that populations increase in geometric ratio, while food supplies increase only in arithmetic ratio, upholds the UN concept of sustainable development.

114. Daniel 11:23 indicates that Antichrist will be strong over those deemed to be "small people." His bidding is that of the Devil, a "murderer from the beginning" (John 8:44).

115. Romans 1:25–28. In Daniel 11:37, we learn this about the Antichrist: "Neither shall he regard the God of his fathers, nor the desire of women." In his regime, traditional family isn't honored.

116. www.un.org/womenwatch/daw/cedaw.

117. Margaret Sanger, "A Plan for Peace" (Birth Control Review, April 1932) 107–108.

118. Although respect of persons plays into the global agenda, the concept is at odds with Bible protocol (Acts 10:34).

119. The notion that animals deserve to become a protected societal class is the myth commonly promulgated by advocates of PeTA. God made garments of animal skin for Adam and Eve to wear, and Christ himself ate broiled fish. Similarly, as a tent-maker, Paul was no animal-rights activist; he fabricated tents from strong goat's-hair cloth stretched over poles and held in place by cords that reached out to stakes driven into the ground. In God's economy, humans are of infinitely greater value than other life forms (Matthew 10:31).

120. Matthew 12:25.

121. Phyllis Schlafly, "Guest Workers Aren't Cheap; They're Expensive" (Alton, IL: *The Phyllis Schlafly Report*, July 2006), Volume 39, Number 12.

122. For more thorough exposure to these concepts, see: Allen Quist, *Fed Ed: The New Federal Curriculum and How It's Enforced* (Maple River, MN: Maple River Education Coalition, September 2002).

123. Frank Aydelotte, *The Vision of Cecil Rhodes (London: Oxford, 1946)* 5.
124. See: Mikhail Sergeevich Gorbachev, *Search for a New Beginning: Developing a New Civilization* (London: HarperCollins, June 1995).
125. The Bilderberg Group is a coterie of elite and wealthy globalists who meet annually to coordinate and disseminate plans for the new world order. Established by Prince Bernhard of the Netherlands (1954), it acts as a sort of international Council on Foreign Relations and is credited for bringing about the Common Market and the EEU. In "dividing the land for gain," and "causing craft to prosper," the antichrist system will "destroy wonderfully the mighty and the holy people" (Daniel 11:39 with 8:24–25).
126. Founded in 1968 by Italian industrialist Aurelio Peccei, the Club of Rome is an occult-driven spin-off from the CFR. Most planning directives for world government come from the COR whose 1972 report, *The Limits of Growth,* served as blueprint for today's bold new economic, military, and political union in Europe.
127. Founded in 1973 by David Rockefeller and Zbigniew Brzezinski, the Trilateral Commission is a multilateral planning commission within the stalwart of the Eastern liberal establishment of insiders. Members from three economic superpowers (North America, Western Europe, and Japan) seek to unite into a one-world, socialist government requiring voluntary demise of America's independence. The intent is to seize control of government and thereby establish "political cosmopolitanism" by grasping her commercial/banking interests (Held, Falk and Miller). See: R. Falk, *On Humane Governance* (University Park, PA: Pennsylvania University Press, 1995); D. Held, *Democracy and Global Order* (Stanford, CA: Stanford University Press, 1995); David Miller, *On Nationality* (Oxford, UK: Oxford University Press, 1995).
128. Revelation 3:14ff.
129. Not to embrace love of truth is to be "strongly deluded," believing instead what literal Scripture calls "the lie" (as opposed to "a lie"). Most likely this lie is grounded in the nefarious claim to Godhood advanced by Cosmic Humanists. At its root is pantheism, belief that all life is part of the impersonal god-force, defined as the sum total of all that exists (2 Thessalonians 2:4, 11).
130. There will come a time when all nations will be made "to drink of the wine of the wrath" of what is tantamount to spiritual fornication (Revelation 14:8).
131. International Community, *Charter of the United Nations and Statute of the International Court of Justice* (New York: United Nations, Department of Public Information, 1985) 80 pages.

132. http://www.pluralism.org/news/article.php?id=14538. The Bible speaks of end-time false teachers who defame truth and forsake the straight path of moral absolutism. The global community acts instead upon whatever suits human fancy (2 Peter 2:1–2, 15; Judges 17:6). Principles as these take form in the *United Nations Declaration of Tolerance*, 2006.

133. Jacobism (The Philosophes) was founded in Versailles (1789) as an extremist republican club of the French Revolution. Its Grand Patriot Adam Weishaupt founded the Illuminati on May 1, 1776. This Enlightenment-era, Bavarian secret society is dedicated to world conquest.

134. To succumb to deception results in spiritual subservience, 2 Thessalonians 2:10, 11.

135. Galatians 1:9–10. Universalism teaches that all religions hold elements of truth and that no religion or religious teacher is right or wrong.

136. Living constitutionalism is dynamic interpretation of constitutional phraseology. With a view to pragmatism, or framers' intent, living constitutionalists always take into account contemporaneous society. While Al Gore favors the concept, Supreme Court Justice Scalia strongly opposes it.

137. Cecil Rhodes' *Confession of Faith*, "Sustainable Development Syllabus" from Radio Liberty at Post Office Box 13, Santa Cruz, CA 95063.

138. Neal Donald Walsch, *Tomorrow's God: Our Greatest Spiritual Challenge* (New York: Atria Books, Simon & Schuster, 2004) Workbook 45.

139. Today's new revelation is seeded in neo-pantheistic syncretism—that being doctrinal mix (syncretism) resurrecting ancient mystery religions with a new *(neo)* take on all *(pan)* life's constituting the God essence *(theo)*. One's divinity is realized in his "higher self," achieved by altered states of consciousness.

140. For an expanded perspective, see: Eckhart Tolle, *A New Earth: Awakening to Your Life's Purpose* (New York: Penguin, Plume, 2006).

141. 1 Timothy 6:12.

142. Dennis Judd, "Cecil Rhodes Legacy," *The British Imperial Experience from 1765 to the Present* (New York: Basic Books, 1998) 117.

143. Richard Harwood, "Ruling Class Journalists" (Washington, D.C.: *Washington Post*, October 30, 1933) A-21.

144. L. Brent Bozell III, "Weapons of Mass Distortion" *National Review Online* (2004).

145. Frazier Moore, "Bill Moyers Retiring from TV Journalism" (Associated Press, 2004) 1.

146. Proverbs 29:11.

147. Daniel 11:32.

148. Arguably the oldest and most influential U.S. organization openly committed to a new world order, the World Federalist Association was the instrumental group responsible for setting up the International Criminal Court. Along with the Counsel on Foreign Relations, major foundations, and money center banks, the WFA is part of the imposing infrastructure of the World Constitution and Parliamentary Association; and it enjoys consultative status at the UN.

149. http://quotes.liberty-tree.ca/quote/david_rockefeller_quote_103d.

150. http://www.ed.gov/pubs/NatATRisk/risk.html.

151. http://www.quotes.liberty-tree.ca/quotes by/dr.+chester+pierce. In his Keynote Speech, Dr. Chester M. Pierce effectively undermined parenthood when he addressed Childhood Education International in Denver, Colorado (1972). In contrast, Scripture admonishes believers to continue in truth, as taught in the home from childhood (2 Timothy 3:14–15 with Isaiah 28:9).

152. Prophetically, end-time global citizens indulge the lower stimulus of enchantments with drugs (*pharmakeia*, or "sorceries"), Revelation 9:21 and 18:23.

153. In a world typified by seemingly limitless knowledge, end-time world citizens continually learn new things, yet they lack weightier knowledge of truth (2 Timothy 3:7).

154. Scripturally, those wise in their own eyes forfeit righteousness by "justifying the wicked for reward" (Isaiah 5:20–23).

155. http://www.youtube.com/watch?v=DDyDtYy2I0M.

156. Robert Müller, *World Core Curriculum Manual* (Arlington, TX: The Robert Müller School, 1985) Preface 2.

157. http://www.learn-usa.com/relevant_to_et/ctd03.htm.

158. http://www.newhorizons.org/future/Creating_the_Future/crfut_frontend.html.

159. Dr. Shirley McCune and Dr. Norma Milanovich, *The Light Shall Set You Free* (Albuquerque, NM: Athena, 1996).

160. Robert Carkuff and Bernard G. Berenson, *The Possibilities Mind* (Amherst, MA: Possibilities, 2001).

161. As reported by Dr. Dennis Cuddy, "The Emperor's Closet," *The Christian Conscience*, December 1997, 31—this, in reference to Drs. Shirley McCune and Norma Milanovich, *The Light Shall Set You Free* (Albuquerque, NM: Athena, 1996).

162. http://thefactsaboutedreform.homestead.com/The_Unveiling_Part_1.pdf. See page 9.

163. Robert Carkuff and Bernard G. Berenson, "The Processing Science," *The New Science of Possibilities* (Amherst, MA: HDR, 2000) Vol. I.

164. http://commonaction.blogspot.com/search/label/ephebiphobia.

165. Jill MacIntyre Witt, "Anita's Activism and Inspiration" *The Body Shop ® Blog,* (2008).

166. Edward Cody of the *Washington Post, "Laissez-faire* Finished" *The Seattle Times* (September 26, 2008) 26.

167. http://www.wto.org.

168. http://www.ifg.org/wto.html.

169. http://quotes.liberty-ree.ca/quote/henry_kissinger_quote_b58f.

170. T.R. Reid, *The United States of Europe: The New Superpower and the End of American Supremacy* (New York: Penguin, 2004).

171. Ross Perot, *Save Your Job, Save Our Country* (Scranton, PA: Hyperion, distributed by HarperCollins, 1993) 41–42, 47.

172. Huang Hua was the foreign minister of China from 1976 to 1982.

173. The U.S. Army is building a huge biometric data base using verification technology (hand geometry, retinal reading, signature dynamics, voice recognition, and fingerprint reading) to identify parties of interest. This is consistent with the biblical mark of the Beast which is a stamp or brand employed by the Antichrist for permanent identification, surveillance, and control of its bearer (Revelation 14:9–11 with 13:16–17).

174. Formerly editor-at-large for *Time* magazine, Strobe Talbott (CFR and Trilateral Commission member) received the prestigious Norman Cousins award from the World Federalist Association. As chief foreign adviser to the Clinton administration, Talbott was known to systematically undermine national sovereignty in favor of a single, global authority.

175. Roger Kotila, *Constitution for the Federation of the Earth* (San Francisco, CA: Democratic World Federalists, 1977).

176. Donella H. Meadows, et. al., *The Limits of Growth. A Report for The Club of Rome's Project on the Predicament of Mankind* (New York: Universe, 1972).

177. Comprised of twenty-eight members, NATO has added new members six times since its founding in 1949. In 1990 NATO added the former country of East Germany to its twelve founding countries. Between 1994 and 1997, wider forums were set up for regional cooperation between NATO and its neighbors. In 1997, three former communist countries were invited to join. After this fourth enlargement in 1999, the Vilnius group formed in May of 2000 to lobby for further NATO membership; and seven more joined in the fifth enlargement (2004). In 2009, Albania and Croatia joined in its sixth enlargement.

178. A professor at Trinity Law School in Orange County, California, James L. Hirsen, J.D., Ph.D., is an internationally recognized attorney

and speaker on constitutional, government, and global issues. See: James L. Hirsen, Ph.D., "The Founding Fathers' Worst Nightmare," *The Coming Collision: Global Law vs. U.S. Liberties* (Lafayette, LA: Huntington House, 1999) 25–26.

179. For Christian believers, Old Testament ceremonial laws were voided once they were fulfilled in the life, death, and resurrection of Christ Jesus. Nevertheless, Christ held Holy Spirit-empowered followers to an even more stringent code of conduct than what Moses delivered in stone. According to new-covenant theology, the law now is written on redeemed hearts empowered to exercise the "royal law of love" (James 1:25; 2:8; Romans 2:14). Founding Father John Adams linked civil government with said principles, and America's legal system established as its overarching worldview the very essence of the Ten Commandments coupled with New Testament amplification.

180. New Age guru Eckhart Tolle underscores "power in the Now," thus enabling transformation of consciousness from illusive thought to Self-God awareness. Thusly awakened, "Custodians of the Plan" watch over and even guide all of humanity's spiritual progress.

181. A multi-billion dollar industry, radical environmentalism is no small player. Deep ecology activists, pandering politicians, and moneyed foundations pull strings to affect what Tom DeWeese of the American Policy Center calls an "ecoligarchy" with no less than one third of all federal laws focused on the environment. Moreover, the scientific community has reached no consensus to warrant need for nearly three hundred environmental treaties already administered by the United Nations.

182. http://www.biomimicryinstitute.org/about-us/what-do-you-mean-by-the-term-biomimicry.html.

183. http://www.garretthardinsociety.org/info/quotes.html.

184. International Community, *Plan of Action to Combat Desertification, PACD* (New York: United Nations Conference on Desertification, 1977), http://www.unccd.int/convention/menu.php.

185. Proverbs 29:26.

186. International Community, *International Covenant on Civil and Political Rights* (New York: United Nations, April 1992).

187. The eco-socialist new world order counterfeits God's true design. In the end, the Lord will assume His rightful, uncontested place on the planet, earmarked by restoration. The coming Millennium on earth is a one-thousand-year theocracy under rule of Jesus Christ (Joel 2:25; Habakkuk 2:14; Isaiah 32:16–20, and Psalm 45:16).

188. 1 Thessalonians 5:3.

189. Isaiah 52:11; 2 Corinthians 6:17.

190. Isaiah 28:10.

191. Ephesians 4:14.
192. Luke 12:48.
193. Amos 5:14–15.
194. Ephesians 6:11–13.
195. 1 Timothy 6:12.
196. John 14:14 and 15:7 (abide and ask in Jesus' name); James 4:3 (in His will).
197. Proverbs 29:26.
198. 1Timothy 1:1.
199. For the Lord's sake, Christians are commanded to respect and obey those authorized to rule over them. Furthermore, they are to submit to rightful laws of the land while staying informed, prone to good works, and of good courage on behalf of the cities of our God. Even as Queen Esther took interest in the rights of her people, and approached King Ahasuerus on their behalf, Christians today are called to proclaim and promote righteous judgments. Indeed, righteousness exalts a nation (1 Peter 2:13; Ecclesiastes 1:13; Titus 3:8; 2 Samuel 10:12; Proverbs 14:34).
200. Matthew 5:16; 1 Timothy 6:18; Titus 2:7; Hebrews 10:24; 1 Peter 2:12.
201. Hebrews 12:2.
202. 1 Peter 3:20; 2 Peter 2:5.
203. Matthew 24:24; 2 Thessalonians 2:11.
204. Revelation 13:16–17.
205. Revelation 17:12–13.
206. For Satan to inflict human harm, he must first clear his intent with God. Even then, the degree of temptation allowed to be meted out is meticulously measured and masterfully limited (1 Corinthians 10:13). An example is found in the book of Job in which a righteous man enjoys God's hedge of protection until God lifts it. Never did God allow temptation beyond what Job could endure. In the process, Job was strengthened. Having endured, he saw his sorrow turned to joy and his blessings in life doubled. Through Job's extended trial, God gave him opportunity to prove his faith.
207. 2 Thessalonians 2:8.
208. John 17:16.
209. 1 Corinthians 7:31.
210. 1 Peter 2:11.
211. Daniel 12:4.
212. In 2 Thessalonians 2, Paul warns of a flood of evil and apostasy to come; however, until a specific event occurs (the Great Outtranslation, or Rapture), evil's full manifestation will be restrained. By way of explanation, verse 6 speaks of "what" (neuter case, or "the thing")

that "withholds" ("restrains" or "holds back") this flood. Verse 7 suggests that the one who "is now restraining" (continuous action in the Greek) will continue to do so until "he be taken out of the way" (Greek: "he suddenly be taken out of the midst of").

213. Esther 2:20ff.
214. Matthew 10:16.
215. James 1:5.
216. 1 Peter 5:8ff.
217. 1 Corinthians 13:1–3.
218. Galatians 2:20.
219. Philippians 4:13.

Chapter 6

220. Picken, Jane. Medical Marvels, *The Evening Chronicle*, (April 13, 2007).
221. http://www.lifenews.com/bio2823.html.
222. http://www.wikipedia.com/transhumanism.
223. Grassie, William. What does it mean to be Human? A John Templeton Foundation Research Lecture Query (2006).
224. Singularity 101 with Vernor Vinge, http://hplusmagazine. com/articles/ai/singularity-101-vernor-vinge.
225. Case Western Reserve University. Case Law School receives $773,000 NIH grant to develop guidelines for genetic enhancement research: Professor Max Mehlman to lead team of law professors, physicians, and bioethicists in two-year project (April 28, 2006).
226. http://www.nickbostrom.com, "Transhumanist Values."
227. http://www.transhumanism.asu.edu/.
228. http://lach.web.arizona.edu/sophia/.
229. Leon R. Kass, *Life, Liberty and the Defense of Dignity: The Challenge for Bioethics* (Encounter Books, 1st ed., October 25, 2002).
230. Rick Weiss, "Of mice, Men and In-between," http://www.msnbc.msn. com/id/6534243/ (November 20, 2004).
231. http://news.yahoo. com/s/cq/20090315/pl_cq_politics/politics3075228
232. Vol. 28, Number 2&3 (2002) 162.
233. Chris Floyd, "Monsters, Inc.: The Pentagon Plan to Create Mutant 'Super-Soldiers,' *CounterPunch* (January 13, 2003).

Chapter 7

234. Transcribed from audio tape of Bob Jones, Kansas City Prophets, "Visions & Revelations" (Fall 1988).

235. Transcribed from audio tape series, "Joel's Army," by Dr Jack Deere, Evangelical Foundation Ministries, North Richland Hills, TX, Tape #1.

236. Transcribed from audio tape of Mike Bickle, Kansas City Prophets, "Visions & Revelations," (Fall 1988).

237. Rick Joyner, *The Harvest* (Charlotte, NC: MorningStar Publications, 1993).

238. Richard Kelly Hoskins, *Vigilantes of Christendom* (Virginia Publishing, 1995).

239. Transcribed from audio tape, "Joel's Army," Paul Cain, Kansas City Fellowship (Fall 1988.)

240. Henry James Mills, *Jesus the Pattern Son,* (Xulon Press, 2007) 36–40.

241. Paul Mueller, *New Beginnings Magazine* (July 1991) 3.

242. Francis Frangipane, *The Three Battlegrounds* (Cedar Rapids, IA: Arrow, 1989) 128.

243. Ibid., 43.

244. Gary North, *Dominion and Common Grace: The Biblical Basis of Progress* (Dominion, 1987).

245. Transcribed from audio tape, "Harvest Conference," Denver, Colorado, Rick Joyner (November, 1990).

246. Rick Joyner, *The Harvest* (Charlotte, NC: MorningStar, 1993).

247. Francis Frangipane, *Exposing the "Accuser of The Brethren"* (Cedar Rapids, IA: Arrow, 1994) 13–16.

248. Transcribed from audio tape, "Vision of the Eagle's Nest Christian Fellowship," Rick Godwin (July, 1990).

249. Transcribed from audio tape, "Holy Ghost Camp Meeting," St. Louis, Missouri (1997).

250. Francis Frangipane, *Holiness, Truth And The Presence Of God* (Cedar Rapids, IA: Arrow, 1994) 128–130.

251. M. Scott Peck, What Return Can I Make? The Dimensions of the Christian Experience (New York: Simon & Schuster, 1985) 152.

252. Tommy Tenney, *The God Chasers* (Shippensburg, PA: Destiny Image, 1998).

253. Rick Joyner, *There Were Two Trees In The Garden* (New Kensington, PA: Whitaker House, 1997) 17–18.

254. John Arnott & Tony Black, "The Sword of the Lord," http://www.revival.com/index.htm.

255. Marc Dupont,"Behold I Am Doing a New Thing," http://www.revival.com/index.htm.

256. Transcribed from audio tape, Benny Hinn, TBN (December 15, 1990).

257. Hank Hanegraaff, *Christianity in Crisis* (Eugene, OR: Harvest House, 1997) 60.

258. Kenneth Copeland, "Substitution and Identification," Kenneth Copeland Ministries, 1989, tape #00-0202, side 2.

Chapter 8

259. Elbert Hubbard, "A Little Journey to the Home of Thomas Paine" as published in *Life and Writings of Thomas Paine* by Daniel Edwin Wheeler (Vincent Parke, 1908) 332–333.

260. Quote taken from the Bauman Rare Books website (http://www. baumanrarebooks.com), on which a copy of Paine's *Common Sense* is offered for $52,000.

261. Thomas Paine, *The Age of Reason*, Part 1, Section 5, http://www.ushistory.org.

262. Ibid.

263. John Adams, as cited in *American Philosophy: An Encyclopedia*, by John Lachs, Robert B. Talisse, (Routledge, 2008) 164.

264. Paine, *The Age of Reason*, Part 2, Section 20, http:www.ushistory.org.

265. Ibid.

266. James H. Billington, *Fire in the Minds of Men: Origins of the Revolutionary Faith* (Transaction, 1999) 3.

267. Ibid., 93.

268. Ibid., 103.

269. Ibid., 96.

270. David Harrison, "Thomas Paine, Freemason?" *Freemasonry Today*, Issue 46 (Autumn 2008) Grand Lodge Publications Ltd. 1997–2009, http://www.freemasonrytoday.com.

271. Ibid.

272. Ibid.

273. Moncure Daniel Conway, The Life of Thomas Paine, With a History of His Literary, Political, and Religious Career in America, France, and England, Vol. 2 (New York & London: Knickerbocker Press, 1893) 450.

274. John E. Remsburg, *Six Historic Americans* (New York: Truth Seeker Co., 1906) http://www.infidels.org.

275. Moncure Daniel Conway, ed., *The Writings of Thomas Paine,* Vol. 4, Appendix M, "The Will of Thomas Paine" (New York: G.P. Putnam's Sons, 1894).

276. Ibid.

277. Andrew A. Lipscomb & Albert Ellery Bergh, eds., *The Writings of Thomas Jefferson*, Vol. XVI, (Washington, D.C.: Thomas Jefferson Memorial Association, 1903) 100–101.

278. Jefferson, in a letter to William Short, October 31, 1819. from *Thomas Jefferson and William Short Correspondence*, Transcribed and Edited by Gerard W. Gawalt, Manuscript Division, Library of Congress.

279. Lipscomb & Bergh, Vol. XIV, 71–72.

280. Samuel E. Forman, *The Life and Writings of Thomas Jefferson* (Bowen-Merrill, 1900) 365.

281. Walter Isaacson, ed., *Benjamin Franklin Reader*, (New York: Simon & Schuster, 2003) 492.

282. M.F., "Ben Franklin and His Membership in the Hellfire Club: Founding Father or Satanic Killer?" Associated Content News, June 27, 2007, http://www.associatedcontent.com.

283. "Benjamin Franklin, the Occult, and the Elite," *The Sunday Times*, February 11, 1998, http://www.infowars.com, (January 11, 2005).

284. Benjamin Franklin, as cited in *The Encyclopedia Americana*, Vol. XII (Encyclopedia Americana, 1919) 11.

285. Ibid.

286. John Adams, *Letter to Thomas Jefferson, September 3, 1816,* as cited by Richard Dawkins, *The God Delusion* (New York: Houghton Mifflin Harcourt, 2006) 43.

287. Article 11 of the Treaty of Tripoli, Annals of Congress, 5th Congress, written by Joel Barlow in 1796, approved by the U.S. Senate, July 7, 1797, then signed by President John Adams.

288. Remsburg.

289. Ibid.

290. Ibid., 193.

291. Ibid.

292. "A Sly Old Fox: George Washington and Religion," from a Talk for Teacher's Institute at Mt. Vernon, July 21, 1999 citing: *The Writings of Thomas Jefferson*, Vol. 1, p. 284.

293. Remsburg.

294. Ibid.

295. Ibid.

296. Peter A. Lillback with Jerry Newcombe, *George Washington's Sacred Fire* (Providence Forum, 2006) 453.

297. David Barton, *The Question of Freemasonry and the Founding Fathers,*1st ed., (Wallbuilders, 2005), 21. Emphasis in the original.

298. "The Secret Mysteries of America's Beginnings" series is available at http://www.adullamfilms.org, or by calling our ministry at 888-780-5049.

299. Vine's Expository Dictionary of Old and New Testament Words (W.E. Vine, 1997) 283.
300. Manly P. Hall's obituary, *Scottish Rite Journal* (November 1990) 22, as cited by Academic Dictionaries and Encyclopedias, http://www.dic. academic.ru.
301. Manly P. Hall, *The Secret Destiny of America* (Philosophical Research Society, 1944, 1972) 77.
302. Barton, 82.
303. Johan Huizinga, *Erasmus and the Age of Reformation* (New York: Harper Torchbooks/The Cloister Library, 1957) 171.
304. Jared Sparks, *The Writings of George Washington*, Vol. XII (American Stationers Co., John B. Russell, 1837) 201.
305. James H. Billington, *Fire in the Minds of Men: Origins of the Revolutionary Faith*, (Transaction, 1999) 99.
306. "Riddles in Stone: The Secret Architecture of Washington D.C." is the second part of the "Secret Mysteries" series, and is available at http://www.adullamfilms.org.
307. Manly P. Hall, *The Secret Teachings of All Ages*, Diamond Jubilee Edition (Philosophical Research Society, 2000) CIV.
308. Johanne Wolfgang von Goethe, "Faust," translated by George Madison Priest, The Alchemy Website, http://www.levity.com.
309. *Freemasonry Today* (Spring 2001) Issue 16, Grand Lodge Publications, http://www.freemasonrytoday.com.
310. Oxford World's Classics, *Francis Bacon: The Major Works, The New Atlantis* (London: Oxford, 1996, 2002) 459.
311. Ibid., 459.
312. Ibid., 461.
313. Ibid., 461–462.
314. Ibid., 463.
315. Ibid., 465.
316. Hall, *Secret Destiny*, 77.

Chapter 9
317. Revelation 3:14–22. Some commentators, as do I, teach that this seventh and last letter to the seven churches has multiple meanings. One of these meanings is a warning that the Christian church will fall apostate, "lukewarm" in its final stage of organizational development.
318. *Iralestine* was released in 2008 by Highway, a division of Anomalos Publishing, and is available at author's website: http://www. prophecydepot.com.

319. Iranian President Mahmoud Ahmadinejad declared on October 26, 2005, at the World Without Zionism conference that Israel must be "wiped off the map."

320. The understanding of "kingdom against kingdom" as referring to regional conflicts rather than world wars is established in Isaiah 19:2 and elsewhere.

321. Revelation 3:15–16 describes the church of Laodicea in a "lukewarm" condition.

322. Daniel 9:24–27 predicted a period of seventy weeks of years, with the seventieth week being a time when Antichrist reigns. Other passages identify this as a period of tribulation—i.e., Matthew 24: 9,15,21 and Revelation 2:22, 7:14. Thus, many eschatologists call this the "Tribulation period" and furthermore suggest that many of the judgments described in the book of Revelation occur in this final, seven-year period.

323. For further study into the prophetic interpretation of the seven letters to the seven churches of the book of Revelation, refer to the Revelation commentaries of Dr. Arnold Fruchtenbaum of Ariel Ministries (http://www.ariel.org) or Chuck Missler of Koinonia House Ministries (http://www.khouse.org.).

324. The date associations for the purposes of this chapter were quoted from http://www.midnightcry.net/PDF/Seven%20Letters%20to%20 Seven%20Churches.pdf on 2/28/09.

325. These are not necessarily clichés of that period, but serve this author's purpose to convey his ideas and understanding of the Pergamos period.

326. 2 Thessalonians 2:8–13.

Chapter 10

327. Related terms include "exogenesis" which, like panspermia, describes the hypothesis that life on earth originated ("genesis") outside ("exo") earth in space. It differs from panspermia in that its claims are less comprehensive (i.e., it does not claim that *all* life on earth originated from space). "Astrobiology" and "exobiology," though part of the panspermia discussion, are terms that refer to the study of extraterrestrial life (in any form). These terms make no claim that such life is or would be related to life forms on earth, or that extraterrestrial life was a cause of life on earth.

328. For a general introduction to panspermia, see "Panspermia," *New Scientist* 189:2541 (3/4/2006): 54; David Warmflash, "Did Life Come from Another World?" *Scientific American* 293:5 (Nov. 2005): 64–71.

Examples of more technical treatments would be Ashwini Kumar Lal, "Origin of Life," *Astrophysics & Space Science* 317:3/4 (June 2008): 267–278; Chandra Wickramasinghe, "The Universe: A Cryogenic Habitat for Microbial Life," *Cryobiology* 48:2 (Apr 2004): 113ff.

329. On proposed mechanisms for undirected panspermia, see P. Weber and Greenberg, "Can Spores Survive in Interstellar Space?" *Nature* 316 (1985): 403–407; H. J. Melosh, "The Rocky Road to Panspermia," *Nature* 332 (1988): 687–688.

330. G. Louis, "The Red Rain Phenomenon of Kerala and Its Possible Extraterrestrial Origin," *Astrophysics and Space Science* 302:1–4 (2006) 175–187. Excerpts of the abstract for this article read as follows: "A red rain phenomenon occurred in Kerala, India starting from 25th July 2001, in which the rainwater appeared coloured in various localized places that are spread over a few hundred kilometers in Kerala. Maximum cases were reported during the first 10 days and isolated cases were found to occur for about 2 months. The striking red colouration of the rainwater was found to be due to the suspension of microscopic red particles having the appearance of biological cells. These particles have no similarity with usual desert dust.... An analysis of this strange phenomenon further shows that the conventional atmospheric transport processes like dust storms etc. cannot explain this phenomenon. The electron microscopic study of the red particles shows fine cell structure indicating their biological cell like nature. EDAX analysis shows that the major elements present in these cell like particles are carbon and oxygen. Strangely, a test for DNA using Ethidium Bromide dye fluorescence technique indicates absence of DNA in these cells. In the context of a suspected link between a meteor airburst event and the red rain, the possibility for the extraterrestrial origin of these particles from cometary fragments is discussed."

331. "Panspermia," *The Internet Encyclopedia of Science*. http://www.daviddarling.info/encyclopedia/P/panspermia.html (March 23, 2009).

332. F. H. Crick and L. E. Orgel, "Directed Panspermia," *Icarus* 19 (1973): 341–348. Crick later authored the book *Life Itself: Its Origin and Nature* (New Work: Simon &Schuster, 1981).

333. Crick and Orgel in part opted for directed panspermia due to their pessimism that random evolution could account for the complexity of DNA. They later tempered their view of directed panspermia (but did not dismiss it) in the wake of advances in biology that postulated an "RNA World" could possibly account for the origin of life on earth.

334. R.B. Sheldon and R.B. Hoover, "The Cometary Biosphere" in *Instruments, Methods, and Missions for Astrobiology X*, Hoover,

Levin, Rosanov eds. Proc. of SPIE Vol. 6694 (Bellingham, WA) 6694-0H, 2007; R. B. Sheldon and R. B. Hoover, "Cosmological Evolution: Spatial Relativity and the Speed of Life" in *Instruments, Methods, and Missions for Astrobiology XI,* Hoover, Levin, Rosanov eds. Proc. of SPIE Vol. 7097 (Bellingham, WA) 7097–41, 2008. Dr. Robert Sheldon is a NASA physicist and proponent of intelligent design (see http://procrustes.blogtownhall.com/2006/09/23/ cosmologists_panic!.thtml and http://www.uncommondescent. com/intelligent-design/life-on-mars-id-and-a-prediction/).

335. This is equally the case for researchers outside the mainstream public scientific community. Claims abound for the reality of intelligent aliens but no hard data has been produced which cannot be accounted for in terms of terrestrial origin.

336. Patrick McCafferty, "Bloody Rain Again! Red Rain and Meteors in History and Myth," *International Journal of Astrobiology* (2008).

337. Debora MacKenzie, "Are They Aliens or Just Humble Earthlings?" *New Scientist* 2291 (May 19, 2001).

338. "Panspermia" and "SNC Meteorites," *The Internet Encyclopedia of Science,* http://www.daviddarling.info/encyclopedia/P/panspermia. html (March 23, 2009).

339. Ibid.

340. Bada, J. L.; Glavin, D. P.; McDonald, G. D.; Becker, L. (1998). "A Search for Endogenous Amino Acids in Martian Meteorite ALH84001". *Science* 279 (5349): 362–365; Becker L., Glavin D. P., Bada J. L. (1997). "Polycyclic aromatic hydrocarbons (PAHs) in Antarctic Martian meteorites, carbonaceous chondrites, and polar ice". *Geochimica et Cosmochimica Acta* 61: 475–481.

341. "Creature Survives Naked in Space," (September 8, 2008) http:// www.space.com/scienceastronomy/080908-space-creature.html.

342. NASA, "NASA Spacecraft Confirms Martian Water, Mission Extended," (July 31, 2008); Phoenix Mars Lander page on the NASA website: http://www.nasa.gov/mission_pages/phoenix/news/phoenix-20080731.html.

343. Vivien Gornitz, "Mars: Signs of a Watery Past," *Science Briefs,* Goddard Institute for Space Studies (2004), http://www.giss.nasa. gov/research/briefs/gornitz_07/.

344. My own experience while a graduate student at the University of Wisconsin, Madison from 1995–2004 is illustrative of this statement. While in Madison, my wife and I were members of a theologically conservative reformed church. The congregation was largely composed of university professors and graduate students, most of whom were in the hard sciences. The congregation was home to the

heads of the botany and environmental studies departments, two
research physicists, two engineering professors, and doctoral students
in the fields of geology, artificial intelligence, and chemistry. We also
had several medical students. Most of these individuals were elders
or deacons in the church, and I knew all of them personally. To my
knowledge, none of them were traditional solar-day creationists. All of
them were serious, theologically-literate Christians.

345. See http://www.michaelsheiser.com/Genesis 1 and creation.pdf.

346. See http://www.asa3.org/ASA/topics/Bible-Science/index.
html#Age%20of%20Earth.

347. See for example, Paul H. Seely, "The Geographical Meaning of
"Earth" and "Seas" in Genesis 1:10," *WTJ* 59:2 (1997): 231–255;
idem, "The Firmament and the Water Above : The Meaning of "The
Water Above the Firmament" in Gen 1:6–8," (Part 1) *WTJ* 53:2 (Fall
1991): 227–240; idem, "The Firmament and the Water Above : The
Meaning of "The Water Above the Firmament" in Gen 1:6–8," (Part
2) *WTJ* 54:1 (Spr 1992): 31–46; Luis J. Stadelmann, *The Hebrew
Conception of the World* (*Analecta Biblica* 39; Rome: Pontifical Biblical
Institute, 1970).

348. Note my example in footnote 18.

349. See the fourth chapter in my book, *The Myth That is True* (in progress
at the time of this writing).

350. See http://en.wikipedia.org/wiki/Animal_cognition, The Animal
Cognition Network, http://www.animalcognition.net/home.html,
and the scholarly scientific journal, Animal Cognition. For an
academic introduction to the field, see D. R. Griffin, *Animal Minds*
(Chicago: University of Chicago Press, 1992).

351. For example, which would make a better guide for a blind person:
an adult service dog or a toddler or severely retarded child? There are
many other obvious analogies and examples in the literature.

352. Artificial intelligence has achieved some of these properties as well.

353. See Genesis 1:21, 24, 30. Genesis 1:30 is interesting in that the text
tells refers to the "living *nephesh*" as being *in* animals.

354. See 1 Samuel 1:15; Job 7:11; Isaiah 26:9. Compare Matthew 6:25
and 10:28 ("body and soul") with Ecclesiastes 12:7 and 1 Corinthians
5:3, 5 ("body and spirit"). Death is described as giving up the soul
(Genesis 35:18; 1 Kings 17:21; Acts 15:26) and as giving up the spirit
(Psalm 31:5; Luke 23:46).

355. See Millard Erickson, *Christian Theology*, 2nd ed. (Grand Rapids:
Baker Book House, 1998) 537–557.

356. For a fairly detailed description of the film, see http://www.
themoviespoiler.com/Spoilers/knowing.html. An earlier feature film

"Mission to Mars" (2000) makes the case for intelligent panspermia, though it is less explicit with respect to planting human life on earth.

357. See Derek Michael Donovan, "Angels and Extraterrestrials in Contemporary Dramatic and Filmic Literature," unpublished dissertation, Stephen F. Austin University, 1996. Donovan's thesis abstract states: "This study examines portrayals of angels and extraterrestrial aliens in the popular entertainment forms of the theatre and film of the twentieth century. It focuses primarily on those works produced after 1947, when a spectacular sighting of several unidentified flying objects (UFOs) by private businessman Kenneth Arnold caught the attention of America and indeed the world.... This study points out thematic similarities in several angel- and extraterrestrial-related plays and films, many of which present their otherworldly characters as benevolent, wise creatures who advise and otherwise assist mankind through the trials and tribulations of modern life."

358. See http://www.youtube.com/watch?v=hxsQrBa0ECE.

359. The plurals of Genesis 1:26 should not be taken to speak of the Trinity, since plural language used elsewhere in the Bible in similar contexts cannot speak of the Trinity without avoiding explicit heresy. See my website, http://www.thedivinecouncil.com as well as Chapters 1 and 4 in my book, *The Myth that is True* (in progress at the time of this writing).

360. The sequel to my novel, *The Façade*, will have this intellectual scenario as a centerpiece. The sequel will be entitled *The Portent*.

Chapter 11

361. This has been extensively addressed on the Internet, in books, and through speakers on radio, with listings of these camps online. But the author of this chapter has not seen such a camp personally, so its authenticity cannot be verified.

362. "U.S. Among World's Worst Surveillance Societies," http://www.aclu.org/privacy/spying/index.html.

363. Insight On The News. In volumes '02, '03; www.insightmag.com/news.

364. David Kravets, "ACLU: U.S. on Verge of Big Brother Society," *The Daily Times*, AP: SF. Salisbury, MD; (January 16, 2003).

365. "Eye Scanners for School Children," BBC News (January 8, 2003). http://news.bbc.co.uk/1/hi/england/2638075.stm.

366. See "News with Views" article, "40 Techniques of the Illuminati," http://www.newswithviews.com/Hayes/gianni25.htm.

367. Dave Eberhart, "New ID Scanners at Borders Raise Privacy Alarm," Newsmax, (December 1, 2008).

368. John Terry, "Beyond Fingerprints: Our New Identification System. Revelation Files," (January 26, 2009) www.fbi.gov/page2/jan09/ngi_012609.html.

369. "Will Israel's 'Bionic Hornet' Fulfill Prophecy?" Revelation File via www.raidersnewsnetwork.comfull.php?news=22766, Springfield, Ohio (January 14, 2009).

370. Mudiaga Affe, "Safe City Project: Gov't set to commence 24-hour surveillance," Punch on the Web (Nigeria) (January 14, 2009) www.punching.com/Article-print2.aspx?theartic=Art200901140434442.

371. Ibid.

372. "Law Enforcement Receives Contract for Surveillance Vehicles from the Federal Government," Marketwire (January 13, 2009).

373. Tom DeWeese, "For Freedom—E-Verify System Must be Stopped," American Policy Center, Virginia (July 30, 2008).

374. May 1, 1937.

375. "Society's Secrets and Sicknesses," by Gianni Hayes, Ph.D.D. Manuscript form. 119.

376. Adrian Sainz, Associated Press writer, The Daily Times. Boca Raton, Florida.

377. John Markoff and John Schwartz, "Many Tools of Big Brother Are Up and Running," The New York Times (December 23, 2002) 3 of 4, http://www.nytimes.com/2002/12/23/technology/23PEEK.html.

378. Ibid.

379. Newsweek Magazine also offers a good overview of today's surveillance capabilities: (December 20, 2002—January 6, 2003) "We Need to Debate a National ID Before the Next Attack," page 46: The Biggest Hole in the Net by Steven Brill.

380. Sainz.

381. Markoff and Schwartz.

382. "High Tech Helpers or Big Brother Surveillance Tools?" The Chief Engineer, http://www.chiefengineer.org/index.cfm.

383. Christian News & Reviews, http://cnview/news_service/cnv_july_1997.htm.

384. As quoted in Christian News & Reviews, "A British Charity Is Offering 'Lunch Break Abortions,'" (July 1997) http://www.cnview.com/news_service/cnv_july_1997.htm#A%20British%20Charity%20Is%20Offering%20Lunch%20Break.

385. Barack Obama, Speech in the U.S. Senate, March 6, 2007; The White House (Report) http://www.whitehouse.gov/agenda/homeland_security/.

386. Ellen Knickmeyer, "Funding House Bill 1017 Could Take $81 Million," *The Journal Record* , (January 19, 1994) http://www. encyclopedia.com/doc/1P2-5641821.html.

387. "Computer Surveillance," Wikipedia, http://en.wikipedia. org/wiki/Spy_software.

388. ACLU, "ACLU Calls on President Bush to Disavow New Cyber-Spying Scheme That Seeks to Put Every American Under Scrutiny" (November 14, 2002) http://www.aclu.org/safefree/general/ 17109prs20021114.html.

389. Steven Aftergood, "Democratic Senators Seek TIA Info," *Secrecy News* (January 14, 2003) 3, http://www.fas.org/sgp/news/secrecy/index.html.

390. Ibid.

391. "Take everyone's DNA fingerprint, says pioneer," *Privacy World—The World's Shrewdest Privacy Newsletter* (January 2009) Issue 2, privacy@ privacyworld.com.

392. http://www.albalagh.net/population/overpopulation.shtml; http:// www.ncpa.org/sub/dpd/index.php?Article_ID=13087 ; http://www. juntosociety.com/guest/sperlazzo/bs_opm1010903.html; and many other online sites list over 20,000 scientists who disagree with the global warming myth.

393. AgapePress News Summary. May 1, 2002. http://www. agapeprivsmple"lyris.afo.net.

394. Wikipedia. "Stargate Project," http://en.wikipedia. org/wiki/Stargate_Project.

395. Wikipedia, "Remote Viewing," http://en.wikipedia. org/wiki/Remote_viewing.

396. Confirmation was attempted by contacting the e-mailer—Xin ZhongqiNanjing—but no response from that party was forthcoming; hence, the author of this paper cannot verify its veracity.

397. _____; sender Xin ZhongqiNanjing City, Jiangsu Province, China. "An Announcement to the Whole World by Chinese Victims" (January 23, 2009).

398. Gianni DeVincent Hayes, Ph.D, *Lucifer's Legion* (Cambridge, MD: Cambridge Books, 2005).

399. Ibid.

400. Ibid.

401. Ibid.

Chapter 12

437. Dale Allen Pfeiffer, "Eating Fossil Fuels," *Energy Bulletin,* From The Wilderness Publications (October 2, 2003) www.energybulletin. net/node/281.

438. Ibid.
439. Matthieu Bonkoungou, "Burkina general strike starts over cost of living," Reuters (April 8, 2008).
440. "Riots prompt Ivory Coast tax cuts," BBC.co.uk (April 2, 2008).
441. "Egyptians hit by rising food prices," BBC.co.uk, (March 11, 2008).
442. "Soaring Food Prices Spark Unrest," *The Philadelphia Trumpet* (April 11, 2008).
443. "Pakistan heading for yet another wheat crisis," *The Independent* (April 1, 2008).
444. "Anger grows over rising prices in Sri Lanka," World Socialist website (April 11, 2008).
445. "SA must grow food on all arable land, says Manuel," *The Times* (April 11, 2008).
446. Julhas Alam, "Bangladesh in critical shape as people desperate for food—30 million poor could go hungry, estimates show," The Associated Press (April 13, 2008).
447. Stefan Steinberg, "Financial speculators reap profits from global hunger," www.globalresearch.ca (April 24, 2008).
448. "Cyclone fuels rice price increase," BBC News (May 7, 2008).
449. Ibid.
450. Interview from Fox News, www.infowars.com (November 13, 2008).
451. Ambrose Evans-Pritchard, "Citigroup says gold could rise above $2,000 next year as world unravels," *The Daily Telegraph* (November 27, 2008).
452. Steve and Paul Watson, "Army 'Strategic Shock' Report Says Troops May Be Needed To Quall U.S. Civil Unrest," www.prisonplanet.com (December 16, 2008).
453. Peter Goodgame, *Red Moon Rising* (Xulon, 2004) ISBN-10: 1594679622.
454. David W. Lowe, *Earthquake Resurrection* (Lulu, 2005) ISBN-10: 1411639707.
455. David W. Lowe, *Then His Voice Shook The Earth* (Seismos, 2006) ISBN-10: 0615136141.
456. John Perkins, *Confessions of An Economic Hitman* (Berrett Koehler, 2004).

Chapter 13

457. The terms "central banking" and "fractional-reserve banking" refer to a debt-based system and regulatory regime that controls money and credit. A powerful aspect of this system is that it can create monetary assets out of nothing and can influence the allocation of these new monies.

458. The definition of total world financial obligations used by the author includes the full notional values available for documented securities and derivatives markets and as well as bank lending. Using this conservative definition, total financial obligations (or "position value") totaled $818 trillion at year-end 2007, or more than fifteen times global economic output for that year (employing the World Bank's current value estimate in U.S. dollars and not adjusted for purchasing power).

459. This statistic is calculated on a per-capita basis, in other words, accounting for population growth over the period being reviewed.

460. Financialization, as a concept, captures the notion of human activities and obligations being expressed in a financial form—i.e., debt, an insurance policy, savings, deposits, etc.

461. Paul Volcker, "We Have the Tools to Manage the Crisis," *Wall Street Journal* (October 10, 2008).

462. Luc Laeven and Fabian Valencia, "Systemic Banking Crises: A New Database," *IMF Working Paper 224* (September 2008).

463. United Nations Conference on Trade and Development, "Towards Reform of the International Financial Architecture: Which Way Forward?" *Trade and Development Report,* (New York, 2001).

464. World Investment Report 2008: Transnational Corporations, and the Infrastructure Challenge, United Nations Conference on Trade and Development.

465. Benjamin Wills Newton, *Thoughts on the Apocalypse*, 1843. Cited in *The Coming Day*, Vol. 2, B.W. Newton [1843] 1853. (London: Houlston & Sons).

466. Jean-Baptiste Say, [1880] 1971, "A Treatise on Political Economy: or the Production, Distribution and Consumption of Wealth," translated by C.R. Prinsep and Clement C. Biddle. (New York: Augustus M. Kelley, 1841).

467. The terms "central banking" and "fractional-reserve banking" refer to a debt-based system and regulatory regime that controls money and credit. A powerful aspect of this system is that it can create monetary assets out of nothing and can influence the allocation of these new monies.

468. "Anglobalization": A term coined by Niall Ferguson, in his book, *Empire: The Rise and Demise of the British World Order and the Lessons for Global Power* (London: Allen Lane, 2002), which outlines the economic and financial impact that the spread of the British Empire had upon the entire world.

469. Carlo Resta, "How to Generate a New Wave of Prosperity," *RGE Monitor, Europe Ecomonitor* (December 18, 2008) http://www.rgemonitor.com.

470. Lawrence Summers, "Obama's Downpayment: A Stimulus Must Aim for Long-term Results," *Washington Post* (December 28, 2008).
471. http://telegraph.co.uk (October 9, 2008).
472. Satyajit Das, "Only Global Action Will End This," *Business Spectator* (October 7, 2008).
473. Roger C. Altman, "The Great Crash, 2008: A Geopolitical Setback for the West," *Foreign Affairs* (January/February 2009).
474. Ibid.
475. Thomas Ice, "The Earth Dwellers of Revelation," *Pre-Trib Perspectives*, February 2008, http://www.pre-trib.org/data/pdf/Ice-TheEarthDwellersofRevelation.pdf.

Chapter 14
476. Henry A. Kissinger, "The Chance for a New World Order," http://www.iht.com/articles/2009/01/12/opinion/edkissinger.php, 1/12/09.

Chapter 15
477. Curlender v. Bio-Science Labs., 165 Cal. Rptr. 477, 489–90 (Cal. Ct. App. 1980).
478. Procanik v. Cillo, 478 A.2d 755, 764 (N.J. 1984). The State of Washington has also recognized wrongful life suits. See Harbeson v. Parke-Davis, Inc., 656 P.2d 483, 496 (Wash. 1983).
479. David Andrusko, "Harvesting the Living," *A Passion for Justice* (Washington, D.C.: National Right to Life Committee, 1988) 87–88.
480. Ibid., 88.
481. Ibid., 88.
482. Larry Thompson, "Fetal Tissue: Should Fetal Tissue from Abortions Be Available for Treatment of Patients with a Range of Diseases?" *Washington Post Health Magazine* (January 26, 1988) 11.
483. Bernard Nathanson, "Obscene Harvest: Selling Fetal Body Parts for Profit," *Liberty Report* (January 1988).
484. HR 2708, "The Patients First Acts of 2007."
485. James A. Thomson, "Standing in the Way of Stem Cell Research" (December 3, 2007) A17; "Stem Cell Discovery Hailed as Milestone: Technique Doesn't Destroy Embryos: Obstacles Remain," *USA Today* (November 21, 2007) 1.
486. Richard L. Berkowitz, et. al., "Selective Reduction of Multifetal Pregnancies in the First Trimester," *The New England Journal of Medicine* 318 (April 1988) 1043–47.
487. *Houston Chronicle* (June 18, 1981).

488. Gina Kolata, "Multiple Fetuses Raise New Issues Tied to Abortion," *New York Times* (January 25, 1988) A1.

489. Dorothy C. Wertz and John C. Fletcher, "Fatal Knowledge? Prenatal Diagnosis and Sex Selection," *The Hastings Report* (May/June 1989) 21–27.

490. John Leo, "Baby Boys to Order," *U.S. News and World Report* (January 9, 1989) 59.

491. Joyce Price, "Prenatal Test of Sex Sometimes Triggers Abortion Decisions," *Washington Times* (February 13, 1987).

492. Ibid.

493. Jo McGowan, "In India, They Abort Females," *Newsweek* (January 30, 1989) 12.

494. Judith Perea, "Sex Seals the Fate of Fetuses in Britain," *New Scientist* (January 22, 1987).

495. McGowan, "The Abort Females," 12.

496. "Feminism's Triumph: The Extermination of Women," The Population Research Institute (January 19, 2007).

497. Joseph Stanton, "Mifepristone RU 486: The Latest Chapter of Chemical Warfare on the Human Unborn" (unpublished article).

498. "French Abortion Pill 90% Effective," *Medical World News* (October 12, 1987) 82.

499. Stanton, "Mifepristone RU 486."

500. Robin Herman, "In France, A New Method of Abortion," *Washington Post Health* (September 27, 1988).

501. Ibid.

502. Ibid.

503. B. Couzinet, et al., "Termination of Early Pregnancy by the Progesterone Antagonist RU486(Mifepristone)," *The New England Journal of Medicine* (1986) 1569.

504. Stanton, "Mifeprisone RU 486."

505. "Abortion at Home." See http://www.abortion-pill-online.com.

506. *Nature* 385, 810–13 (1997).

507. *Roe v. Wade*, 410 U.S. 113 (1973); *Doe v. Bolton*, 410 U.S. 179 (1973).

508. "Partial Birth Abortion," Wikipedia, http://en.wikipedia.org/wiki?Intact_dilation_and_extraction.

509. *Testimony of Brena Pratt Shafer, R.N.*, Committee on the Judiciary, Subcommittee on the Constitution, U.S. House of Representatives, March 21, 1996.

510. Ibid.

511. *Stenberg v. Carhart*, 530 U.S. 914 (2000).

512. Partial Birth Abortion Ban of 2003, 18 U.S. Code 1532.

513. *Gonzalez v. Carhart*, 550 U.S. 914 (2007).
514. "Transhumanism," Wikipedia, http://www.wikipedia.org/wiki/Transhumanism.
515. Wesley J. Smith, "The Transhumanists," National Review Online (September 20, 2007) http://www.nationalreview.com/comment/comment-smith092002.
516. Ibid.

Chapter 16

517. Corinthians 13:5.
518. John 3:3–8.
519. Matthew 15:14.
520. Matthew 13:24–43.
521. Letter from Maj. Larry A. Johnston (Ret.), United States Air Force, to the author (January 26, 2009).
522. The ten episodes of Christian persecution are only a few of the many reported by Christian news services during a one-week period in January 2009.
523. Genesis 3:15.
524. The family line through which Jesus Christ would come was clearly identified: Abraham, Genesis 12:3; Isaac, Jacob, Judah, one of the twelve tribes of Israel, from the family of Jesse, from the seventh one of Jesse, David, the king of Israel, down through generations to the virgin Mary.
525. For the chronology of these end-time events, see my book, *The Sequence of End-Time Events* (Prophecy Watch Books), www.prophecywatch.com.
526. The seal and trumpet judgments are detailed in Revelation 6, 8, and 9. Since all of those killed in the first four seals go to Hades (the place of the lost), and since the trumpet judgments also target only the lost, and because one-fourth killed in the seals plus one-third killed in the trumpets equals one-half, then God's judgment upon the persecutors of Jews and Christians during the Great Tribulation will take at least one-half the world's population. The persecution of believers will be judged, and the record will be set straight in favor of the saints of God.
527. See 1 Thessalonians 1:10, where Jesus rescues believers "from the wrath [Great Tribulation] to come."
528. See Matthew 24:36, which indicates that this "rescue mission," the Rapture, is imminent—that is, it could happen at any moment. Then see Matthew 24:33, which says that Jesus will not come until certain

signs (listed in the previous thirty verses) come first, and that we are expected to recognize those signs. Therefore, all true Christians living at the time of the Rapture (1 Thessalonians 4:13–18) will be taken to heaven to be kept out of the worldwide great Tribulation (Revelation 3:10), while new believers will arise on the earth after they are gone. These new believers will be those who will "recognize that Jesus is near, even at the door" just before His return to the earth (Matthew 24:33). But since prophetic signs cast forth a foreshadow, or a build-up period, then it is probable that even those Christians who are living before the Rapture takes them to heaven will be able to discern that, since Jesus' post-tribulation return to the earth is being signaled by signs, then His pre-tribulation Rapture of the church must be very near. The Rapture is termed a "rescue mission" for the very reason that those taken to heaven will undoubtedly be undergoing increasing persecution as the time of the Tribulation nears.

Chapter 17

529. George Washington's Letters: From the Ends of the Earth-Judaic Treasures of the Library of Congress, pages 231–239.

530. "Clinton Encourages Arafat,"Associated Press (May 4, 1999).

Chapter 20

531. Mimi Hall, "Most people unprepared for disaster," USA Today (updated 12/18/2006) http://www.usatoday. com/news/nation/2006-12-17-prepare_x.htm.